QUIET WARS

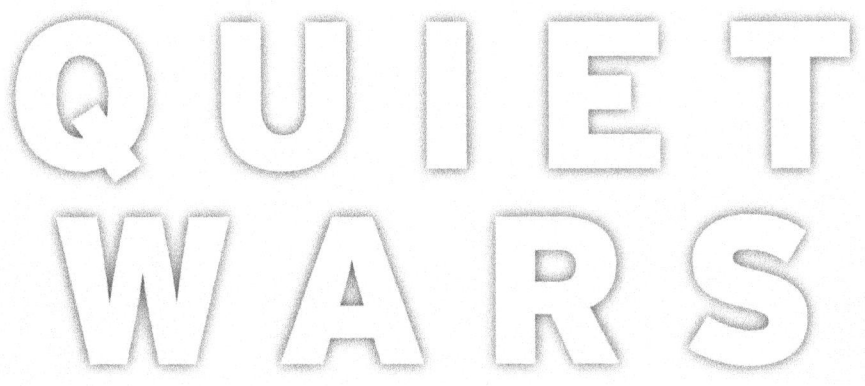

QUIET WARS

U.S. Naval Human Intelligence
Operations during Crises
with China, 1931–1965

BRIAN J. ELLISON

NAVAL INSTITUTE PRESS
Annapolis, Maryland

Naval Institute Press
291 Wood Road
Annapolis, MD 21402

© 2025 by the U.S. Naval Institute
All rights reserved. No part of this book may be reproduced or utilized in any form or by any means, electronic or mechanical, including photocopying and recording, or by any information storage and retrieval system, without permission in writing from the publisher.

ISBN: 978-1-68247-970-4 (hardcover)
ISBN: 978-1-68247-971-1 (eBook)

Library of Congress Cataloging-in-Publication Data is available.

♾ Print editions meet the requirements of ANSI/NISO z39.48-1992 (Permanence of Paper).
Printed in the United States of America.

9 8 7 6 5 4 3 2 1

For
Melissa, Eamon,
and Isla

Contents

LIST OF ILLUSTRATIONS	ix
PREFACE	xi
ACKNOWLEDGMENTS	xv

Introduction: The Challenge and Theory of Naval Intelligence — 1

Part I. Strategic Observation: Prewar in the Far East, 1931–41 — 19

    Chapter 1. Intelligence in the Interwar Years — 21

    Chapter 2. Collection and Observation in the Second Sino-Japanese War — 43

Part II. Damage Control: The World War II Legacy and Preparing for Communist China — 69

    Chapter 3. Legacies of World War II and the Resumption of the Chinese Civil War, 1942–49 — 71

    Chapter 4. Blackout in China: U.S. Intelligence for a New Kind of War — 89

Part III. Active Containment: Intelligence in the Taiwan Crises of the 1950s — 109

    Chapter 5. New Model Intelligence and Holding Steady with the Nationalists — 111

    Chapter 6. Reading the Chinese Communists through Taipei — 128

Part IV. **Clandestine Containment: Intelligence Activities against North Vietnam and China, 1959-65** — 151

    Chapter 7. Kennedy and the Dominoes — 153

    Chapter 8. Preparing Intelligence for Deeper Involvement — 171

CONCLUSION: PIVOTAL LEGACY — 191

APPENDIX: NAVAL ATTACHÉ REPORTS (1930-41) — 203

NOTES — 207

BIBLIOGRAPHY — 281

INDEX — 297

Illustrations

Photos

1. Japanese scheme of maneuver and line of control — 28
2. Capt. William D. Puleston, DNI — 35
3. Capt. Milton Miles and Tai Li, 1944 — 76

Figures

1. U.S. Naval Intelligence Command and Control (1931–41) — 31
2. Naval Intelligence Reporting Chain (1954–58) — 124
3. Naval Intelligence Reporting Chain, Southeast Asia (1960–65) — 167

Preface

When I first arrived in Washington, DC, in 2006 for graduate school, a friend of mine who was an analyst in the intelligence community offered to link me up with a colleague who would soon retire after a couple decades of service in operations. I was contemplating that career track and wanted to collect some perspectives. All I had read on the subject to that point—which, in perspective, was relatively shallow—had indicated that they sought young, hungry, worldly candidates. Surely, I was one of those. After a month or so of phone tag, I spoke with Holly over the phone while I was back in Los Angeles visiting my family for Thanksgiving. She was kind and a little off-putting. As a low-grade test, she asked me what I thought they did in intelligence operations, or human intelligence collection. Fair enough. As I recall, I replied with something I probably believed was a safe answer, such as: *It is the cultivation of foreign sources for the exploitation of information about the intentions, capabilities, disposition, and perceptions of foreign governments.* She politely interrupted with a *nice try*. She said, "We steal foreign information, and convince people to commit treason against their governments." The key word, *stealing*, was something I only appreciated sometime later.

I ended up pursuing a career in naval analysis, wherein "collection" for people like us was more along the lines of what scholarly data collection was in grad school (e.g., structured interviews, constructing and coding spreadsheets for linear regressions, and reading a lot). I quickly decided that intelligence collection was not my life's path. Instead, studying those who collected intelligence was what I wanted to do—essentially, I wanted to study the very group of people who do not want to be studied.

Another experience that shaped my outlook on naval intelligence occurred when I was deployed aboard the *John C. Stennis* (CVN 74) as the Center for Naval Analyses field analyst assigned to Carrier Strike Group 3 (CSG-3), in the winter of 2011. After some time in transit across the Indian Ocean and a series of air-wing operations in the Gulf of Oman, the CSG made its way to the mouth of the Strait of Hormuz. Having spent most of my career thus far studying international security from a Washington desk, I was in a world unknown. The one-star strike group commander wanted to know the kinds of naval activity that would get the attention of a certain government in the region. For a transiting carrier and her cruiser/destroyer (CRUDES) accompaniment, operating in the Strait of Hormuz and the cauldron of the Arabian Gulf meant the ever-present threat of Iranian fast-attack craft and fast-inshore-attack craft (FAC/FIAC) and coastal defense cruise missiles.

The questions the strike group commander was interested in were consequential. When I surveyed the kinds of intelligence available—especially on-demand and timely intelligence—I was faced with highly technical forms of intelligence, the kind one would assess adversary capabilities but not necessarily the circumstances under which capabilities would be used. Depending on the context, all kinds of intelligence can be valuable, but few inform us much in the way of intentions, beliefs, and limitations of an adversary. I wondered why we seemed to care less about good old-fashioned HUMINT—human intelligence. For all its imperfections—and they are many—HUMINT might be the one "INT" that could help answer some of the more nonquantifiable priority intelligence requirements for the Navy, if it were more clearly driven by naval forces in theater. Had HUMINT seen its day? What was the Navy's relationship with it and, for that matter, intelligence in general? These were the questions that drove me to take a seat in the J2, N2, and G2 for the next for several years in my career.

While the answers to these questions are inherently complex and storied, the first thing I needed to get over was a fundamental paradox: The Navy continued to maintain a HUMINT capability in the twenty-first century and yet some in its three main communities (undersea, surface, and air) often seemed to view HUMINT as a fiscal burden and a mission distraction. Warranted or not, it was less-than-satisfying to me to take the petty officer's word for it, as he puffed a Camel filter starboard aft on the USS *Kearsarge* during a Bold Alligator exercise many years ago.

As I studied the Navy and Marine Corps' relationship with intelligence, the circumstances of my career pushed me more and more into the Western Pacific from about 2010 onward, and specifically toward China and the naval underpinnings of Beijing's relationship with the United States. This, of course, was quickly followed by the so-called pivot to Asia, announced in the Barack Obama administration and spearheaded by Secretary of State Hillary Clinton's pivotal article in *Foreign Policy*, "America's Pacific Century," in 2011.

The national security establishment was finally catching up with what the China watch community in the West had been cautioning since at least 1990s. As the commands I worked for slowly shifted from a post-9/11 mindset into one of future crisis and conflict with major economies involved, emerging priority issues gradually became clearer. China was no longer a lower tier concern than how best to conduct counterterrorism, and counterinsurgency. In a sense, our bilateral relationship *was* our future, for better or worse.

As the pivot to Asia became specifically strategic competition with China, problems that the intelligence, strategic studies, and China watch communities faced over the horizon became more pronounced. The questions decision-makers asked became increasingly about the intentions, perceptions, and beliefs of the Chinese political and military leadership in future scenarios. Since future crises and conflicts in the Pacific continue to seem overwhelmingly naval in nature, it seemed wise to revisit some of the questions I struggled with previously from a distant and historical perspective. What had we learned? This book is simultaneously a modern story (from a Western perspective) of China and an institutional reconstruction of the U.S. Navy and Marine Corps, and national-level intelligence institutions' journey into modernity. The selected time span of this book (1931–1965) was evolutional but ultimately deliberate. On one hand, it represented a pronounced period of China's twentieth-century tragic—many Chinese would say humiliating—struggle with external forces (the

Japanese invasion of Manchuria in 1931, foreign occupation, the Second Sino-Japanese War, and civil war), and the beginning of the U.S. Navy's reassessment of its intelligence capabilities, emerging from a period of institutional atrophy in the interwar years. However, it also represented Communist China's adversarial relationship with the West—indicative of Maoist policies toward Taiwan and the American war in Vietnam—and the Navy's early steps into its modern relationship with intelligence.

May the reader take from this book a few considerations as the United States prepares for further unsteady waters ahead with China, while keeping in mind that the cases herein represent a far less technologically advanced—and arguably simpler—world than the one we find ourselves in currently, and in the next several decades. History is not a prologue to the future, despite how some historians may think of it. However, it is a useful roadmap of possible courses of action, given a certain set of circumstances. To this end, context is nearly everything to the historian. For the naval intelligence historian, please feel free to run when the brass asks you to use the past to predict the future. And then quietly walk back into the room when you realize the more things change, the more things change. We are merely humbled by history.

Acknowledgments

I would like to thank several people who supported me throughout the research and in the drafting of this book. My earliest discussions with Dr. Michael Goodman (professor, head of the Department of War Studies, and dean of research impact) at King's College, London, were invaluable, and his advice will never be forgotten. I am indebted to my G2, G5, N2, and N5 colleagues at Marine Corps Forces, Pacific; U.S. Pacific Fleet; Fleet Forces Command; and Carrier Strike Group Three for the discussions that ultimately inspired the research of this book.

As I dove headfirst into the business of archival research, I am grateful for the expertise and vast knowledge of the archivists at the National Archives and Records Administration in Washington, DC, and in College Park, Maryland, particularly Rebecca Collier, Darryl D. Bottoms, and Holly Reed. Together they made a daunting research journey much more enriching and enjoyable. Additionally, I am thankful for the historians and archivists at the Central Intelligence Agency, who have built and maintain the CIA CREST database, a national treasure. I would also like to acknowledge the inspiring online archives of the Naval History and Heritage Command, George Washington University's National Security Archives, the Harry S. Truman Archives, Marine Corps History Division, Texas Tech University's Vietnam Center and Archive, the U.S. Army Center of Military History, the U.S. Department of State's Office of the Historian, and the Wilson Center Digital Archive.

I am forever grateful for the tuition grant I received from the Johns Hopkins University Applied Physics Laboratory and the support of my dear colleagues there, including Ian MacLeod, Michael Moskowitz, the late Dr. Todd Kauderer (Capt., USN, Ret.), John Shissler, and Dr. Jonathan

Bierce. My eternal gratitude is extended to Erin Hahn, managing executive of the National Security Analysis Department, for her continued support, patience, and friendship throughout my research. And, of course, I would like to thank my JHU/APL colleague and fellow King's College, London, alumnus, Dr. Stephen P. Phillips, whose legwork and advice along the way I would be nowhere without. Thank you for sharing the PhD journey with me, and for being such a great colleague and friend. Go Navy!

I was extremely fortunate to have a deeply expert and thoughtful thesis committee at King's College, London. In addition to Dr. Goodman, I would like to thank my dissertation committee members, Dr. Robert Dover and Dr. David Gioe, for their candid, supportive, and thorough feedback on my dissertation thesis. Cambridge will always be a magical place for me, and I thank you, gentlemen. Most of all, I thank Dr. Huw Dylan, whose support, wisdom, humor, and commitment I would have failed without. Your dedication was so generous and life-changing that I do not have sufficient words to convey my appreciation here.

I am indebted to the good people of the U.S. Naval Institute. For the early conversations with Adam Kane and Bill Bray, I thank you for the generosity of your time and advice. I am so grateful for meeting and working with my Naval Institute Press editor, Padraic (Pat) Carlin, and the production team, whose patience and dedication to this project was deeply appreciated along the way.

My family was a consistent support system throughout the research and writing of this book. Thank you to Lisa Ellison, the Greens, the Palmers, the Andersons, Gary and Pam McAdam. My sincere thanks to my father, Jon Ellison, for the long-distance discussions on history for history's sake. Thank you to my mother who lovingly instilled in me a lifelong passion for knowledge, and whose spirit is with me every day. Lastly, I thank my beautiful, loving, and incredibly supportive wife, Dr. Melissa McAdam. Thank you.

Introduction
The Challenge and Theory of Naval Intelligence

The history of the U.S. Navy's relationship with intelligence is paradoxical: Intelligence has always played a fundamental role in naval strategy and operations—sometimes decisively so—but it is often treated as a stage prop (necessary but forgettable) in the broader naval context while the recorded story that naval practitioners and enthusiasts often read is of great battles in which such names as Bull Halsey, Chester Nimitz, Matthew Perry, and others or aircraft carriers, battleships, cruisers, and submarines come to mind. Or it may be the memoir of a decorated naval aviator. Conversely, it is important to never overstate the role that intelligence plays, but it should be placed in its historical context.

This book presents a history of the U.S. Navy's use of human intelligence (HUMINT) in ways that previous works have not. Although often eclipsed by other historical narratives, HUMINT by the U.S. naval services (U.S. Navy and Marines Corps) during crises in the Asia-Pacific has a rich history and deserves substantive examination.[1] Histories of U.S. intelligence have abundantly focused on the Central Intelligence Agency (CIA) while artificially downplaying the HUMINT work of the military.[2] Navies are not based on the intelligence they collect. They are based on surface, undersea, and air platforms and the power these assets can project ashore to affect political and military decisions.[3] However, conducting naval operations and policy and war planning for future threat environments generally benefit when navies have sufficient and timely intelligence with which to make decisions.[4] When the story of naval intelligence is illuminated, it is most often the signals intelligence (SIGINT) and cryptologic histories that are recorded, most likely because they are observable through a navy's shipborne tradition and air- and land-based systems that enable a fleet.[5] The relevance and application of HUMINT gathered during certain historical periods is seldom told, and yet HUMINT was occasionally the primary means of intelligence-gathering.

From the emergence of radio technology and its use in intelligence collection during World War I, navies began focusing much of their intelligence collection efforts on the radio communications domain.[6] Nevertheless, the reality of naval intelligence requirements could not ignore HUMINT (then, and until after World War II, generally referred to as espionage) because when technological means failed, naval officers still needed to deliver critical information. This book addresses how and why the U.S. Navy developed its HUMINT capability between 1931 and 1965 by examining its institutional evolution through the lens of crises with China. As such, it assesses the HUMINT aspects of crises and the Navy's and Marine Corps' roles in each. It traces naval HUMINT over a significantly contrasting period in the Asia-Pacific, organizational and operational changes during that time, and the impact of that intelligence.[7] Ultimately, it reveals that HUMINT has at times influenced the ability to enable decisions in crises, but this fact was largely marginalized because kinetic operations are more culturally indicative of the Navy and Marine Corps, mission than the information that underpins them. While this makes perfect sense broadly, intelligence collection and analysis are not often associated with the lynchpin of naval battles and more accurately belong associated as part of the conditions prior to battle, or in political attempts to avoid conflicts.

The four core parts of this book (each, two chapters) focus on the organization and influence of U.S. and Western naval HUMINT during crises in which the U.S. and China were actively or indirectly involved. A case study approach to studying this subject is useful because a complete history of the U.S. Navy's experience with HUMINT would show considerable gaps in archival records.[8] Additionally, using cases within a discrete period and region offers the ability to examine the discipline more closely. Between 1931 and 1965, naval services collected, analyzed, and applied intelligence in crises in the Asia-Pacific while global politics were rapidly changing and U.S. intelligence needed to evolve in stride. It was also during this time that the Navy transformed from being one of the sole collectors of foreign intelligence, prior to World War II, to losing some of its national influence in this area with the emergence of the Office of Strategic Services (OSS), and later the CIA overseeing HUMINT, as well as the National Security Agency (NSA) overseeing SIGINT.[9] The structure of the Cold War national security complex—which remained relatively intact for seventy years—centralized intelligence under the CIA. The ensuing case studies illustrate the institutional changes for naval intelligence and the effects to the way HUMINT was collected, organized, and prioritized during crises. Important in this evolution are the interactions with the CIA and consequences for the Navy's role in intelligence community over time. Therefore, the examination of naval HUMINT in Asian crises is a richly informative lens about the development, use, misuse, and value of intelligence in general to U.S. foreign policymaking. The Navy's role in this is a missing piece of the puzzle in the history of U.S. intelligence.

Assumptions on War and Crisis Intelligence Research

One will likely appreciate the fact that World War II represents a significant point of distinction in the Navy's and Marine Corps' experiences with intelligence. This book recognizes the role of intelligence in the Pacific and Korean wars in terms of the context it provided in years following them but otherwise eschews those experiences for four reasons. First, general intelligence history in war has been so thoroughly examined that a reexamination at this point with apparently no recent, additional archival records would be superfluous to the body of research.[10] In this book, the existing body of intelligence research is incorporated, is expanded upon, and recognizes the important role wars played on the institution of intelligence. Second, crises during periods of relative military peace (for the U.S. and other Western nations) present a unique context because the rules of engagement and the risks of escalation constrain the ability for intelligence actions to be unbridled—a phenomenon rarely studied.[11] Third, related to the previous point, intelligence is often collected and used differently in peace and in crisis during peace than it is used during war, and it is important that Fleet practitioners study the differences.[12] Fourth, and finally, many changes to the intelligence establishment resulted from systemic institutional perturbations and struggles between wars, whether World War I and World War II, or World War II and the Cold War, or Korea and Vietnam.[13] The latter point is a primary focus in this research, as I will soon elaborate on. While World War II and the Korean and Vietnam (after 1965) experiences are demonstrably operational intelligence cases, they are not the primary concern here. They are acknowledged as wars and thus wholly different in terms of the collection and interpretation of the intelligence they required. Although subtle at times, the body of intelligence research established that war and crisis intelligence differ in many ways (most notably in the access to sources), a point this research enhances within the naval context.[14] Conversely, World War II and its outcomes were so galvanizing to intelligence as an institution that it is necessary and useful to include substantial context within a single case in this work.

Building on an established body of intelligence studies literature, the research focuses on (a) how U.S. intelligence contributed to the evolution, management, and outcome of crises in which the possibility of greater Western involvement was a factor; and (b) the institutional changes undertaken by the Navy and others to refine the way intelligence is carried out. Beginning with the U.S. Navy's presence in China from 1931 with Japan's initial invasion of Manchuria and its full-scale invasion in 1937 through 1964 when the United States entered Vietnam following the Gulf of Tonkin Resolution (August 1964), this period offers contrasting crises in which naval intelligence was required in various forms, yet HUMINT was rarely treated as consequential as electronic and communications intelligence within the institutional Navy, or by historians. Conversely, this book explores, challenges, and contextualizes this notion through an archival case study structure.[15]

The research in this book aims to achieve four goals. First, it seeks to inform and contribute to the existing body of intelligence research by shedding light on an area seldom addressed through four unique cases in a single strategically important region of the world. Second, it presents a renewed explanation of how naval intelligence played a role in crisis management. Third, it aims to challenge some basic assumptions of the use of HUMINT during crises. Fourth, it attempts to serve as an informative resource for HUMINT practitioners in the intelligence community today, particularly as a record of naval HUMINT culture and practice's evolution.

The Approach

What does it mean to understand the practice of human intelligence and its institutional parameters within the Navy? To address these goals, three questions are posed of each case study. First, how did the Navy or Marine Corps collect HUMINT, and what role did this play throughout crises? Second, what were the institutional drivers and underpinnings of naval intelligence during the period in question? Third, ultimately, what value can be identified in the intelligence collected in each crisis? These are the fundamental questions addressed in the chapters ahead.

Following the study of the institutional and security environment contexts in each case, the research explores a large number of archival records and databases. The bulk of data relating to Navy and Marine Corps intelligence reports, operations, and policy in each of the cases derives from over 4,000 pages of records (317 documents) from the U.S. National Archives collections in Washington, DC, and College Park, Maryland, and from the CIA's CREST database.[16] Other archives and databases included the National Security Archives at George Washington University, the Marine Corps History Division at Quantico, Virginia, and several online public and private archives.[17] While these archives have been leveraged to great end in the past, this research presents an original contribution to the body of research in the way it is thematically organized through the relationship between crisis and organizational development. Thus, this effort required a substantial body of records from various archives since no single archive maintains the totality of material on these subjects.

In collecting and analyzing the archival data, the research applies a four-step method. First, a wide net was cast in collecting published works and archival records. This effort went beyond the published accounts of the U.S. Navy and of naval units in East Asia to examine operational, intelligence, and policy documents from Washington, correspondence between the Office of Naval Intelligence (ONI) and its forward units, and War and Defense Department policies. The case studies that follow rely on the substantive merits of archival records to further the book's overarching conclusions. Second, where possible, data related to Navy policy and operations in the Asia-Pacific were compiled in a timeline spreadsheet, indicating the date, description or quote, the source, and portion of the historical record the information addressed. Third, a draft case was then compiled using a thematically based structure. While each case varies considerably from the next, this analysis identified common themes. These include the context of the crisis, the Navy's role in it, institutional considerations for intelligence, command and control of intelligence, and the methods with which individual units collected intelligence. Finally, the questions posed on how and what intelligence was collected, the operational and strategic circumstances, and the institutional changes and constraints helped to render inferences about the value naval HUMINT demonstrated in the crisis.

The Historical Account of Naval HUMINT

This book addresses the subject of naval HUMINT—particularly in crisis—in a way that has not been done previously. An explanation for the dearth of seriously rigorous research on naval HUMINT is that the discipline was institutionalized slowly, over the course of several decades—a primary conclusion derived from examining the literature.[18] Training in this area was often relegated to officers slated to become naval attachés with embassies or special operations personnel rather than those in the general-purpose fleet.[19] As evident in the cases, training for personnel prior to the establishment of the Defense Intelligence Agency (DIA) in 1961 was limited and often nonexistent. As Capt. Wyman Packard shows in his history of U.S. naval intelligence, prior to the 1960s, official career paths within the Navy were established, and the training of sailors to conduct source operations was minimal, reinforcing the notion that, while HUMINT was relied upon, officers often had to learn on the job, a generally common tradition in this discipline.[20] Rare instances of well-credentialed officers are recorded, but they remain rare. This was the case with a U.S. naval intelligence mission in China in 1934, in which the director of naval intelligence, Capt. William Puleston, recruited State Department–trained Chinese linguist Maj. William Worton (USMC), with two previous tours with the 4th Marines in Shanghai, to develop a network of agents in Shanghai that would be employed in Japan.[21] Given the Navy's institutional biases for Fleet assets (e.g., ships and aircraft), the need for secrecy, and the overall cultural disdain for the practice of HUMINT historically, the literature in this area tends to be limited. In general, the historiography of naval intelligence (particularly intelligence involving human sources) has been poorly recorded and analyzed, either for protective purposes, destruction of records, enduring classification, or for other unknown reasons.

As with past historical research in intelligence studies, this book uses a series of crises in the Asia-Pacific as the bedrock for examining how sailors and Marines spied to further tactical, operational, and strategic goals, either in the maritime domain or more broadly, to enhance U.S. and Western national security. Understanding U.S. naval intelligence between the 1930s and 1960s requires a multilayered discussion of how such intelligence fit into naval operations and the national strategic context. The cases here document the evolution of naval human intelligence over a specific period, drawing out the institutionalized bedrock of intelligence whose basic elements can still be found in the Fleet today.

The Bounds of Crisis and Intelligence

Cases in the following chapters concern intelligence during periods of crisis. So what is meant by "crisis"? International relations and political science research have addressed numerous aspects of crisis dynamics, such as escalation.[22] One might consider a spectrum of world affairs in which each country is closer to absolute peace at one end or to total war at the other end, and where crises and proxy wars find an indirectly engaged country somewhere in between. Each of the cases in this book are situations in which the United

States and allied nations were not at that time in major conflict with a country. In each of them, however, the circumstances found naval operating units so perilously close to the war side of the continuum that a miscalculation or a misunderstanding could have led to deeper involvement and even war. In the case of early U.S. involvement in Vietnam, it did lead to war.

Let us consider the characteristics that make crisis dynamics unique for intelligence in this context.[23] First, a dangerous struggle is underway, yet all-out war is not inevitable.[24] This could occur quickly (e.g., U.S.-Japanese relations prior to the Pearl Harbor invasion) or with a longer-term realization (e.g., the deployment of Soviet SA-2 S-75 Dvina missiles to Cuba in 1962 or the Able Archer crisis in 1983).[25] Second, there is the notion that a crisis can, or should, be managed by the countries involved to avoid escalation and undesired consequences.[26] Third, diplomacy—and, thus, the opportunity for strategic intelligence collection—might be possible, but this will not necessarily avert escalation.[27] Fourth, there are crises that have more immediate implications and those that are lower intensity but with the potential to develop into larger crises.[28] Without some careful contextualization, a discussion of crises could inevitably bring one to compare circumstances of unlike characteristics (e.g., Able Archer in 1983 and the threat of nuclear war, as compared with U.S. interests in denying Chinese support to Laos in 1962); thus, it is useful to think of crisis as being on a spectrum. Each fitting within the above definition of crisis, the case chapters in this book consider these common characteristics.

The cases examined in this work evoke the above characteristics even as each of them occurred under significantly different circumstances. In the case of U.S. presence in China in the 1930s, the Navy and Marine Corps were in the middle of a civil war between the Communists and Nationalists and later a full-scale war between China and Japan, yet the United States and Western countries were not directly involved.[29] U.S. naval presence could have contributed to earlier Western entry into the war with Japan prior to 7 December 1941, given the Japanese invasion of Shanghai in August 1937 and, later, following the sinking of the USS *Panay* in December 1937.[30] Instead, the Japanese continued their invasion, and the United States remained out of the war for another four years. Similarly, in 1954 the

United States refrained from full-scale war when the Chinese People's Liberation Army fired missiles at the Quemoy islands, despite its stated policy to defend Taiwan.[31] Generally, historians and political scientists treated each of the cases in this research as crises (if not explicitly stated), even as they tend to be very different in both cause and resolution.[32]

Intelligence has been defined ad infinitum, but it is useful to contextualize it for crises. States maintain national security in spite of not being able to know everything about the actors that threaten security.[33] Generally, intelligence should improve decision-making by reducing ignorance and by uncovering secrets "that other people are trying their best to prevent us knowing."[34] Naval historians have even defined intelligence as "the acquired knowledge on the naval science and developments in all maritime countries; the naval capabilities, activities, and intentions of all potentially hostile and friendly countries; and the characteristics of all possible areas of naval operations."[35] The subtle distinction of military intelligence should not go unnoticed—namely, that, unless under commercial, unofficial cover, military intelligence collectors are bound to military command and control, organizational constructs, and other institutional norms. Building from these parameters, and for covering a geographic region over several decades in this book, intelligence will be defined as secret information collected and analyzed (in this case, often naval or maritime in nature), as well as actions taken overtly, covertly, or clandestinely, by organizations charged with these activities to inform a government's decision-making in relation to foreign entities.[36]

It is generally accepted that intelligence can play a consequential role in international crises, either in escalating or de-escalating.[37] To this end, strategic intelligence has the ability to change the course of crises if it is coupled with sound operational planning.[38] Operational intelligence—information needed to plan and coordinate intelligence, military actions, or political decision-making—is required to account for the possibility that actions could lead to escalation and, thus, war.[39] To make effective decisions, leaders require accurate information. Rather than acquiring *all* information, only the *right* information is necessary. Furthermore, because it is not always possible to collect the right information, yet timeliness is essential, intelligence organizations rely on estimation. For this reason, the collection and analysis of intelligence play important roles in crises because such intelligence can provide leaders with a better understanding of the enemy's disposition, capabilities, and intentions, if properly assessed.[40] Sometimes political leaders require the manipulation of information, events, and political/military processes through covert means, which is also part of intelligence.[41]

What is the role of intelligence in crisis? Considering the precarious nature of international events, one needs a flexible yet meaningful definition. Crisis is the circumstance in which a country is in a political or military struggle with another country in which the near-term consequences could result in war. Likewise, if the intelligence collected and used for policy and response over the course of the crisis is not sensitive to enemy intentions, the result could produce unwanted results (e.g., inadvertent escalation).[42] Assuming the primacy of intelligence in crisis, naval intelligence and naval HUMINT should enable decision-makers to make decisions in relation to naval and other domains to effectively control the crisis. Furthermore, if one merges the two terms (crisis and intelligence) with HUMINT, the result will be defined as secret information collected from overt, clandestine, or covert human sources and the means to enable the fulfillment of objectives in managing a country's interests during a crisis. This is the working definition used in this book to broadly address both theater- and national-level contexts.

Employing Humans for Intelligence

Before the wide use in the last several decades of satellites, unmanned aerial vehicles, and other sensors to collect electro-optical, infrared, synthetic aperture radar and SIGINT, navies have used human means for intelligence collection. Humans were the first means of intelligence-gathering for the Continental navy in the American Revolution.[43] Still, as the age of sail ended in the late nineteenth century and radio as a means of communication in war was in its infancy, navies began to understand and develop new means by which to collect information on enemy navies. In addition, these means proved tactically infallible under the right circumstances. The unique nature of navies, particularly great power navies, is that they are often persistently deployed globally with forward presence in and around nations of interest to the intelligence community and leaders who use intelligence.[44]

In the mid-twentieth century, the U.S. Navy employed naval intelligence officers abroad in three different ways. The first was the sailor or officer afloat, deployed with the fleet and often aloof to the political and military activities of nations until he comes ashore or into port. Such an officer's mission is most often concerned with how events ashore might affect fleet operations, a foreign nation's disposition toward these operations, and tactical and technical information on enemy capabilities. The second kind is the naval attaché assigned to an embassy or consulate overseas, with intelligence activity that generally tends to be of an overt nature.[45] The nation in which the attaché is assigned understands that this is the attaché's mission. Indeed, nearly all modern nations sponsor defense and naval attachés in foreign countries and must accept this as a norm of modern international politics. The overt intelligence work of an attaché is an implied activity, and thus the attaché often finds himself at the hands of the host nation's counterintelligence efforts, which is on alert to limit the value of intelligence overtly collected. In the United States, it is common for the attaché office to remain separate from the CIA station in country.[46] This aspect of the attaché relationship with the host nation is not well understood, certainly unsanctioned, and most highly secret as it deals with sources of clandestine intelligence. Prior to the CIA and OSS, the Navy, Marine Corps, and Army fulfilled this foreign intelligence mission.[47]

Another type of naval intelligence officer is forward deployed and either assigned to a specific unit deployed in country or under clandestine cover. Periodically, since the establishment of the ONI, the Navy managed its own programs, both in peacetime and in war. These programs typically focused on clandestine collection of information on enemy naval technology developments as well as internal political and economic factors. The Navy built and maintained local agent networks, interrogated enemy and non-enemy combatants, investigated counterintelligence cases, liaised with foreign government intelligence agencies, and acquired information of operational, strategic, and technical value to itself and national security decision-makers. A formerly classified 1974 report of the naval HUMINT program illustrated some of the activity of clandestine agents over the course of the previous year:

> In the Far East, sources obtained intelligence on Communist Chinese and North Korean ship construction and naval order of battle. Sources entered the two countries nearly 100 times in 1974. One source observed and sketched for the first time a new class of Chinese missile equipped patrol boat and CIA clandestine photography later confirmed the existence of the new unit. . . . Another source spent nearly three months in a Communist Chinese port and kept a detailed log of all naval and air activity in the port during that period. Several hundred ships identification numbers were recorded.[48]

The Navy's uniquely oriented intelligence capabilities and institutional knowledge supported this kind of activity, even as the CIA emerged as the U.S. leadership's primary intelligence organization during the Cold War. Thus, as Arthur Darling maintained in his history of the formation of a Central Intelligence Group in 1946, the Navy and other defense intelligence organizations continued to stake a claim in intelligence collection. To centralize all collection in a single civilian agency would obfuscate unique capabilities developed over many years.[49]

The dynamics of naval human intelligence interacting with, institutionally adjusting, and operating alongside other forms of intelligence across a series of crises, from the interwar years through the Cold War, are consequential to the evolution of the Navy and of U.S. intelligence community to its current form. The crises discussed trace the activity and organizational changes that occurred within the U.S. Navy and Marine Corps and in the national security community. They serve as vehicles for exploring the significance and contributions of naval HUMINT. The character of naval intelligence—particularly naval HUMINT—identifiably changed as this period evolved. The picture that emerges shows an institution in periodic disarray even as its officers needed to be professionally trained and deployed to collect and provide useful and accurate information to their leaders for efficient and effective decision-making. Institutionally, naval HUMINT played two primary roles across the national security bureaucracy: to serve the needs of the Fleet and to provide intelligence to the broader community—particularly for the president's use through CIA's national intelligence estimates and, later, the president's daily brief.

Strategic Context and the Institutionalization of Intelligence

The study of U.S. Navy and Marine Corps intelligence during mid-twentieth century crises in Asia requires that one consider different contexts over time. The first is the institutional context, by which one examines how intelligence in the Navy changed over time as its leaders refined processes by which its people collect, analyze, manage, oversee, and disseminate information depending on the strategic, policy, and budgetary constraints placed on them by leaders. As Amy Zegart discussed the Navy's role in opposing William "Wild Bill" Donovan's and others' call for a central intelligence organization following World War II in *Flawed by Design*, so too can one find other periods of both a parochial and a practical basis for institutional change.[50] The second context is a strategic one that recognizes the manner in which external and circumstantial phenomena affect institutions within the Navy and broader intelligence community. The period between the 1930s, when the ONI overcame the controversy of domestic spying and recast its mission, and the 1970s, when the intelligence community was held under a close congressional microscope, provide a series of crises in international security in which the maritime services played a central role.[51] Many of these crises, including the ones discussed herein, had long-term effects on regional security and strategic affairs. Each of the cases in this book add further context to both the state of the Fleet (the Navy and Marine Corps) and the institutional and operational nature of its intelligence community.

Institutional evolution is an important factor in tracing how and why intelligence collection occurred. HUMINT in the United States is often associated with the CIA, and the research here will contextualize this finding. Historical records show that from the early twentieth century, as predecessors to the OSS and CIA and later alongside them, the Navy and

Marine Corps (under the direction of the ONI) conducted a wide range of intelligence operations that surpassed their now commonly known missions (e.g., SIGINT). The institutionalization of HUMINT has hardly seen a consistent trajectory, however. It is possible that a disconnection exists between the Navy's primary mission—to project power at sea, protect maritime commons, and win naval battles—and the collection of information that enables the success of that mission. At times, as the cases show, this disconnect has led to the ad hoc use of HUMINT for the Fleet's sake of simply collecting intelligence by any means necessary.[52] As the national security establishment evolved, however, degrees of professionalism and institutionalized refinement occurred.

The ensuing chapters partly focus on the institutionalization of intelligence with an eye toward the Navy and Marine Corps' tendency to ascribe aversion to change as an institutional norm. The continuance of traditions plays a large part in this mentality. In his book on the Navy's culture, Roger Thompson addresses the status quo culture.[53] No warfare discipline better exemplifies the Navy's inability to change than intelligence. Moreover, this underscores a paradox: although intelligence, particularly HUMINT, has played a central role in enabling the Navy to advance objectives, it is not a discipline generally rewarded with senior promotion and accolades by the Navy. Nevertheless, periodic silent victories in this area yielded important operational, situational, and strategic awareness for both the Fleet and political leaders. As the case of the Navy and Marine Corps' experience in Indochina in the early 1960s shows (chapter 7), cultural aversion to change tended to yield to acceptance to change when failure was imminent, as the establishment of the Navy's clandestine Task Force 157 would suggest.[54]

Case Studies in this Book

Examining naval intelligence in crises enables both an operationally as well as an organizationally focused study. The cases range in intensity, duration, and strategic and operational outcomes. They underscore four distinct roles that Western policy was fulfilling at the time: strategic observer, damage control, active containment, and clandestine containment. The research is structured sequentially starting with the Western role in China prior to World War II and during the Sino-Japanese War, when U.S. naval forces were largely observers, even as the possibility of deeper involvement increasingly seemed imminent. This is followed by the crisis that U.S. policy immediately faced in China following World War II, when Communist influence was taking greater shape and yet damage control was necessary when direct involvement was not desired. This occurred against the backdrop of a quickly changing national security community. Then, as containment policy became the Western grand strategy, active military engagement became necessary in the face of Taiwan potentially falling to the Communist mainland forces, where open war was still not the desired course. Finally, in U.S. policy in Indochina in the early 1960s, clandestine intelligence and activities were necessary, and the national security community increasingly accepted this broadening of mission as the direction the Navy was headed.

The cases take an intuitive structure throughout, with occasional case-specific sections added for clarity.[55] For example, in the post–World War II Chinese Civil War case, a significant amount of effort was placed on bridging the role of intelligence in the war to the institutional vacuum that occurred in its aftermath. Each one includes a contextualized background to the crisis in which the role of intelligence and the Navy's presence are explored. Each case discusses the command, control, and organization of intelligence. Where there are archival data, the cases discuss trends in intelligence training that occurred during the period. Each of the cases follow a thematic base generally centered around the organization of naval units collecting intelligence, the kinds of intelligence collected, and the potential value it had in resolving or changing the crisis. Following the summary of each case's objectives is a description of the archival records used and explanation of how they helped or hindered a greater understanding of sources, methods, and tradecraft.

A Theory of Naval Intelligence?

The history of the years before World War II and into the Cold War serves construct a few narratives of naval intelligence, its evolution, and naval HUMINT's role as a discipline. First, while the interwar years were transformative for naval strategy, doctrine, and technology—including SIGINT technology—the act of sailors and Marines collecting intelligence by human means was highly informal and only minimally institutionalized.[56] Second, while World War II was pivotal for the development of long-term naval intelligence practices, this was most notably appreciated in the area of SIGINT and codebreaking because of its consequential effects to battles, such as Midway, and other strategically significant issues such as the economic blockade.[57] Third, because of an institutional bias toward signals, collection through human means continued to be under leveraged during the Cold War, even as the intelligence community underscored HUMINT in other areas.[58] Finally, the Navy failed to clearly institutionalize HUMINT until the mid-1960s, even when instances of success were realized and failed opportunities called for formalization.[59] This failure resulted not only from the primacy of SIGINT within the naval intelligence community but also from the fact that the Navy's leadership (often colloquially referred to as Big Navy) seldom treated intelligence as a means for its officers to gain senior leadership positions, vice the surface warfare officer's career trajectory.[60] The intelligence officer—whether SIGINT specialist or human intelligence collector—has more often been relegated to positions of specialty without room for greater advancement within the broader Navy, an area the literature has rarely highlighted.[61]

This work proposes that the reader consider a few overarching claims inferred throughout, specifically whether they may be timeless or merely circumstantially dependent on the cases presented. First, the main idea of this book is that the role that naval HUMINT played in a series of crises involving China—directly or by proxy—is only partially related to the role of the United States in it, that access to sources more often drives the value. Assuming we know the significance of a crisis, the effect of its outcome on national security, and the Navy's proximity and role in relation to information that matters (either in the short term or in the longer-term strategic context), one can then deduce the operational and strategic value of intelligence. This approach varies greatly across each case study and by no means follows a quantitative line of inquiry but a descriptive one. For instance, the stakes in the Far East crisis were significantly opaquer than the stakes in the Taiwan crises, where the possibility of the use of nuclear was real. The contrast between the contexts in each case is the catalyst for broadly evaluating naval intelligence.

Second, the nature of navies—specifically, great power navies—is to be forward deployed in areas of national interest. This presence enables the collection of information from unique sources (human, but also electronic, imagery, and others) that might otherwise be unavailable to other entities throughout the intelligence community, and even in the diplomatic realm. However, this composition and proximity of this access advantage can vary significantly, depending on the intensity of the strategic competition, crisis, or conflict.

Third, institutional changes—both those directly related to intelligence and those affecting a broader community—can yield significant effects on the prioritization of intelligence, its collection and analysis thereof, and the customer base. The research will show that the Navy and national security community's periodic shifts in policy, approach, and leadership significantly impacted the value of naval intelligence during each of these crises. When needed, and with the institutional wherewithal lacking, the foundation for change was established. The World War II experience was greatly enabled by SIGINT operations at sea, and this set the Navy on a course of increasingly relying on it more in the ensuing Cold War. As through its entire history, however, the Fleet also relied heavily on intelligence collected ashore—primarily through HUMINT. The postwar years, however, were an inflection point for national security. No greater change occurred to the naval intelligence community than the passing of the National Security Act of 1947 and the subsequent establishment of the CIA.

Fourth, in addition to access, the kind of crisis partly determines the kind of intelligence leaders require. The cases underscore four different kinds of crisis roles in which the United States was involved: strategic observer (the Asiatic Fleet in the pre–World War II era), damage control (Chinese Communist Revolution), active containment (Taiwan crises), and clandestine containment (U.S. policy in Southeast Asia in the early 1960s). The cases will explore each of these roles further. The unifying theme in all crises discussed in this research is the threat of escalation and deeper involvement, a factor that intelligence informed in each case.

Finally, access to political and military personnel, facilities, and other factors in enemy or third-party territory ashore is a primary factor in the ability of an intelligence body to collect accurate information and develop reliable sources. When access is acquired and then lost due to deterioration in foreign relations, resuming control over regular intelligence channels can be difficult. Transparency is lost. The number of potential sources diminishes. Moreover, the likelihood that a hostile nation protects itself through improved counterintelligence increases, along with its desire to increase its own foreign intelligence collection abilities. Although imperfect in terms of explaining the history of naval HUMINT overall, these cases offer an opportunity to explore a wide range of explanations for its role in a discrete region and an institutional community that saw tremendous change over the course of thirty years.

Part I

Strategic Observation
Prewar Intelligence in the Far East, 1931-41

Chapter 1

Intelligence in the Interwar Years

The case evaluates the circumstances and rudimentary employment of human intelligence (now referred as HUMINT but called "spying" and "espionage" at the time) collected by the U.S. naval services during the Second Sino-Japanese War, 1931–41, and the organizational changes in U.S. naval intelligence that occurred during this period. It is a case in which intelligence played a fundamental role, but one where the United States and Britain were not ready to become involved militarily. Primary concerns were averting the likelihood of becoming embroiled either in the Chinese Civil War (which a few Marines and sailors had already been in earlier years) or, more importantly, in Chinese war against Japan.[1] If a war had broken out between the United States and Japan earlier than 7 December 1941—given the limited number of forces in the region—history might have been radically different, at least prior to the use of the atomic bomb in August 1945. The collection of HUMINT was not employed consistently or explicitly during this period—but more an implied necessity; thus, subtleties and nuances are important.

There are two main components to the argument. First, it exposes a contrasting view of how the naval services viewed intelligence, the idea that human-derived intelligence was a low form of information collection and that rapidly evolving radio technology was the future of the Fleet.

In the case of the Marine Corps, prior to World War II, intelligence by human means doctrinally enabled amphibious operations, merely requiring scouting and reconnaissance prior to a landing and in establishing a command post ashore.[2] Neither naval service seemed to give significant value to HUMINT in helping military and political leaders make strategic decisions, much less in averting crises, even though it was often a fundamental input to decision-making. Still in its institutional infancy, naval HUMINT in the Far East prior to World War II served as an exploration in the ad hoc development of a discipline that was otherwise taken for granted by Navy leadership.

Second, as one will see, the Office of Naval Intelligence (ONI), led by the director of naval intelligence (DNI), employed several units to collect the information it required to render estimates of the situation, but the ones of consistent reliance were those present in the Far East theater—namely, subordinate units of the Asiatic Fleet and naval attachés.[3] The mission of naval presence in the Far East in the 1930s was to protect U.S. and Western citizens in the international settlement in Shanghai and at embassies (first in Beijing and then in Nanking), Japan, and elsewhere.[4] It was also, however, about understanding a growing threat from Japan and staying as close as possible to the lifeline of Tokyo's imperial expansion. Therefore, intelligence benefited the Franklin Roosevelt administration tremendously in this sense. Although it also helped that President Roosevelt himself was a voracious reader of naval intelligence, specifically HUMINT.[5] At the same time, the fact that the U.S. Navy and the Royal Navy were clearly present in the region did not have a significant effect on the outcome of events within the crisis, which could have (and did) lead to escalation, albeit one-sided prior to the Pearl Harbor attack. Intelligence did what it was supposed to do, however; it informed leaders of the disposition, posture, capabilities, and activity of foreign nations.

This case comprises seven overarching parts. First, the issues of sources and methods are briefly discussed as they relate to archival records and the methodological approach in this case. Second, the context in which developments occurred is important for understanding why the Sino-Japanese war constituted a crisis for the United States and Britain and why intelligence was increasingly important. This section includes a brief historical account of the U.S. Navy presence in China. Third, the case presents the issue of command of naval intelligence in the Far East and its organizational structures. Ultimately, the centralized managing intelligence agency (the ONI) often relied on emboldened personnel far from its central headquarters to feed its ability to produce intelligence. Fourth, the research addresses the evolution and significant reforms of the ONI in the 1930s in the Navy's attempt to adapt to a unique period of strategic changes in relation to Japan. Fifth, the case delves into the kinds of intelligence naval units in the Far East collected and the possible impacts on leadership's understanding of the situation. Sixth, this case explores each of the major sub-crises during this period related to the collected intelligence. Finally, the case concludes with the argument that, while the institution of naval intelligence observed fluctuations during the 1930s, naval HUMINT was a particularly unique aspect of the crisis in the Far East, but its effects on U.S. policy in relation to Japan were limited.

When contemplating the value, or perhaps relevance, of examining the human dimension of naval intelligence, a number of themes are evident in the case that the existing body of literature has failed to underscore.[6] First, the notion of not knowing the unknown intensifies in a security environment in which the primary fighting forces are not one's own. Like the British and French, the Americans were simply visitors on the verge of war in the region later.[7] Intelligence during this period for the West was used very differently than wartime intelligence was for the Japanese, the Kuomintang Nationalists, or the Communists. Second, intelligence processes (including disseminated products) improved and became more consistent over time, but this does not necessarily mean the intelligence improved as a result. It is widely understood throughout naval intelligence literature that the ONI (including the Fleet's intelligence officers collecting for the ONI overseas) greatly atrophied in the years between World War I and World War II.[8] There is, however, significant evidence to show that the Navy anticipated the need for better intelligence at least a few years prior to Pearl Harbor and began institutionally changing as early as 1935 under

DNI Capt. William Puleston.[9] Third, in the course of the Navy's preparation for a war footing, the importance of accurate intelligence intensified, but in spite of significant changes in the late 1930s, capabilities were not fully institutionalized to meet the apprehensive demand. Finally, given the number of reported subject intelligence units and the lack of insight into the utilization of the bulk of the information collected, one will likely conclude that intelligence had an ambiguous effect on averting a preemptive war from the Japanese.

Sources and Methods in the Interwar Period

The most sensitive aspects of any kind of intelligence are its sources and methods, and humans were still the main source of intelligence during the 1930s. It is not surprising, then, that the record is still limited in this area during the prewar years. The story of *how* intelligence was collected is intriguing, but it is unreasonable to expect a transparent picture of operational methods. Indeed, a few of the most exhaustive naval intelligence histories say very little about sources and methods.[10] However, in some cases, documents uncovered traces of sources and methods, which is evident in the case of the Navy in the pre–World War II Far East, but hardly enough exists to draw robust, empirical conclusions as to the quality, effects, and institutionalization of practices. It is perhaps ironic, then, that the conclusions drawn in this research are very similar to an intelligence estimate: conservative, purposeful, tailored, and circumstantially specific.

The limited number of sources and methods the research can identify also disables one's ability to infer the differences between them in terms of reliability or authoritativeness. One sees very little ability to assess the qualitative contrasts between the sources a Marine from the 4th Regiment developed from those a naval attaché in Nanking developed with little more than anecdotal evidence. The dearth of archival records undoubtedly results from the ad hoc nature by which sources developed as well as the secrecy entrusted to them and naval intelligence personnel running them. For instance, while sources were consistently not assigned source serial numbers, descriptions in reporting often spoke directly to each one's credibility, albeit subjectively applied in each reporting unit's assessment.[11] With some consistency in reporting throughout this period, terms such as "observation" or "confidential" were used in relation to sources, as was the case with reports from the South China and Yangtze patrol units.[12] In the case of the former, one assumes that the reporting individual refers to himself as the observer. In the case of the latter, however, because there is no affiliated serial code with each confidential source, an evaluation of the individual's credibility or reliability over time—outside of the individual naval intelligence officer who originally developed the source—cannot occur. This undoubtedly presented significant consequences on collection management and oversight for the ONI.

While forward-deployed intelligence officers—in Shanghai, Chongqing, Nanking, Beijing, and Tokyo—originally developed many of the ONI's sources, nearly every *Weekly Summary* report (which began publication in the summer of 1939) during the prewar years included confidential, restricted, or secret sources.[13] The work of foreign press correspondents from the United Press, *New York Times*, the Associated Press, and from foreign press corps were the sources of a substantial portion of the reporting that the ONI, attachés, and others often exploited. As with the other issues mentioned regarding sources, this hindered the evaluation of sources from a collection management perspective.

The Sino-Japanese War as a Crisis for the West

"Crisis," in this case, is defined as (a) a dangerous struggle in which all-out war is not inevitable but (b) can or should be managed by third countries involved (i.e., the United States, Britain, and France), (c) diplomacy will not necessarily avoid escalation, and (d) this can have potentially immediate implications. All of these factors are present in the archival records of the State Department's Office of the Historian, which used the term "crisis" to describe the period at least as early as 1934.[14] It was a unique crisis, however, because it was simultaneously a war for Japan and China and, even as Japan's bellicosity was increasingly evident, a circumstance significantly different for the United States.[15] The initial driving factor for the increasingly adversarial relations between the West and Japan was the fact that Japan openly violated the Washington Naval Conference agreement of 1921–22 in which the United States, United Kingdom, and Japan agreed to set a cap on the ratio of naval tonnage between them.[16] At first the violation was not seen as openly hostile, but Japan's actions in relation to China, Korea, and other nations in East Asia later proved the contrary.

For the United States and Western nations engaged in China, the Sino-Japanese War consisted of a series of sub-crises and points of potential escalation in which the intelligence coinciding with each further explains the Western role. These sub-crises included the initial Japanese invasions of Manchuria and, later, Shanghai; the Nanking invasion and massacre; the sinking of the USS *Panay*; and, finally, the Pearl Harbor attack. Also in this context was the frequent threat to Western commercial shipping, which itself was a crisis for the United States and Britain.[17] As long as militaries of the West occupied China, the threat of crisis loomed because at least since the Boxer Rebellion—when the Navy and Marines first increased their presence in the country—Chinese aversion to foreign military presence was certain.[18] All the while, U.S. forces in the region and the naval intelligence infrastructure overseen by the ONI were charged with collecting intelligence in the face of uncertain national policy. If China fell to the Japanese, this would make it easier for the Imperial Japanese Navy to turn its attention to the United States and the eastern Pacific.[19]

The Japanese invasion of Manchuria in September 1931 through 27 February 1932 and the subsequent acts of aggression against the international settlement in Shanghai might have been considered the first act of World War II in the Asia Pacific. Weakened by years of civil war, China was ripe for invasion. Nationalist and Communist forces focused on each other and on staving off greater Western influence and thus were not prepared to fight an external threat—certainly not one as industrially advanced for the time as Japan. The Kuomintang leader, Chiang Kai-shek, often thought the greater threat to China resided internally from the Communists rather than the Japanese, the former of whom had their roots in the uprisings in Wuhan (and elsewhere) by trade unionists aligned with the Chinese Communist Party in July 1927 (referred to as the 715 Incident).[20] This predisposition points to the Nationalists' inability to fend off a full-scale invasion of the Chinese mainland in 1937, which led to all-out war and the genocide of hundreds of thousands of Chinese in Shanghai and in the Nationalist capital, Nanking. Eventually, Communist leader Mao Zedong proposed that the Nationalists and Communists agree to cease the civil war and first fight their common enemy. While the civil war paused until 1946, the two sides hardly joined together in their efforts. Instead, as the so-called Nanking decade progressed, and the country plunged further into chaos, both sides further consolidated territorial and political control.[21] Ultimately, the dynamics of Communist and Nationalist relations became a preoccupation of U.S. intelligence units observing China during this time.

By January 1932 the United States realized the problem with its forward positions in Shanghai, Nanking, and Beijing after the Japanese government indicated its long-term imperial ambitions of expanding its territory into China and sustaining its presence on the Korean Peninsula.[22] Japan's policy was for the separation of Manchuria from China, which began in September 1931, and this fanned the flames of anti-Japanese sentiment throughout China. The Chinese boycotted Japanese goods and cotton mills. In January Japanese forces at the international settlement in Shanghai attacked the Chapei district. While Chinese popular and military resistance was significant, the Japanese bombed Chenai, setting fire to a densely populated area. The United States and Great Britain diplomatically protested the act and, together with several other foreign governments, rushed additional troops to Shanghai.[23] The 4th Marines, per their primary mission, occupied and defended the international settlement, while the U.S. Army 31st Infantry defended the American portion. Intelligence units observing these events were charged with deciphering the collapse and occupation of China for their governments' interests and involvement in the region. This core mission established the rationale for intelligence requirements for the duration of the crisis.

Finally, followed by a set of events typifying the intensity of the crisis from a Western perspective, the Japanese invasion of Shanghai (13 August

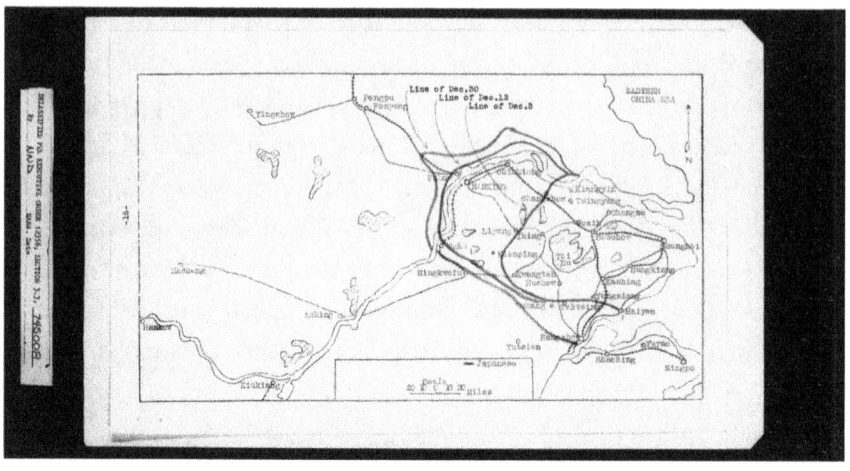

Photo 1. Japanese scheme of maneuver and line of control: Haiyan/Shanghai to Nanking *NARA*

through 25 November 1937) began with a landing at Hongjo Bay (south of Shanghai), followed by a strategic bombing campaign. The landing enabled Japan to outflank Nationalist forces amassed to the southeast of the city. From Shanghai, with Nationalist ground forces weakened and taking nearly 300,000 casualties, Japanese forces made their way to the Nationalist capital of Nanking, approximately three hundred kilometers northeast of Shanghai. Photo 1 depicts the Japanese army's scheme of maneuver from Haiyan to Nanking.

From the north, the Japanese then invaded the Shanxi and Shandong provinces. These campaigns were the first they had experienced against a combined Nationalist and Communist force. Japan's move into China and increasing expansion into the Pacific islands indicated clear signs that Tokyo did not intend to curb its imperial intentions beyond its immediate territory. The U.S. Navy, as the primary U.S. force in the region, collected and reported intelligence that, in hindsight, seems significantly disconnected with the reality of the intended purpose of U.S. foreign policy in the prewar years.

Intelligence needed to play a central role in U.S. involvement in the Far East during the 1930s as the crisis clearly concerned whether

Japan would continue to invade the better part of Asia and effectively diminish Western influence in the region. Short of initiating an undesired conflict, intelligence fulfilled a fundamental part in the United States' ability to observe Japan. Naval intelligence was the most valuable type of information in informing leaders of Japan's imperial ambitions because the Imperial Japanese Navy represented the greatest potential threat to Western presence in the Asia Pacific. Although the U.S. Navy and Marine Corps were not the only U.S. players in the crisis, they held the main U.S. focus because the U.S. presence in the Far East prior to World War II protected maritime interests. This is coupled with the fact that an enormous amount of intelligence was collected solely on land and in the urban, chaotic settings of Shanghai, Beijing, Nanking, and Tokyo by naval attaché in Nanking, Beijing, and Tokyo and by Marines in Shanghai. While one could debate the overall significance of this presence, during the span of the Sino-Japanese War—as to its ability to predict and warn on individual events—the U.S. Navy valued the continuous evolution of knowledge of a rapidly advancing enemy preceding World War II even though it failed to convince policymakers of the inevitability of war earlier than the attack on Pearl Harbor.[24] Given the notion that intelligence in democracies tends to be a customer-based function (i.e., it guides policy through the analysis of collected information rather than following an inductive approach), this was never its purpose.[25] Thus, the key factors during this crisis included Japanese expansion and the danger of inadvertent escalation between the West and Japan.

Command of Intelligence in the Far East

This section shows the arcane state of how naval units collected, analyzed, and managed intelligence in the Far East in the decade prior to World War II, and the fact that the naval intelligence enterprise would inevitably require organizational change and modernization. It is necessary to preface this with the fact that the ONI endured tremendous disarray by 1931 from more than a decade of budgetary neglect and eventual atrophy. Still, it was the nation's first and—to that date—only foreign intelligence body other than the Department of State's attaché system, in which the ONI also controlled the naval attachés. By 1931, however, the ONI lost some of its direction and control over its personnel and policy globally.[26]

In the early 1930s, the Navy was slow in developing an intelligence approach to situations brewing in East Asia and in Europe specifically as it related to the Japanese invasion of Manchuria and the Nazi rise in Germany. Finally, in May 1933, the Navy articulated its information policy: "To acquire through naval and other agencies accurate information concerning the political, military, naval, economic, and industrial policies and activities of all countries. To select, analyze, and preserve information for ready reference and for historical purpose. To acquire and to disseminate expeditiously appropriate information in time of war. To disseminate appropriate information systematically throughout the Naval Service."[27] The statement seems relatively innocuous. The fact that human means and foreign news clippings yielded most of the intelligence in those days, however, required either a significant investment or risks in other areas of warfare to reverse the Navy's atrophied ability to collect intelligence. Additionally, an inconsistent pattern of accounting of circumstantial contexts under which intelligence was collected at the time made it difficult to evaluate potential impacts. In other words, much of what might have been referred to as intelligence was simply information.

As previously explained, the case addresses sources derived from U.S. Navy and Marine Corps operations primarily in China but also in Japan, the Philippines, and other regions in the Pacific. The data discussed here, however, suggest some possible explanations about the nature of intelligence collected and used for decision-making—particularly in relation to the decaying situation in China and the increasing threat of war with Japan in the 1930s. Given that policies to counter Japan's expansion were arguably escalatory (even as they were gradual)—such as military assistance to the Nationalists and, later, the 1941 embargo on oil exports to Japan—intelligence was less useful for crisis resolution and more for the purpose of continuous situational awareness and continuity of the enemy situation.

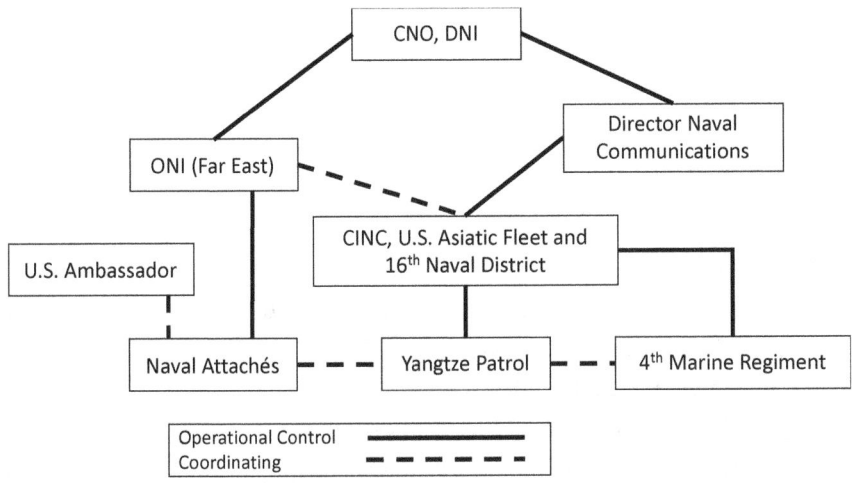

Figure 1. U.S. Naval Intelligence Command and Control (1931–41) *Created by author*

The Command and Organizational Structure

In many ways U.S. intelligence in the Far East during the pre–World War II period can be understood through the Navy's presence in China and each level of command's relationship with the ONI and DNI. Ultimately, the naval intelligence command structure in the Far East consisted of five components, each with its own subcomponents. First, regardless of the ONI's poor condition and the way it evolved over these years, it always remained at the top of the command structure, with the DNI as chief of all naval intelligence. Under him sat the naval district commanders, with the Far East being the sixteenth naval district. Uniquely, however, the sixteenth district was also the regional area of the commander in chief, U.S. Asiatic Fleet (CINCAF), headquartered in Manila. Operationally subordinate to CINCAF were the Yangtze Patrol, the South China Patrol, and the 4th Marine Regiment (Shanghai). The naval attachés in Beijing, Nanking, and Tokyo, as well as other capitals in the region, reported directly to the ONI (B-13, Far East). However, the qualitative nature of command relations became more centralized in 1935 under DNI Captain Puleston; command and control of intelligence across the 1930s generally followed this structure.[28] Figure 1 shows a notional architecture of the naval intelligence command structure in the Far East during this time.

Between the wars, the ONI was organized in five main sections: administrative (which included naval reserves); mail and translation; intelligence (OP-16-B-1, with domestic and foreign bureaus); public relations; and historical library and archives.[29] The Foreign Intelligence Bureau (OP-16-B-1) divided into regional sections, including the Far East (B-13). As Figure 1 implies, the DNI held some level of authority over all realms of naval intelligence. As discussed below, Captain Puleston (DNI, 1934–37) further reinforced a centralized command structure. In addition to the oversight and ability to prioritize and task operational units in the Fleet with intelligence collection, the DNI could also task and manage the embassy naval attachés and consulate generals. While CINCAF had operational control over units and could regularly task intelligence sections throughout the Asiatic Fleet, the ONI regularly tasked (particularly following Captain Puleston's tenure) CINCAF's subordinate units as well.[30] This ultimately contributed to a greater degree of centralization after 1935, with Puleston's reorganization. In addition to subordinate units of the Asiatic Fleet, the ONI periodically deployed individual augments to the Far East to embed with units or live among the population for a time.[31]

Intelligence reporting during this period ultimately served three chains of command. First, the ONI prioritized and tasked the various components; therefore, raw intelligence returned directly to the ONI to conduct headquarters-based analysis. Second, for finished intelligence products produced in the field (i.e., Fleet units), this reporting came directly from the originator and was disseminated to the DNI and the secretary of the Navy, who then shared the report with the secretaries of war and state as well as the president, if required. Finally, subordinate to the DNI, the naval attachés also often shared their intelligence reporting with the ambassador.[32] These dynamics were not perfect, and they often overlooked key people (e.g., CINCAF); however, this was a period change for a naval intelligence enterprise that had grown out of its previous standard practices. Naval intelligence in the Far East was very much the testbed for how the Fleet would prepare for a quickly evolving naval threat from Tokyo while observing the unfolding invasion on the Chinese mainland.

The Interwar Office of Naval Intelligence

The ONI represented the focal point and driving force for naval intelligence for both the Navy and Marine Corps, but the interwar years and the effects of the stock market crash in 1929 left it underresourced and without a clear mission. It is important to understand the power of the Navy—and, thus, the ONI—in the 1930s in terms of affecting interagency relationships. On the one hand, its units in the Fleet produced intelligence (with some minimal, periodic, analytic support from the ONI Far East section). On the other hand, however, being far away from sources of intelligence meant the ONI played the role of centralized coordinator, manager, and final adjudicator of intelligence distributed to customers across the establishment—namely, the president and the secretaries of war, state, and the Navy. In 1937 the assistant secretary of the Navy, Charles Edison, requested a report from the U.S. trade commissioner in Shanghai, China, on Chinese industrial explosives.[33] The resulting deliverable detailed a myriad of naval-relevant issues, from port and warehouse capacities to specifications of containers required for transport, to the ammunition capacity per city on a daily basis.[34] The report was most notable for its valuable use of interagency access to information in an area of expertise (industrial capacity) that ONI and Fleet intelligence officers might not have been able to collect and analyze as quickly. Although its subordinates were often the primary collectors, the ONI oversaw, managed, and evaluated final intelligence. Often a raw report was not intelligence until OP-16 analysts critically analyzed multiple reports and assessed source credibility and implications. This fundamental practice generally continues today. Management of intelligence processes and policies was an evolving dynamic across the 1930s.

However, even as the ONI's influence increased, it demonstrated serious institutional deficiencies. While the DNI held official authority over the naval attachés globally, many of them did not provide him with the quality of reporting as that provided in China and Japan. One aspect of the attaché system not evident in the research was the coordination and sharing of intelligence between naval attachés in the Far East. For instance, perhaps naval attachés in Tokyo, Nanking, Manila, Seoul, and elsewhere periodically sent intelligence summaries to their regional counterparts. This dissemination of intelligence would have been difficult to direct from Washington, but the research does not support evidence of this trend during the prewar years. While Puleston attempted to streamline dissemination processes, abysmal recordkeeping at the ONI (particularly on sources) created another problem.[35] Intelligence priorities were driven not by national priorities but by the DNI and his perceived interpretation of priorities.[36]

Given the fact that the ONI's capabilities atrophied following World War I and further deteriorated with the onset of the Depression, its leadership in the early 1930s (led by DNI Capt. Hayne Ellis, June 1931–May 1934) was noticeably passive at times in its tasking of subordinate units.[37] Captain Ellis often responded to intelligence reports from subordinates with critical thoughts but did not proactively task them in a way to suggest naval intelligence at the time actively attempted to shape strategy. For instance, in response to a report from the USS *Stewart* following a port call in Hong Kong, Ellis wrote an airy thank-you note, stating, "Please go ahead and shoot us any information that you get that occurs to you or could be of interest to us."[38] This response speaks to the significance of delineating between the "push" and "pull" aspects of an intelligence customer versus a producer. Generally, although the DNI received reports from subordinate units, he was not a customer; ultimately, the customers included the president, Congress, and the secretary of the Navy. Instead, Ellis' ONI tended to act as a customer who regarded his subordinate unit's reporting as finished intelligence. Additionally, more instances occurred of Ellis yielding to the CINCAF chain of command rather than directly to the subordinate unit, as demonstrated later under Puleston and Adm. Ralston Holmes. It is possible that Ellis saw himself and the ONI as coordinators of information between the Navy and the War Department as opposed to the producer of intelligence. Either way, the Ellis campaign further underscores the ad hoc and still maturing nature of naval intelligence prior to World War II.[39]

Puleston's Modernization Drive

Historians have sometimes referred to the changes undergone from Captain Puleston's time as the DNI (starting in 1934) as desperately welcomed, but some context and elaboration is required.[40] The ONI is a highly centralized agency, but such a construct holds different connotations for the Fleet in the mid-1930s versus that serving in previous times. Reporting by Fleet units operating in foreign waters and inside foreign countries prior to the buildup of Japanese naval power was not regularly mandated to push all intelligence reports up a chain to a single central repository. In the case of the Asiatic Fleet, CINCAF's subordinate units would report all intelligence to their commander in Manila, and when it appeared to be of interest to the DNI, they would then send it to him through regularly encrypted naval traffic. While preceding DNIs, including Captain Ellis (1931–1934), exhibited individual styles of command, mechanisms to institutionalize a centralized management system did not exist. As a result,

Photo 2.
Capt. William D. Puleston, director of naval intelligence
Naval History and Heritage Command

it is likely that at least some intelligence of value to the DNI was lost by prerogative of naval district commanders.[41] Additionally, while this level of reliability remained until DNI Puleston's tenure, informal measures were used to better coordinate intelligence at least as early as Captain Ellis' time in office, just following the violence in Shanghai in January 1932.[42] This did not necessarily mean that data flowed more comprehensively but rather more easily when the DNI desired. Informality, however, would not last as the crisis became more and more intense in years before the Pearl Harbor invasion.

Under DNI Puleston, the ONI began to focus on more than simply Japanese military capabilities. Puleston wanted the Fleet to focus on the intentions and perceptions of emerging adversaries in a way the agency had not done in years past. In one report the ONI indicated that "a firm belief exists in the minds of the Japanese Army and Navy that they have had considerably more training in night flying than the air services of the United States and that as a result of this training they are considerably superior in night flying."[43] The report identified significant implications in battle wherein Japan might overshoot its operational expectations, thus serving as an Achilles' heel later.[44] While informal, the report resulted in the underpinnings of an earlier version of the national intelligence estimate, later developed by the CIA. From the beginning of the crisis the ONI remained a powerful entity in the United States' ability to collect, analyze, and disseminate intelligence to leaders, although its interwar-atrophied capabilities required changes to support a shifting security environment, which slowly developed over the 1930s.

The institutional challenge of modernizing the practice of intelligence to better handle the crisis in the East was one of collection prioritization, analysis, and dissemination—all increasing concerns for DNIs throughout the 1930s. For the Navy to address this, it had to determine the important factors in the crisis that could be collected upon by units operating in the region. Puleston and his successors were interested in situating ONI intelligence reporting in a strategic context and in the systemic support of the naval intelligence establishment in strategic war planning and operations rather than the largely tactical situational awareness role it had evolved into after World War I. Given the Japanese buildup, the chief of the War Plans Division at the Office of the Chief of Naval Operations wrote to the president of the Naval War College (the repository at the time for many large, strategic intelligence studies conducted by the Navy) regarding the issue of destruction of analytic materials and the relevance of several of the studies on the Far East.[45] The War Plans Division demonstrated difficulty in determining whether each on-hand study (most dating from 1935) held relevance to its current war-planning effort vis-à-vis Japan.[46] This was a metaphor for the broader institutional challenge of how to modernize the intelligence establishment while simultaneously requiring useful intelligence.

The ONI periodically assessed Axis naval strength, which could then be used for strategic decision-making. In 1939 a report showed comparisons of total naval tonnage, data largely collected by Marines and attachés at ports in theater.[47] At the time the United States owned 1.5 million in total tonnage afloat globally. This value was compared to Japan's 1.1 million (primarily in the western Pacific) and combined Italian–German tonnage, 1.1 million. As past works suggests, counting naval tonnage was rudimentary in nature. Naval officers counted ships in harbors, recorded hull numbers, and totaled each class of ship. It is reasonable to assume, however, that this effort did not require a significant amount of unit resources and time. To maintain continued accuracy, however, units in theater continuously monitored shipbuilding and maintenance activity. With the limited number of personnel available and the amount of other regular intelligence reporting, the feasibility of conducting such levels of effort with regularity seems questionable. Ultimately, this led the CNO to increase the number of personnel conducting collections in the Fleet prior to World War II, as described by W. J. Holmes.[48]

One of the areas the ONI attempted to fix in the prewar years was in operational warning intelligence—timely intelligence required by U.S. and British governments had they declared war on Japan prior to Pearl Harbor, which was often seen as possible. While no evidence of actual policy change in this area exists, regular reporting became increasingly focused on the need to provide current enemy dispositions. For instance, a *Weekly Summary* in April 1941 read, "Five thousand Japanese troops, 3500 of whom had received special instruction in jungle maneuvers, left Haiphong during the week. A strong concentration of Japanese transports and light naval craft were reported off Hankow Bay. Troops from Japan continued to arrive at Shanghai while veteran units left the same point, believed bound for Formosa."[49] The Western powers did not intend to invade mainland China, but additional forces leaving Japan represented a potential indication of Tokyo's commitment to seizing greater China, rather than furthering its expansion in the Pacific.

Ultimately, one questions the value of naval intelligence in warning of a Japanese initiation of war. Certainly, volumes are written on the subject, but the important issue to consider here is whether the aggregate pieces—the net strategic meaning of events—could be assembled and deciphered from the West's perspective. For instance, the ONI reported the Japanese foreign minister stating, in October 1940, that Japan would declare war on the United States if it entered the European war or insisted on the status quo in the Pacific.[50] Following this, in late December 1940, the ONI reported that Japan extended its blockade of the China coast to the southeastern ports of the Kwangtung Province.[51] This measure could be taken as a sign that the Japanese were nearly satisfied with their territorial advancement and holdings in the Chinese theater and that there were no indications FDR and British prime minister Winston Churchill would enter the war in the Far East. Actions from the West, such as British and Dutch merchant ships suspending operations north of Hong Kong and women and children evacuating from Thailand in February 1941, further emboldened this notion.[52] All of these instances needed to be reported to contextualize the regional situation, but this required a bit of a revolution in how the ONI and the Fleet effectively coordinated and disseminated information.

The ONI refined its report production practices in 1940 to more clearly communicate the kinds of reports various intelligence customers received, deciphering between individual reports including letters and tabulations (Class A) and those of general interest compiled from time to time (Class B).[53] Furthermore, The ONI's position regarding its products was that "certain evaluation can only be made by competent specialists beyond the ability of the Division of Naval Intelligence."[54] Furthermore, oversight was ultimately—and continued to be—a mission of the customer—namely, the CNO and the executive branch of government.

The amount of information generated in the intelligence services on the Japanese and Chinese situations was vast, but the proper and timely dissemination throughout the Navy of potentially important analysis was a potential problem. What good is intelligence if the right people have out-of-date products? Clearly, this would continue to be a problem in the years leading to the attack on Pearl Harbor; however, the DNI and the War Plans Division viewed it as a major challenge earlier. Operators transferred intelligence from Asiatic Fleet headquarters using the cryptologic system, but it lacked standard operating procedures to determine when intelligence needed to be transferred. Additionally, units operating in Chinese waters and on the mainland did not have the same system (for fear of it falling into Japanese hands), so intelligence reporting was often routed by ships in the Fleet or secure mail.[55]

The ONI changed to more effectively accommodate a wartime footing (as opposed to strategic surprise by attack from the Japanese Imperial Navy), which yielded important implications for the Fleet in the Far East. In 1939, as DNI Rear Adm. Ralston Holmes (1937–39) continued to attempt reforms begun under Captain Puleston, the ONI mandated changes to regular Far East intelligence reporting. The new reports—*Weekly Summary, Far East*—consisted of clear fusions of open (news media), confidential, and secret sources, which closely resembles the current concept of "all-source." Instead of the *Weekly Summary* being a compilation and summarization of raw reports—the way preceding ONI assessments had been—they became analytic assessments conducted by the regional sections (e.g., Far East Section) and based on multiple sources.[56] They included strategic updates of the rapidly changing situation in the region, with contributions from naval attachés and fleet intelligence officers in the region. While intelligence today is more often collected from forward positions, reported, and then analyzed from a distance far away from its source, the weekly summaries often comprised finished intelligence upon arrival because the intelligence personnel in the Far East could more easily verify sources and disambiguate facts. This field-based and seemingly ad hoc approach did not solve the lack of analytic oversight apparently lacking at ONI headquarters in Washington.

Naval Intelligence Preceding Pearl Harbor

Under Rear Admiral Holmes and continuing under Rear Adm. Walter Anderson, the ONI increasingly exploited Japanese press and media for more reliable information on Tokyo's view of the strategic situation due to the limited number of credible sources in Tokyo. For instance, in 1941 a Joint Intelligence Activity press representative wrote that a so-called ABCD line encirclement blockade strangled Japan economically, and Japan will break it "without delay . . . by force if necessary."[57] ABCD was a series of embargoes against Japan by foreign nations—namely, the United States, Britain, China, and the Netherlands. The British government indicated its intention to conduct a mass evacuation of British personnel from Japan with the announcement that its embassy had arranged for a ship to transport all British nationals desiring to leave, a signal that came through confidential embassy-to-embassy exchanges.[58] Around the same time, the U.S. ambassador assessed that "Japanese people are alarmed, apprehensive and in dread of war."[59] Additionally, and contradicting previous statements, ONI confidential reporting discussed the possibility of the establishment of a Japanese "ocean safety zone . . . for the purpose of prohibiting US supplies to the Soviets at Vladivostok."[60] Intelligence officers in country obtained and disseminated this earlier-day version of document exploitation for many years until foreign press became more widely available.[61]

Given the previously mentioned changes in requirements and priorities, the approach the ONI and the Fleet took with collection and source targeting in this period evolved as well. Because units were either ashore or on the Yangtze and South China littorals, nearly all intelligence was derived from human sources as SIGINT technology was still maturing and not widely used as a primary means of collection the way it would be later. Examination of the National Archives records of the Navy during the 1930s (namely, Record Group 80) confirmed this assessment. A persistent paradox, however, existed in the simultaneous need for information and the risk that the ONI would accept in guaranteeing the reliability of sources. While Marines and sailors collected a portion of the intelligence through regular interactions with the Chinese and observations of Japanese occupation forces, more sensitive collections required indigenous sources.

For instance, ONI reporting often indicated that U.S. intelligence relied on Chinese sources to provide battle damage assessment of Sino-Japanese battles.[62] While understandable, the reliability of such sources is difficult to ascertain. As the Sino-Japanese War intensified and the crisis deepened, and as U.S. involvement became more likely, the level and methods of evaluation of reports of guerrilla artillery batteries sinking Japanese war and transport vessels on the Yangtze are unknown. Additionally, the archive records provide very little evidence of the ONI questioning the validity of sources in theater related to Sino-Japanese battles. The lack of scrutiny could be explained as either a lack of policy or a policy of hindsight evaluation by officers conducting the reporting, but this is unknown. Either of these, however, point to an underdeveloped process.

Despite the often-questionable utility of much of the information that naval units ashore reported in prewar intelligence, the nonnaval nature of such reporting lent itself to the notion that allied leaders knew the conflict would eventually need to be resolved in relation to the political situation ashore. Some of these reports provided utility to the Navy's ability to later establish the U.S. Naval Group, China, in Chongqing in 1942 in order to set up the bilateral intelligence-sharing and advisory Sino-American Cooperation Organization. These efforts also undoubtedly enabled the Office of Strategic Services to establish the Dixie Mission in Yenan later in 1943.[63] The ONI and the Asiatic Fleet's intelligence detachments in Shanghai and Beijing maintained situational awareness in the East preceding the Pearl Harbor attack. Upon the signing of Japanese-dictated peace treaties in March 1941, confidential source reporting noted that French Indochina and Thailand "promised not to enter into any agreements or understandings with third powers which would be disadvantageous to Japan," indicating the coercive nature of Tokyo's regional approach.[64] Furthermore, the ONI concluded that this insight was consequential to reducing the obstruction of Japanese actions in Indochina.[65]

While these examples allude to a competent ONI in terms of collections and the availability of much of the intelligence needed to properly assess Japanese and Chinese dispositions prior to World War II, it is less evident the degree to which the ONI underscored the value of analysis.

As discussed later, the fact that Japan first invaded upper and lower Manchuria and Shanghai, brazenly attacked the USS *Panay*, and continued to expand eastward in the Pacific collectively yielded high-level intelligence U.S. estimates of Tokyo's willingness to escalate. Whether this was simply disregarded by Fleet commanders or not aggregately understood is unknown. More than enough human-derived intelligence was available to render an estimate of some value to strategic policymakers. Ultimately, the ONI's ability to aggregately analyze the data and then reprioritize depending on the resulting intelligence played a role in the breakdown of making sense of Japanese actions, at least from ONI headquarters' products.

As the Japanese occupation of Manchuria and islands in the Pacific continued and the likelihood of deeper U.S. involvement increased, the ONI refined its intelligence collection policy—particularly in relation to the territories in which the Japanese expanded.[66] For instance, in 1935 the CNO released tasking to the Asiatic Fleet to conduct scouting intelligence collections on the Pacific islands. It stated that an "intelligence report on the Bougainville side of Bougainville Strait is desired."[67] Subsequently, other scouting instructions were released for similar Japanese positions. The DNI also released guidance and instruction for intelligence personnel engaged in espionage, counterespionage, and passport control to address source operations in a controlled manner.[68] However, another memorandum announced impending training for senior officers necessary for communications intelligence secrecy and security.[69]

The 1930s led to an inflection point in which the ONI experienced a renaissance through trial-by-fire with the Sino-Japanese War. While the DNI often required strategic intelligence on the disposition, quality, intentions, and national perceptions of the enemies, units in theater more often reported on the tactical and operational situations. However, as the following chapters show, there were exceptions to this notion. The ONI's ability to manage collections and turn reporting into intelligence was limited to the Fleet's access to the sources in the Far East. While the enemy was present in China—and much could be learned from this—his leadership extended to Tokyo, where the Fleet's assets were few. Collection and analysis relied on an indirect approach to developing a broader strategic picture. The naval units in the Far East collected what information they could from the access granted to them.

Chapter 2

Collection and Observation in the Second Sino-Japanese War

Intelligence Collection by Naval Units

Continuing in the context of the Navy's role in China and the western Pacific during the Sino-Japanese War, this chapter examines the kinds of intelligence naval units in the Far East collected and how institutional reforms of naval intelligence gathering over the course of the 1930s affected these units. It begins with an examination of the Asiatic Fleet headquarters and the limits it faced in producing useful intelligence for the Fleet from its standoff position in Manila. The discussion then contrasts those findings with substantial intelligence experiences of the 4th Marine Regiment in Shanghai and the naval attaché's office in Nanking. This is followed by a section discussing a different kind of observational intelligence reported by the South China and Yangtze patrols. Finally, some conclusions are drawn from the analysis of the archival record.

The Asiatic Fleet Headquarters

Headquartered at Subic Bay in Manila, the commander of CINCAF—the Navy's Far East theater commander—oversaw patrol operations in and around Chinese littorals and protected U.S. interests and citizens in China.[1] While the DNI certainly centralized the institution of naval intelligence, CINCAF regularly tasked its operating units as well. Unlike the ONI, however, it could not task the attachés, who often received the bulk of intelligence tasking. In many cases the subordinate units, such as the 4th Marine Regiment in Shanghai, were not bound by a specific guiding directive to direct its intelligence reporting specifically to the DNI. Such ad hoc procedures were contradictory at times, and despite the ability for the DNI to maintain a centralized, task-subordinate relationship with CINCAF's units, sometimes Washington recognized CINCAF as the Fleet commander with operational control over the units.[2] This demonstration of power depended on the particular DNI.

Early on, under Hayne Ellis as the DNI, reporting from CINCAF and its subordinate units also tended to be more conversational and undisciplined, characteristic of the fact that, in the early 1930s, the CINCAF headquarters N2 (intelligence) section consisted of a single intelligence officer.[3] A survey report of the British-occupied island of Wei Hai Wei (at the mouth of the Bohai Gulf) demonstrates the ambiguous tone of such intelligence as the report either intended to inform future U.S. operations or provide a general awareness.[4] Although informative, reports were often long and meandered without an explicit point, an indication that they were not explicitly solicited by higher headquarters compared with more succinct reports of the attachés, patrol units, and Marines. Such reports often were equivalent in form to an after-action or trip report today. Additionally, CINCAF could also process and analyze longer-term intelligence products that might have overburdened the busier patrols and 4th Marine staffs. For instance, on direct assignment from the DNI, the Asiatic Fleet reported in December 1935 on the Ta Wah Petroleum Company in Tientsin as possible oiling facilities for future operations and found that the facility carried no fuel or diesel oil in its stocks or storage tanks.[5]

Bearing in mind that the period of 1931 to 1941 was a crisis in U.S. and Western policy toward the Far East, it was officially considered peacetime, both factors affecting command and control and the subjects ultimately useful to intelligence customers. In peacetime, it is not always necessary for the theater commander to closely control forces collecting intelligence.

Instead, given the lack of enemy hostility toward U.S. forces in the region, especially in the early 1930s, CINCAF's role in the chain of command for intelligence was often disregarded, presumably by units needing to pass or inquire about intelligence to other units.[6] This recognition signifies the distinction between prewar intelligence and the in-theater command and control of intelligence apparent later during the war under Admiral Nimitz of the U.S. Pacific Fleet.

The 4th Marine Regiment and Second Marine Brigade

The headquarters of the 4th Marine Regiment and, later in 1938, the Second Marine Brigade resided in Shanghai until the command structure changed in the months following the Pearl Harbor attack. The number of official Marine intelligence personnel maintained on mainland China was around sixteen (six in each of the regiment's two battalions and four at its headquarters) with the regiment, and it increased only with the brigade.[7] In many ways the ONI and CINCAF relied more on the 4th Marines for intelligence (especially in and around Shanghai, with the international settlement) than any other unit—arguably even as much as the attaché's office in Nanking.[8] The reason for this reliance was threefold. First, the location of the 4th Marines headquarters in Shanghai held great importance to the Japanese; therefore, it was very much the heart of activity in China for much of the war, both politically and militarily. Second, with greater capacity than the naval attaché office (which normally consisted of four persons: the naval attaché, his deputy, and two junior officers or enlisted), the Marine regiment covered more territory and sources in a shorter amount of time. Finally, the ability of the Marines to quickly deploy to remote and often harsh locations with heightened levels of danger gave them an advantage over attaché and patrol units. Because boats operating on the Yangtze also occasionally embarked Marines, the Marines could land, move quickly inland, and observe situations.[9] The Marines were the single most expeditionary of intelligence collectors in China during the 1930s, and the information they provided the Fleet was unique in a way that the intelligence of afloat units could not compare. It nearly achieved the intimate detail that attaché reporting often evoked.

Because 4th Marine Regiment units in Shanghai and Nanking were often the only U.S. naval assets able to clearly assess the war unfolding in China, they were important in the three years before the United States and Great Britain entered the war in the Pacific following the *Panay* incident, when patrol units seemed increasingly vulnerable to attack. The form of intelligence engaged by Marines often resembled reconnaissance scouting operations rather than source development and what would later come to be known as HUMINT. For instance, Marine sources in ONI reporting in May 1941 indicated the shear strength of Japanese forces "carrying on five offensives . . . three in the deep interior and two in coastal regions," continuously keeping up to date with each unit's numbers and dispositions.[10] Furthermore, the sources ascertained that along the Yellow River in Honan, at least four to as many as six divisions attempted to dislodge Chinese forces from their positions in the Chungtiao Mountains as well as other units on the offensive in the Han River valley.[11] This assessment undoubtedly required sources in the Chinese National Revolutionary Army (Kuomintang Army), and possibly even Japanese sources, but as evidenced by much of the reporting of the time, source delineation was limited. The ONI weekly summaries that the 4th Regiment contributed to reported a continuous running assessment of the fighting in China, including dispositions of the Nationalists, Communists, and the Japanese.[12] Marine intelligence, expeditionary as it often was, meant that the end product was often less formal than source-developed intelligence and was approached with an ad hoc nature. Despite such a seemingly informal result, this mode of intelligence gathering demonstrated disciplined methods; this era preceded what would later be termed "collection management." Ultimately, while the naval intelligence enterprise processes under the ONI were becoming more formal, informalities inherent in the Navy and Marine Corps, organizational culture continued.

Naval Attachés, Beijing, and Nanking

Adjacent to the 4th Marine Regiment, the naval attaché office served as a heavily relied-upon source for the DNI's intelligence during this period. It enjoyed a natural diplomatic relationship with not only the Kuomintang government but also the British and French legations in both Shanghai and Nanking. Although the U.S. embassy (1928–August 1936 in Beijing and thereafter in Nanking until 8 December 1941) actively participated in typical overt intelligence activities such as official state dinners and functions at the Beijing Club, its naval attachés were subordinate to both the Fleet and the heads of missions at the embassies for whom they immediately served.[13] During the period 1935 to 1939, then-colonel Joseph "Vinegar Joe" Stilwell was the military attaché for China.[14]

Given the range of subjects that naval attachés addressed and the kinds of high-level sources discussed, three explanations about intelligence management during this period exist. First, the units in-theater often drove the agenda by the kinds of intelligence they were able to most easily and expediently produce. Second, by subordinate units driving the collection process, the DNI and other decision-makers (e.g., secretary of the Navy and chief of naval operations) could carefully refine the kinds of intelligence targets they believed were important, given their distant, yet unique bias. Finally, the apparent absence of clear and consistent priorities from the ONI lends itself to the notion that overseeing the quality and reliability of intelligence personnel was a challenge at best.

Intelligence officers at the embassy in Nanking and the installation in Shanghai also acted as covert deliverers of enemy material. In November 1937, as Japan's war against the Chinese mainland was in full bloom, Assistant Naval Attaché J. M. McHugh (Lieutenant Colonel, USMC) delivered a cache of Japanese aviation equipment, seized by a source in the Nationalist 88th Division, to the USS *Panay* for exploitation later by direction of CINCAF.[15] McHugh wrote: "I have this date delivered on board the USS Panay, upon oral instructions from Commander, Yangtze Patrol, certain articles of Japanese aviation material.... It is my understanding that instructions as to the eventual disposition of these articles will eventually be received from the Commander in Chief, Asiatic Fleet, and that in the meantime it is the intention of Commander, Yangtze Patrol, to leave them in the custody of the Station Ship at Nanking."[16] According to McHugh, permission to view the material was granted by the secretary of the commission, Madam Chiang Kai-shek (Generalissimo Chiang Kai-shek's wife), who constituted the highest-level source of the prewar years, rivaled only by Nationalist Jun Tong head (or Bureau of Investigation & Statistics, BIS) Tai Li (戴笠).[17] With some interlocution by a Mr. Donald (a civilian close to Colonel Chenault aboard the USS *Panay*), some articles were released to U.S. custody, one of which was a German-made bombsight the Japanese used that the United States had apparently not yet encountered.[18] The cache consisted of equipment from radio receivers and transmitters to wireless generators and a Vickers air-cooled machine gun.[19] No further data were found as to the purpose of the eventual exploitation, but at the very least, CINCAF wanted to understand enemy fighting capabilities firsthand.

While the acquisition of the enemy articles was not uncommon, the source reliability spoke for itself. According to McHugh—who, as it became apparent through his intelligence reports, was prone to speaking highly of his own collection of work—he convinced Mr. Donald that the "impending departure of the [Nationalist] Government from Nanking might necessitate the abandonment of the exhibits."[20] Madam Chiang then followed this by issuing an order to let "young" McHugh have whatever he wanted of the cache. McHugh commented on the fact that the Japanese used carburetors that embodied the "latest principles of American design," which were still in experimental stage a year and a half earlier and certainly not available for export, as well as a metal fabric that McHugh asserted was much lighter than that used by the United States and would not "support the weight of a man on a wing."[21] Due to the weight and the helpful, yet impatient, Chinese attendants, McHugh could not remove the entire cache.[22] Whether this particular incident was a one-off opportunity is unknown, but the fact that the naval attaché office secured Madam Chiang's approval in exploiting it is significant, for no other reason than it showcases the Navy's relationship with Kuomintang leadership, later enjoyed by Milton Miles and the U.S. Naval Group, China, during World War II.

As in the case of the assistant naval attaché, J. M. McHugh (Captain, USMC), some correspondence from the naval attaché offices shows that higher headquarters did not always drive intelligence requirements, and forward base afforded the customer in Washington an eyes-on perspective of intelligence otherwise not obtained or deemed relevant if stationed elsewhere. In one instance a reporting naval officer wondered about leadership's interest in Chinese information on breaking Japanese codes and its willingness to trade valuable information or goods to the Chinese in exchange.[23] Furthermore, the reporting officer under McHugh stated: "I learned . . . in Nanking that they had just broken a message from the Japanese Consul General in Shanghai to Tokyo which stated that an American named Epstein in the employ of the United Press, who had recently arrived in Nanking, had promised to give them information on the situation in Nanking. . . . I turned the conversation to the basic question of breaking the codes."[24] In another instance, the naval attaché office secured a high-level source (apparently through his relations with Madam Chiang) in the Nationalist government, Dr. Y. C. Wen, the director general of communications, who would later occupy several other high-level positions in the government during the war.[25]

In speaking with Dr. Wen, who had worked on the issue since 1930 and employed over one hundred people, McHugh and his team further deduced that in their diplomatic work alone, the Japanese used from ten to twelve different codes and ciphers; "that their codes are phrase codes almost exclusively with alternative meanings or interpretations; and that they shift codes within messages sometimes as many as four or five times."[26] Furthermore, Wen offered to travel to Washington to educate leaders on the bulk of his knowledge in exchange for help in procuring the machines needed to assist future breaking of Japanese codes and technical advice.[27] This example demonstrates HUMINT enabling SIGINT and the emergence of the intermingling of disciplines for greater effect.

McHugh finished his report on the prospect of Japanese codes to the DNI with an appeal: "Frankly I would like to do a little something for them if possible in return for the many favors and inside information that Madam Chiang has extended to me. Thus far I have been riding on my face and getting away with it, with China progressively awakening to the realization that the United States is not going to do anything to help her and never has had any intention of so doing."[28] While one should always scrutinize the validity of any source, the existence of a consistent record of Chiang Kai-shek and his inner circle reaching out to the United States prior to this—and U.S. policy certainly supported Chiang Kai-shek's regime during FDR's administration[29]—represents a strong example of strategic intelligence, arguably right at the time the Navy became deeply interested in Japanese codes.[30]

Across the 1930s and prior to the United States' entrance into the war, the naval attachés at embassies and consulates in Nanking, Beijing, Shanghai, and Tokyo collected a tremendous amount of intelligence on a wide variety of issues.[31] Intelligence was primarily collected through human means at the time.[32] Because of its vulnerability to interception or mail manipulation by the Japanese, the DNI changed Navy policy to disseminate intelligence through encrypted naval message traffic. The most revealing aspect of the National Archives collection of U.S. naval attaché reports between the years 1930 and 1941 is not the sheer number (although, it was expansive, at 822 just for U.S. embassies in Tokyo and Beijing/Nanking) but the fact that each of the three- to five-person attaché teams covered so many different areas of potential interest to the DNI. Where one might otherwise assume that subjects generally covered enemy orders of battle and shipbuilding plans, these subjects composed only 15 percent of the total. The appendix provides a complete overview of subjects covered by the naval attaché teams in Japan and China during these years.

In lieu of priority intelligence requirements—not found in the archives as part of Navy policy in the 1930s—subjects in the appendix serve as a general list of priorities for the naval intelligence community in the Far East during this time. Additionally, one would consider the fact that a certain portion of intelligence was pushed to the ONI that did not necessarily fulfill the DNI's priorities but was nonetheless useful. For instance, consider economic intelligence.

While the role of the naval attaché can be exaggerated, an appraisal of the work achieved during this period raises the notion that the DNI likely received his most important intelligence from attachés.[33] Moreover, one might consider the freedom by which the attaché office engaged with officials of state. Beyond the position of the intelligence officers assigned to the 4th Marine Regiment—who also enjoyed considerable access—it is difficult to ascertain how afloat units, much less the Asiatic Fleet intelligence officer located in Manila, performed on a similar level. This institutional difference is by design, but it results from the period in question and the kinds of intelligence required. While afloat units produced general studies of ports, enemy laydown, and movements, political and military activity ashore held more persuasive value to customers in Washington. Clearly, this focus changed as the war drew closer and the likelihood the Navy would engage in a battle with the Imperial Japanese Navy increased.

The South China and Yangtze Patrols

Another important component of the primary actors collecting in the Far East was intelligence gathered by the Asiatic Fleet's patrol groups—namely, the South China Patrol and the Yangtze Patrol. Both subordinate units of the CINCAF were uniquely situated to provide a wide array of intelligence on enemy and friendly naval units and infrastructure in ways the 4th Marines, the attachés, or other ONI personnel could not; they stationed in the littorals and near inland rivers where they regularly encountered both Japanese and Chinese forces. Their collections largely derived from firsthand observation, as opposed to that developed through foreign sources, and their frequent movement from port to port.

The subjects the patrol units could cover indicate an outgrowth at times of the ability to move across larger areas in short periods. For example, in November 1936 the USS *Augusta* reported through a confidential source in Singapore that an aircraft plant originally built for the Kuomintang by the U.S. aero-defense company Douglas was then being "sponsored" by the Italian government.[34] As time went on and the United States considered an alliance with Chiang Kai-shek, intelligence targeting the Chinese Nationalists and Communists became nearly as important as intelligence on Japanese forces operating in China, for no other reason than the protection of information from the hands of enemies. The access the ships of the Fleet garnered through their frequent port calls and inlet dockings was qualitatively different from the access of the Marines in and around Beijing, Nanking, and Shanghai because the Fleet covered a more expansive littoral territory. While the record is limited, according to John

Prados, the Navy employed sixty-five linguists from 1920 to 1940; therefore, it is unlikely the patrols extensively used Chinese-language skills, hindering further the ability to develop local sources.[35] Additionally, Yangtze and South China patrol sailors were not trained in intelligence, and intelligence officers were rarely embedded, except when Marines or attachés engaged with them. Where the attachés were often given some basic language training prior to service in-country, it was hardly enough to prepare them for the dialectical intricacies of a language such as Mandarin. No evidence was found in the archival records that the intelligence officers at the Asiatic Fleet or the Marines ashore could provide language skills to the patrol units as well.

The patrol units also observed coastal installation and port facilities that land-based units could not always access as easily. For instance, on a port visit at Chefoo (6–9 December 1935), the USS *Barker* (Destroyer Division 13) conducted an extensive survey of the Bay of Wei Hai Wei and its military characteristics to assess its suitability as a future temporary base for major ships in the Fleet.[36] Relying on local Chefoo sources and "eyes-on" observation, the report discussed indigenous availability of food and water supplies, sanitation, medical resources, and roads.[37] On all accounts, the port and city around the bay would have made a sufficient base for operation, except for the lack of a communications infrastructure. There were no radio stations in operation and no electric lines. Although ships of the China Navigation Company, China Merchant Navigation Company, and Jardine Matheson and Company all stopped there due to a rule when passing between Tientsin and Shanghai, the report found the port too antiquated to sustain naval ships for any period. The report found, however, that Northern Pier at Wei Hai Wei could be used in a landing. Given the pier's strategic position, the report indicated an expectation of a forthcoming Japanese invasion of Shanghai.[38] When the major amphibious landing occurred on 12 October 1937, however, it transpired at Jinshanwei on the northern bank of Hangzhou Bay, south of Shanghai. Conversely, the report could have had equal value for U.S. and British amphibious forces conducting a landing north of Shanghai, nearly equidistant to Beijing, but it is unclear exactly how it was used. The patrol intelligence officers showed some success with collections inland and in the littoral areas in which they collected, but overall, they were disassociated from the sources their Marine and naval attaché counterparts ashore developed.

Alternative and Surrogate Means

Another way the Navy and U.S. government collected intelligence in the Far East was through the explicit or surreptitious employment of U.S. and Western nonmilitary personnel. Some willingly served as sources from the start, while others unwittingly provided information. Others, such as journalists, simply did their jobs, and their work inevitably helped gain a greater sense of the political and security environment. Such quasi-collectors should be clearly distinguished from private industry sources in proximity to foreign information for which the ONI periodically consulted as well.[39] The Navy record, however, of the number of each of these groups used during the 1930s is incomplete. Furthermore, the unofficial nature of such a collection invariably leads one to question the reliability of these sources.

Considering the crisis and that the United States could not dismiss eventual war with Japan, it is perplexing why the ONI waited until 1940 to call to the CNO's attention the importance of leveraging merchant marines in proximity to Japanese naval forces for intelligence, as they had been present in the region for many years prior.[40] Indeed, personnel shortfalls alone might have otherwise warranted an earlier alert that regularity of the merchant marines' position was of high value to intelligence.[41] In a memorandum to the CNO found in the National Archives, DNI Anderson stated that "additional useful information could probably be obtained for the Office of Naval Intelligence and, at the same time, the interest of merchant marine Naval Reserve officers in the Navy might be stimulated if they were invited to supply observations of interest made while on foreign cruises."[42] While the ONI did not intend to interfere with the Weather Bureau of the Hydrographic Office in its use of merchant marines, the DNI acknowledged that the information they observed and collected on a regular basis should be exploited. Furthermore, merchant marine observations offered the guise of a more innocuous presence to the enemy than the often heavily armed units of the Fleet, whereby the Japanese could understandably let down their guard.

On 28 March 1940, the DNI appealed to the CNO to make this information partnership official, and to make it "easy and convenient for them [the Merchant Marines] to get in personal touch with the representatives of the Naval Intelligence Service."[43] In a memorandum dated the next day on implementing merchant marine intelligence collection, the Navy captain in charge of the U.S. Naval Reserve (USNR) merchant personnel affirmed the value in assigning merchant marines with collection tasking.[44] The captain warned, however: "If any steps are to be taken in this direction merchant marine officers should be carefully instructed concerning the extreme care that must be taken to avoid the making of written notes or records, and the same extreme care that their activities ... could not be successfully accused of espionage or service as the agent of the government as regards the securing of information of military value."[45] This statement and the entire counterintelligence effort in relation to merchant marines seem to indicate ignorance or misinformation because, as the evidence shows, both the Japanese and Germans had been engaged in such activity for several years prior to this point.[46] A reasonable assumption is that each of them would have conceived of the idea of the U.S. Navy engaging in similar activity as well.

Despite the well-documented record of missionaries being exploited for intelligence purposes in the Far East prior to the war, no record of naval personnel engaging the clergy for intelligence purposes was found.[47] The Japanese government was certainly aware of the missionaries potentially influencing its ability to maintain strict control of domestic politics. As the ONI reported in 1940: "many Occidental missionaries were dismissed by Japanese churches during the week and it is expected that, in a short time, foreign influence will be entirely removed from Japanese Christianity."[48] The quote demonstrates the ONI's interest, but this is likely more a commentary on the deteriorating security environment in Japan for Westerners.

As with missionaries, the record shows no official Navy use of its own journalists as intelligence sources. It is unlikely journalists were employed by intelligence units; however, the Marine Corps deployed its own journalists with the *Leatherneck* and the *Gazette*, and the Navy sometimes deployed journalists of the *Proceedings* of the U.S. Naval Institute to China throughout the 1930s.[49] Journalists' ability to collect information on the enemy was impressive from an intelligence perspective. In addition, even though their published reports were not secret intelligence, the ability to gain access to details of warfighting strategies, tactics, and plans was undeniably useful to the Fleet. For instance, one report detailed the maneuver warfare tactics used by the Japanese army to attack the 100,000-strong army of Shansi from the rear.[50] Another account reported on weaknesses within the Japanese army, such as "clashing political ideas of various groups."[51] If one considers the audience to which the Marine Corps disseminates its publications, the implicit value of such information rests in it preparing personnel for service in the Far East, although its use as actual intelligence for which the Navy made decisions is limited at best.

A complete and definitive account of the Navy's use of non-Navy personnel for intelligence purposes during the 1930s has not been published for two possible reasons. As alluded to earlier, it is unlikely one will find explicit policy outlining the processes through which this was achieved, for no other reason than its sensitivity. Second, while the merchant marines clearly fulfilled an intelligence-gathering purpose, much intelligence gained by the Navy and Marine Corps from journalists, missionaries, and private corporations during the 1930s supplemented the foreign-source intelligence collected by units in-theater. However, unless otherwise clandestinely managed by the ONI Intelligence Branch for the Far East (OP-16B-11), the ONI's Public Information Office in the Public Relations Branch (OP-16-C1) coordinated this information. Ultimately, evidence exists of the use of non-Navy personnel for intelligence during this period, but the degree to which one could produce a complete record remains unclear.

The units operating in the Far East were both enabled by an ONI undergoing reforms. There were flaws in how the Navy executed its intelligence mission, and the 4th Marines and the Yangtze and South China patrols were perhaps the clearest testbeds for this. While the naval attaché was technically under the DNI, his mission was fundamentally different from that of the Fleet because the attaché operated in a diplomatic context. The Asiatic Fleet headquarters' role rarely put its intelligence officers in close contact with sources in-theater; rather, they acted much as the role of a modern service component, producing finished intelligence and liaising between higher headquarters and the operating units. Broadly speaking, for the flawed system that the prewar naval intelligence enterprise was, it increasingly showed signs of modernization and closer alignment with what the DNI expected, which often resulted in intelligence of significant potential value.

Crisis Culmination and Intelligence

Building off how and what naval intelligence units collected, this section pulls together the major events and themes occurring in the 1930s Far East and focuses on how U.S. naval intelligence addressed each in the years preceding the attack on Pearl Harbor and America's more pronounced alliance with Chiang Kai-shek and the Kuomintang. One might view some of the events of the 1930s individually as mini crises within an overarching crisis. Conversely, because none of them pushed the United States and the West into a sudden escalatory cycle with Japan, collectively they added to a growing strategic tension precipitating the oil embargo on Japan in the summer of 1941 and, later, the Japanese attack on Pearl Harbor.[52] Clearly, however, no amount of intelligence seemed sufficient to push the United States into a preemptive war with Japan.[53] Other aspects of Japan in the prewar years that naval intelligence tracked created escalation in a subtler way, such as through foreign relations and territorial claims. The value of intelligence during this period might seem dubious in the absence of countering military action, but it provided situational awareness to operational units and built a comprehensive understanding of the political and military crisis evolving between the United States and Japan during the 1930s, which was useful to the DNI and the Roosevelt administration. Ultimately, considering the intelligence produced, the prewar period observed a myriad of lost opportunities for intelligence customers in Washington, despite the well-informed Asiatic Fleet sailors and Marines.

This analysis warrants a word on the semantics of the term "crisis." It is often used, in the media and even in intelligence, as if it is commonly understood. Moreover, although a well-established discourse on "crisis" exists, the word is generally misused or at least liberally used.[54] For instance, in November 1935, citing intelligence reporting solicited from CINCAF, DNI Puleston wrote to the commander, U.S. Fleet (CINCFLEET) that, given the attempted assassination of the Chinese foreign minister, Wang Jingwei, the Japanese arrest of several prominent Chinese officials, and the Chinese nationalization of silver (an attempt to keep the Japanese from stealing silver), the situation in North China was "rapidly approaching a crisis."[55] Importantly, as if a signal to CINCFLEET to alert his higher authorities, the DNI stated that there was popular support for the Chinese government's decision to refuse to yield to Japanese demands and to fight them if necessary.[56] Events in foreign countries are only as crisis-worthy as the importance that leaders place on a change in policy, and intelligence informs this. In short, crises can continue to intensify, as demonstrated by the Sino-Japanese crisis, even when the interests of foreign nations with the wherewithal to intervene are threatened.[57]

Prior to the 1930s the Asiatic Fleet's approach to the unfolding crisis established U.S. fortifications throughout the Pacific, showing that a long-term view of a possible war with Japan would undoubtedly include fighting over islands in the Pacific. Subsequently, intelligence aided in the preparation for such circumstances for the United States and Great Britain. For instance, reporting in 1929 indicated that "the Commandant doubts if the island could be 'Secretly' fortified without the knowledge of Japanese now on the Island and it is extremely doubtful if any work done by other than service personnel could be kept a secret, and even that would be questionable while Japanese are on the island."[58] The memorandum discussed Japanese naval and industrial presence on Guam and in Saipan in great detail and cited governmental personnel on Guam as the source.[59] This example reveals a broader perspective on long-term Japanese planning on the part of the Navy. Its importance holds value in hindsight associations when comparing Japanese buildup in the Pacific over time.

In a similar case, in March 1941 the ONI determined an increase of Japanese forces from forty-five thousand to sixty thousand on Hainan Island as well as three hundred Japanese planes, a sign of a possible escalation of force in the region given the fact that the laydown and posture of forces in an area tends to be deliberate.[60] Meanwhile, two months later the Japanese navy occupied Lema Island, near Hong Kong, as well.[61] A Western Pacific rivalry in the 1920s evolved into a crisis with the Japanese invasion of mainland China, and the Fleet—unprepared at first—recognized this shift even as its ability to collect intelligence to mitigate it required a formalized change to address the threat.

The Japanese Invasion of Manchuria

The Japanese invasion of Manchuria in September 1931 surprised the Western powers, as did the ensuing attack on Shanghai in early 1932 which, considering the paralysis of the naval intelligence system at the time, means the failure of foresight is not surprising. In February CINCAF had provided an estimate of the situation to the ONI, stating that his "general impression of the Japanese Army is that it is overconfident, has poor estimate of the enemy [presumably the Chinese Nationalists]; is slow unwieldy, careless in choosing gun positions and in saving equipment ammunition etc. in exposed positions."[62] The United States did not respond much at first until the American portion of the international settlement in Shanghai was also threatened with violence in January 1932 and the realization that Chinese (both Communist and Nationalist) forces were ill-equipped to defend themselves, which constituted a fundamental mechanism of the crisis.[63] Although policy dictated that the Marines guarding the legation there and in Beijing exclusively defend Americans, discreet operations took place, such as a detachment from the USS *Houston* landing at Shanghai on 3 February to reinforce the 4th Regiment.[64] The bigger question was apparent: Would the Japanese stop at China and the western Pacific? Or would Japan continue trying to expand its empire further into the Pacific? The Marines in Shanghai temporarily sought reinforcement by a single Army regiment.[65] Subsequently, the DNI continued to set intelligence requirements related to Japanese units operating in northern China, which ultimately enabled leaders to develop a deeper understanding of the course of the crisis.[66]

The ONI's and CINCAF's interest in the ability of Chinese forces to fend off further Japanese invasion seems to be one of the primary purposes of the intelligence gathered during the early period (1932–35) primarily because U.S. policy would not yet allow for direct confrontation with the Japanese (except in situations where units defended themselves). The movement of Chinese Manchurian forces to the northeast was significant because it signaled a retreat rather than an immediate confrontation.[67] Additionally, however, the Japanese clearly intimidated the patrols on the Yangtze.[68] The War Department desired basic information: the numbers of Japanese forces in northern China, their capabilities, and details about their command leadership.[69] In this, tasking came in a typically traditional way: War Department to DNI (ONI) to CINCAF to the 4th Marines in Shanghai and then back to CINCAF to ONI and the War Department. Crisis intelligence in this case evolved because the institution was still immature in responding to the nature of the threat, but the reforms that came in years following the Manchurian invasion originally stem from the Navy (and War Department) being caught off guard by Japanese intentions. Demobilization following World War I had allowed the naval establishment—and, thus, its intelligence capabilities—to atrophy. While the ONI was the premier intelligence agency for foreign intelligence, it was undermanned prior to Rear Admiral Puleston's leadership).[70] Of course, this continued to be an institutional challenge at least through the Pearl Harbor attack.

Shanghai to Nanking and the Pre–World War II Buildup

The Japanese began an offensive in the summer of 1937, marking the official beginning of the Sino-Japanese War, instigated when Chinese Nationalist forces near Shanghai killed two Japanese marines.[71] Following months of fighting, the Chinese forces withdrew from Shanghai. On 4 December 1937, CINCAF reported substantial Japanese troop movement sixty kilometers from and toward Nanking.[72] CINCAF also reported (likely from units on the Yangtze River) that Chinese forces had evacuated

Kiangyin forts on the night of 2 December and withdrew westward from Tanyang, Kintan, and Liyang.[73] In addition to CINCAF subordinate units (Commander, Submarine Squadron 5; Commander, Destroyer Squadron 5), the ambassador in Nanking was notified. Although it was likely that other word-of-mouth sources alerted the embassy on the Japanese force presence near Nanking, CINCAF did so starting seven days before the Japanese marched on the center of Nanking. Still, the evacuation of the embassy began then and continued until 12 December, a day before the massacre occurred. The same day, CINCAF reported that Japanese planes actively bombed the Nanking perimeter as refugees crossed the north bank of the Yangtze.[74] In the process, Japanese bombs also struck two British steamers on the river.[75]

The Japanese became bolder in their actions against U.S. interests in the East. Following the *Panay* incident on the Yangtze River in December 1937 in which Japanese fighter planes sunk the U.S. gunboat, apologized, and later paid an indemnity, Tokyo was less selective about its actions, such as commerce and island raids. For instance, a May 1941 ONI weekly summary reported that the Japanese military "broke open two warehouses in Haiphong and seized American goods, originally destined to Chiang Kai-shek's government, valued at $10,000,000," stating that Japanese freighters traveled en route to Haiphong to transport the merchandise to Japan.[76] Having warned against provoking Japan in the past, the U.S. ambassador in Tokyo, Joseph Grew, communicated to the State Department that little more could be avoided, and Tokyo was already provoked to such actions.[77] The crisis escalated, and the Navy entered a time in which intelligence was no longer a quaint matter of situational awareness but a necessity for monitoring prewar conditions. There is little evidence to suggest that the increase in prewar intelligence of Japanese activity in China greatly affected U.S. policy on Japan in China, other than acting as a monitoring function for the Roosevelt administration. This is likely because China was always a sideshow and not the main act, which would remain true even through World War II, mainly a result of the close relations the United States, Great Britain, and greater Europe naturally and historically shared.[78]

While the ONI's attention to warning intelligence littered the archive records for 1939–41, there is little to indicate how Washington and London actually used it. For instance, on 20 October 1940 the ONI reported that Japanese foreign minister Yōsuke Matsuoka indicated that Japan would "declare war on the U.S. in case the U.S. enters the European war, or insists on the status quo in the Pacific."[79] One knows, however, that this was ultimately not the case; Japan entered only after the oil embargo in the summer of 1941 further altered the status quo in the Pacific. Prior to this, CINCAF warned the secretary of the Navy that the situation in the Far East was "steadily and swiftly deteriorating," and as the Japanese assumed greater control, U.S. interests would disappear.[80] He recommended either "consent to our expulsion from China" or "in conjunction with other countries serve notice on Japan that her conquest of China will not be tolerated."[81] If the mission of the Navy was to provide ready forces capable of defeating an enemy at sea, the job of naval intelligence was to prepare naval forces at any moment for this mission—and with accurate information.

The ONI noted a shift in Japanese grand strategy in 1941 in relation to increasing Western pressure through oil and trade limitations, eventually amounting to the U.S.-imposed embargo. "The Tokyo Government placed Japan at a full economic war foot by implementation of the remaining provisions of the national mobilization law."[82] Japanese citizens began leaving India, Australia, New Zealand, Singapore, and Hong Kong, and the Canadian Pacific bureau closed its offices in Japan.[83] One of the more ominous signs of economic warfare was the fact that a Japanese tanker left San Pedro empty even as Tokyo needed oil more than ever following the July oil embargo enacted by FDR.[84] While it is not clear where the port authority in San Pedro reported the departure, the report began a dangerous series of coercive economic actions prior to the attack on Pearl Harbor. Japan had little oil of its own, and losing roughly 88 percent of its total regular supply forced it to import from nations it had originally confronted.[85]

In 1941 strategic intelligence began to flow with regularity. First, Japan formed an unsaid policy in relation to the Russo-German war and the crisis in the East it created, leading naval intelligence analysis to speculate whether this apparent shift could include a blockade of

Vladivostok.[86] The move caused additional problems in the event the United States and Great Britain declared war on Japan as it limited the number of eastern ports the U.S. Navy and Royal Navy could use to protect those vulnerable to attack in the south, such as Subic Bay. Second, the Japanese attempted to consolidate power in southern China. Troops landed in South China and "occupied six ports along the coast from near the mouth of the Pearl River to Pakhoi . . . driving inland from these points with the objective of closing Chinese supply routes."[87] The ONI reported that the Japanese navy strengthened its blockade of the Guangzhou (Canton) area "by establishing an office in the Portuguese colony of Macao, where all seaborne traffic must obtain permits."[88] An offensive on the Kiangsi Province was launched "in an effort to break up a concentration of some 80,000 Chinese forces."[89] At the same time, Japanese troops in central China moved southward while reinforcements arrived from mainland Japan to the Yangtze River in the central region, and the imperial navy intensified its blockade of the South China coast. Furthermore, an ONI detachment in Shanghai assessed indications that Japan would soon attack Siberia and advance into southern Indochina (Vietnam) to establish air and naval bases.[90] Although assessments such as these aided in a greater understanding of the adversary's trajectory, they do not appear to have prompted a strategic shift in U.S. naval presence to counter such activity prior to Pearl Harbor.

As the crisis evolved and the situation in East Asia transformed into more of a prewar environment, intelligence reporting became more about warnings, indications, and preparations of the battlefield. This entailed reporting on Japanese troop sizes, the actions they undertook in the region, and possible intentions—all subjects that could often only be reported on through human sources. While operational units had gained significant experience in the region in the previous several years, the intelligence mission became a lot more difficult for two reasons. First, access to credible sources was challenged with increasing hostility. Second, while naval intelligence units in China learned a lot about the Japanese military from that vantage point, truly high-value sources resided in Tokyo, where the U.S. Embassy assigned too few intelligence officers. Overall, the highest-value intelligence collected during this period in the Far East seems to have been from the 4th Marine Regiment in Shanghai and the naval attachés in Beijing and Nanking.

Reporting Territoriality and Foreign Relations

An important theme of prewar intelligence included deciphering Japanese territorial claims and adversarial actions at sea in the months preceding the Pearl Harbor attack as the United States increasingly assumed a war footing. As one report clarified, Japanese territorial claims extended from the Spratley Islands west to Half Moon Shoal (seventy miles from Panama), and the territory from North Danger Reef to just north of Swallow Reef in the south; this report aimed to show to leadership in Washington the geographic degree to which the threat extended.[91] Reporting from afloat units of the South China Patrol, the Imperial Japanese Navy began using pirates (in stolen Filipino fishing boats) to harass seafarers near Palawan.[92] In August 1941 the naval attaché in Tokyo indicated that Japan tolerated the passage of U.S. war matériel to Vladivostok for the USSR without use of force or diplomatic protest.[93] The reasoning for this tolerance likely stemmed from indications by the Soviet government to Tokyo that it regarded any act to hinder such support as an unfriendly act, as well as Tokyo's desire to avoid influencing a greater alliance between Moscow and Washington. Still, such behavior contrasted the thrust of Japanese actions elsewhere in the region. Meanwhile, the director of the Japanese ministry of foreign affairs (U.S. bureau) indicated to U.S. ambassador Grew in Tokyo that "contemplated actions by the US and Britain" would strengthen the hands of those in Japan favoring a stronger policy.[94] Analysts sorting through these indications in Shanghai, Tokyo, and elsewhere faced the ambiguous complexity of observing diplomatic hyperbole in a period of heightened tension. Indications that the U.S. and Japanese delegations would meet to discuss worsening relations made such statements even more consequential for intelligence analysts observing the events.

One of the elements that the ONI consistently watched from the beginning of the Sino-Japanese conflict and the Japanese naval buildup was Tokyo's foreign relations and specifically connections to the broader strategic context.⁹⁵ Alliance and foreign policy monitoring of foreign governments is a fundamental aspect of intelligence. This tendency manifested itself in a few ways in the Far East. First, in several instances, the ONI reporting tied the Pacific theater to the crisis in Europe. The ONI reported in January 1941 that the Japanese government possibly assisted German raiders in the Pacific.⁹⁶ This support implied a political alliance between Tokyo and Berlin. The ONI reported that the Japanese minister of foreign affairs, Yōsuke Matsuoka (松岡 洋右), traveled to Italy to confer with dictator Benito Mussolini and Pope Pius XII before going to Berlin to meet with dictator Adolf Hitler.⁹⁷

Second, the ONI found reason to question Britain's relationship with Japan, noting, "British quarters insist that possible arrangements for British-Japanese trade is not an 'appeasement' measure"—a subtle acknowledgment that the sovereignty of allies dictates that disagreements occur as part of reality.⁹⁸ Third, the Japanese feared a grand alliance between the United States, Britain, and the Soviet Union. In May 1941 the ONI Shanghai uncovered evidence of collaboration between Japan and Russia along the China coast and reopened shipping services between Vladivostok and Shanghai.⁹⁹ Feeling the impending doom of a counteralliance, the ONI alluded to the fact that "Japan has shown great concern and fear over preparations for an American-British-Soviet Military conference in Moscow with a cry of encirclement."¹⁰⁰ Either in protest or in the context of general U.S.–Japanese relations, Tokyo refused the evacuation of one hundred U.S. private citizens, an unprecedented act in defiance of international norms.¹⁰¹

Further considerations included the assessment of the Chinese and whether the United States should further align with the Kuomintang in an ensuing conflict. Despite the fact that the Nationalists and the Communists agreed not to fight each other until they defeated the Japanese, this proved to be a far-flung aspiration that placed particularly troublesome pressure on U.S. intelligence to decipher such intentions. Even in the months preceding World War II, Western missionaries and citizens on international assignment often collected and delivered intelligence on political issues of interior China. For instance, the ONI reported that a missionary report from Beijing showed increased friction between Chiang Kai-shek's troops and the Communists "so severe in south Hopei and south Shansi that no operations are being conducted against the Japanese in these districts."[102] Although the Nationalists and Communists were never a unified alliance, pronounced long-term differences in how to run the country dominated their ability to operate with a single voice. U.S. Army and OSS support of the Communists (under Mao) in Yenan later exacerbated this tension, while the Navy established SACO with Tai Li.

Ultimately the United States decided to support the Nationalists prior to entering the war, and naval intelligence units in China served an integral part of enabling this through continued reporting on Chinese capabilities, dispositions, and perceptions through close contact with senior Kuomintang sources. For example, in June 1941, the ONI reported, "the Chinese Army Staff informed the American military attaché that China faced an acute small arms shortage. 150,000 rifles and 15,000 automatic rifles together with ammunition are necessary to enable the Chinese to continue resisting Japan for another year."[103] Additionally, reporting on primary inter-theater logistics route availability, such as the Burma Road, was important.[104]

As ONI reporting became more sophisticated and customer-focused in 1940, and as Washington became more aligned with the eventuality of war with the Japanese, some reports in August 1941 included enemy activity occurring in several subregions of the Far East theater, such as the heavy bombing attacks on the Burma Road, the cessation of foreign travel in Manchukuo, and the Japanese troop reinforcement in Indochina.[105] Another important fact concerned the United States' intention to establish a military mission in China at the advice of Chinese military leaders in Chongqing (particularly Tai Li), led by Brig. Gen. John Magruder, U.S. Army, which represented an important milestone in the prewar establishment of an intelligence base. While the Asiatic Fleet and the Army had been in China for several years by this point, no official military relationship had yet been established with either Nationalists or Communists.

Collectively, these events contributed to the intensification of a crisis already years in the making. Naval intelligence units operating in the Far East reported on them, worked with allies, and developed sources inside the Chinese Nationalist community and among the general population to produce continued intelligence, which interpreted meaning for U.S. policy in the region. While the latter seems like a fool's errand in the broader context (given the eventual attack on Pearl Harbor), it is reasonable to conclude that naval intelligence accomplished its purpose—namely, to provide useful information for senior decision-makers to consider in making policy decisions. Customer policymakers could do with that information what they chose, but that was a separate issue from the naval intelligence mission. Considering the span of naval intelligence efforts and the fact that the War Department's Military Intelligence Division was the only other recognized intelligence agency at the time, naval HUMINT progressively became more valuable to Navy leaders and civilian political leaders in the period preceding the Pearl Harbor attack if for no other reason than it enabled the administration to build a clearer case for countering Japanese expansion.

Conclusion

As the likelihood of war with Japan increased during the crisis, the Roosevelt administration's reliance on naval intelligence grew, as evident in the naval mobilization that began as early as 1939.[106] As a result, this required greater refinement of intelligence policy, organizational structure, and the readiness of intelligence officers. The research uncovered a great deal of foreign policy development and oversight at the national and Fleet levels. Even as the ONI attempted to modernize and improve its collection and reporting practices in the 1930s, there were fewer records on tactical and operational policy. Intelligence officers developed reports with a significant amount of autonomy, as evidenced in the sources they developed and the kinds of insights they provided to the DNI. They were often free to collect by any means necessary within the bounds of U.S. priorities in the Far East. As long as the operation did not compromise U.S. relations with the Chinese Nationalists or initiate hostility, tradecraft was minimally managed at higher levels. This produced mixed results, however. Sometimes the level of risk appeared to be greater (e.g., the incident with Madam Chiang) depending on the means of collection. More often, however, intelligence reported during this period suggests only a moderate risk.

The DNI and subordinate commanders infrequently issued priority intelligence requirements, often in an ad hoc manner, and they seemed to take less of a central role than in the intelligence community in later years. Like the autonomy intelligence officers often enjoyed, they sometimes proposed issues as potentially important to Washington. When the CNO or DNI requested information from units of the Asiatic Fleet, such requests often clarified particular details rather than providing strategic information to the Fleet. This indicates a possible lack of subject-matter insight in collection management at the ONI. This should not, however, be taken as a sweeping conclusion, as there is some evidence that the ONI's tasking to the Fleet occasionally focused on other important issues as well.

Considering the nature of navies and the information they generally require to operate both in war and peace, the number of subjects reported on in this period is remarkable. Subjects such as economic resources and infrastructure as well as internal politics and leadership issues later became synonymous with CIA reporting—in other words, they were considered nonmilitary issues. While the range was seen more clearly through the work of the naval attachés in Nanking, this was also apparent in the work of the 4th Marine Regiment and Second Marine Brigade in Shanghai.

It is doubtful whether any amount of HUMINT could have prevented the inevitability of war with Japan, but this was not the intended purpose of the intelligence that was collected largely in Japanese-occupied China. The United States under Roosevelt in the 1930s did not intend on becoming embroiled in a war on the Chinese mainland. That is the nature of crises, however. Nations often aim to monitor a crisis with limited military presence, to look after national interests, and to avoid greater calamity. Intelligence is the fundamental mechanism for providing this monitor. The value of intelligence by human means in the decade prior to the attack on Pearl Harbor was largely not for warning but rather for strategic awareness over Japan and the general situation in China. It was for understanding a rapidly improving adversary and monitoring the likelihood of eventual war. Still, the focus on Japan seems like an intelligence tragedy, given the attack on Pearl Harbor. The attack might not have even been for lack of information about Japanese capabilities or even strategic intentions. The

ONI and its units collected and reported on exactly what one would expect of a naval intelligence organization, but given the misunderstanding surrounding warning intelligence, failure was inevitable.[107] It is unreasonable to blame the quality of human intelligence. Prewar intelligence prepared the Navy for its eventual occupation of the region and provided future organizations—Naval Group, China, for example, and the Joint Intelligence Center Pacific Ocean Area—with an established baseline of sources, repositories, and relationships with the Kuomintang Nationalists. As shown in this research, intelligence units operating in the Far East prior to the war produced tremendously robust intelligence. Intelligence officers and organizations are not judged on volume but accuracy and credibility of sources. On the latter, it appears the Navy and Marine Corps contributed significantly.

Part II

Damage Control

The World War II Legacy and Preparing for Communist China

Chapter 3

Legacies of World War II and the Resumption of the Chinese Civil War, 1942-49

Northeast Asia in the post–World War II years represented both a crisis for the remaining Western military forces and a microcosm of the burgeoning cold war.[1] The Chinese verged on resuming a civil war, interrupted in 1937 by the Sino-Japanese War. Postimperial Japan gradually became peacefully reintegrated into the region. The Soviet Union gained greater regional influence after the invasion of Manchuria in August 1945. The Harry Truman administration did not intend to respond militarily to the Chinese Civil War or to the Soviet presence in East Asia, but the potential spread of Communism became increasingly unacceptable to the West. The Navy's mission in China during this period, however, included several opportunities to observe and collect intelligence to inform leadership in Washington on developments in a highly consequential region.[2] Moreover, although the deployment of the Marines in northern China in September 1945 was primarily to "accept the surrender of Japanese troops for the Chinese Central Government and supervise the repatriation of Japanese military and civilians," as was their experience in China prior to the war, intelligence gathering remained uncelebrated, although it was an important and necessary byproduct.³ For a naval intelligence establishment in transition, the period after the war was both chaotic in its policy adjustments to a new security environment and an opportunity to gain greater insight into a rapidly changing environment.

This chapter argues that the World War II and post–World War II institutional changes that occurred in national security (culminating with the National Security Act of 1947, and the subsequent establishment of the Central Intelligence Agency, the National Security Council, and the Joint Chiefs of Staff) had significant implications for the collection and production of naval intelligence in a more national context, but archival data show only limited evidence of this immediately affecting how the Navy and Marine Corps fulfilled their missions in East Asia. Policy and organization on the use of the military services in national-level intelligence was incomplete to date and still evolving. This unsettled evolution inherently affected how the Fleet and Marine Corps perceived the intelligence mission at the service level in Washington, which was generally aloof to the day-to-day realities of Fleet operating forces in the Far East.⁴ Ultimately, this disconnect created the effect of two (or more) naval intelligence contexts existing simultaneously: the one in Washington, in which the services fought for ever-dwindling (at least until 1947) postwar resources in a newly formed national security construct, and the one in which the Fleet operated in the existing national security framework.⁵

This case is explored in two parts. First, important background context from naval intelligence going into and during World War II is provided. This includes how intelligence was integrated in the Pacific campaign and how it changed institutionally to meet the needs of the warfighter. Second, the case examines the war's aftermath and legacy on the naval intelligence community. This includes an exploration of the final days of the Sino-American Cooperation Organization (SACO) and Naval Group, China (NGC), the bilateral intelligence-gathering and -sharing organization.⁶ Both of these sections provide pertinent background for why the disparate approach to intelligence going into the war needed to be revamped for a new and very different postwar era.

Pacific Naval Intelligence during World War II

Globally, the Navy's approach to intelligence during World War II was necessarily robust, and it evolved into a multifaceted and prioritized discipline concerned with the timely and predictive in value of information. The fundamental driver of this was the difference between the proximity that intelligence collection of any kind stood to gain during peacetime and the access that was denied during wartime. In general, there was far less HUMINT in the Pacific than in the European Theater. This is due to the obvious geographic isolation of much of the Pacific campaign's island-focused battles. In Europe, intelligence officers (both under the ONI and under the Office of Strategic Services, or OSS) were ashore operating at embassies and cover facilities years in advance of the landings in Italy and in northern France. The Pacific campaign was a different story entirely.

As discussed in each of the cases in this book, access to sources is an essential lynchpin for intelligence, and when denied, it is an Achilles' heel for HUMINT. During the period of the Sino-Japanese War, when American naval personnel were stationed in China, Japanese forces certainly operated with violent impunity in the region, but run-ins with them by U.S. forces did not yet run the risk they would later, when open conflict was at hand.[7] When war broke out for the United States in December 1941, there was suddenly a clear denial of territory (the U.S. Embassy in Tokyo was closed 8 December) and a need to maintain a standoff position for safety reasons. This difference of environment invites one question, the subject of this chapter: How will naval HUMINT in World War II be represented in the historical record? This will be addressed below, both broadly across the Fleet as an institution and within the East Asia regional context to align with the subject of this book.

Intelligence after 7 December 1941

The days and weeks following the Japanese attack on Pearl Harbor were a chaotic and yet unifying time for the United States, its allies, and its Fleet.[8] There was little time to ask why or how the attack had occurred, as now the country was at war. In time, however, it would become clearer that Fleet intelligence had failed.[9] As some have pointed out, Japanese bellicosity in preceding years—for example, in the *Panay* incident—should have at least been considered strategic warning signs.[10] Failures aside, the attack put the Fleet on a war footing, which meant operational intelligence would soon be of higher priority than HUMINT, the latter being less relevant to immediate movements of ships and other forces than the former. While HUMINT is often about the intentions and perceptions of the adversary, this was less relevant after the adversary's intentions were clear with the attack on Pearl Harbor.

Operational intelligence was the product of electronic signals, radio communications intercepts, and code breaking and would remain steadily vital to the afloat forces of the Fleet in both the Pacific and Atlantic campaigns for the duration of the war.[11] The intelligence that preceded the Battle of Midway—arguably the most important naval battle of the war—was entirely enabled by Station HYPO's (officially known as Fleet Radio Unit Pacific, or FRUPAC) attack on the Imperial Japanese Navy's JN-25 code groups.[12] HUMINT could not produce—at least not as efficiently—the intelligence needed to prosecute target sets in large swaths of operational boxes the way code breaking could.

While operational intelligence was important in both the European and Pacific theaters, HUMINT was not entirely forgone during the war. It was of broad utility in each of the Japanese-occupied areas in Southeast Asia, including in the Philippines and Burma, both of which were strategically important (especially after the Battle of Leyte Gulf) but still peripheral to the main island campaign.[13] Still, the value rarely matched that of the operational intelligence collected through signals and code breaking. In Europe—where the ONI had a minor footprint compared to the Pacific—the OSS was able to operate inside the enemy's country, often collecting similar tactical intelligence. Moreover, unlike the Tai Li network that the Navy was cut off from following the war, OSS officers (and, later, directors of central intelligence) Richard Helms and Allen Dulles managed to keep strong relations with Reinhard Gehlen (chief of the Wehrmacht Foreign Armies East, or FHO) and later create the so-called Gehlen Organization, which became a paid CIA source network.[14]

Intelligence in the Pacific Campaign

Led by Commander in Chief, U.S. Pacific Fleet, Fleet Admiral Chester Nimitz, the Pacific Theater was a complex intelligence challenge. Nimitz established the Joint Intelligence Center Pacific Ocean Area (JICPOA) in 1943 to coordinate and prioritize intelligence collection and analysis in the Pacific.[15] As chapter 2 pointed out, this obfuscated the director of naval intelligence's (and, therefore, the ONI's) established centralized authority, even as JICPOA often shared intelligence with the ONI. In terms of collections, Nimitz had an opinion of how intelligence should be organized and executed, at least in war.[16] He favored a regionalized approach, the way JICPOA was aligned with Pacific Fleet.

The NGC, under the command of Capt. Milton Miles, enabled access to sources in the Chinese Communist guerrilla army as well as some in the Japanese occupation of central and northern China.[17] The NGC was an integrated U.S.–China (Kuomintang) intelligence agency under SACO.[18] The intelligence that it produced, however, was arguably of little value in relation to the primary objective, which was to defeat and roll back Japanese territorial advances, primarily in the Pacific island region. The access it garnered U.S. naval intelligence was a double-edged sword, however, due to the Navy's overreliance on Tai Li's network. When World War II ended, the Nationalists and Communists resumed their civil war, Tai Li was assassinated, and the sources Miles and his team had relied upon dried up. It is debatable how useful the intelligence was that NGC collected in enemy territory. War is primarily concerned with destroying the enemy, or at the very least destroying the enemy's will to continue fighting. Where the value of the intelligence during the war was questionable, one could clearly see that ties to the Tai Li network would have been valuable (vis-à-vis the Chinese Communists and the Soviet Union).

While it is difficult to find copious examples of traditional spy work during the war outside of the Tai Li relationship, that is not to say other forms of what today would be considered a form of HUMINT did not occur; they did—and with regularity.[19] In addition to the typical intelligence personnel of Marine landing forces, the Special Intelligence Section (OP-16-F-9) of the ONI was set up in January 1941 to focus solely on

Photo 3. Capt. Milton Miles and Tai Li, 1944 *United States Naval Academy, Special Collections & Archives*

interrogation of Japanese prisoners of war.[20] In the process of standard post-battle interrogations, Fleet intelligence officers would uncover troves of Japanese documents, in some cases highly classified plans.[21] Finally, although arguably a form of passive reconnaissance, coast watching was a valuable form of intelligence; the Pacific Fleet relied on Australian-led coastal networks to provide warnings and indications of Imperial Japanese Navy ship movements in particular island areas.[22]

While war and HUMINT are not entirely incompatible, one can see that collecting intelligence from human sources in enemy territory is directly threatened by one's permissive proximity to the enemy. The fundamental difference between HUMINT and the other clearly more utilized disciplines in the World War II Pacific campaign is that it is a patient man's game. War—at least major state-on-state war, as opposed to counterinsurgency—does not lend itself to patience. Instead, commanders prioritize fires, targeting, and maneuver, all of which require gaining intelligence quickly, and often without warning. The fact that the Chinese state during World War II was in transition, with the Nationalists expending the bulk of military capabilities against the Imperial Japanese Army, and with Mao letting that largely occur concentrated on unifying and consolidating the Chinese Communist Party for a stronger position following the war.[23] Additionally, this also set up a context in which the U.S. presence during the ensuing Chinese Civil War was increasingly unpopular.

Relatively less HUMINT was collected in World War II in the Pacific for three reasons, but it was clearly used with some success. First, outside of the periodic interrogations of Japanese personnel and the recovery of classified documents following a battle, the lack of access to Japanese sources made collection prohibitive. Second, HUMINT was secondary to signals and code breaking because they required long source development periods. Third, the Fleet primarily required operational intelligence to maneuver around and destroy enemy targets in a timely and lethal manner. For these reasons, one could characterize HUMINT's role in the Pacific campaign as being a supportive enhancement to the Fleet's broader intelligence mission. Arguably, it often played a similar role in peacetime, and even in crisis, but for different reasons explained throughout this work.

Post–World War II Intelligence Conditions in the Far East

While the war in the Pacific primarily occurred at sea and in amphibious storm landings of the island-hopping campaign devised by Adm. Chester Nimitz, Gen. Holland Smith, and others, the postwar period in the Far East was politically chaotic and required a new intelligence focus ashore. Whether the naval services were up to this task is a matter of debate, but, as was evident in implementing containment, a new system was emerging to address concerns emerging out of the burgeoning rivalry between Western democratic powers (namely, the United States and Great Britain) and the Communist Bloc.[24] On one hand, the services greatly contracted due to the postwar drawdown; thus, they showed difficulty sustaining their capabilities. On the other hand, the Navy remained present and engaged in the Far East with postwar security missions. As in the interwar years of the 1930s, HUMINT demonstrated significant value because more technical forms of intelligence (signals intelligence, or SIGINT, and cryptology) could not always show similar value to the ability to understand the intentions of China, Japan, Korea, and the Soviet Union.[25] While a human source requires vetting, the information produced is a direct result of his credibility. Whereas other intelligence often requires further interpretation, the means with which to assess technical sources (e.g., radio frequency sources) are more straightforward.[26] Following wars and the drawdown of forces from a region, it is important—although often not acted upon—for countries to ensure that opportunities for intelligence collection and the access to source networks remain in place. An insurance policy was only partially acknowledged by the Navy and others in national security during this period. Despite occasionally ambiguous foreign policy toward China in the immediate years after World War II, engagement efforts with Chiang's Kai-shek's regime continued, as was historically common following an occupation. It was not immediately apparent, in the intelligence of the years through 1947, that the days of the Kuomintang reign on the Chinese mainland were numbered.[27] As reinforced in this case—and explored elsewhere on the last years of the Nationalists' presence on the mainland—the situation quickly deteriorated in 1948.[28]

To frame the challenge that intelligence faced in the East, one might consider HUMINT as a threefold paradox. First, it requires sources of high reliability. Second, these sources need to be close to the information they collect and report. Third, often when specifically sensitive intelligence is most required, source reliability becomes more susceptible to foreign tampering or lessens with a lack of proximity to the target.[29] While Marine and naval units (including the naval attachés) remained in the region through 1949, access to sources and increasingly precarious security affected intelligence. By the end of 1949 access ceased entirely when the Communists defeated the Nationalists, Chiang Kai-shek retreated to Formosa, and the People's Republic of China was established. Access to sources became a paradox in times of peace, war, and crisis; more than other intelligence disciplines, access and proximity to the source are important for HUMINT collections, yet violence inhibits both.[30] Moreover, wartime intelligence often requires an operational focus, whereas peace and crisis intelligence often require higher-level strategic intelligence, necessitating longer-term patience in developing sources of value and credibility.[31] If an adversarial target increasingly occupies a standoff position—the way the Chinese Communists under Mao became in relation to the West—access to sources decreases and strategic intelligence is more difficult to produce.

Another important factor that ultimately drove the ability to collect intelligence—of particular interest to the Navy—includes the issue of U.S. policy and the renaissance undertaken in national security policy in the postwar and early Cold War years, in which the Truman administration recognized the need to fundamentally transform the national security paradigm to counter a growing Soviet threat. The National Security Act of 1947 initiated the paradigm and the development of the Truman Doctrine and the policy of containment, culminating in April 1950 with National Security Council Memorandum 68 (NSC 68).[32] The act created the National Security Council, the permanent establishment of the Joint Chiefs of Staff, and the CIA. Unlike the years when the ONI and the War Department's G-2 (Intelligence Division) were the only national foreign intelligence agencies, intelligence now held sufficient relevance that it needed to be modernized and coordinated through a unifying authority to leverage all data gathered by three disparate agencies (War, State, and Navy).[33] Months after Truman signed an executive order disbanding the OSS, his administration began work on its successor.[34] The debate over the organization and direction of the national security establishment—particularly the transformation from a federated intelligence system to a centralized one—continued for over a year before Congress passed the National Security Act of 1947.[35] During this time the Navy spoke against centralizing intelligence primarily because leaders thought it meant ultimately relinquishing some of its authorities and thus limiting its ability to collect intelligence vital to the Fleet.[36] These institutional changes came at the expense of the Navy's historical role in which it served few but the DNI and the president. Ultimately, however, the perturbations gave way to a burgeoning relationship between the CIA and ONI.

The crisis in this case comprises a number of subcomponents, each of which could be considered a distinct subcrisis. First, it includes a postwar disintegration of the Chinese state, its currency devaluation, and the general chaos that ensued with accepting the Japanese surrender and the demobilization of its forces. In this case, this analysis uses terminology such as "postwar period" or "in the years following the war." Second, the Chinese Civil War, which re-erupted in the spring of 1946, held particularly consequential importance to the West because a Communist victory implied that the whole of Asia would become Communist aligned. Third, the crisis of Soviet influence and subversion enabled the slide into Chinese Communism while extending Moscow's reach into Asia. In this case, the term "cold war" is used.[37] Although these refer to the exact same period, subtle differentiation is intentional, depending on when each is referenced. Furthermore, although a crisis in postwar Japan occurred at the same time, this research only addresses Japan peripherally in relation to the intelligence collected on its military forces demobilizing in the region.

The War Is Over, and Its Aftermath

As the war with Japan ended, China imploded, and the civil war that Chiang Kai-shek and Mao Zedong postponed to fight the Japanese soon resumed.[38] The fundamental point that made this a crisis for the West was the fact that the Truman administration was already facing a vacuum of Soviet influence in Eastern Europe and similar trends were occurring in China as well, with the Chinese Communists gaining greater power over the population.[39] A central concern in the immediate aftermath of the war was China's economy—namely, its currency devaluation and the ability of the Kuomintang government to maintain trade partnerships. Economic aid to China was at the forefront of this problem.[40] Part of the intelligence mission during this period was to ascertain the degree to which the Chinese economy suffered and the implications for trade relations with the West.

U.S.–Chinese diplomatic histories shows that U.S. forces maintained relations, but intelligence networks built by the West during the war—with the Nationalists in Chongqing and the Communists in Yenan—were disestablished in April 1946.[41] This became an important inflection point later when they needed to be reestablished during the Korean War and Taiwan crises. The JICPOA, established by Pacific Fleet during World War II, was also dissolved in April 1946.[42] The Truman administration's idea of creating an organization for centralized intelligence was in its infancy.[43] Moreover, the Navy struggled to maintain long-term presence in China, a region quickly controlled by Mao's Communists, while the postwar demobilization was in full force. All of this postwar dissolution served to break down valuable access to mainland sources at a time when the fate of Nationalist China, a potential ally, was threatened by Communist encroachment.

Meanwhile, while naval attachés in the Far East contributed some meaningful intelligence at the national level for policymakers in the first years of the Cold War, the attaché system in general was broken, and gaining source contacts in the Soviet Union, China, and in other Communist-leaning nations was more difficult than ever. Due to violence, the American Embassy moved several times (from Chongqing to Nanking in May 1946, to Guangzhou in August 1949, back to Chongqing in October 1949, and finally to Taipei in December 1949) between the end of World War II and the Nationalists' retreat to Taiwan in October 1949.[44] This period of transition inevitably disrupted the intelligence relationships that U.S. intelligence officers had cultivated along the way in each region of China. The British and French embassies remained, with consulates in Guangzhou and elsewhere, which served as an irreplaceable supplement for the lack of access to agents for the Navy's intelligence collection. Literature on this period in East Asia exists mainly in the final chapters of works on World War II or the introductions of books about the Cold War.[45] This is perplexing for the simple fact that much of the course of the Cold War was determined in the period between the end of World War II and the Communist takeover in Beijing in 1949.[46] This case fills a gap in research on U.S. naval intelligence contributions to national security during an important period of enormous changes, both geopolitically and organizationally, in which the institutional transition demonstrated lasting effects on the Navy's role in intelligence production.

Four specifically different issues marked the postwar period of the U.S. Navy and Marine Corps' presence in the Far East during the late 1940s: (a) A more violent and chaotic relationship between the Communists and Nationalists eventually erupted into civil war; (b) Communists engaged in violence against the Americans in a way not comparable to that during the cease-fire of the 1930s and World War II; (c) U.S. strategic interests in China were in flux as Chinese Communist influence grew with the hegemonic support received from Soviet assistance; and (d) U.S. national security strategy, policy, and organization imminently changed in a way that eventually affected naval operations—and, therefore, conducting naval intelligence.[47] These dynamics resulted in the national security apparatus' slight inability to become too invested in a region that would soon be a primary cold war battleground.

Naval Group, China, and the End of SACO

The slow withdrawal from China ultimately uncovered some challenges, both institutionally and operationally, in the event the United States continued to require intelligence from sources inside China in the initial years of the Cold War. First, it showed the brittleness of the relationship with the Kuomintang. Second, it foreshadowed the service-based parochial interests (namely, between the Navy and Army) that played a major role in the postwar rebuilding of the national security community. Finally, it showed that the Truman administration sent mixed messages on its policy and role in China, which later resulted in significant negative consequences for maintaining sources on the mainland. Chiang's frustration with America's wavering commitment led him to lash out at times, typified by his perception that the Marshall Mission—the diplomatic effort led by George Marshall (Truman personally chose the newly retired five-star general for the mission) to negotiate a peace treaty between Nationalists and Communists—was a disingenuous vote of no confidence for his leadership.[48]

In August 1945 Fleet Admiral Nimitz conceded that the terms of the SACO agreement dictated its dissolution upon the signing of the surrender by the Japanese but that its end would be an "extremely bad impression with the Chinese Government."[49] The implications of what Nimitz was saying were significant. SACO was at the heart of U.S.–Chinese relations and fostered tremendous intelligence sharing, coordination, and combined activity during the war, including clandestine operations against the Japanese and training of Nationalist guerrillas, the latter of which the NGC (discontinued on 5 July 1945, pending V-J Day) conducted.[50] As close advisers to the Chinese Nationalist leadership on matters of intelligence and operations, Rear Adm. Milton Miles (commander, NGC, and codirector of SACO) and his staff enjoyed the highest level bilateral relationship with the Chinese during the war, developing close relationships with Chiang Kai-shek and Tai Li.[51] Indeed, the Chinese were not happy about the prospect of losing U.S. support in the face of an impending resumption of the civil war. This dissatisfaction demonstrated itself when, prior to being notified, Chiang's president of the Executive Yuan (or premier), T. V. Soong, contacted the secretary of the Navy requesting that the United States upgrade the status of the NGC to a "Naval Mission to China," complete with implied additional resources.[52]

From the end of the war when Japan surrendered, the Army and Navy differed considerably on their views of discontinuing the SACO agreement.[53] They debated a proposed SACO termination agreement for three months, ultimately proving a moot point in the absence of an official stance from the Truman administration.[54] Gen. A. C. Wedemeyer, commander of U.S. forces in the China Theater, thought the agreement should be terminated on V-J Day and that no further activity should occur.[55] Writing to Gen. George Marshall, Army chief of staff, Wedemeyer admonished the Navy's activity in China for hindering his position: "I do not feel that Navy Group should be involved in clandestine activities or in intelligence. Intelligence should be conducted by a joint Army and Navy organization and should not be permitted to have any contacts whatsoever with the Tai Li organization."[56] Marshall supported him, maintaining to Fleet Admiral Ernest J. King that Miles should be relieved of duty and that NGC's functions under SACO duplicate that of the Army in China.[57] This perceived duplication was false because both efforts focused on very different targets—Chongqing and Yenan.

Internally, Navy leadership struggled with its position on its role in China as well. In a memorandum written by the Seventh Fleet commander, Adm. Charles M. Cooke Jr., and passed to the CNO from the commander of the Pacific Fleet, the former admonished Miles' position of consistently hailing Tai Li as an "honorable and perfect gentleman" and that perhaps he should begin admitting he has "attributes which were not the best" in communicating with the Truman administration.[58] In a memorandum to Admiral Cooke in September 1945, Navy captain J. C. Metzel (deputy commander, NGC) appealed: "Wedemeyer and his staff have crusaded against three obligations to which . . . Miles was bound by government agreement; association with the Tai Li organization, integration of U.S. and Chinese commands below the Theater GHQ [general headquarters] level, and gratis exchange of materials without lend lease procedure."[59] One of the officers in the naval attaché office further supported this sentiment in a memorandum to Metzel, maintaining that Amb. Patrick J. Hurley thought Wedemeyer's opinion of the NGC and SACO was primarily based on his jealously of Miles and the close relationship he maintained with Chiang Kai-shek as opposed to some practical aversion to continuing intelligence activity in China.[60] The discussion between Metzel and Miles in Nanking identified the Army's deep aversion to integrated command structures in which the forces of one nation are under the direction of another—the way NGC operated under Chiang and Tai Li.[61]

The main issue between the Navy and Army centered on whether to terminate SACO activities immediately or to extend them for a year to transition Chinese intelligence into the postwar environment; the Navy favored the latter option.[62] In October the Joint Chiefs of Staff instructed to take the former action, pending attention at higher levels (in other words, Navy leadership might appeal to the administration); this order was largely ignored.[63] The NGC eventually dissolved in January 1946.

The status of the U.S. military in China could not go unresolved for very long. On 20 December 1945 Truman assigned U.S. Army general George C. Marshall to head a mission (the so-called Marshall Mission) to negotiate a peace between the Nationalists and Communists with the possibility of creating a unified government.[64] The final hammer for the Navy dropped on 22 December when Acting Secretary of State Dean Acheson wrote Secretary of the Navy James Forrestal a forceful instruction that read in part: "I desire that all conversations with Chinese officials regarding extension of American economic of financial aid to China, in which officers of your organization may be participating, be suspended, and that for the time being no member of your staff engage in conversations with Chinese officials, which might encourage the Chinese to hope that this Government is contemplating the extension of any type of assistance to China, except in accordance with the recommendations of General Marshall."[65] The cease and desist order from the Truman administration clearly addressed the Navy. The record is incomplete, however, on the dissolution of SACO, the suppression of Navy officers' interactions with Chinese government officials, and the implications for the strategic relationship, particularly in relation to creeping Soviet influence in China.

On 3 January 1946 Adm. Raymond A. Spruance, commander of the U.S. Pacific Fleet, instructed Seventh Fleet that—even though SACO would be terminated—the intelligence relationship with China continue as directed. Referring to the administration's new policy—specifically the Joint Chiefs of Staff memorandum from October 1945—naval forces in China should continue "to arrange jointly for an interim continuance of U.S. weather communications and intelligence activities now being conducted by SACO which in their [Joint Chiefs of Staff] opinion are of post-War military value."[66] Despite the implied value of this correspondence, Spruance likely referred to the increasing influence of Soviet Communism in the region and therefore the need for better intelligence. While the SACO experience provided the Navy and political leaders with substantial human source–based intelligence throughout the war, it showed in the end the parochial disposition of the Navy at a time when resources quickly became scarce. Due to language barriers, cultural understanding, and sheer numbers of personnel, the loss of a formal organizational relationship between the Chinese Nationalists and the Navy meant the loss of institutionalized access to sources the United States would not likely otherwise develop on the mainland.

The Legacy of SACO, Miles, and Tai

To understand the stakes for intelligence collection in China during the early Cold War and the implications of a drawdown of U.S. naval presence for collection of priority intelligence, one should understand the inroads made during World War II in the region. The experience of the Navy in

China during the war—specifically U.S.–China relations following the war—is important because it partially enabled U.S. Cold War policy in East Asia for many years. The bond the Navy and the Chinese Kuomintang government leadership forged prior to and during World War II in a common fight against the Japanese manifested itself by the SACO, led by U.S. intelligence officer Capt. Milton Miles (as commander, NGC), and the so-called Dixie Mission (and the OSS unit assigned to it, External Survey Detachment #44) in the northern city of Yenan.[67] While SACO's mission mostly focused on developing spy networks and coordinating special operations with Chiang Kai-shek's Jun Tong (Bureau of Instigation and Statistics), Gen. Tai Li, (the Dixie Mission) focused on liaison intelligence work with the Chinese Communists. During the war, the NGC (headquartered in Chongqing during the war and in Nanking following the Japanese surrender) frequently squabbled with the Dixie Mission, which was largely a creation of Maj. Gen. William "Wild Bill" Donovan, director of the OSS.[68] Although they both aligned under presidential leadership, parochial rivalries and their respective Chinese alignments dissuaded them from sharing intelligence and coordinating operations.[69]

Some Navy leaders viewed China and the NGC's (and therefore Miles') relationship with Tai Li as far more than a means to the end of the war.[70] Although it primarily focused on developing intelligence and coordinating operations with the Chinese Nationalists in the defeat of Japan, Miles saw the continuation of the U.S.–China intelligence relationship as an opportunity for naval and military access following the war, assuming the Nationalists retained power.[71] Building the relationship early and with a shared common history brought the two countries closer together, and both benefited. It should be understood, however, the Chinese Nationalists' aim ultimately remained as it was prior to the U.S. involvement in the war: stopping Communist advancement.[72] While the civil war paused during World War II, it remained Chiang Kai-shek's priority and would be given full attention when the war ended.

Meanwhile, of growing importance to Western policy—even before the war officially ended—was the influence and increasing threat of Communism. In November 1944, diplomat John Service—who worked with the Dixie Mission and was later accused of spying for the Communists, although the charges were eventually dropped—received a proposal from Mao's deputy, Zhou Enlai, that he and Mao come to Washington to meet with Roosevelt.[73] The United States considered this proposition under the logic that shifting full diplomatic support to the Chinese Communists could tip the postwar balance away from the Soviet Union, a prospect already anticipated well more than a year before the end of the war.[74] There was a belief that Communist takeover following the war was inevitable, and to continue futilely supporting Chiang at the expense of letting Moscow influence Mao's regime was a most unwanted outcome.[75]

As Linda Kush showed in her book about SACO, U.S. diplomatic dissent did not dissuade the meeting between Mao and Roosevelt; instead, Tai Li influenced Miles and SACO.[76] Miles sent a number of cables to Washington stating that Donovan and OSS encroached on the NGC and even compromised the overall war effort with their support for the Communists. He was supported by the staunchly anti-Communist U.S. head of diplomatic mission, Major General Hurley.[77] For his part, Tai Li took the information Miles supplied him to Chiang, who then protested to Washington, even threatening to side with Japan.[78] Under these extreme pressures, Washington began to reevaluate its relationship with China and the resulting consequences for its relationship with Moscow.

Although U.S. and Western policy toward China changed—largely manifested in a decrease in military aid[79]—it is inaccurate to depict this as a complete ejection from the region. To start, the U.S. Marine Corps' Third Amphibious Corps deployed in northern China through 1947, after which it downgraded to the 9th Marine Brigade until May 1949.[80] The Navy's Seventh Fleet headquartered in Tsingtao until May 1949 as well. The embassy—and, thus, the naval attaché office—moved to Nanking in May 1946, to Guangzhou in August 1949, then to Chongqing in October, before finally moving to Taipei when the Nationalists were defeated.[81] Tokyo at this time also quickly became a source for collection efforts. Additionally, Navy and Marine Corps intelligence collection returned to the sea, where infrequent encounters with PRC boats occurred. A focus of the case will be to develop an understanding of the practices that the

Navy and Marine Corps established to mitigate the loss of valuable access gained across the 1930s and during World War II.

Following their defeat in 1949, Chiang Kai-shek and the Nationalist forces escaped to Taiwan, and the Navy and other intelligence agencies established surrogate access to the mainland, such as the Navy's Intelligence Liaison Office in Shanghai.[82] On 1 October 1949 Mao declared the birth of the PRC. The U.S. Embassy shut down, and the last of the U.S. military forces remaining on security detail were forced out. The Cold War and Truman's NSC 68 also ushered in a new and dangerous game in which the CIA and other intelligence agencies planned and conducted various covert actions against Beijing's interests both inside China and on its periphery.[83] At the same time, U.S. policy was never more convoluted and contradictory than in the years following World War II. However, the access to both Communist and Nationalist leadership that these units fostered became increasingly limited, and important observations enabled Western intelligence to gain a better understanding of Chinese Communist motivations, the Kuomintang will to fight, and Soviet influence in the region. All of this posed enormous challenges to the naval HUMINT mission in collecting and producing a coherent intelligence picture, which was further complicated by both a quickly changing region and a whiplashed U.S. national security establishment that was both in a postwar demobilization process and ramping up to counter a growing Soviet threat. The latter dichotomy came to typify the nature of how the national security community dealt with the situation in China, both at arm's length in terms of commitment and with fortified presence, underscored a paradox of crisis spectrum mentioned in this book's introduction.

Chapter 4

Blackout in China

U.S. Intelligence for a New Kind of War

This chapter exposes some of the institutional factors that postwar intelligence was faced with the in emergence of the Cold War, the National Security Act of 1947, and the centralized intelligence system. It addresses Navy and Marine Corps intelligence operations in the East, the results of such operations, and their overall utility. Following this, the case explores information gathered by naval intelligence units regarding Soviet clandestine activities and influence in China during this period as well as the consequences on the strategic environment. Finally, given the changes to intelligence policy—both nationally and within the Navy— the case presents conclusions on the contributions naval HUMINT made—both through collections in the Far East, and through institutional changes—during the post–World War II crisis and during preparations for a bipolar world.

The strategic shift that occurred with the onset of the Cold War, however, held significant consequences for the naval intelligence mission. This case research focuses on the transition in foreign and national security policy following World War II and the result on the ability to collect, analyze, and produce meaningful intelligence. As one will find, the transition to a centralized intelligence system, culminating in the National Security Act of 1947 and the establishment of the Central Intelligence Agency (CIA), yielded minor immediate effects at the collection level and subtle yet important ones institutionally. The Navy—along with the Army and State Department—witnessed a shift never experienced in its history that permanently altered overall national policy, but the transition took time to infiltrate the institutionalized fibers of the naval intelligence establishment.[1] For once, national security policy was managed centrally, as was the intelligence that supported it. At the same time, all departments and agencies were expected to individually prepare the establishment for a new enemy in an age of nuclear weapons. The Navy held less influence than in intelligence prior to the war, but it played a role during the development of a centralized intelligence system. While its leadership role in intelligence diminished since times prior to World War II—including having less central authority over the types of information gathered and the methods with which it is collected—the Navy (particularly the Office of Naval Intelligence [ONI]) assumed an increasing role in the intelligence viewed daily by the president. This was particularly true with the DNI taking a position on the Intelligence Advisory Board, which, under the DCI's direction, was established in January 1946 to advise President Truman on intelligence matters.[2] This transition did not come without its challenges and required several years to fully mature.[3]

Changing Command and Control of Intelligence

While command and control of intelligence and operating forces in the Far East experienced significant changes following the war, some policies remained the same. The position of commander of the U.S. Pacific Fleet (PACFLT) had existed since 1907, although his responsibilities extended to the entire Asia-Pacific region following the defeat and subsequent dissolution of the U.S. Asiatic Fleet in the early months of the war.[4] PACFLT had operational control (OPCON) of all naval forces in the Pacific. Under PACFLT sat the sub-unified commander of naval forces in the Far East, who controlled the Seventh Fleet (headquartered in Tsingtao until 1949), naval forces in Japan, and naval forces in Korea. Directly under PACFLT was the Third Fleet (headquartered in San Diego) and the Fleet marine forces in the Pacific (in Hawaii). This structure continued following the war.[5] During the war the Fifth Fleet was under the command of the Central Pacific Fleet, which also served as OPCON to PACFLT.

The Pacific under Nimitz also created a burgeoning legacy of joint intelligence that appeared to ultimately inform decisions, even as primary parochial interests of the services continued for many decades. At the beginning of the war, PACFLT developed the JICPOA to address critical intelligence gaps in the Fleet's understanding of Japan and other countries in the Asian subcontinent. Unlike in the past when an intelligence unit ultimately served as OPCON to the DNI and ONI, the JICPOA strictly fell under the control of commander of PACFLT, Admiral Nimitz.[6] The JICPOA was composed of four groups, each with individual subsections: Group I (geographic, photographic, terrain model, reference, medical, hydrographic, cartographic, and target analysis); Group II (enemy shipping, enemy air, enemy land, enemy flak, and estimates); Group III (psychological warfare, and escape and evasion); and Group IV (bulletin, production, administrative, translation, interrogation, and operational intelligence).[7] While each group had its own subordinate field teams, the degree to which they developed human sources and collected HUMINT was minimal, generally relying on the intelligence of operating units throughout the theater. Although the overwhelming bulk of the JICPOA's efforts focused on Japan, its geographic section (fifty-six officers, twelve yeomen, and four "women accepted for volunteer emergency service"), the geographic section of Group I consisted of desks specifically focused on Nansei-shotō, Formosa, Japan, China, Korea/Manchuria, Nanpō Shotō, and other special projects.[8] The JICPOA disbanded immediately following the Japanese surrender, and the degree to which this was a loss to the Fleet's postwar intelligence capability is unknown.

Because of the JICPOA and the OPCON that commanders in each theater had over their respective forces during wartime, the ONI experienced a loss of influence during the war.[9] With the National Security Act of 1947, under Rear Adm. Thomas B. Inglis (September 1945–September 1949), the ONI experienced some of the most far-reaching changes in its history, ultimately placing it in a more powerful role than during the war.[10] First, the resources and personnel formerly under the intelligence officer of commander-in-chief of the U.S. Fleet shifted to the ONI's control, and the title of DNI changed to chief of naval intelligence (CNI).[11]

Second, although the ONI had existed since 1882, it survived until the postwar period without any official delineation of its duties or an official budget. This status changed with the publication of *Advanced Changes to the U.S. Navy Regulations* (signed by President Truman on 20 June 1946), which codified the ONI as "the organization charged with the execution of the intelligence and counterintelligence mission of the Naval establishment."[12] This important policy development established the CNI as having cognizance and authority over all aspects of planning, collection, analysis, and dissemination of naval intelligence. This role further changed with the evolution of centralized intelligence in late 1947.

Third, the CNO informed the commandant of the Marine Corps (an adjacent service to the Navy but within the Department of the Navy) of his intention to fully integrate Marine Corps intelligence activity within—and thus under—the CNI. These activities included planning and doctrinal contributions for amphibious operational intelligence, assignment and training of Marine officers in the naval intelligence establishment, and the selection and training of Marine reserve officers to act as specialists in the event of mobilization.[13] Despite the occasionally strained relationship between the Navy and Marine Corps, the bureaucratic and institutional truth is that the Marine Corps is a part of a broader naval force, subordinate to the Secretary of the Navy. This integration likely did not sit well with the commandant, Gen. Alexander Vandegrift, but evidence does not exist to indicate any substantial perturbations due to this hierarchy at the time.[14]

Finally, in a November 1948 memorandum to the CNO found in the National Archives, the title CNI changed back to DNI with the rationale of consistency, and thus standardization, with the other agency heads throughout the intelligence community.[15] The Marine Corps' III Amphibious Corps deployed to Hebei Province (Beijing, Tianjin, Qinhuangdao) in the days after the Japanese surrender and the Soviet invasion of Manchuria. They first served as OPCON to U.S. Forces, China, but when that disestablished in the spring of 1946, the Marines fell under the commander of the Seventh Fleet. When Fleet Marine Force,

Western Pacific, was later established in Tsingtao, it assumed tactical control of the Marines and became OPCON to the Seventh Fleet. Still, as in years prior to the war, OPCON was slightly different from intelligence command and control relationships. As with the sailors of the Seventh Fleet and the naval attachés who collected intelligence, they ultimately served the CNO and his deputy, the DNI. This organizational makeup of the naval intelligence community remained as the Navy faced great uncertainties, both in the Far East and in the emergence of a new national security construct.

Multiple institutional shifts occurred while naval forces in the Far East still needed to maintain security and collect intelligence. The dissolution of the SACO and the reemergence of the ONI as the central authority and clearinghouse for intelligence restored a prewar construct, as did the reaffirmation by the CNO that Marine Corps intelligence would also be centralized again under the CNI/DNI. Just as traditional Navy intelligence relationships returned, however, the broader national security challenges began to emerge, as the following sections show. The Truman administration opted for a centralized intelligence system overall, a construct the Navy and Marine Corps were familiar with from the ONI's earliest days. Centralized under whom and with what authority, however, soon became the national security community's fundamental question.

The Navy in an Age of Centralized Intelligence

When Truman dissolved the OSS in September 1945, there was a clear desire to establish a central agency for coordinating intelligence. In January 1946 the administration established the Central Intelligence Group (CIG), the immediate predecessor of the CIA.[16] While the conversation evolved from this time through the eventual creation of CIA in 1947, the parochialisms that occurred—particularly from the Army, Navy, and State Department—did not occur within a vacuum. Indeed, the creation of the CIA brought out intense competitiveness among them, but it also enabled each of them to have a voice within the emerging community, even as the CIA inevitably subjugated their power.[17] The CIG regularly coordinated and shared intelligence with the ONI, such as that concerning emerging rocket-propelled artillery technology the Soviets developed in 1946.[18] Still, the CIG demonstrated a dynamic that expanded its mission into territory traditionally assigned to military services and the State Department; for example, in May 1947 the CIG established posts at embassies, including those in East Asia, such as in Manila (a territory previously off limits to the OSS).[19] Having no similar agency with which to compare historically, the military services naturally opposed this institutional shift.

The ONI in the Postwar Period

The ONI benefited from a postwar renaissance in intelligence and national security affairs. This occurred for two primary reasons. First, although the ONI continued to collect intelligence during the war, it contributed to the war effort much the way it did to the prewar effort, with activity of a largely noncombat nature. The operating units in the Pacific, the Atlantic, and elsewhere relied largely on (a) their own intelligence sections and those of units operating in other areas of the same theater; (b) networks of foreign sources, including coast watchers; (c) intelligence from close proximate foreign and allied navies; and (d) the timely establishment of joint intelligence centers, such as the JICPOA.[20] These activities almost entirely ceased following the war, yet the conflict still required naval intelligence due to the growing Communist threat, as clearly shown in the National Archives records.[21]

Second, the ONI's centralization efforts could be restored given that the war ended. The Truman administration empowered the centralization of intelligence in general, as CIA CREST postwar archives show.[22] Soon after the war the Secretary of the Navy indicated to the commandant of the Marine Corps that he intended for Marine Corps intelligence to be overseen and managed centrally by the same entity that managed the Fleet's intelligence—the ONI and the CNI.[23] In some ways, this represented the Navy leadership's anticipatory action to shore up Navy parochial interests in light of Truman's intention to centralize intelligence because it did not know the future for the myriad federated Navy intelligence units throughout the Fleet. The Navy did not know what to expect given its inexperience with a centralized system (the ONI was highly centralized but exclusively Navy oriented). Nevertheless, with the demobilization, the ONI once again became the central body managing naval intelligence, ultimately eschewing responsibility for collection of any non-naval–related subjects (e.g., political and economic) referred to in chapter 2.

Postwar and Cold War Institutional Perturbations

As separate events, the end of the war and post-Potsdam relations between the West and Moscow inevitably changed U.S. national security dynamics, at least partially exacerbating the institutional challenges of the crisis in the East. Together, however, they ushered in the greatest institutional changes in U.S. history. This research presents a third less-studied Western national security dynamic: Far East Asia (more specifically, China) as a testbed for the changes that occurred from 1945 to 1949.[24] One should first consider the roles the services played following the war and the jockeying that occurred in the run-up to the 1947 act.[25] Second, other considerations included issues of inertia and naval intelligence bodies, such as the NGC, the joint U.S. Army–Navy intelligence collection agencies, and the Joint Intelligence Agency, set up during the war (the latter two disestablished in the months following the war) and, some would argue, exclusively *for* the war. Third, the institutions that existed prior to the war changed as a result of the war and continued to exist following the war—for example, the ONI. Fourth, the war—and the dynamics of Western–Soviet relations—produced an institutionalized intelligence relationship between the United States and Britain for which the ONI and the Royal Navy's Naval Intelligence Division contributed significantly.[26] Finally, the postwar era saw the dissolution of the OSS and joint intelligence organizations (e.g., JICPOA) and nearly immediately gave way to a new era of centralized intelligence.[27] The initial years of the Cold War in Asia represented a venue for which all of these changing tendencies occurred, wherein HUMINT fundamentally shaped aspects in policy, if only realized in hindsight. Although bifurcated from day-to-day activities, the bureaucratic crisis over the future of intelligence writ large going on in Washington would eventually have deep effects on intelligence in the Far East.

Following the National Security Act of 1947 and James Forrestal's confirmation as secretary of defense, Forrestal publicized agreements reached by the Joint Chiefs of Staff at Key West, Florida. Principal decisions entailed the following: (a) The Air Force became responsible for strategic air warfare; (b) the Navy assumed primary responsibility for antisubmarine warfare; (c) the Marine Corps, under Navy Department direction, took primary responsibility for the development of amphibious warfare; (d) the Air Force supplied most air transport for all services; and (e) the Army's functions included land, joint amphibious and airborne operations, intelligence, defense against air attack, and military government.[28] This codified the general mission areas of each of the services for the first time since the drafting of the U.S. Constitution. Given the direction the country was headed in the Cold War, in many ways the Constitution's wording on the military was arguably out of date.[29] The problem with Forrestal's precise language was that it set the groundwork for future parochial infighting among the services. In the area of intelligence, the Navy and Marine Corps experienced long-established relationships. To be relegated to antisubmarine and amphibious warfare—and, therefore, the intelligence that supports only those missions—forced them to accept a diminished role at a time, following the victory in the Pacific, when the naval services were quite popular.

Because of the need to coordinate amphibious operations in the Pacific, the war forced the Army and naval services to frequently depend on one another, even though this relationship hardly resembles joint command and control in the modern sense.[30] Within the Department of the Navy, the Marine Corps and Navy had experienced the greatest battle victories in their history, despite the institutionalized resentment and abandonment the corps experienced during the Guadalcanal campaign.[31] For defense intelligence coordination, the War Department created the Joint Intelligence Study Publishing Board in early 1946 for Navy and Army intelligence to coordinate and jointly produce frequent, strategic, and operational analyses (joint Army–Navy intelligence studies) based on each one's intelligence contributions.[32] At the same time, the Truman administration was going through a metamorphosis in its thinking of how to organize intelligence for the Cold War era. This transition reinforced the difficulties that operating forces experience in post–World War II China, undoubtedly affecting how intelligence personnel maintained source relations.

Naval Intelligence Operations in East Asia

This section addresses Navy and Marine intelligence in China by examining the kinds of intelligence they produced and the manner in which they collected it. Bearing in mind the dictates under which foreign forces could operate (particularly the Marines in northern China), one should consider the context in which they gathered intelligence. For at least the first year of the Cold War (1945–46)—and then later, when the force size reduced—intelligence was collected in reasonably stable security conditions, often in garrison or in liaison with Chinese Nationalist Army (CNA) and Navy counterparts. Several noteworthy exceptions exist, evidenced below. Ultimately, these source relationships informed the Truman administration on the totality of the crisis in the Far East: the status of the withdrawal of Japanese forces, the ongoing civil war between the Kuomintang and the Communists, and, most importantly, Soviet influence on the Chinese Communists' ability to defeat Chiang's military and grow popular support for the Communist movement.

Postwar Fears of Communist Power

Following the Japanese surrender, and despite reasonably stable relations with Mao during the war and with his deputy, Zhou Enlai, and his intelligence chief, Kang Sheng, the Communists intended to return to the civil war previously forgone with the Japanese invasion of Shanghai in August 1937.[33] While Communist forces generally refrained from attacking Western forces during the war—given their cooperation with the Dixie Mission and Amb. Patrick Hurley—this quickly changed, including attacks by Communist guerrillas on U.S. intelligence units.[34] The ONI reported in December 1945 the combined end-strength personnel numbers of the Chinese Communist army at approximately 2,130,000 (8th Route Army at 1,580,000 and New 4th Army at 550,000), twice the size as in July upon the surrender.[35] The number of forces raiding individual villages in the south (previously held by the CNA) seemed to rapidly increase by September 1946; similarly, acceptance of Communist spies grew among the populations of those villages.[36]

As in the 1930s, fear of Communist influence permeated the U.S. foreign policy establishment, evidenced in attempts to infiltrate Western governments working in the region. This was demonstrated when offices and personnel of the U.S. Information Service (USIS) moved by ship on the Yangtze from Chongqing to Shanghai in November 1945, wherein a credible source indicated the "handling of tickets by USIS favored known Chinese Communists over other individuals friendly to the Central Government."[37] At least three of the individuals were affiliated with (and one working for) Zhou Enlai.[38] The source also indicated that in Chongqing most of the Chinese staff of the USIS were Communists, including the chief Chinese editor, Loo Tseng-chi.[39] While the naval units operating in China eventually took a similar view, prior to its disbanding in September 1945, the OSS was likely the earliest intelligence agency to collect and document the growing Chinese Communist threat.[40] As discussed in the section on attaché intelligence collection in chapter 2, Communist influence and subversion continued to threaten the Western presence in China during the civil war.[41] Based on reporting from forces from the East, Washington was becoming more and more concerned with Soviet influence in China and with how this could tip the scales against the West's ability to maintain a postwar foothold.[42]

Nationalist Disintegration

It was apparent to the ONI and the naval attaché in Nanking, long before October 1949 when Mao declared victory and the establishment of the People's Republic of China, the Nationalists were headed to their defeat. Naval intelligence reporting depicted this military downfall in two ways. First, speculation surrounded the abruptness of Soviet drawback of forces from Manchuria in the spring of 1946 based on the perceived intention to enable Chinese Communist forces "to entrench themselves before Nationalist troops could arrive in sufficient number."[43] Whether this was indeed the Soviet impetus, the Soviets felt safe leaving the region in Mao's hands without risk of losing it to the Kuomintang. Additionally important to this point, the 50,000 Marines in northern China were ultimately deemed unthreatening to the overall Communist cause, given that the Chinese

Communist forces vastly outnumbered them, even with CNA support in Hopei Province.[44]

Second, the naval attaché in Nanking claimed a few months later, after the Chinese Communist forces filled the military vacuum left by vacating Soviet forces, that CNA forces departed their positions on Hainan Island to reinforce positions in Manchuria already occupied by Communist forces.[45] The slow response to redeploy these forces meant that CNA would likely not displace an already entrenched Communist force (especially given the guerrilla nature of the Communist way of war in which parts of the nonuniformed population implicitly contributed to the belligerent force). The naval attaché reporting does not capture this trend. To add to the loss this ultimately produced for the Kuomintang, the unfortified positions on Hainan indicated Chiang's weakened position for continuing to rule at least southern China by 1949. In 1946, however, intelligence did not demonstrate these intricacies of the conflict because any information-gathering efforts of the crisis—from a Western perspective—focused on Soviet Communist influence in the north.

Marines in Northern China

Confusion came to characterize U.S. policy toward China during the years of the civil war, which undoubtedly yielded negative consequences for the ability to collect intelligence and clearly understand the state of the Kuomintang in relation to the increasingly strengthened Chinese Communists. Chaos was evident in the deployment of the Marines to northern China. The mission was straightforward—protect Americans in and around Nanking and on the trains transporting U.S. personnel and supplies throughout the northern portion of the country.[46] The fact that the Marines were often in proximity to Soviet and Chinese Communist forces (often attacked with small arms and artillery[47]) created confusion, but the problem stemmed from a lack of direction from Washington.[48] This manifested itself in George C. Marshall's failure to negotiate peace between the Nationalists and Communists in January 1947 as well as in the announcement of the withdrawal of 12,000 forces (including 2,000 Marines) from the mainland.[49] As academic research asserts, this raised the question of whether the United States would continue to support the Chinese Central Government under Chiang and the Kuomintang.[50]

Despite the U.S. withdrawal, the Fleet Marine Forces Western Pacific established in Tsingtao four months later.[51] Then, after another month, the 1st Marine Division closed its post at Tientsin and then headquartered aboard the USS *Renville* in the Bohai Gulf.[52] Robert Lovett, as acting secretary of state, reiterated the United States' hands-off policy in December 1948, which maintained that the Marines were in China only to protect Americans; however, the simultaneous establishment of command structure, additional reinforcements, and the signal sent following the Marshall Mission confused the Kuomintang leadership. Overall, the Marshall Mission was a colossal failure in that it did not succeed in bringing peace between Mao and Chiang.[53] The U.S. military commitment to the region, however, continued unabated.[54] As a result, this negatively affected bilateral intelligence sharing.

While SACO discontinued in 1946, the Friendship Project, bilaterally run by the Navy and the Chinese naval attaché in Washington, maintained the U.S.-China (Nationalist) intelligence and military assistance relationship. The National Archives records show that the Friendship Project coordinated all matters affecting U.S. responsibility under the SACO agreement and acted as the liaison vehicle when the United States engaged Chinese government officials.[55] In some of the chaos that drove postwar restructuring of intelligence, the ONI moved from its previous OPNAV OP-02 (Intelligence) designator to OPNAV OP-03, which subsequently left a foreign liaison gap in the former. Records from the National Archives also revealed that, as a Friendship Project officer, Capt. J. C. Metzel (formerly deputy commander of the Naval Group, China) stated in a memorandum to the vice chief of naval operations, Adm. D. C. Ramsey, this gap led to problems in bilateral relations: "I have found that our present organization is exceedingly vague . . . and that it is necessary in the case of most specific problem to talk somebody into stretching his precept a little as a favor to me in releasing a dispatch and doing whatever else is to be done."[56] In another memorandum to Ramsey in August 1946, Metzel requested permission to send Colonel Sinju Pu Hsiao (the current liaison officer and acting military attaché in Washington[57]) to the Navy's intelligence course after he was informed by his commanding officer, Lieutenant General Yung-Ching Kwei, his next assignment would likely be as DNI.[58] Whether he honored this request is unclear, but Colonel Sinju served as the acting military attaché when he wrote Admiral Ramsey directly seven months later, repeating Metzel's same request.[59]

HUMINT and Marines on Patrol

The primary mission of the Marines in the III Amphibious Corps' deployment in Hebei (October 1945–May 1949) was to guard the train lines in Beijing and the surrounding area and provide security to U.S. citizens and property (embassies, consulates, and businesses). Occupying forces in the middle of a civil war, however, will at times encounter hostile forces and ultimately yield at the very least an intelligence opportunity. On several occasions, the Marines in northern China experienced this obstacle. For instance, on Christmas Day 1947, five Marines disappeared in China on a hunting trip in the vicinity of Wang Tan Yuen, ultimately passing into Communist territory despite warnings by Nationalist guards on post at nearby Ling Chan (near Tsingtao).[60] After weeks of an unsuccessful search, on 13 February 1948 the Chinese Communists confirmed the capture of the five Marines. The five men were accused of participating in the civil war. Pfc. Charles J. Brayton Jr., aged nineteen of New York, was fatally wounded and the four survivors were held until the U.S. Navy apologized.[61] By April 1948, after the release of the four and the murder of the fifth man by the Communists, the ordeal yielded some explicit intelligence about the willingness and capabilities of Mao's guerrilla force.[62] It is unclear, however, the degree to which the ONI and CIA used the intelligence produced by the Marines in China because national estimates generally did not include reference and source lists, and the ONI's contribution to them only referenced the Department of the Navy.

Another incident occurred in which Marines of the 2nd Battalion, 1st Marine Division, mounted a search-and-rescue operation after seven

Marines went missing from their outpost at Liu-Shou-Ying on 13 July 1946 when they were searching for ice to fill their beer cooler.[63] Although the operation was ultimately unsuccessful in finding the Marines, the battalion—with extremely limited intelligence capabilities—collected substantial area reconnaissance and HUMINT from both Nationalist army and Communist-aligned elements of the population. Consider the following, in which author Henry Aplington II refers to Communist guerrillas as "irregulars" and Nationalist and foreign forces as "regulars":

> The irregulars are supported by the whole body of the native people who are an effective intelligence net for them and, through feigned or actual ignorance, are a negative source for the regular troops. . . . Irregulars, with a complete knowledge of the countryside, are capable of utilizing all cover and short cuts while the regulars are confined largely to obvious road and rail nets and their information to the limits of their visibility or reconnaissance. Even guides are capable of misleading and procrastination. Not only is the regular's intelligence limited, but his mobility is hampered by his equipment and his method of making war.[64]

Other incidents occurred in late 1948 when Marines responded to events in Nanking and Shanghai, both cases in which they provided accounts of Communist actions against Nationalists and foreigners. In keeping with their primary mission in China, a platoon of Marines maneuvered to Nanking in November to protect the U.S. Embassy when the fall of the city appeared imminent.[65] Remaining there until April 1949, when the Communists completed their looting of the city center, the Marines encountered a unique experience—they were the last Western military unit to operate in proximity to the Chinese until two years later, when the Chinese People's Liberation Army (4th Army) crossed the Yalu River during the Korean War. In December 1948 Vice Adm. Oscar C. Badger, the commander of naval forces in the Far East, announced the movement of a contingent of Marines from Tsingtao to Shanghai to protect 2,500 Americans as the Chinese Nationalists fought to break a Communist encirclement.[66]

Naval Attaché, Nanking, and Soviet Encroachment

More than the Marines and naval forces in China, the ONI relied upon the naval attaché in Nanking in the years following the war, possibly because of growing Soviet influence in the region. The mission, however, was increasingly limited in its access to Chinese sources, due in part to the fact that the Nationalist government was at odds with the United States, and Mao's Communist forces were steadily more hostile to the West.[67] Nevertheless, the ONI's reliance included three overarching areas important to the West's ability to prepare for the cold war ahead. First, the naval attaché office regularly profiled Chinese leadership in response to calls from the CNA and others. Second, the ONI was interested in the fast expansion of Chinese Communism—particularly in relation to Chiang Kai-shek's Kuomintang regime—and the impact to U.S. relations with China. Third, given the number of reports that outnumber those of other issues, the Truman administration clearly directed the naval attaché to collect as much information as possible on Soviet influence, intelligence, and military presence in northern China. Therefore, the naval attaché was the single most important intelligence collector in the years between 1945 and 1949 in China. The value of this role is further supported by the amount of space devoted to the mission and tradecraft of the naval attaché in the June 1949 *Naval Intelligence Manual*, published by the ONI.[68] In some ways the attaché office represented the last opportunity for national security leaders to gain an understanding of the direction of China's political system before Mao closed it to the outside world for many years.

As the Chinese people experienced the horrific effects of World War II and the Sino-Japanese War, and as the Chinese Civil War resumed, Soviet influence in northern China grew to unprecedented levels. The archival record is inconsistent in the first couple of years after World War II (especially given Soviet military presence in the northeast), but Stalin both benefited and was at odds with a Communist succession of power in China.[69] Eventually, when the Communists won a series of battles, particularly in the second battle of Siping (1946) and the Liao–Shen Campaign (1948), Stalin's position shifted more in direct support to Mao's cause and ensuring a Communist succession in Beijing.[70] Remaining U.S. naval forces in the region observed and collected tremendous amounts of intelligence on the Soviets in China during this time. This resulted in the ability for Western intelligence to maintain an understanding of the rapidly shifting security and political environment in East Asia.

As early as August 1945, following the Soviet invasion of Manchuria, Soviet intelligence services conducted influence operations, clandestine actions, and other intelligence activities in northern China. In November the U.S. naval attaché stationed in Chongqing reported that the OCGU (translated as "joint staff political directorate") unit in Shanghai, led by A. A. Alexandroff, was "responsible for the dissemination of Communism among the various Nationalistic groups [in Shanghai]."[71] Under his direction and with financial support from Moscow, the naval attaché reported that the OCGU's propaganda unit proceeded secretly with support to the Chinese Communist Party using "Soviet newspapers as a guide for communist propaganda."[72] This activity seems mild and even primitive, but the early penetration of the region led to the ability of Soviet intelligence to establish long-term, robust networks. Likewise, this report indicates that the U.S. naval attaché—as part of the embassy—was pushed south to Chongqing and to that time was able to maintain sources north in Shanghai. Intelligence reporting over time tended to rely on access to sources south in the Nationalist capital, such as the War Department Strategic Service Unit's comprehensive report (one of its last ones before its dissolution) on intelligence services in Guangzhou, Hong Kong, and Macau.[73] Despite the chaos in the southern region in the modern Guangzhou Province at the time, the area was far safer than in the north, where forces endured intimately closer violence.

As U.S. Army observer John Service uncovered through sources in Communist-held Yenan in March 1945, Soviet planes had not landed in the area since November 1942, and no Soviet weapons were identified on Chinese Communist guerrillas in the last year of the war.[74] As Service also claimed, though, Mao clearly maintained at least moderate ties to Moscow throughout the war, evidenced in the letter published by the community news agency's paper from Stalin to Mao thanking the chairman for congratulations on Red Army Day. This global Communist revolution resulted in the significant reemergence of Soviet activity in the fall of 1945.

The military and naval attaché offices in Nanking tried to maintain a complete understanding of Soviet influence in China, but this became an insurmountable task as the number of Soviet plainclothes officers from the People's Commissariat for Internal Affairs and the other agencies grew—the number of potential intelligence officers in country decreased since VJ Day. Conversely, reporting was consistent and often novel in sources and subject matter. No other naval attaché in East Asia following the war demonstrated as much influence, consistency in quality, and prolific output as Navy captain William T. Kenny and his office. For the period that the Kuomintang government remained in Nanking, Captain Kenny and his successor maintained sources—government, Communist, nonaligned civilian, and even Soviet—in northern China. Reported by Cdr. Gould Thomas in April 1946, the naval attaché in Nanking confirmed the existence of Soviet ammunition and firearms in the cargo of four merchant ships headed for Shanghai, Tientsin, and Guangzhou.[75] Kenny and his team also identified Soviet positions as forces in central Manchuria moved across the Yalu River into Rashin and Seishin and occupied the Dalian Harbor.[76]

The Soviets also engaged in establishing cover organizations in collusion with the Chinese Communists for recruiting Chinese nationals to the party. The U.S. naval attaché in Nanking reported in April 1946 the establishment of the Sino-Soviet Philanthropic Association to help "'international refugees' and the unemployed in order to induce them to become members of the Communist Party."[77] In this case the Soviet news agency (TASS) set up the organization, but in other cases, Soviet Internal Affairs (Министерство внутренних дел, МВД, MVD[78]) became more explicitly involved, such as when one Mr. Patrikeef of the Soviet Embassy in Beijing summoned a group of Soviet nationals from Tientsin to organize political and other activities inside China, coercing the individuals as "each owed his country a definite obligation and that orders were to be followed to the letter."[79] Given the lack of an aggregate assessment, the naval attaché and ONI did not have a holistic perspective on these activities and thus did not understand them in their collective context (i.e.,

Moscow attempted to establish a puppet state under Mao). The equivalent of the Berlin blockade and airlift (June 1948–May 1949) in northeast Asia was the Soviet Union's military support to China and North Korea that enabled the Korean War's initiation. This initial intelligence baseline allowed for some foresight among the U.S. and UN forces in June 1950.

The environment in China after World War II proved a highly chaotic period. The fear of a Communist takeover (either by Mao or by the Soviets) typified the period, exacerbated by the slow but clear Nationalist government disintegration. The United States and the West needed intelligence in order to assess where China was headed, the degree to which Moscow would assist Mao's forces, and whether China would be increasingly hostile toward the West. Intelligence collected during this period was limited to source development and reconnaissance observation access that Marines operating in Northern China and the Naval Attaché in Nanking could maintain, which was ultimately limited in producing strategic intelligence on Chinese Communist and Soviet intentions.

Conclusion

HUMINT serves a different function in crisis than in war. As the Marines in Manchuria and the naval attaché show, HUMINT is a unique kind of intelligence that requires the safety, security, and access that wartime is often unable to provide, particularly regarding the most sensitive of sources and targets. Unlike in war—when men often die to obtain the intelligence required for their decision-makers and operating forces—crises like the Chinese Civil War show the illusive cover enabled by officialdom. Other forms of intelligence (e.g., SIGINT), which can be collected at will, adhere to a more standoff position to administer the application of collection, but the record of these being present in China during this period is extremely limited, if available. In war, HUMINT is susceptible to open targeting by counterintelligence forces and the outright killing of agents. The post–World War II case of U.S. naval intelligence in China illustrates these points.

Crises such as the early years of the Cold War in the Far East complicate the development of human sources when access is constrained, as it was for the Western powers in the years following World War II. Nevertheless, demand for HUMINT remained high, if for no other reason than that it was the primary intelligence capability present. As the Chinese Communists gained greater power, the Kuomintang under Chiang fought to hold on to power. In addition, increasing Soviet influence in China greatly hindered the ability for U.S. naval intelligence personnel to gather intelligence. At the same time, the contested presence of Navy and Marine Corps forces in the country afforded valuable intelligence insight into the direction by which Communist presence proceeded in the region.

All of these events occurred while the entire national security apparatus underwent a historical modernization. The centralization of intelligence institutionally affected the Navy intelligence community, which resulted in a degree of chaos surrounding the ability to manage and prioritize intelligence. While the Washington bureaucracy rapidly changed, the field units charged with collecting intelligence continued, often applying practices learned and institutionalized from years past. The practice of intelligence did not maintain pace with the policy and institutional changes within the bureaucracy before the Chinese Communists forced the last U.S. military units out of the country in 1949, which enabled the final victory over the Nationalists and the establishment of the People's Republic of China.

Part III

Active Containment

Intelligence in the Taiwan Crises of the 1950s

Chapter 5

New Model Intelligence and Holding Steady with the Nationalists

This chapter addresses U.S. naval HUMINT during the Taiwan crises of the 1950s, in which Chiang Kai-shek and the Kuomintang Nationalists faced the threat of invasion and unification with mainland China by Mao Zedong's People's Liberation Army (PLA).¹ It highlights some unique dynamics of the U.S. intelligence experience that most previous research has overlooked.² The U.S. Navy was on a different footing than it had been prior to entering the Korean War, at which time Truman ordered the U.S. Seventh Fleet to begin regularly patrolling the Taiwan Strait.³ Korea reoriented the Navy and Marine Corps to the new reality that the threat of war was again nearly inevitable, which required them to constantly prepare, especially following the signing of the Mutual Defense Treaty between the United States and Taiwan in December 1954, and then with Chiang's *fangong dalu* (counteroffensive against the mainland, 1955–57) plans.⁴ Preparation meant acquiring highly credible intelligence. The establishment of the intelligence community in 1947 immediately placed exceptional authorities in CIA, under which each of the military services played a fundamental yet subordinated role in national intelligence estimates (NIEs), the nation's premier classified intelligence reports on issues most consequential to national security.[5]

While the Communist Bloc was collectively the West's primary threat, U.S. intelligence was never able to recruit any high-level agents within the Chinese Communist government or military after the post–World War II drawdown of forces.[6] Because of the threat of the use of nuclear weapons, it was a time unlike any other in Western history and one in which strategic intelligence (based on human sources) could have been decisive.[7] HUMINT played an important role in the crisis, especially driving U.S.-Taiwan policy, but yielded little effect on resolving issues with Beijing that were advantageous to the United States over the long term. It notably showed that the issues most affecting crisis outcomes—that is, foreknowledge one would most likely require to make informed decisions—were related to the often disconnected dynamics between the United States and Taiwan, and it taught us very little about how the Chinese Communist Party thinks about war.[8]

The naval HUMINT record is limited but discernible, and the standoff position the West held in relation to the mainland reduced access to Chinese Communist sources often resulted in intelligence of limited value. Intelligence in a broader context and the circumstances of the United States lacking access to sources on the Chinese mainland at times created a fog of understanding during the crisis. The Nationalist sources that the Navy, CIA, and others developed in Taiwan often hindered these conditions. While some human sources proved valuable (particularly those in Taipei), Navy and CIA leaders often relied on newer intelligence disciplines (e.g., IMINT and SIGINT), effectively limiting insight into patterns of life, decision-making rationales, intentions on the use of force, and the Chinese (both on Taiwan and the mainland) understanding of enemy intentions.[9] Because of this tradeoff, intelligence prior to and in the crisis often focused on capabilities as well as less elusive evidence gathered through aerial reconnaissance and coastal patrol.[10] However, because of the uniqueness of HUMINT, it still served as a highly employed discipline during this time, albeit often flawed under the circumstances.

The conflict between the People's Republic of China (PRC) and Taiwan between 1949 and 1958 was actually a single continuous set of provocations, two instances in which the intensity reached a crisis level and war was likely.[11] Intelligence played an essential yet problematic role because Western governments needed to ensure their adversary's intentions and disposition. The U.S. Navy was a primary actor in the crises—both inherently naval—and, thus, Fleet intelligence was fundamentally relevant to the courses both crises took.[12] This importance brought challenges and limitations, however. This chapter addresses three basic questions. First, what did the Navy and CIA need to know about the enemy? Second, how did they conduct information gathering in the human domain? Finally, what value did the resulting intelligence have in resolving the crisis? The case answers these questions by examining archival records of naval intelligence in the Far East and the burgeoning intelligence community given CIA's primacy at the time.

The chapter organizes around an evolving set of crises, interrelated but distinct in beginnings and ends, as well as the Navy's approach to naval HUMINT at the time, its relationship with CIA, and its effect on strategic outcomes in the crises. The case begins an examination of superpower competition and Western containment strategy and crisis in the Cold War, including an analysis of crisis intelligence in this context. Then a discussion of challenges and changes in U.S. intelligence during this period and the subsequent Navy adjustments follows. From there the analysis presents an examination of naval intelligence command structure. A few years following the establishment of a centralized intelligence community, the case then explores how Navy training and integration with the CIA progressed, building on the previous chapter's exploration of the organizational impacts of the National Security Act of 1947.

Bipolar Competition and Taiwan

In a speech on 12 March 1947, just months before the National Security Act of 1947 and the establishment of the CIA, President Truman declared that the United States would assist any country threatened by Communism, which ultimately amounted to his doctrine.[13] While not necessarily groundbreaking at the time, like the chargé d'affaires in Moscow George Kennan's "long telegram," it was the bedrock of U.S. containment policy for the rest of the Cold War.[14] To fulfill the objectives of containment and the Truman Doctrine, nations in the free world needed an expansive view of intelligence. The Soviet Union and the PRC were largely black boxes in terms of understanding leadership intentions and strategic capability developments. In addition, while the United States maintained an embassy in Moscow—from where Kennan penned his telegram—the U.S. Embassy in China moved to Taipei in December 1949, effectively losing complete access to sources on the mainland.

To fulfill the Truman Doctrine, an overall containment strategy required an enormous amount of accurate intelligence from sources who could speak authoritatively on Communist Bloc leadership decisions. Almost from the beginning, the CIA did not operate in a vacuum with organic capabilities of its own but recruited, developed, and trained them over time.[15] In addition to collection, the military services—mostly through each one's intelligence agency—participated in nearly all estimates.[16] For example, in the CIA's estimation of the likelihood of Chinese military activity in various regions in the Far East in 1950, the ONI offered that, while the Communist Chinese had a limited naval capability, they were capable of mounting an amphibious invasion of Formosa with about 200,000 forces.[17] However, the same estimate also inaccurately concluded—just days before it actually happened—that "while full-scale Chinese communist intervention in Korea must be regarded as a continued possibility . . . such action is not probable in 1950."[18] While intelligence the Navy produced strictly for the Fleet in the early Cold War held tactical and operational value, the ONI's participation in NIEs with the CIA often demonstrated its strategic value. In the early and mid-1950s, these estimates were generally the DNI's finished naval intelligence inputs from around the world.[19]

It is easy today to pass off the issue of Taiwan's independence in the early Cold War as only peripherally important to the West. The entire nature of the Cold War centered on the idea that if Moscow influenced one country to turn Communist, this could then in turn influence other regions to espouse Communist ambitions.[20] Consider, however, a statement by William "Wild Bill" Donovan (former director of the OSS) in a lecture at the Naval War College in 1953: "Once China is consolidated, Stalin's conquest will be extended throughout Southeast Asia, down the same path the Japanese followed through Indo-China, Hong Kong, the Philippines, Siam, Malaya, Indonesia and Burma—all the way to India."[21] While Donovan remained an influential figure in the intelligence community, he simply communicated similar sentiments of leaders, such as DCI Allen Dulles.[22] In short, Taiwan's independence or Nationalist reunification with the mainland was commonly understood as directly tied to Communist strategic influence vis-à-vis Moscow in Western containment policy; if Taiwan fell to the Communists, other countries around it could as well.[23] This clearly represents deeply flawed logic considering Taiwan, though, given the history of China since 1911.

While relations between Washington and Taipei strained after the Kuomintang's move to Taiwan—owing primarily to the tenuousness of the U.S. commitment to the Kuomintang and the island's defense—the Navy's relationship with Nationalist intelligence (stemming from the days when Tai Li had significant influence over Chiang's intelligence enterprise) continued to be strong.[24] Nationalist agents in Taiwan or clandestinely inserted on the mainland derived or enabled the majority of human sources that the ONI and the Seventh Fleet relied upon for intelligence on Communist China. This is directly related to the fact that U.S. intelligence officers no longer enjoyed direct access to mainland China.

In a fatalistic atmosphere that followed the Truman Doctrine and the onset of the Korean War, Donovan's words, and others', likely colored the CIA's and the military's approach to intelligence in the 1950s, possibly affecting a variety of aspects from assumptions to perceptions of those analyzing it and customers using it.[25] Bias is generally inherent in intelligence analysis, but agencies tend to control the amount of bias to eliminate inaccuracies and skewing in analysis. In addition, while much of the discussion of bias in intelligence focuses on the analyst in finished intelligence products, bias presents itself in the management, planning, and execution of intelligence collection. Operational commanders often directed intelligence requirements based on the gaps in information they might have in relation to a necessary operational decision.[26] More often than not, such guidance focused on capabilities rather than adversary intentions, beliefs, and perceptions, which perpetuated a monolithic view of the Communist Bloc's threat to the West.[27]

Two challenges drove the nature of the intelligence relationships the United States established and maintained in relation to Communist China during this period. First, the move of the U.S. Embassy to Taipei in 1949 and the withdrawal of the last of the U.S. naval forces and Marines in Manchuria, China, severely constrained access to the mainland, which was ultimately available only through clandestine means (such as watching coastal activity from the sea and reliance on clandestine sources in Taipei and by Kuomintang intelligence assets on the mainland). These circumstances thus underpinned the U.S. relationship with Taiwan.

Second, in spite of the continuing intelligence relationship with Taipei, Chinese Nationalists' trust in the United States that existed prior to the 1949 split with the mainland was strained due to Taipei's uneasiness with the United States' commitment (both politically and militarily).[28] There is little doubt that U.S. sentiment at times impacted Taipei's trust concerning the reliability or willingness of Kuomintang sources to reciprocate with frankness. Likewise, the CIA and ONI applied skepticism to the intelligence their officers acquired from Taipei-based sources.

The West relied on Taiwan, more than Taiwan relied on the West, and the Navy played a central role in this dynamic primarily because of the inherent naval nature of the relationship. The naval aspect of any crisis or conflict between Beijing and the West was clear given that activity would most likely occur in the western Pacific, in the Taiwan Strait, or in China's littoral approaches. To prepare for that eventuality, the CIA and Navy planned and conducted sensitive, clandestine, and covert operations.[29]

Crisis Intelligence in the Cold War

Following the Chinese Communist revolution and civil war that ousted Nationalist Kuomintang rule, pushing Chiang Kai-shek and his regime to the island of Taiwan, the newly established PRC under Mao Zedong quickly became embroiled in a conflict on its northeast border with North Korea in October 1950 to expel U.S. and United Nations forces.[30] Mao's decision to focus on Korea as the immediate problem (at the expense of resolving the Taiwan problem) and the United States' ability to commit a portion of U.S. Seventh Fleet's assets to the strait while prosecuting the Korean campaign postponed the Taiwan conflict. At the time, however, Mao's intentions were unclear and Western leaders required intelligence based on reliable sources to assess the situation. As discussed in chapter 4, the United States lost direct access to sources on the Chinese mainland when Embassy Chongqing shut down and the last Marines in Manchuria were ejected following the Communist victory on 1 October 1949, exacerbating the difficulty of gathering intelligence.

To gather intelligence in the Cold War, particularly when it came to crises involving the possible use of nuclear weapons, requirements were based on dangerous terms, and leaders made requirements and decisions based on dangerous terms that potentially affected millions of people.[31] In the context of the naval crisis in the Taiwan Strait, the potential intervention by the Soviet Union ultimately threatened nuclear war between the West and Moscow. Collecting intelligence against this required first an understanding of the Chinese Communist forces (the PLA) in the region and then their leaders' intentions.[32] While naval intelligence certainly focused on Communist intentions at sea first, some of its support to the CIA's national mission also yielded strategic intelligence about Mao's regime. Furthermore, Western intelligence attempted to clarify the projected path of the crisis and the implications for U.S. involvement. To understand the nuances of this conflict, intelligence needed to uncover the experience level and knowledge among the Chinese Communist leadership regarding crises, but in lieu of high-level sources on the mainland, such efforts often attempted this required context by observing and interpreting Chinese military actions.[33]

Past works have examined crisis dynamics specific to the U.S.-China relationship. Michael Swaine characterized the problem inherent in the Western interpretation of Chinese *weiji* (危机, crisis) many years after the Taiwan crises of the 1950s.[34] In examining Sino-U.S. crises, he described six variables that influence crisis behavior: (1) elite perception and belief; (2) domestic politics and public opinion; (3) decision-making structure and process; (4) information and intelligence receipt and processing; (5) international environment; and (6) idiosyncratic or special features.[35] Swaine's model provides a rough roadmap for a structured and critical discussion of intelligence in the crises. Understandably, given the context of the Cold War, some of these factors are more clearly observable than others. Elite perceptions and domestic politics were certainly of interest to the intelligence services in the 1950s—evident in some of the subjects reported on by the CIA—but the level of primary source access was limited in comparison to, say, an allied country or a country in which the U.S. maintained an embassy. Thus, with a limited amount of information garnered on a subject, such as Premier Zhou Enlai's perceptions of U.S. involvement in Korea, intelligence analysts pursue a structured estimation, based on what is known, what is unknown, and what is likely given historical activity.

While intelligence was collected against many aspects of the PRC, some targeted intelligence benefited the CIA, ONI, and naval operating units on fundamentally different levels. For instance, would the Chinese Communists attack Taiwan unprovoked? Would Mao and the PLA back down if the United States intervened and applied some level of military force? Would the Soviet Union intervene, either covertly in support with arms or overtly with the Red Army? These questions plagued decision-makers but often fell short in the priority list for the operational Fleet, which focused instead on the capabilities and disposition of Chinese Communist forces in the strait.[36] For example, the Intelligence Advisory Committee—headed by the DCI—on which the DNI was a full member, often discussed Communist leadership as a part of its agenda.[37] While important, this contrasts with the Navy and CIA's ability to actually collect and report on strategic subjects such as this given the lack of access to the Chinese mainland.

Intelligence Community Changes

To examine how naval intelligence changed a few years into the Cold War, this analysis highlights the primacy of the CIA at this time, but it would be a mistake to consider the CIA's role as rendering the military services irrelevant. Indeed, an April 1955 memorandum from the chief of naval operations (CNO) to the chief of naval personnel indicated that the Navy and CIA had reached an agreement to introduce officers from Langley into intelligence staffs within the Fleet to garner much-needed naval perspective information at lower levels for incorporation into national-level intelligence estimates.[38] Contrary to the notion that the CIA was monolithic in producing intelligence during the Cold War, however, the services' intelligence contributed to nearly every NIE published by the agency, certainly when featuring domain-specific areas (e.g., naval warfare).[39]

The purpose of centralizing intelligence was not to box out the military or other producers of intelligence (e.g., the Federal Bureau of Investigation) but rather to foster a central repository and arbiter of finished intelligence at the national level. The intention was to avert strategic surprises, such as another Pearl Harbor or the Soviets' development of the hydrogen bomb. This aversion to surprise served as an enormous catalyst to the postwar reorganization of the intelligence community, discussed in the previous chapter.[40] In a speech that President Harry Truman delivered to the CIA's eighth training orientation course for representatives of various government agencies in 1952, he said: "When I became President . . . there was no concentration of information for the benefit of the President. Each department and each organization had its own information service, and that information service was walled off from every other service in such a manner that whenever it was necessary for the President to have information, he had to send to two or three departments to get it, and information of vital importance to the President in his hands."[41]

The way intelligence was managed in the Taiwan crises resulted from enormous changes that the Navy and Marine Corps underwent in the years following the establishment of the CIA, when the services were racing to catch up, as well as following the 1950 intervention on the Korean Peninsula.[42] Where naval intelligence was historically centralized, in that reporting inevitably served the DNI, the structure broke down somewhat with the CIA's establishment, and the adjustment yielded significant challenges.[43] The Korean War showed several problems in the naval intelligence establishment (as well as in the young intelligence community overall), even as newly successful operational relationships, such as the one the Navy developed with the CIA, gave way to a new era of clandestine intelligence.[44] For instance, Navy air units, such as the battle-hardened Carrier Air Group Two, continuously reported shortages of nonflying air intelligence personnel, those who liaised with allied Korean intelligence services.[45] The shortages of trained intelligence personnel resulted in "inadequate briefing and de-briefing" during the early stages of the war.[46] Naval air units also pointed to the need for "photo coverage and intelligence information, collected by other sources" to be disseminated to lower echelon units, such as at the squadron level.[47] The demand for intelligence was as high as ever—now serving multiple authorities—but the capacity and preparation to deliver it was not keeping pace.

While the notion of a centralized intelligence institution theoretically produced more accurate and holistic intelligence, this created institutional perturbations in a Navy with an insular hierarchy deeply embedded in its history. Never before had Navy intelligence been prone to the scrutiny of any other agency or service but the Navy leadership and the ONI. While naval intelligence continued its traditional mission of supporting the Fleet with operational intelligence, the ONI contributed the Navy's input to NIEs managed at Langley. Intelligence priorities in this dual-natured context clearly conflicted at times and often expanded. Operational collections also changed as the Navy forged a field-based relationship with various emerging CIA stations around the world. Naval intelligence collection priorities were periodically published in the early 1950s, but with some seeming irregularity.[48]

As much as the intelligence community became centralized under the CIA, one should recognize that, even when different institutions operationally integrate, the fundamental differences in missions produce different intelligence (e.g., strategic political intentions versus naval capabilities).[49] The Korean War represented an initial case of this, in which naval intelligence personnel assisted the CIA's operations against Communist China on the Yellow Sea and Sea of Japan coasts.[50] Power shifts in the community changed the naval intelligence establishment permanently, and the

1950s experience in the Far East was an early test of how the Navy adapted and continued to provide meaningful intelligence. For example, while the CIA came to use the military in operations under the DCI's authority, the agency sent a clear message that only one agency managed and oversaw covert action. Such was the case when Far East Command was compelled to discontinue covert action in 1950, a move that likely was result of the CIA's consolidation of such activities.[51] In another case, in 1950 DCI Roscoe H. Hillenkoetter sent a memorandum to Rear Adm. Felix L. Johnson, then DNI, lambasting the ONI for suggesting (in a recent collection instruction) that the Navy conduct covert collection, which was a direct violation of National Security Council Intelligence Directive 5 (NSCID-5, "Espionage and Counterespionage Operations").[52] This indicated that the Navy held the position that the clandestine and covert operating space was not only the CIA's, as the NSC directive intended. Still, it would be several years before this activity was formally sanctioned for the Navy to officially conduct. The challenges posed by the changes to intelligence writ large five to ten years into the Cold War pushed the Navy to approach its intelligence mission differently, which resulted in the Fleet accepting more risk when the stakes were higher in the pursuit of adversaries even less transparent than its German and Japanese enemies had been during World War II. The risks, however, yielded mixed results in the context of the Taiwan crises.

Another development in the intelligence community during this period emerged from the 1948 National Security Intelligence Directive 9 making the CIA a member of the United States Communications Intelligence Board, the highest authority in the United States on communications intelligence (COMINT).[53] Due to growing communications interception cryptologic capabilities in both the Army and Navy, the Armed Forces Security Agency was established in 1950.[54] Because these capabilities continued to grow and the Armed Forces Security Agency had neither its own facilities or authorities (authorities remained at the service level), the National Security Agency (NSA) was established in November 1952 to handle and oversee the military's SIGINT mission. The NSA's significance to the Navy quickly became profound. While the Navy regularly collected voluminous amounts of ELINT and COMINT, the ONI and the Navy's Bureau of Communications were overwhelmed by the job of processing the data and producing SIGINT reports.

Navy Thinking on Intelligence

It is useful to consider the Fleet's viewpoint on intelligence at this point in the Cold War. The experience of World War II and the changing requirements in relation to the Communist Bloc following the war shaped the Fleet's views and use for intelligence. Whereas intelligence fulfilled an operational end before the war, the need for strategic intelligence became greater as the stakes in maritime power and the Soviet nuclear threat became greater. In a 1953 lecture at the U.S. Naval War College, Capt. George R. Phelan noted that naval strategic intelligence focuses "on the capabilities, vulnerabilities and intentions of possible or actual enemies within the field of naval warfare."[55] Likewise, he said that operational intelligence was intelligence "needed by commanders in planning and executing operations including battle," and the ONI might send the Fleet strategic intelligence when the Fleet uses it as operational intelligence.[56] The dichotomy of intelligence as either static or dynamic, overt or covert, old or new, and derived from secondary or primary sources became a new way for the Fleet to think about intelligence—possibly a result of the CIA and Sherman Kent's (director of the office of national estimates, 1952–67) influence on the entire U.S. intelligence analytic community at the time.[57] The Marine Corps even integrated Kent's work in its discourse, in one case noting Kent's stark debunking of the romanticism of espionage in place for the value of the organization and coordination tenets of the effective intelligence agency.[58]

As the Navy adjusted to the National Security Act of 1947 and the Truman Doctrine, it cannot be overstated how the CIA changed nearly the entire intelligence establishment, a new reality not fully appreciated during the course of events in the previous case's events. Organizationally, and in terms of driving intelligence policy for the course of the Cold War, centralization meant greater control over intelligence priorities, starting with the president. The management of naval intelligence in this context implied that a greater number of leaders and entities could ultimately use naval intelligence products, but this also meant a greater demand for them, which inevitably taxed the Navy's limited resources. This was further reinforced with the advent of the NSA. Intelligence prioritization became a driver, but the Navy and CIA did not always agree, either on priorities or on the Navy's role.[59] On the one hand, the Navy was oriented to collect directly on enemy capabilities and intentions in relation to its operational mission. On the other hand, the CIA had a national mission to fulfill for its primary customer, the president. Fundamental differences underpinned each institution, even as the Cold War intelligence mission seemed increasingly unified. Intelligence to the Fleet in the early Cold War was comparable to the pre–World War II era, but with the vexing addition of nuclear weapons and higher stakes in relation to the Communist Bloc.

Intelligence Command Structures

As in previous times, the command and control of naval operations were vastly different from the command structures of intelligence in terms of structure and reporting. Prior to World War II, all naval intelligence reporting was centralized in that it went through the ONI (with the DNI as its head), from the lowest level units to the Fleet level of command. During World War II, units operating in the Pacific were required to report to both the ONI as well as Admiral Nimitz's (commander in chief, U.S. Pacific Fleet) Joint Intelligence Center, Pacific Ocean Areas.[60] This chain of command changed following the National Security Act of 1947 and the establishment of the CIA. While the ONI continued to be the central repository and coordinator of all finished intelligence internal to the Navy, the CIA now centralized intelligence at the national level. If an NIE or national-level intelligence report included intelligence on enemy naval activity, Navy intelligence was involved. While the CIA coordinated such efforts as the final arbiter, the ONI served as an obligatory contributor, similar to the other services in their respective warfare areas. This relationship means that the CIA, rather than the ONI or the Navy, published many of the finished products.

Similar to the past, however, reporting went two ways and ultimately produced two tiers of intelligence. Units at the tactical level (namely, the Taiwan Patrol Force, Military Assistance Advisory Group, Taiwan [MAAG-T], and Taiwan Defense Command[61]) reported both to their higher Navy commanders in the Fleet (to the Seventh Fleet and then to Pacific Fleet) and to the ONI.[62] While the Far East Command, Seventh Fleet, and Pacific Fleet produced finished intelligence for the CNO and ONI, their finished reports were often then used to produce further-refined intelligence at the ONI's headquarters at the Navy Yard in Washington, DC.[63] As the ONI produced intelligence for the CNO and the secretary of the Navy as well as a regular naval intelligence board, these reports also contributed to NIEs. Figure 2 shows the intelligence command-and-control structure during this period specifically as it related to Navy intelligence and Taiwan.

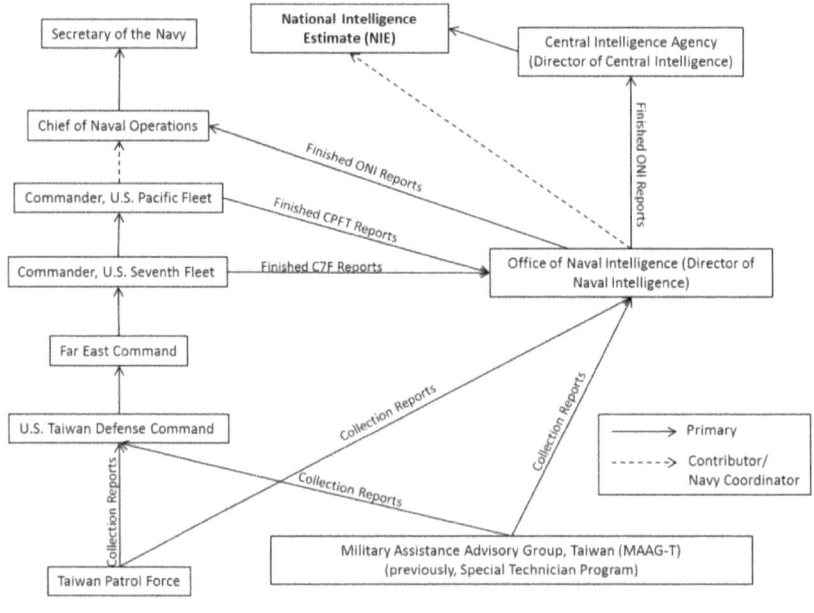

Figure 2. Naval Intelligence Reporting Chain (1954–58). This figure was constructed from many of the documents cited in this case as well as from Packard, *A Century of Naval Intelligence*, 415–18. *Created by author*

Reporting changed only slightly over time between 1954 and 1979, when the Jimmy Carter administration disbanded the Taiwan Patrol Force.[64] Generally, however, the CIA maintained the hierarchy of the community through the period of these crises. Internally to the Fleet during the 1950s, in July 1954 the DNI completed a Fleet-wide assessment of intelligence organization and operations.[65] The First Fleet (the command charged with conducting the assessment) concluded that the Pacific Fleet's organization and personnel were sufficient for its mission.[66] However, this assessment occurred concurrently to the ramping up of the Taiwan crisis. Given the timing, it is difficult to say whether the Fleet's intelligence enterprise was optimally organized and manned in the first Taiwan crisis.

The Pacific Fleet endured command changes within its intelligence enterprise during this time, however. Whether a result of CIA appeals or an internal defense examination (via the Joint Chiefs of Staff's direction), the Pacific Fleet notified the CNO in December 1954 of a reorganization and overhaul of clandestine and covert operations within the Far East Command (including the Pacific Fleet and Taiwan Patrol Force) "for the purpose of improving coordination and control over the various activities of the component services in these areas."[67] The Far East Command now maintained command over plans, policy, and day-to-day operations (in nonwartime environments) and coordinated with the Special Plans Branch of the Joint Staff J2.[68] The reorganization also established the Special Support Activities, Naval Forces (Far East) unit, directly under the command of Far East Command.[69] This effectively created greater regionalized centralization of these activities where—before multiple commands shared this responsibility—the possibility of operational failures was more likely. Almost immediately the new unit requested additional resources, but the degree to which the CNO granted this is unclear.[70] Just a few months earlier the Pacific Fleet requested additional personnel for the so-called Formosa Liaison Center (subordinate to the Military Assistance and Advisory Group Formosa, MAAG Formosa, a.k.a. Task Force 74), an activity in Taipei known to develop sources within the Taiwan government.[71] As will become evident, the majority of the valuable sources U.S. intelligence relied upon during the strait crises derived from sources either within the Taiwan government or sources on mainland China developed by Taiwan government intelligence.

Training and Integration with the CIA

Naval intelligence in the Fleet in the 1950s experienced more changes than any time since the ONI's establishment in 1882, and this was reflected in training and integration with the CIA. To conform to its evolving practices, the CIA also dictated the methods to collect naval intelligence. For example, one memorandum in early 1950 indicated the desire to "make arrangements with the Navy so that they won't get too far out of line" when following the collection directive, the so-called 5009—Contact Register.[72] More important is what this memorandum did not say—namely, exactly what the agency did expect from the Fleet. Because the national security complex evolved over the early Cold War, no one single guiding charter existed for the Navy–CIA relationship but rather several disparate memoranda. Illustrating this, the Navy occasionally appealed to the CIA for the release of intelligence not already forwarded to the ONI, but the agency returned any documentation with redacted references to sources and methods.[73] It was a time of establishing norms between the Navy and the agency, and this started with how the Fleet prepared its intelligence personnel.

The CIA increasingly weighed in on the methods used by the Navy to collect intelligence, but it also wanted to derive expertise from the Navy that its training program could not organically build. In terms of collections, consider the 1951 NIE titled "Chinese Communist Capabilities and Intentions with Respect to Taiwan."[74] The agency tasked the Navy with overseeing the following highly broad and all-encompassing categories:

> communist China's capabilities for securing control over Taiwan, Chinese communist resources available for an assault on Taiwan, military strength and disposition of forces (including air and naval support), watercraft capability, demands on Chinese communist resources made by other major commitments, Nationalist capabilities to repel an assault, deficiencies of the Nationalists that require U.S. aid to repel an assault, external factors that affect communist China's intentions with respect to Taiwan in 1951, considerations of an over-all Soviet policy, consideration of U.S. counteraction, and probable place of Taiwan in Chinese communist over-all planning during 1951.[75]

This priority list reflects the fact that the CIA cast a wide net in tasking the Navy and perhaps a level of trust in the Fleet's ability to collect national-level intelligence, evident as well in its contributions to NIEs discussed in the following sections.

The Navy's intelligence school became more sophisticated in 1954 (albeit limited in depth) and began inviting a select few students from the CIA in addition to the three dozen the Fleet sent annually at that time.[76] The curriculum for the six-week course included world geography and resources; international relations and foreign policy; world organization; international trade, transportation, and finance; current international relations problems; fundamentals of intelligence; national intelligence organization; strategic application of intelligence; counterintelligence; psychological warfare; photographic interpretation; prisoner of war interrogation; technical and scientific intelligence; foreign intelligence systems; briefing; and various naval applications of intelligence.[77] Unlike the CIA's "Farm" at Camp Peary, which trained and prepared case officers for overseas duty, including covert action, the Navy's school focused solely on tradecraft and the skills required to collect intelligence.[78]

The Navy began revamping its approach to intelligence as a naval profession in the postwar years, but it operated in a much different world than before. The ONI began a new year-long training course in July 1950 at its Anacostia location, in which candidates studied naval intelligence, a foreign language, and a foreign area—the first time the Navy formally included the latter two.[79] To create more symbiosis, however, between political and naval intelligence, the CIA reached out to the Navy in October 1951 to create a program to expose new case officers to naval operations matters, provide reserve-status cover for them, and release them into environments in which they collected naval HUMINT.[80] Additionally, as naval officers, they were then assigned clandestine missions at the CIA "insofar as it is practicable for Navy to do so. Types of duty contemplated by the CIA includes sea duty, and assignment to the CIA as part of its regular active-duty Navy quota."[81] This relationship evolved and matured across the next several years, likely giving impetus for the clandestine HUMINT programs that emerged in the 1960s. The record of how successful this training was is limited, but it at least partially attributed to the fact that the ONI later pushed for greater clandestine capabilities, as discussed in the next chapter.

Chapter 6

Reading the Chinese Communists through Taipei

Given the contextual and institutional factors discussed in the previous chapter, this chapter delves into naval HUMINT's role in the Taiwan crises, jumping off from the end of the Korean War, followed by a reconstruction of each of the crises. It shows the near impossibility of determining Chinese Communist intentions when access to mainland sources dries up or is filtered through intermediary allies in Taipei with questionable access themselves. Finally, the chapter provides some conclusions on the value of naval HUMINT in the outcome and comments on how naval intelligence and HUMINT continued to mature since the period of the first case in this book.

The Crisis before the Crisis

The Korean War and the Taiwan Strait issue in the early 1950s cannot be separated because the former could not be prosecuted while ignoring the latter, and yet the United States could not devote full military resources to both situations at the same time.[1] Neither could Communist China, with its still immature military capability. The end of the Korean War brought a reduction in pertinent intelligence related to China and the Soviet Union in that region of the world.[2] At the same time, Communist China soon focused its attention on the Taiwan issue, partly as a Mao-driven political diversion for domestic upheaval, later including the Great Leap Forward. The Navy and CIA faced Chinese Communist intelligence capabilities undergoing developments as well. Based on Navy-developed sources in Taiwan, the CIA reported in 1951 that the PLA established a naval intelligence school of its own in the Kwangtung Province.[3] At first, when the Seventh Fleet increased its attention toward Taiwan, its intelligence primarily included air and surface reconnaissance.[4] This trend changed as the Truman administration's intelligence priorities evolved in relation to the unfolding crisis environment, and human sources became increasingly relevant.

Taiwan was clearly a brewing crisis from the beginning. From the moment Chiang and the Kuomintang fled the mainland for Formosa in June 1949, Mao and the PLA attempted to take the island back under Communist control. The question was when this would happen. While the Communists outstripped the Nationalists in terms of personnel numbers, Chiang's navy retained much of its capability. Previous research on the Taiwan Patrol Force showed the optimism of the British Intelligence Division of the Admiralty in July 1949 that the Nationalist Chinese Navy could successfully conduct a blockade in the event of a Communist attempt to take Formosa.[5] The report comparatively assessed the Nationalists' fleet of thirty-two ships to the Communists' and concluded the Nationalists' retention of the Miaodao Islands north of Formosa enabled them to blockade the majority of ports on the Bohai Gulf and "provided them with 50 percent coverage of Qingdao."[6] As with much of the intelligence relationship between the admiralty and the U.S. Fleet, this report was shared with the U.S. Seventh Fleet. Under the Radford–Collins Agreement (the ANZUS Treaty), the U.S. Navy shared and exchanged SIGINT with Australia and New Zealand as well.[7] From the summer through the fall of 1949, the Nationalist fleet defended the offshore islands, allying with indigenous guerrilla forces to enforce the blockade against the Communist forces by mounting attacks on passing ships. Later in 1953, however, the ONI reported that the Nationalist fleet did very little to counter Communist activity for fear that it would "undoubtedly lose them the guerrilla support in the coastal islands."[8] It was increasingly clear that the Nationalist forces alone could not stave off the Chinese Communist forces in the long term.

For several months it appeared that war reignited between the Communists and the Nationalists would effectively draw Western intervention. That possibility was postponed, however, when North Korea invaded South Korea on 25 June 1950. While U.S. and UN forces almost immediately became involved in the Korean conflict, Truman announced that the Seventh Fleet would send surface combatant ships and a formation of aircraft from the USS *Valley Forge* to neutralize the Taiwan Strait on 27 June to signal preventive measures to Beijing in the event of an attack on Taiwan.[9] Truman understood that both the Korean situation and the Taiwan issue could not be solved simultaneously, primarily because the Seventh Fleet could not commit enough forces to both of them.[10] Due to the forces committed to the Taiwan Strait, however, Chen Jian stated, "this created the perception in the minds of the leaders in Beijing that Korea and Taiwan were inseparable issues for the Americans."[11] CIA estimates tended to note this as well.[12] Nevertheless, Seventh Fleet and Taiwan Patrol Force intelligence units observed maritime traffic on both sides of the strait. In late 1951, for instance, the DNI sent a report of non-Communist merchant shipping to the DCI, likely resulting from the need to understand the degree to which a blockade affected commerce from the Far East in the event of a conflict.[13] Similar to the Americans, however, the Communist Chinese leadership could not address the Korean and Taiwan issues simultaneously.

Zhou Avoids a Two-Front War

On 30 June Zhou Enlai ordered "the PRC's Navy Commander, Xiao Jinguang, to suspend plans for the invasion of Taiwan, because of the intelligence network uncovered by the Kuomintang that would have otherwise supplied the PRC with strategic intelligence in support of the campaign."[14] In July 1950 PLA commanders were told that the campaign to resist U.S. intervention in Korea should proceed, and the Taiwan campaign would likely postpone until 1952.[15] This shift in priorities depended on the duration and intensity of the Korean conflict. It is unclear whether this information was shared with the ONI or Seventh Fleet at the time because of some of the assertions that U.S. intelligence soon concluded afterward.

A 17 July CIA report, which the Navy contributed to, concluded that the PLA "could launch a successful amphibious assault on Taiwan in spite of U.S. opposition" based on sources from a British merchant ship that witnessed a mass of junk ships in the Taiwan Strait.[16]

On 18 July 1950 officers from the U.S. Far East Command in Tokyo "learned that a Nationalist agent on the mainland had attended a meeting at which Communist leaders discussed an assault on Taiwan in the near future."[17] A national intelligence estimate in October underscored this fear.[18] This kind of source with high-level access in Beijing was rare, and the fact that naval officers cultivated relationships of this caliber is enlightening in the context of the CIA's tendency to maintain strict control over political leadership sources. The perceived threat prompted the Joint Chiefs of Staff to direct the commander of the Far East Command to conduct a naval show of force in the strait. Intelligence reports delivered to Vice Adm. Arthur Dewey Struble and Vice Adm. C. Turner Joy (commanders of the Seventh Fleet and Far East Command, respectively) from submarines USS *Pickerel* and USS *Catfish*, returning to their home station at Yokosuka on 30 July, contradicted other reporting at that the time that the PRC was prepared to invade Taiwan.[19] A few days later, on 4 August 1950, the commander of the Seventh Fleet established the Formosa Patrol Force (Task Force 72), which later operated for almost three decades as the Taiwan Patrol Force.[20] The antiaircraft cruiser *Juneau* (CLAA 119) and two destroyers composed the primary units of the Formosa Patrol Force, by which radar and eyes-on observation most often served as the sources of the regular intelligence reports delivered to the Seventh Fleet commander in Yokosuka.[21]

Korea as a Diversion

Meanwhile, the Korean campaign pressed forward with the 15 September Incheon landing, an operation preceded by an exemplary intelligence gathering operation that the Navy and Marine Corps employed later in the Taiwan Strait crisis in 1954. As the landing force approached the channel leading into the Incheon harbor, a previously out-of-service lighthouse suddenly illuminated, the result of a clandestine operation by the Far East Command.[22] Navy lieutenant Eugene F. Clark, placed in charge of the prelanding intelligence mission by General MacArthur, executed a clandestine intelligence mission behind North Korean lines beginning in August. Operating from Yeongheung Island with a small support group of South Korean forces, Clark and his team learned about local hydrography, tides, currents, and any North Korean military capabilities.[23] This example—perhaps the most notable at the time, given the ensuing success of the Marines in the Incheon campaign—represents the kind of risks naval intelligence personnel often took in preparation for battle. Less often studied, however, were the risks intelligence personnel took in crises in which war was not what it enabled, such as the Taiwan case.

The U.S. landing at Incheon in September 1950 and the ensuing march to Seoul pressured Mao and the Communists to enter the war. Indeed, "Mao decided to enter the Korean War [1 October] not for the cause of the international communist revolution against the threat of capitalism, but to protect China's physical security and to defeat U.S. influence surrounding its sovereign borders."[24] The CIA station in Taipei reported on 13 October that Mao fired and replaced Ch'en I, his commander for the Taiwan invasion.[25] Upon learning this, Navy intelligence sources provided insight into specifics of the potential Chinese Communist invasion: "The invasion force will consist of 600,000 combat-trained troops of the 3 Field Army (whose approximate strength is now 1,050,000). These troops have already been selected and are undergoing amphibious training at Amoy, Wenchow, and Shanghai. Results are Favorable. The vanguard of the invasion force will be landed from Soviet submarines, the second wave from landing craft and small gunboats, and the main force from a fleet of motor junks protected by sandbags and steel plates and armed with machine guns."[26] China entered the war on 15 October 1950; the PLA 4th Army crossed the Yalu River border with North Korea.

At the end of October the Revolutionary Military Council directed Admiral Chang Ai-p'ing and the East China Navy Command to move from Nanking to Shanghai, an indication of a lack of faith among the Communist leadership in the naval forces from southern China to stave off a potential conflict with Taiwan and the United States, especially considering the conflict unfolding in Korea.[27] Beginning in early 1951 intelligence reports from Task Force 72 of a Chinese troop and junk boat concentrations in and around various mainland ports once again indicated the possibility of an invasion of Taiwan. This conclusion was based on the premise that the PLA Navy likely wanted to avoid the monsoon season and would employ several thousand smaller motorized and sailing junk boats irregularly against Taiwan, as opposed to its larger, more modern ones, some of which were delivered by the Soviet navy.[28]

While U.S. intelligence continued to speculate whether the PRC would attack Taiwan, the Chinese leadership continued to hold to its intention of not pursuing the straits campaign prior to expelling the United States from the Korean peninsula. In case Mao's intelligence was aware of it, this speculation persisted, with the threat of U.S. B-29 bombers potentially using tactical nuclear weapons against ground infantry units after October 1951. Nevertheless, in March 1952 the Seventh Fleet began developing operational plans for a Taiwan campaign to break the blockade that was in place.[29] In this effort, Taiwan Patrol units regularly updated intelligence annexes for the plans, which necessitated a substantially increased effort in collections against mainland coastal units operating opposite in the Taiwan Strait.[30]

In the April 1954 talks in Geneva between the United States, China, and the Koreas, the parties failed to reach an agreement on the reunification of Korea. The implication of these talks was that the United States remained uneasy about the status of Communism in East Asia, Soviet influence in China, and intervention in a future Taiwan conflict. The United States, in relation to Taiwan, was ultimately in the same situation after the Korean War as it was prior to June 1950. Conversely, while the PLA 4th Army was understandably devastated, the Beijing leadership had not exhausted the bulk of its resources simultaneously in Korea and Taiwan. Instead, Mao exercised strategic patience and the PLA generals focused on one campaign at a time. While obvious now, this common assessment does not appear in the intelligence estimates of the time.[31]

Based on the desperate need for better intelligence on activities of the Chinese mainland, the CIA and the Navy issued an interagency agreement on covert and clandestine collection activities in May 1954.[32] This important development codified the Navy's role in HUMINT in the region prior to the crisis. It is important to underscore the fact that, while the CIA was formally inviting the Navy into the world of clandestine collection and activity, the agency still owned the mission. The partnership was an essential aspect of the Taiwan crises to come, even as the Fleet retained its traditional intelligence mission as well.

Intelligence in the 1954–55 Crisis

The 1954–55 crises brewed following the Nationalists retreat from the mainland in 1949. From that time, it was expected that the Communists would attack Taiwan and attempt to physically bring the island back under its control.[33] However, Mao's decision to enter the war in Korea put these efforts on hold in his aversion to a two-front war. For naval intelligence units operating in the area around Taiwan from the moment Truman ordered the Seventh Fleet to patrol the strait, indications and warnings (I&Ws) intelligence was of the utmost importance. Based on known (albeit limited) Communist Chinese naval capability, the Navy concluded that a concentration of naval forces, junks, and merchant ships outfitted with weapons in the strait constituted a move to seize the main island, potentially prompting war.[34] The Strait Patrol was nearly a constant effort, except when units were forced to evacuate due to poor weather. Mao ordered PLA commanders in the Fujian Province (opposite Taiwan) to "pay attention to seizing Taiwan immediately."[35]

The U.S. was slow to appreciate—and thus lacked caution at times in its reliance on intelligence sources—the Communist Bloc's penetration of Taipei. This evolved over the course of the 1950s as the CIA, ONI, and Fleet began to wise up. On one hand, Taipei sources were most often the best chance the West had to gain access to assets on the mainland. On the other hand, they were also potential vehicles for disinformation campaigns. Mao's approach to intelligence was the steady recruitment of Communist-sympathetic agents in the Kuomintang (some turned) while attempting to continue the PRC's client relationship with Moscow, evident in correspondence between Mao and Zhou Enlai in 1949 in which they appeared to manage both with caution.[36] Taipei's vulnerability to Communist Bloc intelligence (including Soviet MGB [Ministry of State

Security] presence in Taipei) and the Cold War onset of a lack of access to the mainland further hindered the U.S. intelligence mission during the crises. However, the operational alternatives that often produced suboptimal results emerged in lieu of what might actually have led to strategic intelligence of Chinese Communist intentions and perceptions. This would be a consistent tendency throughout these crises, ultimately barring U.S. intelligence to gain a clear perspective of Mao's course.

According to one ONI report in February 1953, the Nationalist interception of Communist-armed junks led to "numerous junk battles" at sea directly aimed at controlling the disputed islands.[37] Still, as one U.S. Navy report stated, none of the offshore islands could be called essential to the defense of Taiwan and the Penghu Islands in the sense of being "absolutely necessary" militarily.[38] Their importance to the Nationalists was mainly psychological, aside from the usefulness in "pre-invasion operations, commando raiding, intelligence gathering, maritime resistance development, sabotage, escape and evasion."[39] This assessment invariably enabled Navy planners to eliminate some important operational gaps and focus on conventional strengths to overcome Chinese Communist forces in a contingency.

While the Navy served as the primary military service involved in Taiwan during the early 1950s, the Marine Corps played an important role as well. From their experience in Korea and northern Manchuria in the late 1940s, units such as the 4th Marine Regiment had an institutionalized regional understanding that Navy intelligence officers generally did not, primarily due to their proximity to intelligence sources. During the years prior to and during the Taiwan crises, Marines encountered Chinese Communist sea bandits, guerrillas, and refugees, sometimes in the midst of conducting raid exercises in the islands north of Taiwan. During Operation Big Comeback, 15 January 1954, Marines of the 3rd Battalion, 4th Marines, guarded 14,500 Chinese Communist prisoners of war requesting asylum and citizenship in Taiwan.[40] As interrogation and debriefing became a more central feature in Korean War intelligence operations, Marines relied more on these tactics in the Taiwan area of operations.[41] However, the record of interrogations and debriefings during this operation is limited.

July 1954 was an exceptionally chaotic and decisive time in the Taiwan Strait and, indeed, served as the initiation of the crisis. Chiang Kai-shek applied pressure on Washington to enter a treaty for the defense of Taiwan, ultimately hoping to replace and expand the directive signed by Truman for U.S. Seventh Fleet protection of the offshore islands.[42] His rationale was based on the fact that both his own intelligence as well as the CIA's and ONI's showed increased Chinese naval and air activity inside and north of the strait, signifying a Communist intention to invade.[43] Chinese Communist MiG fighters attacked a Seventh Fleet P2V Neptune (an aerial reconnaissance plane) in the strait, and the pilot barely managed to escape with his plane intact.[44] Later that day, however, Mao ordered the PLA Air Force to cease firing upon U.S. ships or aircraft unless under direct attack.[45] Mao likely applied similar restraint in relation to the PLA Navy during this period as well. There is no known record, however, that indicates whether U.S. intelligence knew of this restraint at the time. While potentially tested by tactical operating units, the Seventh Fleet still operated in a gray area in relation to China's willingness to escalate.

Mao Calls Seventh Fleet's Bluff

In keeping with Chinese military philosophy, Mao attempted to weave doubt and deception into the U.S. calculus of the situation.[46] Showing restraint for the better part of two weeks, the PLA Air Force accidentally shot down a British airliner over Hainan Island on 23 July. This prompted a retaliation by Seventh Fleet fighter planes on 26 July.[47] The CIA, ONI, and others had considered Chinese Communist approaches to strategic communications, deception, and political warfare in the past.[48] It is unclear, however, whether plans discussed in a telegram from the Chinese Communist Party (CCP) Central Committee to Zhou Enlai on 27 July 1954 on actions to break up the U.S.-Taiwan treaty and liberate Taiwan (through the use of propaganda) were considered.[49] From the intercepted cables and communications between the Chinese Communist leadership and subordinate units in the PLA, an uncertain degree of success surrounds the U.S. and Taiwan forces during this time as they discerned the Chinese leadership's understanding of the situation.[50] The naval intelligence records from this time do not seem to have factored in the role of deception in the Chinese plan. This underscores the immature understanding, on the part of analysts, of the long history of deception in Chinese military discourse.[51]

Western intelligence also observed the potential for deeper Soviet involvement. U.S. naval intelligence units in Taipei reported seeing a Russian tanker (the *Tuapse*) possibly waiting to rendezvous with China Communist navy ships one hundred nautical miles south of Formosa.[52] Soviet premier Georgy M. Malenkov and Chinese premier Zhou Enlai discussed the incidents between China and Taiwan as well as the United States' support of Taiwan, but this information was unavailable to U.S. intelligence at the time.[53] An National Security Council brief from 13 July contemplated various means through which China could prevent further provocations by Taiwan and disassemble the Western bloc. While the Navy and CIA reported on the *Tuapse* (eventually seized by the Chinese), intelligence does not indicate a Sino-Soviet discussion on the matter.[54]

The crisis continued into August, when the PRC's central military commission instructed the PLA commander in Fujian to conduct a bombardment of the Kuomintang force in the Kinmen Islands based on the perceived imminence of a U.S.–Taiwan mutual defense treaty.[55] Bombing and artillery fire did not begin immediately—it was delayed until 3 September—but the delay provided the Kuomintang sufficient time to place 58,000 troops on Kinmen (Quemoy) Island and 15,000 on Matsu, both strategically situated on the western side of the strait.[56] Having received some degree of strategic warning of an impending crisis, the Seventh Fleet deployed around three hundred fighter sorties against the Dachen Islands, north of Quemoy.[57] Mao's PLA forces began shelling the Kinmen and Matsu islands then held by Chiang's Nationalist forces.[58]

Unfinished Matters and Termination

The crisis stumbled into September and October 1954, with little more than a Seventh Fleet commitment to mount shows of force and limited, measured counter-battery fire against the PLA forces. On 19 October, using the excuse of Navy vessels integrated in a Nationalist navy convoy, the PLA announced the initiation of an imposed, unilateral, alternate-day cease-fire for Quemoy beginning 3 November.⁵⁹ Thus, like clockwork, the PLA began shelling Quemoy on odd days of the month, allowing twenty-four-hour intervals for the threat of the next round of shelling to coerce Taiwan into submission and the U.S. leaders into appeasement. Oddly, however, nowhere in the naval intelligence record is it suggested that the Fleet questioned the reason for the alternate-day approach.

While the shelling of Kinmen (Quemoy) and other islands continued through November 1954, Eisenhower reversed his earlier July decision and signed a defense treaty with Taiwan in December, clearly indicating to the Communist Chinese leadership that its approach in the odd-day bombardment plan yielded the opposite effect Mao intended.⁶⁰ This agreement intended to show resolve and signal to the Chinese the United States' willingness to commit additional forces if the PLA did not relent. The United States Taiwan Defense Command (USTDC) was established to institutionalize the new treaty. Soon naval units evacuated U.S. civilians and military personnel from the Dachen Islands, resulting in debriefings of little strategic value because the Communists had not occupied the islands.⁶¹ Headed by Vice Adm. Alfred M. Pride, the USTDC, as well as its subordinate Taiwan Patrol Force, provided I&W intelligence to the Seventh Fleet of a Communist Chinese amphibious assault on Taiwan, its western islands (Quemoy and Matsu), or the Pescadores Islands.⁶² These signals generally came directly from Taiwan Patrol Force ships to the commander of the Pacific Fleet, potentially facilitated by the USTDC.

As the political situation between Taiwan and the PRC intensified, the potential for the conflict to progress into a full war also escalated. In March 1955 the assistant director for national estimates at the CIA, Sherman Kent, wrote a memorandum to DCI Allen Dulles indicating that the Joint Staff and the G2 (Army intelligence) were at odds on the issues related to Communist China and the Soviet use of nuclear weapons. The Joint Staff's position was that a recent estimate understated the likelihood of the Communists' use of nuclear weapons in the Taiwan crisis, while the Army G2 believed this likelihood was overstated. The Navy does not appear to have weighed in explicitly either way. The NIE report, released the same day, did not discuss Communist nuclear intentions.⁶³

Just as suddenly as Mao precipitated an armed confrontation with the United States and the Republic of China in 1954–55, he ended it. Party officials announced on 23 April 1955 that the PRC was willing to negotiate, and on 1 May the PLA ended its shelling of Kinmen and Matsu. Chinese archives show "the People's Republic of China maintains that the Taiwan issue was an internal issue of China, and it was the U.S. who created tension by invading and occupying Taiwan."[64] This underscores the historical yet sensitive value of intelligence collection in relation to Taiwan independence. As long as the CCP views Taiwan as an internal issue, it views the collection of intelligence on the subject as preparation for war. Intelligence (naval, CIA, or otherwise) did not widely acknowledge this trend at the time, potentially as a result of U.S. commander biases and the effect to influence collectors' and analysts' perspectives in reporting on the 1954–55 crisis. Attribution for this rests in the general tendency during the Cold War for the U.S. intelligence community to focus more on strategic capabilities and major movements of the Communist Bloc rather than the perspectives of the leaders behind them. This is a direct result of the lack of access to the mainland, circumstances that led the intelligence community to infer things from capabilities and observable actions, laying the possibility of extrapolating more from this kind of information about intentions than was verifiable.

Following the crisis, naval source reporting indicated that China built new operational airfields in the Fujian Province opposite Taiwan; it was feared that the situation became "extremely grave [and] pregnant with most disastrous consequences" and the advantage was "in [the] hands of our enemy."[65] Overall, however, considering the dramatic loss of direct access to sources on the mainland following the Chinese Civil War and the war in Korea, the intelligence the Navy collected—in conjunction with the Taiwan intelligence services and the CIA—helped inform senior decision-makers to better mitigate the crisis and successfully prosecute a non-escalatory dynamic. Still, it is difficult to avoid the glaring fact that the Chinese Communists largely controlled the pace and escalation of the crisis into a full-scale conflict.

Intelligence in the 1958 Crisis

The 1958 Taiwan crisis represented a more kinetic and escalatory continuation of the 1954–55 one. While it shows some notable advances in the practice of HUMINT and its sister disciplines, it also reveals a degree of continued immaturity in the intelligence process, ultimately a shortfall, and with ambiguous effects.[66] For decades, the sole publication of the U.S. goverment's account was M. H. Halperin's official history, redacted for unclassified publication, which included very little information on the planning and collection of intelligence.[67] Several other historical and international relations works touched on strategic aspects of both the 1954–55 and the 1958 crises but stopped short of exploring the very aspect of crisis that can directly drive decision-making, namely the intelligence on which leaders based decisions.[68] Nevertheless, since these publications, many more archival resources are available, and some focus on intelligence of the Fleet. This crisis preceded a significant set of changes in the collection and prioritization of intelligence. First, in 1956 the Taiwan Patrol Force established a land-based reconnaissance squadron, based at Naha, Okinawa, and with the increase in Soviet merchant shipping activity along the Chinese mainland coast, shipping surveillance by coastal and port-based personnel became a primary Taiwan Patrol Force mission.[69] While Soviet support to the PLA was limited in preparation for the 1954–55 crisis, by 1958 the Sino-Soviet alliance was fully militarized. Second, by 1956 the Seventh Fleet and Taiwan Defense Command intelligence staffs worked closer together to produce intelligence of high utility. Establishing official exchange agreements with the Chinese Nationalist intelligence services, they received increasingly accurate targeting data and activity by Chinese Communist forces on the mainland. The fundamental improvement in intelligence preceding and during the 1958 crisis in comparison to the previous crisis was the expansion of the liaison relationship between the U.S. military command and its Taiwan counterparts.[70]

The National Archives records (RG 313) clearly show that Task Force 72 served as the primary naval unit in charge of collecting operational intelligence (enemy dispositions, maneuver, and infiltration by mainland agents) prior to and during the 1958 crisis.[71] This evidence resides in the description of responsibilities and mission objective in which the command's intelligence personnel prioritized, managed, and conducted collections and analysis of forward-deployed, operating, continuous liaising of units among the Taiwan navy and briefing the commanders of the USTDC and Pacific Fleet.[72] This amount of tactical control over intelligence by Task Force 72 later yielded a significant advantage primarily because its units embedded themselves close to the enemy position.[73]

Following the 1954–55 crisis—likely a major result of the Korean War experience—U.S. Navy capabilities for collecting electronic intelligence, communications intelligence, and imagery intelligence (referred to as photo reconnaissance) advanced and played a major role in future crises, particularly those in which the enemy is at a stand-off position. HUMINT is not necessarily the desirable or even practical vehicle for gaining a greater understanding of the situation. A simple explanation is that these types of intelligence, in theory, enabled the Fleet to fight with a clearer view of the enemy, whereas HUMINT often enabled a more nuanced understanding of the enemy's intentions, perceptions, and dispositions. That is not to say the Fleet consciously chose one type of intelligence over another; such a rationale makes sense because of its proclivity for readiness in naval battle. In December 1956 the Far East Command issued its first official policy on electronic intelligence, describing the methods and the circumstances under which naval electronic warfare units should collect it.[74] The first use of the AN/ALQ-23 electronic warfare package was also introduced around this time, a standard in naval air electronic warfare for several decades.[75] The Far East Command also established the Joint Electronic Countermeasures Center.[76] In the spring of 1958 the commander of the Taiwan Patrol Force issued a directive on the use of a new magnetic tape recorder to be installed on destroyer units for collecting communications intelligence at sea.[77] The options for the Fleet to gain a greater understanding of the PLA Navy expanded, and deployed units no longer restricted intelligence collection to archaic forms of code-breaking and coast-watching often used in World War II.

On the Brink

By the spring of 1958, the U.S. intelligence community learned of Mao's discontent with the stalemate resulting from the 1954–55 crisis.[78] The hastiness of his actions in that crisis demonstrated that his plan required revision. Subsequently, in July 1958 Mao sent a letter to his regional military commanders, delaying the planned bombardment of the Nationalist-controlled Kinmen Island in the Taiwan Strait.[79] While his uneasiness with pushing forward was not captured in U.S. intelligence reporting at the time, as Halperin's RAND history of the crisis later showed, an NIE from August 1958 "estimated that Chinese communist troop movements could take place rapidly and probably without detection. It was estimated that the Chinese communists would be able to obtain a three to one superiority for an amphibious assault and could be expected to mass approximately 200,000 troops before attempting an attack on Quemoy."[80] While the U.S. Strategic Air Command already deployed nuclear weapons forward in the Pacific (at least as early as January 1958[81]), Eisenhower's early contemplation of nuclear use in the crisis was likely a reaction to the perception that the PLA was building up forces faster than previously thought and that the West might not overcome an early conventional strike.

In some respects, high-level interactions enabled more strategic intelligence in the 1958 crisis than in the earlier crisis, partly because of the sensitive nature of nuclear weapons and escalation. On 12 August a CIA report from the Intelligence Advisory Committee (IAC), based on information from officials on Quemoy and Taiwan, indicated that the Taiwan government expected a squeeze on the offshore islands and made a strong private bid for a public U.S. declaration of support.[82] While the DNI, Rear Adm. Laurence Frost, was present when Taiwan officials believed the United States would be "drawn into the defense of the Islands in the end and that a public declaration was most likely to prevent an attack," the Navy did not take issue with this likelihood, even though the Fleet served as the primary U.S. operating force in the region.[83] Another instance occurred when the Taiwan minister of defense attempted to obtain U.S. support when he told Adm. Roland Smoot (commander of the Taiwan Defense Command) that "he expected the

Chinese communists to continue their actions following the activation of the airfields in the following phases: (1) winning air control, (2) bombing GRC supply vessels, (3) assault on the weakest Offshore Islands, and (4) an attack on all the Offshore Islands."[84] This was not the course of action the U.S. intelligence community—namely, the Navy units operating in forward positions in the Ryukyu Islands—estimated as the PLA preference, especially the idea that winning air control preceded other objectives.[85] On 18 August 1958 Mao instructed Chinese minister of national defense Peng Dehuai to halt military maneuvers and prepare air forces for the planned bombardment of Kinmen Island in the Taiwan Strait, ultimately implementing his plan in July, contradicting the intelligence Admiral Smoot received from the Taiwan Ministry of Defense.[86] Of course, this calls into question the reliability of at least a fraction of the sources the Navy developed in Taiwan at that time.

From the beginning, Navy intelligence and the CIA did not assess that the PLA would mount an all-out attack on the main island of Taiwan.[87] Instead, RAND's official government history of the 1958 crisis noted that "prior to the 19th [August] Army Intelligence [Taiwan's army] provided Chiang with his last brief prior to PRC's initial artillery shelling," in which it was believed Matsu would be attacked rather than the more strategically important Quemoy. The report provided the following reasons for this assessment: "(a) the Chinese communists had numerical superiority in the Matsu area but not in the Quemoy area; (b) the Chinese communists had a slightly better air capability over Matsu; (c) the Chinese communists would have to bring naval units south from Shanghai to support an assault."[88] While U.S. intelligence mirrored this assessment, CIA and Navy reporting of the time did not share information on air superiority.[89]

While naval intelligence did not contradict the Taiwan intelligence assessment, none of the U.S. reports specified one island over another. However, on 22 August, with the support of the ONI, the CIA published a net assessment comparing Taiwan and Chinese Communist military capability in the event of a war in the strait.[90] Ultimately, Taiwan's amassed naval capabilities in and near the strait—coupled with the prospect of U.S.

naval support—led intelligence to assess the possibility of a frontal assault by the Chinese Communist forces on the island of Taiwan versus the likelihood of smaller attacks on peripheral territories—namely, the outer islands.

There were mixed results when it came to the utility of intelligence to the customer—namely, the Eisenhower administration—in preparation for kinetic operations. While the USTDC prepared to respond from positions on Taiwan, farther out in the Philippines and from Yokosuka an IAC estimate of the period shows that Fleet intelligence and the CIA were not surprised by the Chinese Communist initial attack on Quemoy, and this corresponded to previous assessments.[91] There is some question, however, as to whether the intelligence cycle effectively provided estimates in time to affect theater decision-making. For instance, the version of the regular product the CIA developed since July (on probable developments in the Taiwan Strait area), published on 26 August, referred to probable events that had occurred four days prior (on 22 August) as well as other events leading up to it.[92] The nature of the crisis had similar precursors to later Cold War crises, such as the Cuban Missile Crisis and the 1983 war scare, in that reliability and timeliness of intelligence were extremely necessary and consequential to avoiding inadvertent escalation. Lives were on the line, immediately, in Taiwan. The opaqueness of source reliability on short timelines—as a by-product of HUMINT's nature—on the part of Navy and CIA source networks and individual assets shows an immaturity in the intelligence cycle and showed that *this* kind intelligence did not work for this customer's time requirements.

The Crisis Goes Kinetic

The crisis then suddenly escalated when, on 23 August 1958 at 6:30 p.m. Taiwan time, the Chinese Communists launched a heavy-artillery attack against the Quemoy islands. The PLA fired 2,600 rounds in the first minute, killing six hundred Kuomintang ground force officers and soldiers.[93] While reporting clearly shows that Taiwan and U.S. intelligence believed the likelihood of an eventual attack on one or more of the outer islands, the PLA executed a sudden surprise attack on the island that virtually no one believed would be the initial target. As Halperin asserts in his history of the crisis, "although anticipated by a number of planners, the attack provoked a re-evaluation of American policy toward the Offshore Islands."[94] This reassessment likely originated from the fact that the intelligence gathered prior to and during the course of the crisis did not indicate the precise island or the level of the PLA's initial use of force.

Some of the failure on the part of U.S. intelligence to foresee the attack on Quemoy is understood. I&W intelligence—especially overseas I&W—demonstrated known shortcomings. Intelligence methods did not yet use the satellite and ground sensor networks that comprise modern advanced tactical warning systems. The Fleet and CIA relied on signal indications from ship and aircraft movement, but the primary indication for advanced force movements and intentions by an adversary still required human sources, as suggested by intelligence prior to and during the crisis.[95] The crisis underscored a broader problem with I&Ws, revisited by the Navy and CIA in months following the crisis.[96] Soon following the kinetic portion of the crisis, the CNO, Adm. Arleigh Burke, formally requested the DCI continue daily overflight coverage (presumably including flights by the new U2 reconnaissance plane).[97] There is some evidence his request was approved.[98]

In all of the postcrisis discussion—including Halperin's official history—little discussion considered the Chinese propensity for surprise and deception or its context among crisis management and escalation control. While the desire to increase and modernize I&W was a logical and practical action, the naval intelligence community did not increase its attention to the PLA's use of deceptive tactics, particularly those with strategic consequences. To understand an adversary's abstract approach to war, HUMINT should have targeted PLA planners, strategists, and commanders. Instead, as Admiral Burke's memorandum to the DCI suggests, the Navy defaulted to a technological solution that ultimately only revealed a partial explanation in future crises. Of course, this underscores the point made in the introduction to this book, that navies are primarily defined by their systems (weapons) and platforms (ships and aircraft) rather than their people.

In light of the surprise attack, members of the National Security Council drafted position papers during the weekend of 23 and 24 August for a meeting held at the White House on the 25th (also shared with the IAC on 26 August).[99] The basic position paper of the Joint Chiefs of Staff, similar to most of the subsequent papers, urged the defense of the offshore islands initially only with conventional weapons for political reasons, such as the Soviets' intention to draw in earlier if the crisis escalates to a nuclear level.[100] The sources of the intelligence for this paper came directly from U.S. Navy personnel in Taiwan, most likely from the Navy section of the MAAG-T.[101]

Still, in the aftermath of the 25 August 1958 meeting, the intelligence community released an NIE stating that the Chinese Communists would not likely be deterred from further aggression with conventional military (largely air and naval) response options.[102] The logical conclusion for policymakers entailed the eventual necessity of nuclear strikes against the Chinese mainland to quickly and effectively stop Chinese Communist aggression against the offshore islands. According to the RAND history of the crisis, the Navy paper was approved, authorizing the commander of the Pacific Fleet to reinforce U.S. capability and to prepare to escort supply ships to the offshore islands.[103] Communist shelling of the island continued, and the U.S. Navy proceeded on its escort mission of the Taiwan navy. During this period, naval intelligence became subsumed with operational intelligence and maintaining situational awareness on enemy positions and disposition. Intelligence conducted little assessment of the possible Chinese—and the Soviet—response to a nuclear attack because the Fleet had not yet been included as part of the so-called nuclear deterrence triad.

By the first week of September, the crisis appeared to escalate into an eventual war with the potential use of nuclear weapons. Eisenhower reinforced the U.S. Seventh Fleet, headquartered in Yokosuka, Japan, with additional surface and subsurface ships and ordered Adm. Herbert Hopwood, commander of the Pacific Fleet, to defend the Kuomintang navy in the region through additional escorts.[104] On 8 September 1958 Marine Aircraft Group 11 from Japan established its command post on Taiwan to reinforce the island's air defenses.[105] The United States prepared to defend

Taiwan, considering intelligence assessments that proved deterrence efforts unsuccessful against a committed PRC.

Given the U.S. fear of escalation from the PRC's provocations, Soviet foreign minister Andrei Gromyko traveled to Beijing to discuss the Chinese leadership's intentions in the conflict.[106] Also on 8 September, Mao Zedong spoke to an international press conference about U.S. foreign policy and the situation following the Chinese decision to begin shelling Kinmen [Quemoy] Island in the Taiwan Strait, maintaining the stance that Taiwan was an internal Chinese issue.[107] Public addresses such as these offered a rare, and valuable, opportunity for the intelligence community to observe Mao—even if manufactured. Soon, as NIEs previously warned, the Soviet Union officially promised to intervene in the event of a nuclear attack on China from the United States, effectively raising the stakes of the crisis yet again.[108]

The crisis continued through September, and intelligence struggled to fully appreciate the Chinese Communist end game. On the one hand, it was clear that unification was the ultimate goal. On the other hand, Mao's willingness to pursue this goal was unknown. HUMINT on the part of the Navy, CIA, and others was unable to secure sources to uncover the fact that Mao sent a memorandum to a delegation of six Communist countries urging firm unity against Western imperialism under the leadership of the USSR, a statement likely intended for internal consumption just as much as for external messaging.[109] This important PRC position lends credence to the dynamics of the relationship between Moscow and Beijing at a crucial time. On 5 October Mao instructed that the shelling on Quemoy should cease; Zhou Enlai discussed the U.S. response to the Chinese island bombing with the Soviet chargé d'affaires, S. F. Antonov; and the Chinese defense minister, Peng Dehuai, issued a message to the compatriots in Taiwan to unite the Chinese against "the American plot to divide China."[110] Occasionally, when HUMINT focuses on low-level sources to collectively tell a broader story, it misses higher-level adversary perspectives. The ability to target and collect from meaningful sources becomes challenging and even prohibitive when a crisis—particularly involving the potential use of nuclear weapons—is ongoing.

In the wake of the first wave of Chinese Communist shelling of Kinmen in September, Commander Task Force 72 assessed the Taiwan navy's ability to resupply its forces (mainly air defense and counter-lodgment forces) and concluded that the Nationalists required substantial additional resources and trained personnel to maintain a resupply effort for an extended period of time.[111] The capacity of the Nationalist forces to stave off a PLA attack weighed heavily on the Eisenhower administration's calculation of U.S. involvement. Around the same time, naval forces in the Far East compared PLA Navy capabilities to those of the Taiwan navy, ultimately concluding the Nationalist forces were considerably outnumbered and the PRC held a major geographic advantage.[112]

More than at any time during the 1954–55 crisis, the 1958 crisis entailed confusing strategic decisions and behavior on the part of the Chinese Communist leadership. While this could be reasoned with various trains of logic (e.g., Mao was also focused on the initial policies of the Great Leap Forward, and thus his and the party's leadership displaced their attention), the Taiwan issue holds significant value in the Chinese Communist lexicon. The intelligence lessons of this crisis still hold value today. However, U.S. intelligence was unprepared for (a) the PRC's actions preceding and during the escalation with the PLA's attack on Quemoy, (b) the apprehension of the Taiwan navy to maintain a defense of the islands, and (c) the likelihood of a Soviet response in kind if the United States used nuclear weapons to end the crisis. Instead, the Chinese use of deception and surprise led to a misunderstanding in U.S. intelligence. Collectively, this equated to a strategic intelligence failure. As this case shows, the failure is most likely a result of the fact that the best sources the Navy and CIA used during the crisis in Taipei—and any of the Kuomintang sources in Beijing—hardly enabled the collection of intelligence on Chinese Communist leadership intentions.[113]

Conclusion

While the Korean War offered the U.S. Navy and the early Cold War intelligence community a new kind of layered adversary—the primary North Korean client, backed by a Chinese- and Soviet-allied apotheosis—in conflict, the Taiwan crises brought the much more significant threat of the use of nuclear weapons between the West and the Communist Bloc. While the 1954–55 crisis displayed the challenges and advantages of the intelligence community preparing and developing sources in and around Taiwan, the 1958 crisis showed that perhaps sources generally hold less relevance in the event of escalation and conflict termination. When a crisis begins to spin out of control (even as the 1958 crisis ended as abruptly as it began), the identification of new sources and the exploitation of existing ones may be of little value when decisions must be made at a heightened pace. Despite the importance of Admiral Smoot's high-level sources, they ultimately revealed more about the Taiwan leadership than Chinese Communist decision-making. Whether through the Taiwan Patrol Force or MAAG-T, human sources were not integral to revealing the degree of Beijing's reliance on deceptive tactics for strategic gain (e.g., alternate-day bombing of the islands). The loss of access to sources on the Chinese mainland following the Communist takeover in 1949 only added to the darkness that Western intelligence found itself in during the first half of the Cold War. Ultimately, while HUMINT discerned how Western support for Taiwan should continue, it did not decisively produce an advantageous resolution to the 1958 crisis. The problem of the offshore islands continued in the years that followed, along with the need for better intelligence.[114] Furthermore, despite all of the post-1947 reforms and a closer relationship between the ONI and CIA, access to sources was still a fundamental problem. While these crises certainly raise lessons for HUMINT to learn—particularly in the partnership between the CIA and the Navy as well as with the government of Taiwan—they underscore the importance of physical presence in developing sources.

Part IV

Clandestine Containment

*Intelligence Activities against
North Vietnam and China, 1959–65*

Chapter 7

Kennedy and the Dominoes

When President John F. Kennedy took office in January 1961, the U.S. military was focused on Soviet development of long-range ballistic missiles, nuclear warheads, space exploration, and the wider spread of Communism across Europe and Southeast Asia. Grand strategy was intensifying in focus, however, on preventing Soviet- and Chinese-backed regimes from tipping the balance of power in favor of Communism through indirect—and direct, where necessary—action to ensure favorable outcomes. Specifically, the legitimacy in Southeast Asia of burgeoning Communist regimes in Hanoi, Vientiane, and, later, Phnom Penh was unacceptable.[1] Indeed, as previous research has inferred, deeper military and intelligence engagement in Southeast Asia was specifically aimed at denying Beijing (and Moscow, to some extent) advantages of friendly regimes in its immediate periphery.[2] In fact, additional past work has concluded that American leaders' fear of Chinese entry into the conflict "precluded full-scale use of U.S. military power against North Vietnam."[3] This chapter illustrates the duality of this national-level concern being divorced from the day-to-day missions of military and intelligence personnel in theater prior to the Gulf of Tonkin resolution (August 1964), and makes the point that changes eventually occurring to naval intelligence authorities were an attempt to correct this.

As such, national clandestine intelligence collection and covert activities placed high-priority focus on Soviet and Chinese support for Communist movements around the world, in what Mao referred to two decades prior as "national wars of liberation."[4] This evolved into the concept that a war for Communist liberation beyond China's borders was a common war for liberation that established Communist powers had a duty to support. Containment, or Truman and Dwight D. Eisenhower's established strategy for countering the so-called domino theory, was a mirror image that maintained the fall of democratic regimes to Communist ideology would cause others to follow, resulting in set of counteracting Western policies.[5]

By the Kennedy administration, the preference to contain the dominos through indirect means had increased, certainly given the nuclear stakes involved in the 1958 Taiwan crisis. Given that the West and the Communist Bloc often accessed common sources in countries in the midst of political struggles, the nature and importance of intelligence—specifically HUMINT—became intensely essential.[6] Frankly, the CIA did not have enough Farm-trained case officers to fulfill containment's demand.[7] The unfolding crisis in Southeast Asia illustrates this point as well as the role of the military in the region in the years prior to the 1965 escalation. The Navy's role in activities in the developing world during the early 1960s would eventually lead Secretary of the Navy Paul Nitze to approve the establishment of a clandestine naval intelligence capability, followed by the establishment of Task Force 157 (the organization tasked to carry out clandestine intelligence actions).[8] The decision would officially bring the Navy intelligence mission into a modern era, to complement the CIA's mission.

While HUMINT was by no means new to Navy at that point, the Indochina crisis case demonstrates that the mission went through a deeply needed and formal renaissance because the military became increasingly involved in clandestine operations in Southeast Asia, historically more suited for the CIA and its predecessors, the CIG and OSS. Units involved in Vietnam, Laos, and Cambodian operations learned new collection techniques and tradecraft and discovered better working methods over time. While the ONI played a central role in previous conflicts and crises, operational units such as Task Element 79.3.3.6 (Operation Shufly) and others under the Military Assistance Command–Vietnam (MAC-V) and Seventh Fleet became the primary intelligence operators during this period. Likewise, intelligence was a primary overall mission in the early years in Vietnam and during the Laos crisis.[9] The CIA (and the DIA as of October 1961) deeply involved themselves in the crisis as well, but unlike in crises in the 1950s, products developed by military units distinctively influenced certain events, particularly after the watershed moment of the Bay of Pigs crisis. Following the failure of the April 1961 CIA-directed invasion, the Kennedy administration employed greater caution with the use of the agency to direct paramilitary operations and instead empowered the military to share in the burden of irregular warfare. Nowhere was this more experimentally conducted than in Indochina, where the United States was not yet at war.[10] The situation in Vietnam and Laos was indeed thought of as a crisis that could only be managed with an unofficial, clandestine hand. Naval units operating in the region ran agents, developed sources, and operated in a similar—albeit, less resourced and mature—manner. This was a theme of a number of the leading works on the subject of the early 1960s in Southeast Asia.[11] Later in 1965 the experience in Southeast Asia culminated with the realization that the Navy and Marine Corps required the authority to operate clandestinely (defined as "an activity necessary to remain secret and concealed to ensure its success and its revealment could lead to failure") in a broader context.[12] The threat from Chinese and Soviet intervention activities in regions of Western strategic interests—in countering Communist expansion—was a catalyst for change in naval HUMINT in a more pronounced way than in previous crises.

Part IV makes two arguments. First, while the Navy lacked a modern HUMINT capability to the address the overarching concerns of North Vietnam victory and Chinese support to the Viet Cong (VC), the security environment and the Fleet's and Marine Corps' operational circumstances in the crisis in Indochina—as well as their evolving relationship with the CIA—forced them to adapt in ways seldom experienced before. This led to Fleet intelligence officers eventually conducting clandestine missions that previously were solely the domain of the CIA. In a vast archival body on the period of U.S. intervention in Indochina, this case attempts to isolate the contributions of the Navy and Marine Corps to the HUMINT mission while placing the evolving capability properly within the context of CIA and MAC-V missions in the region. Furthermore, the outcome of both operations in Southeast Asia and the preceding decades of organizational reform and capability refinement collectively completed the maturation of the modern era of naval HUMINT, setting the stage for how the Navy would generally view, plan, carry out, and use it.

Second, the case argues that naval units provided vital intelligence on foreign assistance to, and the disposition and capabilities of, Communist forces in Vietnam, Laos, and Cambodia in the years immediately preceding the massive escalation and buildup of general-purpose forces in 1965. These countries were not simplistically satellites of the PRC and Soviet Union but were consequential governments in a crisis that mattered significantly to both the Communist Bloc and the West; they were also frequently influenced from the outside by propaganda and through arms and equipment. In other words, the influence of Communism permeated across borders, and as a primary instrument of national security, intelligence was deeply preoccupied with such phenomena. This is a common theme throughout the written history of the Indochina region during this period, and many assume that because the West ultimately unsuccessfully repelled Communism in Southeast Asia, intelligence was lacking and failed to call attention to certain developments.[13] This perception is false, however. The absence of success in operations—naval operations are not unique—does not suggest the failure of intelligence. The quality of planning efforts and the degree of risk acceptance play major roles as well. In general, intelligence—and specifically HUMINT by naval units during the early years of the crisis in Indochina—was not placed in its proper context. While it did little to stem the creep of an eventual escalation by President Lyndon Johnson, intelligence in an irregular warfare environment showed that a greater degree of necessary risk allowed units to acquire enemy-sourced information. Eventually the Navy and other military services became empowered with historically unprecedented authorities to conduct clandestine intelligence that the CIA previously was unable to manage and conduct.

The paradox of opposing truths in the crisis was evident—the U.S. strategy assumed that limited military power could compel the North Vietnam regime and the VC—and, by default, substantial support from China beginning at least as early as 1962—to discontinue support for the insurgency in South Vietnam, and the VC in turn committed to fight for unification of North and South Vietnam at all costs.[14] The same applied to the CIA's and the military's approach to the Pathet Lao forces in Laos. While many of the histories of the crisis (and the eventual U.S. war) allude to the Ho Chi Minh Trail as the primary route by which China, North Vietnam, and others moved arms, equipment, and personnel from the north to south, much of the distribution of support to the insurgency occurred in the maritime domain in coastal and littoral waters.[15] Clearly, however, as in all naval operations including the Marine Corps, a major portion of the intelligence was indeed collected on land, both as part of the MAC-V and Seventh Fleet afloat operating units in the Mekong Delta and in support of CIA operations in the region. The results of the intelligence collected did not necessarily lead to more successful operations or victory, as history clearly recorded.[16] However, the results served to institutionalize intelligence practices the Fleet would not likely have gained otherwise. Moreover, the early period of U.S. involvement in the region—prior to all-out war—depicts a case in which naval HUMINT fundamentally maintained situational awareness and manipulated the enemy in pursuit of strategic advantage. As in other cases, a central lynchpin was access to and the reliability of sources. The Indochina crisis greatly differs from the previous ones discussed, primarily based on the level of active involvement of—albeit in a noncombat capacity—U.S.- and Western-aligned forces, which underlined how the utility of naval HUMINT (i.e., HUMINT beyond the CIA) had evolved.

The remaining sections begin with discussion of the strategic context for intelligence and the crisis quickly becoming a war in Indochina.[17] They outline command of intelligence and command relationships during the early years of the war, (1960–65). From there they examine some of the Navy and Marine Corps' training initiatives aimed at expanding intelligence capabilities in preparation for the kind of environments Marines and sailors faced in Southeast Asia. An examination of specific archival records follows on intelligence collection in the Indochina crises by units such as the Military Assistance and Advisory Group (MAAG), its successor the MAC-V, the Studies and Observations Group (SOG), Task Element 79.3.3.6, and the Naval Advisory Group (NAVGP), among others. Then the chapter explores China's role in the crisis. It discusses the institutional dynamics of naval intelligence at the time and the maturity of naval HUMINT because of a greater reliance on bodies beyond the CIA. Finally, the chapter identifies some conclusions on archival evidence of this period, telling us more about the modernizing role of naval HUMINT.

Intelligence and the Slide into Intervention

There are several reasons why HUMINT played a central, if thorny, role in Indochina in the early 1960s. Kennedy came into office with an apparent bias toward special operations and clandestine activities, believing that they offered a viable alternative to significant numbers of boots on the ground. With this came counterinsurgency and the use of CIA and paramilitary units to affect the enforcement of containment.[18] A common misunderstanding, however, concerns the idea that conducting counterinsurgency against the Viet Cong began with Kennedy's presidency. It preceded the Kennedy administration by at least a year. In June 1960, the commander in chief of the Pacific (Pacific Command) submitted to the secretary of defense, Thomas Gates, a draft plan for counterinsurgency operations by the government of South Vietnam.[19] While it was a plan for South Vietnam, intelligence would be a fundamental mechanism in carrying it out, and HUMINT is a fundamental aspect of counterinsurgency. In a maturing relationship with the CIA, Navy and Marine Corps missions expanded to support the political/military unconventional side of containment policy.[20] For instance, the ONI played a fundamental role in the Bay of Pigs invasion as a cutout (in the form of the Military Sea Transportation Service) for the Navy's protection of the landing force.[21]

HUMINT's increasing value stemmed from the fact that as the Cold War expanded beyond Europe and beyond the vast resources of the CIA, military capabilities were leveraged. In October 1961 Secretary of Defense Robert McNamara established the DIA in response in part to CIA's—and, most notably, Allen Dulles'—rogue actions in the Bay of Pigs invasion. Officially, however, the DIA was established to unify Defense intelligence across the services and eliminate duplication.[22] The systems analysis and econometrics approach McNamara applied to department planning would eventually lead the services to pursue clandestine capabilities, at least for the efficiency of conducting their relevant intelligence and not being at the mercy of the agency. This would later backfire in the 1970s for all parties involved, but especially the CIA.

The Cold War in the early 1960s experienced two extremes in international affairs, collectively owing to layers of a single massive crisis. At one level of the Cold War, the Communist Bloc and the West established a dangerous long-range nuclear relationship. While intentions and perceptions of the enemy were mistaken before in pursuing the policy of containment, the nuclear threshold was less established, and foreign policy elites dissuaded nuclear use. On the heels of the apparent "missile gap," intelligence mistakes became less acceptable. At another level, the Communist and Western policies played out in the postcolonial territories in which proxies, without U.S. or Britain direct assistance, violently opposed Communist ideologies, evidenced in Indochina and elsewhere.[23] More often than not, the Soviet and Chinese regimes supported, in the form of training, arms, funding, and so on, the Communist movements opposed by the West.[24]

Through the 1950s, the Cold War adversaries increasingly infiltrated the third world, but this was not yet the norm it would later become. Responding to clandestine action with force—especially in third world countries—gave nuclear powers pause. This also meant clandestine actions were heavier handed in third world countries because they were the primary battlefield of the Cold War, but they were not the primary motivation for why the Communist Bloc and the West fought.[25] The threat of Communist influence in the developing world affected Western decisions there, and this further intensified nuclear relations between the West and the Communist Bloc. U.S.- and Soviet-conducted nuclear tests grew in their signaling power. The threat of nuclear escalation raised the stakes, dissuading overt counteractions by the Communist Bloc against U.S., British, and Western intelligence activities in Communist-aligned countries.

When the Bay of Pigs occurred in April 1961, Gen. Maxwell Taylor—on behalf of the commission assigned to him by President Kennedy—recommended a global review of CIA operations.[26] If any transformed into operations beyond an intelligence collection mission—and several had—Taylor recommended they transition to military control. This recommendation initiated a debate about the nature of HUMINT intelligence (i.e., running of sources versus action in relation to political targets) that continued at least until the Church Committee's deliberations of 1975.[27] Kennedy acted on Taylor's advice, but the transition came with enormous challenges. Simply stated, the military had little experience in clandestine operations or background in resourcing them to avoid revealing covers, human sources, and money trails. The transition was named Operation Switchback, and each of the station chiefs were ordered to work with military commanders to ease disruptions.[28] Switchback commenced on the very day—1 November 1963—the South Vietnamese president, Ngo Dinh Diem, was overthrown.[29]

The evolutional change for HUMINT during this period was that intelligence became more than the collection of often sensitive information. It collected sensitive information in sensitive situations and occasionally necessitated activities beyond those considered traditional collection activities. These activities included, for instance, breaking into enemy facilities, sabotage, and other manipulating actions to exacerbate the enemy's situation. The CIA was established for this very kind of activity, but the military services were forced to develop such tactics because of the Cold War's circumstances.[30] Thus, the stakes in the Cold War were high, and few regions in the world required the use of the U.S. naval services in clandestine activities more than in Indochina. Access to sources remained a primary driver of whether HUMINT could be collected. Most of the intelligence activities conducted by the Navy and Marine Corps in the past were not sensitive or clandestine but were more often overt and based on their training. Intermingling these gave way to a new era in naval intelligence. The story of the Navy and Marine Corps in Vietnam, Laos, and Cambodia shows this progression as well as the unavoidable fact that successfully conducting the overall military mission necessitated gathering information in an environment in which the enemy was close, but it was often difficult to distinguish between friend and foe. While in previous crises the Navy and Marine Corps accessed sources among the enemy in Vietnam and in Laos, the VC and Pathet Lao often ran agents among the people.

The Indochina Crisis Contextualized

The Indochina crisis was unique because the military was officially assigned an advise-and-assist mission while conducting low-intensity combat, but it was not yet a declared war.[31] It was, by character of the times, *cold*. Unlike any time since World War II, Marines, sailors, and their Army and Air Force counterparts operated close to the enemy. Few in uniform who deployed during the Eisenhower administration came in close contact with enemy combatants. While not yet a conventional war, the Kennedy administration was determined to subdue the crisis through military means, although servicemembers were ill-equipped or trained to confront the intelligence problem. In terms of U.S. policy, there was no apparent desire to escalate to a full-scale war at this point, contrary to the obvious slope that its course took.

As in any military operation, intelligence was not the central U.S. and Allied mission in Southeast Asia in the early 1960s.[32] Since the Geneva Conference in 1954, which effectively settled France's postcolonial role—partitioning Vietnam into two separate north (Communist) and south (Western-aligned) nations—the United States under the Eisenhower administration established the MAAG-Vietnam (MAAG-V) to aid the Army of the Republic of Vietnam in the south in developing a viable capability in the event the North Vietnamese military and the so-called Viet Cong seized control of large swaths of the South.[33] At the same time, Communist movements aided by the Chinese and Soviet regimes and from North Vietnamese influence and military campaigns emerged in Laos and Cambodia, which the CIA and U.S. military attempted to suppress. The U.S. objective in Southeast Asia was to counter Communist activities (both indigenous and exogenous) without causing war to erupt. This necessitated political engagement to prop up the Ngo Dinh

Diem regime in the South, psychological operations against Communist influence, training and liaising with the South Vietnamese military, and the development of a greater understanding of future Communist intentions in the region. These activities necessitated a robust intelligence effort, including running agents, developing sources, and other clandestine HUMINT activities.[34] Intelligence collection in this crisis was not concerned with the risk of the initiation of direct war with the Soviet and Chinese Communist regimes but rather with the Communist takeover of otherwise Western-leaning societies.

For containment policy, Indochina represented a single crisis to the United States, underscored by four unfolding subcrisis contexts. First, the postcolonial Communist movements—namely, the Pathet Lao in Laos, the VC in Vietnam, and the tendency for the regimes following Sihanouk's rule (after 1955) in Cambodia to lean toward Communist-friendly relations—collectively enabled a Communist wave in Southeast Asia.[35] Second, the VC's military arms and operational support for the Pathet Lao necessitated that the Kennedy administration address Laos first, through the expulsion of the VC, before fully prosecuting the containment of the North Vietnam regime. Of course, we know now that the removal of the VC largely failed, and Laos was consistently used to infiltrate arms into South Vietnam. Third, Chinese support and influence—arms, propaganda, and other means—for all three of the Indochinese Communist regimes fostered a detrimentally unacceptable outcome (according to the United States), which increased the possibility of waging a covert war against the Chinese and the Soviet Union. Finally, successful and sustained governance by Communist regimes implied a victory for the Communist Bloc overall and gave way to a trend across the region.[36]

The history of the Vietnam War has been widely researched. While some works focused on intelligence and the earlier, less-known parts of U.S. involvement in Indochina, they more often shine a light on the CIA's role, such as Max Boot's portrayal of Col. Edward Lansdale, chief of the station in Saigon (1953–57).[37] Rarer are the works that specifically focus on HUMINT, the Navy and Marine Corps' role, and the broader Southeast Asia context, including Cambodia and Laos. A recent, updated edition of the *Pentagon Papers* includes two hundred pages on the period of the war prior to the Tonkin Gulf resolution—citing authoritative, original sources—but largely avoids the tie-in to the situation in Laos and Cambodia and the tremendously important role of intelligence.[38] In addition to operating against postcolonial regimes, such as the Viet Minh under Ho Chi Minh and the Pathet Lao in Laos, the intelligence mission also provided perspectives on Chinese and Soviet support for these movements. The histories of the period rarely articulate this because it is treated as a sideline issue even though tacit support from the Communist Bloc alone warranted focus as a central issue.

The field of intelligence exploded in the early 1960s, and the Department of Defense committed more to it, highlighting specific domains and specialties. While the DIA's establishment in October 1961 did not have the broad and immediately sweeping effect of the establishment of the CIA in the late 1940s, a new era of military-derived intelligence neared.[39] The naval HUMINT intelligence discipline required some evolution because the Fleet's intelligence officers needed to remain relevant to both the joint intelligence and the national intelligence (CIA) missions. In reality, however, the HUMINT mission inched along on the fray—largely without institutionalized standards and with little oversight and a questionable mandate—for several decades. The discussion of policy and organizational change, however, was very much divorced from the immediate operational realities on the ground.[40] The word "HUMINT" was still not used within the Navy in the early 1960s, and the organization of a mission around the term, by all accounts, was still immature.[41] The rapidly changing situation in Indochina, for which the Navy and Marine Corps played a major role, required a fresh examination of how the Fleet collected intelligence through human sources, particularly because the crisis placed them in constant, close contact with the enemy in a way previous crises did not. The enemy was hostile, the United States was not yet officially in a combat capacity, and yet it was clear that U.S. policy was to defeat the North Vietnamese advancement.

Intelligence changed rapidly in the Kennedy years. While the CIA suffered some notable losses in its earlier years, none was more galvanizing than the Bay of Pigs operation, planned prior to Kennedy's inauguration to overthrow Castro's regime in Cuba in April 1961.[42] Conducted by the agency's trained and financed Brigade 2506 launching positions from Nicaragua and Guatemala, Castro's Cuban Revolution Armed Forces defeated this U.S. force in a matter of days. In the aftermath, McNamara argued successfully that so much power, control, and secrecy should not be trusted in the hands of a single agency, and the Department of Defense should also be given the responsibility of overseeing covert operations.[43] This mindset initiated a shift in the minds of national security elites to pursue Western interests against the Communist Bloc with the presumed structure and attention to detail the military historically applied in war planning as opposed to the perceived idealism applied by the agency (through its Office of Policy Coordination; Office of Special Operations; and, later, the Directorate of Plans) under Allen Dulles and covert action chiefs such as Frank Wisner.[44]

Diem's hold on power was precarious, and coupled with gaining influence of the Viet Minh, the U.S. commitment "would demand as much intelligence as possible on North Vietnamese and Viet Minh capabilities and intentions."[45] To uncover a unilateral collection network required both working with South Vietnam's intelligence agencies and training them by working with intelligence leaders, exemplified by the relationship the CIA cultivated with Tran Kim Tuyen, head of the Service for Political and Social Studies.[46] Much of the remaining portion of this research focuses on the MAC-V and its subordinate Navy and Marine Corps units, most of which operated ashore and in the littoral and coastal areas against the VC. This was often where the adjoining sources were located.

The Vietnam and Laos crises were collectively a single crisis in which Western policy called for assistance to regimes opposing the spread of Communism. As tragic as the course events were, they also served as the catalyst for long-term changes in intelligence. It was a petri dish for the development of the Navy and Marine Corps' HUMINT capabilities. This included both overt and clandestine intelligence. Deployments to the region saw increased demand for intelligence from human sources in a way not previously experienced by the Fleet.

Units and Command of Intelligence

The reconstruction of command and control of intelligence during any given period is potentially highly contentious, and the early years of the Vietnam War are no exception. A specific and aggregate naval intelligence estimate in this period has not been conducted. When one discussed any unit or set of units in the context of command and control, this more often refers to an operational relationship (e.g., operational control [OPCON] or tactical control). In the context of intelligence, command and control refers to both the mandatory reporting chains through which intelligence reaches higher headquarters and to the coordination of sensitive activities between units and the sharing of intelligence with higher headquarters and adjacent commands. In many cases there are no available directives in the archival records to suggest the mandatory sharing of intelligence. Therefore, one must extrapolate, based on the orientation of units in an area of operations and any historical, institutional operations. This is particularly true in the relationships between operational units in Southeast Asia (Task Element 79.3.3.6 and the NAVGP) and the national-level intelligence agencies, the CIA and ONI. Of particular note for distinction is the fact that a command in theater, such as TE 79.3.3.6 (the actual unit name was MAG 16), holds a different higher authority while operating (MAC-V) than when in peacetime (3rd Marine Division, headquartered by the Fleet Marine Force–Pacific).

The MAAG-V served as the military lead in Vietnam (a similar MAAG-Thailand also focused on Laos) until MAC-V established in February 1962. Eventually, in May 1964, when the number of U.S. military forces in Vietnam exceeded the command capacity of an advisory group, the MAC-V absorbed MAAG-V.[47] With the exception of a few Special Forces units, such as the Naval Advisory Detachment and occasionally the SOG, which was OPCON to the CIA, the MAC-V four-star Army general commanded all military forces in Vietnam (and some in Laos).[48] The intelligence mandate reflected this relationship as well, in that the MAC-V established intelligence priorities, oversaw intelligence operations, and received regular reports. In turn, MAC-V's higher headquarters was the commander in chief of the Pacific, who reported to the Joint Chiefs of Staff and the secretary of defense.[49] This was similar to the relationship that the U.S. Taiwan Defense Command had with its higher headquarters (Commander of the Pacific) and the Naval Advisory Group, China (to U.S. Pacific Fleet) before it.

Obscure relationships most likely resulted from the need to delegate OPCON to a low, in-country level. For instance, the NAVGP commanded the Seventh Fleet Combined Task Forces 76 and 77 until they became too large to command.[50] Additionally, while the SOG served as OPCON to the commander of the MAC-V, it maintained an operational coordination relationship with the Saigon station chief. While all of these command relationships evolved over the course of the war, the one mainstay through the course of it was that the commander of the MAC-V remained the military commander. Figure 3 illustrates a general depiction of the OPCON, intelligence sharing and coordination and the operational coordination relationships during the years 1961–65.

Training and Expanded Capabilities

The Navy and Marine Corps observed a period of expansion in the area of intelligence in the late 1950s and early 1960s. Acoustic intelligence was an emerging field, and signals intelligence continued to evolve into a powerful weapon in several different areas, the latter generally centralized under the National Security Agency.[51] Parametric data from electronic intelligence platforms gained greater insight into the enemy's radars and other emitters. HUMINT also developed into a discipline far beyond that previously used by the Navy. The Navy and Marine Corps adopted different viewpoints, specifically as this related to dirtier, more unconventional forms of warfare beyond the blue-water navy kinds of warfare the Fleet often conducted. While the Marine Corps was accustomed to operating in close contact with the enemy, the Navy's community-based institutional culture shows that only the Seabees and Sea, Air, and Land Teams (SEALs)—and, later, as a result of the Vietnam War, the Coastal Riverine Forces—regularly operated in direct contact with an adversary nation's population.[52]

The Navy knew it would be called to support operations beyond the great surface battles of World War II. As Adm. H. E. Yeager acknowledged, "The problem of anti-guerrilla operations is extremely complex and

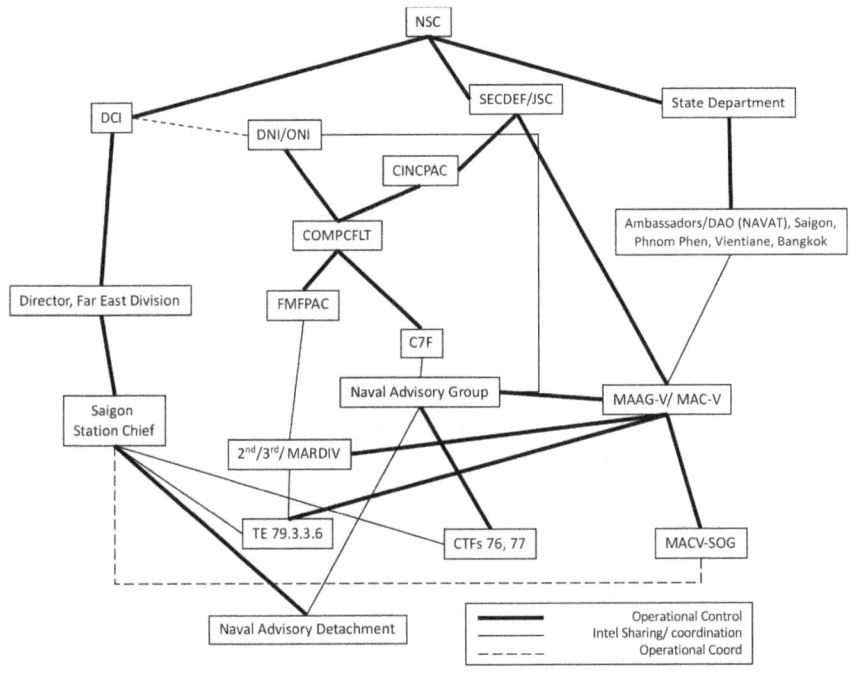

Figure 3. Naval Intelligence Reporting Chain, Southeast Asia (1961-65) *Created by author*

magnified. It requires intensive study, beginning with the highly technical specialty of control and coordination between political, intelligence and the military operations of divisions of the ground forces. It was in this area that the Germans failed completely . . . and it was in the solution to this problem that the British were finally able to win the anti-guerrilla operation in Malaya."[53] While this accurately depicted the problem set the Fleet faced with containment-related policy in the third world, it lacked specificity in what the Navy actually needed to accomplish. The Navy knew its mission in the broad sense, but the early years in Indochina proved the institution was far more capable to meet the challenge than Navy leadership thought.

The Navy experienced shortfalls in personnel, however. For instance, considering a major exercise in 1961 in which the Navy evaluated intelligence human resources and capabilities, an after-action report stated: "During the period of operation of the Exercise Intelligence Center a total of eight enlisted personnel, both Marine and Navy were assigned to the EIC . . . of the total assigned only one had previous intelligence experience."[54] The Navy had experienced shortfalls in intelligence personnel before but, as an institution, began to see the necessity of forward deploying well-trained intelligence collectors to fulfill its own role in national security affairs. As one will recall, the Sino-Japanese War as a crisis for the West did not demand large numbers of additional personnel in the U.S. policy aversion to becoming more involved. The Chinese Civil War of the late 1940s, too, did not prompt additional but rather fewer forces. Moreover, the Taiwan crises focused on a naval battle with relatively fixed numbers of personnel ashore. The crisis in Indochina was different, however. Clearly, the United States was committed to the containment of Communism. Presence in the region supported by consistently strong intelligence and assistance (often in the form of clandestine warfare) to the South Vietnamese was imperative.[55]

Within time, the intelligence community and Department of Defense set up training courses in theater. The MAC-V reported in 1964: "Agents and interrogators were trained in Saigon for use at company, battalion, and sector level. The ultimate goal was to have two trained interrogators at company and battalion level for immediate battlefield information. It had been found that at sector the untrained interrogator was easily fooled by hard-core Viet Cong captives. A course was designed and presented in an effort to prevent this from happening."[56] While in-theater training such as this proved useful, it did not replace the basic "schoolhouse" training that intelligence officers otherwise received at home commands. Conversely, many aspects of the Indochina experience required in-theater preparation.

While the Navy expanded its human intelligence capabilities during World War II and in relation to the Korean War, the Marine Corps only did so on the margins in the early Cold War. It was time, however, to match the Corps' expeditionary ethos with the inherent need to collect intelligence for the operations faced in the ensuing years. Traditionally, the Fleet Marine Force, Atlantic (FMFLANT) set the stage for future capabilities. FMFLANT focused on four areas: photo/imagery interpretation, interrogation translation, interpreter teams, and counterintelligence, the latter of which was deeply associated with HUMINT.[57] This effort began in March 1961 and evolved across the next few years.

On the issues of interrogation and interpretation, the FMFLANT G2 connected the Marine Corps future operations—and training for that environment—with the CIA. Much debate surrounds the importance of these subjects to the Corps as an institution, however. Consider an anecdote of a Marine unit's handling of VC captives in which a "Marine who participated in the actual capture almost never accompanied the captive to the collecting point to permit debriefing by the interrogators."[58] The FMFLANT G2 identified language proficiency and interrogation training as fundamental to future Marine Corps operations and asserted that the CIA, Army, or indigenous personnel could augment the pool of U.S. Marine Corps interpreters. CIA or Army schools conducted all interrogation training, however. In the words of the FMFLANT G2, "interrogation-translation teams should periodically be sent to various countries to enhance their psychological and sociological familiarity with the people of their language specialty."[59] Not since the early 1920s when then-commandant Maj. Gen. John Lejeune sent Lt. Col. Pete Ellis on an extended clandestine information-gathering trip to several of the Micronesian Islands in anticipation of future conflict with Japan had the Marine Corps thought about similar emersion training.[60]

The Marine Corps' renewed focus on counterintelligence acknowledged that "the probable enemy will be capable of conducting extensive guerrilla, sabotage, espionage, and subversive operations by utilizing the civilian masses."[61] As historically was the case with other forms of intelligence, counterintelligence ultimately supported combat operations of the landing force and specifically focused on counterespionage, countersabotage, and countersubversion. Furthermore, rather than organically attaching to the Marine divisions, counterintelligence teams assigned to detachments for specific operations and commands, depending on the circumstances.[62]

The Navy and Marine Corps collaborated with the CIA as well, and training and development of skills and expertise was not a one-way relationship. While the CIA invited a select few officers from the Fleet to the

Farm at Camp Peary, the secretary of the Navy annually invited the DCI to nominate one official to attend the Naval Warfare course at the Naval War College in Newport.[63] In turn, the agency regularly presented informational briefs to the Naval Intelligence School at Anacostia on the organization of the CIA, National Security Council, the intelligence community, and special field relationships.[64] Also around this time, the director of the Navy's annual Operational Intelligence Course for Foreign Officers requested that the CIA's director of training send a particular individual to teach Sketching—an Aid to Observation.[65] Overall, a convergence of clandestine intelligence capabilities emerged, and the experience in Southeast Asia served as a testbed for such collaborative efforts in coming years. The period fundamentally altered how the Navy viewed HUMINT, creating a community for the discipline akin to the historically celebrated air and surface community but, due to its inherent secrecy, still one on the fringes of the Fleet.

Chapter 8

Preparing Intelligence for Deeper Involvement

Navy and Marine Corps Intelligence

This chapter presents archival data on the U.S. operating intelligence units in the early-1960s portion of the war—before it became a full-fledged war for the United States—and the role the HUMINT activities played during this period. It begins with a brief discussion of the MAAG-V, followed by the establishment of the MAC-V. It also discusses the operations of Task Element 79.3.3.6 and Operation Shufly, the NAVGP and Operation Market Time, and other naval intelligence units in the region. The picture that emerges is one of a deeply rich intelligence experience and of a naval intelligence community more oriented to clandestine operations than ever before.

MAAG-V

In August 1954 Lt. Col. Victor Croizat became the first Marine in Vietnam when he assumed the position of adviser to the commandant of the Vietnamese Marine Corps under the U.S. MAAG-V.[1] Like its successor (the MAC-V), Army generals led the MAAG-V, but it included subcomponent commands by service. Its size continually grew throughout the late

1950s and early 1960s to the point that it began forward-deploying advisers with Vietnamese army (ARVN) units in various hamlets in central Vietnam. As indicated by President Diem's appeal to Vice President Johnson in May 1961, the demand to increase the size of the MAAG-V past its 685-man level continued.[2] Intelligence was a natural by-product of the MAAG-V, and leadership in Washington regularly desired to gain a pulse on the disposition and capabilities of the South Vietnamese.

Generally, as might be expected, intelligence reporting did not emanate from higher-level commands, such as the Pacific Fleet and the Fleet Marine Force in the Pacific (FMF-P).[3] While subordinate commands in the Pacific theater were obligated to share intelligence with their higher headquarters, reporting was generally intended for the operational chain of command, such as task force commanders, and for Director, MAAG-V, and later MAC-V.[4] Component commands, such as Commander, Pacific Fleet, and Commander, Fleet Marine Force, focused on the readiness, manning, training, and equipping of forces stationed in the theater of operations.[5]

MAC-V and MAC-V SOG

While the MAAG-V continued to exist for a couple of years, the MAC-V essentially replaced it in February 1962. The MAC-V hosted a name more suitable for combat operations and contained the potential organization structure to increase in size if required. With this transition, the United States' role in combat operations arguably began, even though legally and officially this resulted from the Gulf of Tonkin Resolution in August 1964.[6] By March 1962, however, the Kennedy administration announced that U.S. pilots had flown combat missions, and the first "clear and hold" operation (indicative of counterinsurgency operations) had begun.[7] The debate over whether the war remained a crisis or a war for the United States is unending, but if one accepts the assumption that the administration did not yet desire to go to war but rather wanted to aid the South Vietnamese in their own war, the murkiness of language is worth wading through.[8] The nature of the collection of intelligence certainly changed over this time, expanding to build networks in North and South Vietnam and in Laos and Cambodia.

While the Navy and Marine Corps units subordinate to the MAC-V also worked with the CIA at times to run agents as far north as Hanoi, with units such as the Naval Advisory Detachment and the Maritime Studies Branch of the SOG, forces observed plenty of opportunities to collect valuable intelligence in the south as well.[9] Viet Cong fighters wearing plain peasant clothes and carrying French weapons began appearing in the south following the monsoon season in 1959. When the Ho Chi Minh Trail neared completion in 1961, it was not immediately clear that this served as the reason why the VC supported the Pathet Lao over the course of the previous two years—a complex logistics artery.

Naturally, a major part of the J2 intelligence section of the MAC-V collected and assessed North Vietnamese military capabilities, tactics, techniques, and procedures. One major effort in 1962, a push to penetrate the North Vietnam military centers, focused on the air-defense and anti-aircraft capabilities of the Viet Cong.[10] It used reconnaissance units (both U.S. Marines and ARVN soldiers) to uncover the VC's ability to fire "low altitude bursts that could have been caused by rockets or other ammunition fired from a launcher or mortar type weapon," effectively a threat to rotary aircraft.[11] At the time, this reversed the previous thought that the VC only used small arms to take down aircraft.[12] Collection requirements subsequently included the "location of person observing the burst or weapon" and the untampered acquisition of any such systems for exploitation by the MAC-V J2 and others.[13]

In 1962 Secretary of Defense McNamara ordered that the MAC-V take command of covert programs under a subordinate body, the SOG, "a supposed gathering of analysts devoted to academic study."[14] The SOG was only administratively associated with the MAC-V. It reported directly to the Joint Chiefs of Staff, with day-to-day reporting to the two-star special assistant for counterinsurgency and special activities.[15] Its charter authorized operations in Vietnam (North and South), Laos, Thailand, Cambodia, Burma, and south China, including the strategically important Hainan Island.[16] The SOG's budget was hidden within the Navy's annual budget. Likely an effect of William Colby's (once the CIA station chief in Saigon and then the chief of the CIA's Far East Division) influence on

Switchback and his long history with covert programs dating back to his time in the OSS, the SOG was organized into air, maritime, and psychological sections.[17]

While the SOG officially functioned as a Department of Defense organization, its operations and secrecy resembled those of the CIA's (perhaps by design) and, in fact, often fell operationally subordinate to the Saigon station chief. The agency also provided its logistics base at Camp Chinen, Okinawa, as a resource for importing unique hardware, such as suppressors and personal signals intelligence packages.[18] More importantly, the CIA provided the three-year-old agent program that Colby and his team developed for airdrop infiltrations into North Vietnam and Laos with help from U.S. Navy SEALs.[19]

Based in Da Nang, the SOG's Naval Advisory Detachment consisted of a dozen SEALs from SEAL Team One and Boat Support Unit One from Coronado and five Marines from Force Reconnaissance.[20] While this detachment ran assets, trained and vetted agents, and conducted regular reconnaissance of the enemy positions in the South and along the Ho Chi Minh Trail, none of them crossed the 17th parallel into North Vietnam, for no other reason than the likelihood of compromising plausible deniability.[21] In fact, the Naval Advisory Detachment was accused of luring the North Vietnamese to attack the *Maddox* in what became the Gulf of Tonkin incident on 3–5 August 1964.[22] To some extent the SOG was the military's entrée to modern HUMINT and covert operations cultivated previously by the agency and OSS for many years prior. While many failures were documented—including the avoidable deaths of Marines, sailors, airmen, and soldiers long before the escalation of the war in 1965—the SOG began a foray into clandestine intelligence, institutionalizing practices that previously were taken for granted or applied with ad hoc recklessness. By bringing HUMINT into officialdom, the Navy and Marine Corps recognized it as a valuable piece in support of the Fleet's mission.

In the fall of 1962, MAC-V intelligence estimates began to include substantial reporting on the VC and People's Army of Vietnam (PAVN) troop numbers throughout both the South and North, many of which were based on sources gained from the MAC-V and ARVN National Pacification Program.[23] In addition to the conventional forces of the

PAVN—that were significantly easier to estimate—the MAC-V J2 estimated that the VC comprised 120,000 supporting guerrilla fighters in the South.[24] While this number could be based on credible reporting, it is problematic in the face of other estimations around the same time.[25] MAC-V reporting also attempted to estimate the number of VC personnel in Laos and Cambodia, but these territories often served only as a transit for VC units traveling to and from the North, a realization that became evident with the finalization of the Ho Chi Minh Trail along the Laos border as early as 1959.[26] Because Commander, MAC-V, banned photo reconnaissance over North Vietnam in August 1962 (although, it is unclear how long this ban continued), the majority of the intelligence reporting on the numbers of North Vietnam fighters came from HUMINT reports, either through sources at the district and hamlet level or through the capture and interrogation of VC and PAVN soldiers.[27] This meant not only a significant increase in MAC-V's dependence upon the HUMINT mission but also an increase in the danger of operating in proximity to the enemy.

As it became increasingly obvious the United States would remain in Vietnam for an extended period, the MAC-V intelligence underwent some extensive changes. The 1964 command history reflects this:

> During 1964, to keep pace with intelligence requirements and possible extensive U.S. involvement in Southeast Asia, the U.S. intelligence effort in Vietnam was reorganized and expanded. When the decision was made in March to extend the U.S. effort in Vietnam, plans were developed for degrees of expansion and possible eventualities.... That resulted in the J2 section increasing from five to six branches as follows: Collection Branch (formerly Plans and Operations); Counterintelligence and Security Branch; Production Branch; Reconnaissance and Photo Intelligence Branch; J2, High Command, Advisory Branch; and Current Intelligence and Indications Center.[28]

This reorganization also implied a greater demand of the Navy and Marine Corps units operating from Da Nang and along the coastal littorals. The demand for ground truth was an increasing pressure from Washington.

Other changes that occurred during this period included the increased emphasis on targeting intelligence for prosecution against VC officers. This represented yet another sign that the one-time crisis was becoming a war, and "assistance" turned into force employment. The 1964 command history states,

> In September, a realignment of functions within J2 placed the Analysis Section under Production Branch and added a Plans and Targets Section to the [Current Intelligence and Indications Center]. The latter section prepared and updated intelligence estimates and target lists for Southeast Asia contingency plans, and undertook special studies. A major project was the preparation of proposed target lists for the Laos Panhandle.[29] These lists were approved and a combined Embassy, Vientiane—HACV list compiled. In October, these lists were used to initiate interdiction of communist infiltration.[30]

This also embodies one of the earliest signs that the MAC-V participated in operations in Laos, an admission well beyond the stated mission.

As a result of Secretary McNamara's urgent need to show results in an increasingly unpopular war, intelligence reporting from the MAC-V started to become sterile, often focused on statistics. For instance, "In Binh Dinh Sector in early '65 the SOIC noted a Viet Cong buildup; this intelligence resulted in 200 Viet Cong deaths. In April 1965, Kien Hoa Sector sent four intelligence agents to locate Viet Cong units. They returned with definite information. As a result, Operation Tien Mang 1965 was launched. This operation resulted in 86 Viet Cong killed with negligible RVNAF casualties," a bottom-line reporting tone that signified the mission was to identify and kill as many VC as possible.[31] Subsequently, intelligence reporting should show its value in reporting this. The MAC-V then reported that naval intelligence by J2/High Command greatly improved, and "accurate reporting supplemented by active collection resulted to the capture of many documents and weapons. Navy Intelligence Summaries are now disseminated country-wide and are considered quite valuable."[32] To whom it was of value is debatable: to the prosecution of the war on the ground or to political justifications in Washington?

Preparing Intelligence   177

What constituted intelligence began to gray because the enemy himself was illusive and, similar to the Army and Air Force, the Navy and Marine Corps became part of this. The MAC-V's broad intelligence mission was to run "an intensified program of harassment, diversion, political pressure, capture of prisoners, physical destruction, acquisition of intelligence, generation of propaganda, and diversion of resources, against the Democratic Republic of Vietnam."[33] To enable this mission, most of its early intelligence work against the VC entailed human source operations and the seedlings of clandestine activities.

Intelligence in Operation Shufly

One of the most important naval units during the early years of the crisis in Vietnam was Task Element 79.3.3.6, which became associated with Operation Shufly.[34] The element landed in Soc Trang (on the Mekong Delta) on 9 April 1962 and soon thereafter repositioned to a base in Da Nang, close to the border with North Vietnam.[35] TE 79.3.3.6 comprised the Marine Aircraft Group 16 (MAG 16) from the 1st Marine Aircraft Wing supplemented by units such as the 7th Counterintelligence Team. The Shufly deployment occurred at a very uncertain time, as Vietnam's National Assembly soon pledged full support to Diem's "Strategic Hamlet" plan, in which the ARVN and its benefactors engaged with the population on a hamlet and village level.[36] Shufly Marines worked in close contact with the ARVN, garnering much intelligence from these liaison relationships. The units flying CH-53 and UH-34 helicopters often flew missions in support of naval riverine units on the Mekong Delta and along the coastal littorals, sometimes dropping fire teams from 1st Recon into areas of known VC presence.[37]

Task Element 79.3.3.6 had three primary means of intelligence, which substantially expanded in late 1962. As the intelligence office reported in January 1963, this was "primarily through closer liaison with senior and parallel intelligence collection agencies within I Corps [ARVN in the northern area of South Vietnam] and the addition of an aerial observation capability to the Task Element."[38] Additionally, while often vague in its reporting, the Task Element 79.3.3.6 intelligence section developed a broad network of sources among the population "with the additional advantage of a rapid cross reference to confirm or deny any particular item of information" by using its liaison relationships in the U.S. Army, SEAL teams, and the ARVN.[39]

In one of its periodic intelligence reports, the task element's S2 (intelligence division), identified some major problems that hindered its success in operations. It stated: "There has been a serious disregard of the intelligence capabilities of the Task Element by operational squadrons," and the "failure to properly use intelligence during the planning phase stems from near universal lack of understanding of the role of combat intelligence, years of peacetime neglect of realistic intelligence training, and the delusion that this particular counterinsurgency campaign is not a real war in the true sense of the word."[40] While a complaint, the statement speaks volumes to the nature of the U.S. involvement in Indochina during this period because combat intelligence was unnecessary if the mission was to "assist and advise" the ARVN, as previously stated. In hindsight, this is a flawed assumption because the United States was clearly sliding into a war.

Around the same time that intelligence uncovered the North Vietnamese air-defense capabilities, intelligence officers from Task Element 79.3.3.6 seized an enemy document that discussed in detail the subject of countering helicopter-borne raids.[41] It exposed the VC's understanding of U.S. and ARVN helicopter operations. The VC viewed U.S. assistance to the ARVN through helicopter logistics and raids as the primary center of gravity in defeating the South, saying, "Therefore if we can destroy or greatly reduce the enemy's heliborne capability we will, in essence, have destroyed the mobility necessary to the aid tactics."[42] The document discussed the advantages and disadvantages that the United States and ARVN experienced in these kinds of operations, not least of which pertained to the fact that the "population in our rear areas is on our side and will resist the enemy in every way."[43] The document continued to identify a set of solutions to mitigate the lethality of helicopter-borne operations, which included a campaign to educate the population on ways to counter them as well as a renewed counterintelligence effort to deny U.S. and ARVN units' foresight on PAVN/VC activities. Just like the threat to the helicopter mission, the sources to support this effort were not possible without having personnel on the ground, in country.

An important part of the Task Element 79.3.3.6 S2 intelligence mission was the debriefing of MAG 16 pilots following missions. This provided a systematic way to track and record battle damage assessments but also to learn more about hostile enemy ground fire and antiaircraft capabilities.[44] The several hundred post-mission after-action reports, however, documented little to no evidence that the pilots experienced regular contact with local villagers or direct contact with VC personnel, a trend that undoubtedly changed as the war escalated in years to come. The aversion to engage with the local population was also reinforced by the S2's suggestion that pilots and crew did not properly use intelligence.[45]

Because of the political nature of the crisis, serious considerations were made on the part of the TE 79.3.3.6 of strategic- and national-level actions and circumstances, unlike in other wars in which the stated objective(s) were black or white (i.e., the resolute destruction of an enemy). For example, the S2 published a report in early 1963 on the problems the task element faced in the event of a coup d'état in Saigon against the Diem regime, including the disruption of normal military channels, the increase of danger to U.S. personnel in the Da Nang area, and the increased tactical importance of the airfield and surrounding area.[46] Relationships between the MAC-V leadership in Saigon and its South Vietnamese counterparts could fracture. The implication of this report was that TE 79.3.3.6 personnel—namely, the S2 intelligence officers—should maintain close and reliable sources in the Da Nang area to exploit them for information in the event of a surprise coup d'état. Staying close to members of the ARVN and political leaders paid dividends for Marine intelligence, such as the case in May 1963 when the Ba Xuyen Province chief received intelligence that "a meeting of some Viet Cong leaders would take place in a village about 12 miles southeast of Soc Trang," enabling the MAC-V SOG to target it.[47]

In the context of subjects such as coups d'état and other political warfare activities by North Vietnam, intelligence could not avoid the obvious and growing subject of anti-American activity on the part of the North and its supporters in the South, which became increasingly prevalent as U.S.

involvement in combat operations increased. The Office of the Senior Advisor to I Corps (a Marine detachment from the MAC-V) in Da Nang published a report in November 1962 on this: "Information has been received from a reliable source that the VC may infiltrate CYCLO-DRIVERS into Da Nang for the purpose of conducting terrorist activities against unwary Americans."[48] As the Da Nang Security Office claimed, the VC tracked U.S. personnel, behaviors, and activities.[49] Terrorism activities against U.S. military personnel in the Da Nang area increased, and units were not prepared. Later in April 1964 the director of security in South Vietnam shared a report with TE 79.3.3.6 S2 on VC techniques of assassinating Americans, gathered from Vietnamese population sources who had witnessed these activities in the recent past.[50] These asymmetric tactics included throwing grenades concealed in loaves of bread into parked cars (after repeated observations of the drivers' regular activities) of U.S. personnel.[51]

Another trend in the early years of the war entailed the kidnapping and interrogation of U.S. personnel, as evidenced in two instances in June 1964. First, in the hamlet of Bich Tram and days later in the hamlet of Bin Nam, Privates First Class Greer and Schreckengost (of Task Element S2) were taken while on a reconnaissance mission.[52] A reliable informer reported in both instances the Marines were displayed in the hamlet, and the VC captors announced each would be given five months of political training before being returned. Due to the limited training in escape and evasion the command had received (identified by the S2), the Marines could not likely withstand VC pressure for the limited amount of intelligence a private first class was privy to at the time.[53] Often when VC units kidnapped friendly or U.S. personnel, Marine intelligence used existing source networks to help with search and rescue. The VC's announcement that personnel would eventually be returned, pointed to their (VC) objective that released personnel would then have the desire to the fight for the VC and kill Americans, having been fully indoctrinated.[54]

As part of the regular mission of the intelligence section at TE 79.3.3.6 headquarters in Da Nang, periodic security assessments were conducted—a quasi-force protection and counterintelligence routine. In a survey that an intelligence officer conducted at the end of 1962—in which he found "serious deficiencies regarding internal security"[55]—he concluded that there was either a level of duplicity or an overabundance of pride in his Vietnamese army counterparts. "ARVN officials maintain the position that they are responsible for the security of the air base and have been reluctant to authorize this command [TE 79.3.3.6] any discretion in establishing an effective program to ensure the safety of personnel and equipment from overt or covert acts of hostility from insurgent forces."[56] This regular security assessment uncovered an element of pride or stubbornness, or both, on the part of the Vietnamese army leaders at Da Nang toward relinquishing control over aspects of security, a point that further complicated relations between the task element and the ARVN, particularly on intelligence.

Due to the task element's mission, intelligence focused on improving helicopter operations in relation to the VC. TF 79.3.3.6 pilots garnered very little intelligence from air observation, however. For example, in a two-week period (fifty-four reports in total) in November 1963, the reports' field stating "pilot sightings of intelligence value" consistently declared "none."[57] Likewise, the two-week period after this (15–30 November, a total of thirty-seven reports) showed zero after-action reports in which the pilots identified any data collected of intelligence value.[58] As a study by the Center for Naval Analyses suggested in 1962, "Reaction time might be reduced by certain measures. Routine and methodical reconnaissance of areas known to be subject to Viet Cong operation would help provide positive intelligence. The establishment of additional alert forces or the designation of certain units within a given tactical area (e.g., Ranger companies) to be available for helicopter lift during a given period to the exclusion of other duties, should reduce the planning cycle."[59] The alert forces on standby could theoretically ensure greater ability to prosecute a target. In reality, however, this scheme would only work if reconnaissance of VC areas and HUMINT source development were a consistent mission, which does not appear to have been the case at that time.

There was the dark side of intelligence as well: the fact that occasionally it painted a prettier picture than what existed. For instance, one task element report in 1963 alluded to the relationship between the command's S2 and the I Corps region, which included the Army, Navy, the Australian

MAAG adviser, Special Forces, and the Vietnamese army.[60] "The close liaison resulting from this support has enabled the Task Element to maintain a complete, current estimate of the enemy situation based on the latest intelligence available from a broad range of sources, with the additional advantage of a rapid cross reference to confirm or deny any particular item of information."[61] The report's tone implies the intelligence office was telling the commander what he wanted to hear, which some would claim reflected a broader trend.[62]

The reality of Operation Shufly's fate is multifaceted. The TE 79.3.3.6 pilots operated in the heart of the VC's territory in the northern region of South Vietnam. The fact that leadership had a seeming aversion to source collection and reconnaissance did not make it easy to capitalize on the unit's proximity to the enemy. Liaison relationships with the Army and Navy SEALs, along with the collection work the task element's S2 did with its limited resources, showed that intelligence was vital during this period, but it was not seen as important as supporting South Vietnam's attrition war against the North. Knowing the enemy (including his next moves and long-term intentions) and killing the enemy were separate and contradictory efforts, where they could have been complementary.

Naval Advisory Group and Operation Market Time

The NAVGP served as the Navy's main command in the Vietnam theater, for a time even commanding the various afloat units, such as Seventh Fleet's (or, "the Tonkin Gulf Yacht Club," as it became known) Combined Task Force 77. Like the rest of the primary Marine Corps, Army, and Air Force units, intelligence was not its original primary mission, but it represented an enormous part of its operating time. Intelligence also acted as a primary touchpoint for naval special warfare's future utility to the Navy as an institution.[63] As with Task Element 79.3.3.6 and Operation Shufly, NAVGP's mission—referred to under the moniker Operation Market Time—fell under MAC-V's purview.[64] Market Time's mission objective was the combined U.S. Navy / Vietnamese Navy (VNN) interdiction and infiltration of the VC and PAVN-Navy supply of weapons, personnel, and equipment to inland waters in the South by way of the coastal, littoral, sea, and delta waters. Its primary means of conducting this mission included the use of riverine forces, SEALs, and Marine reconnaissance (generally, 1st RECON), coast guardsmen, and other specialized detachments of explosive ordnance disposal teams, surface units, and intelligence detachment. Additionally, NAVGP also oversaw a subordinate Marine advisory unit, with a mission to advise the VNN specifically on amphibious operations.

As the NAVGP was established in 1964, the commander, Capt. William H. Hardcastle, wanted to ensure that the intelligence collected suited the mission. In the past, the Navy had used indigenous coast-watchers (paid and unpaid) to provide information on enemy ships approaching an area. The problem set in the inland and coastal waters of Vietnam, however, was more complex because the VC's strategy entailed embedding themselves among the general population, which led to serious questions of trust and source reliability. Of the ships coming directly from North Vietnam to deliver arms and equipment, these were often junks that looked similar to nearly every other noncombatant fishing community vessel in those waters. As Hardcastle communicated in his first NAVGP concept of operation: "More than any other item, the development of a naval intelligence network depends on the cooperation and enthusiasm of VNN. NAVGP has recommended that the VNN intelligence T.O. [Table of Organization] be increased. . . . MAC-V J2 has authorized funding for an agent net to be operated by VNN."[65] The latter move represented one altogether new for the Navy because, historically, naval intelligence units rarely approached a collection environment from an agent network perspective. More often, sources had been developed in a manner of singular opportunity. The approach suddenly alluded to the possibility that the Navy's intelligence enterprise was beginning to think of its mission in the way the CIA approached its mission—through clandestine means using Vietnamese assets.[66]

As a MAC-V history revealed, upon its establishment, the NAVGP quickly studied the problem of infiltration of arms and supplies into the South and concluded, "(1) VC infiltration of personnel and equipment was taking place in undetermined but sufficient quantities to successfully support and sustain operations and (2) the primary source of supply continued to be from the DRV [Democratic Republic of Vietnam] via

Laos and Cambodia with delivery by porters via foot trails, by boat and sampan on the rivers and canals, and along the coast by larger seagoing craft."[67] At the time this was an epiphany because it was previously thought that the VC only used the road networks of the Ho Chi Minh Trail, and infiltration by sea would not benefit from concealment—a fallacy soon revealed.

In February 1965 the NAVGP experienced its first significant success, directly a result of the village- and hamlet-based agent networks facilitated by the VNN intelligence liaison relationship. Intelligence provided the location of a sunken junk ship, positively identified as VC-affiliated and carrying arms and supplies bound for the South. The operation included a SEAL adviser and diver (Lt. Franklin Anderson), Special Forces on the nearby beachhead to suppress enemy fire opposing the team, and five other divers including two intelligence officers (Lt. Cdr. Ralph Channell and Lt. Cdr. Joseph Perez).[68] The mission was to conduct the dive, retrieve the intelligence material, plant demolition charges, and destroy the ship. An after-action report stated,

> The discovery of a Viet Cong supply ship in Vung Ro Bay on 16 February represents a major turning point in the history of naval operations in Vietnam. Large scale infiltration by sea of arms and men had long been a tantalizing, but unconfirmed, explanation for the puzzling problem that lies at the heart of the Vietnam conflict: How do the VC successfully transport large quantities of men, arms and munitions undetected? Although fairly frequent intelligence reports of sea infiltration were received, few were confirmed, and of those few that indicated large scale activity, practically none were believable.[69]

The recovery operation at Vung Ro Bay revealed a "new family of weapons" as well as the fact that 7.62-round ammunition periodically found on the battlefield in the South indeed originated from the North by way of sea.[70] More significant than the cache of weapons were the list of crew members (i.e., potential sources or targets in the future), a captain's log book, a propaganda manual, and some items affiliated with the PRC.[71]

By all accounts, the Vung Ro incident represented a resounding intelligence and Special Forces success even though the ashore Special Forces company commander reported taking enemy fire, returning fire, and killing eighteen VC members in the process.[72] As a result of the Vung Ro incident, the NAVGP and Operation Market Time continued to pressure the VC in the inland waterways for the duration of that year, ultimately stopping several other infiltrated shipments from reaching the South. While responsibility over Operation Market Time transferred to the U.S. naval forces in Vietnam in the spring of 1966, the NAVGP's approach to network HUMINT-enabled counterinfiltration continued as a common approach used by the Navy during the crisis. Emerging from much of this is the subtle paradox of the militarization of intelligence and the intelligentization of the military, both concerns that would reemerge again and again in later years.[73]

Naval Special Operations

As William Colby, station chief in Saigon, found, the unmapped, rich vegetation of the Laotian and South Vietnamese jungles hindered the ability of flyovers and aerial photography to disclose the enemy hiding below, so prior to the more expanded use of napalm and Agent Orange to clear dense foliage later in the war, he drew from his knowledge of activities conducted by men on the ground.[74] The National Security Council soon signed National Security Memorandum 52, authorizing Colby and other CIA stations in Southeast Asia to employ Navy SEALs and Green Berets for CIA covert missions in South Vietnam and against the Viet Minh and Pathet Lao.[75] This relationship only expanded in the years to follow, as the CIA Directorate of Operations realized that the paramilitary operations it oversaw could not originate from a solely organic capability. While SEALs trained junk ship crews in Da Nang to land agents in North Vietnam, their CIA cover organization was named Combined Area Studies.[76] Also closely associated with the MAC-V SOG, SEALs experienced more command autonomy than during previous missions since their beginnings in World War II.[77]

In January 1964 the MAC-V officially assumed control of covert special operations missions in Vietnam (previously run from the CIA station in

Saigon), first under the name Special Operations Group, but the unit's name was quickly changed (for operational security reasons) to the innocuous Studies and Observations Group (SOG).[78] Although the name suggested a solely intelligence-focused mission, HUMINT represented only a portion of the SOG's mission. Political warfare, sabotage, assassination, and psychological operations were also part of the unit's mission. The shift in control of the mission to MAC-V was the most significant sign yet that the military was moving to include a greater reliance on Special Forces and clandestine intelligence in its overall mission. Simultaneously, one begins to see the graying of military missions and intelligence missions wherein each relied heavily on the other and became less transparent. This would later evolve into a predecessor of the CIA's clandestine Phoenix Program, a localized interrogation and assassination effort aimed at striking fear and intimidation into the Viet Cong's efforts in the South.[79]

Institutional Lines in the Sand

Initially, the watershed moment ushered in by the Bay of Pigs event affected the military in two ways. First, for the president and secretary of defense, it underscored the need for the military's organic intelligence capabilities beyond its traditional roles, which were to gather and analyze data on the militaries of foreign governments.[80] In the past this simply meant that the agency (or military service) might be reorganized, or another agency would be tasked with future missions. However, this was not the first time the national security complex reacted to the unfolding environment with the establishment of a new agency in lieu of the inability of existing ones to provide the needed capability. The National Security Agency, which was established in 1953, became the product of the Navy and Army's inability to man, train, equip, and operate the forces necessary for the amount of signals collection and processing required during the Cold War.[81] Second, U.S. containment policy evolved and therefore continued to blur distinguishable actions taken by the intelligence and special operations communities in the kinds of missions in which they increasingly became involved, such as those in Indochina. For example, it was not only the CIA and the National Security Council that had to, at least tacitly, endorse the brutal and oppressive policies of leaders such as Diem (particularly his policies on the Buddhist population); military leaders in theater had to as well.[82]

Large portions of the entire national security community increasingly participated in the clandestine containment game, as evidenced in many of the Indochina records previously discussed. For example, while the Army and Navy had experienced times of change in the past, the Air Force—still in its early years—also underwent a period of change. The Air Force was the biggest contributor of pilots to the CIA's so-called Air America, operating between Thailand and Clarke Airfield in Luzon, Philippines, in the agency's arms deliveries to rebel groups in Indochina. This afforded pilots unique access to human sources that other intelligence and general Fleet and infantry were not exposed to in their day-to-day operations. To prepare intelligence airmen for deployment to the Southeast Asia theater, the Air Force's 1127th Field Activities Group's mission was to "conduct collection operations and develop and maintain force and training programs, operational plans, and combat ready HUMINT collection forces to fulfill ACS/I HUMINT responsibilities . . . in cold, limited and general war."[83] Similar to the Navy and Army, the Air Force officially conducted the HUMINT mission, eschewing the ad hoc nature of prior-day intelligence collected by officers for recognized capability, complete with doctrine and standard operating procedures.[84]

Institutional Opposing Forces

One must be even-handed about the impact of HUMINT and the circumstances often beyond the control of naval intelligence units that invariably affected the ability to collect and maintain situational awareness in Vietnam. Access alone was not the lynchpin for gaining credible sources. The host nation—in this case, South Vietnam, the country theoretically benefiting from presence during a crisis—plays a massive role in determining credibility and legitimacy, among others. For example, in September 1963, Ngo Dinh Diem's sister-in-law publicly declared that the U.S. Army officers in Vietnam were irresponsible "little soldiers of fortune."[85] In another instance in October of that year, Diem's brother, Ngo Dinh Nhu, declared that the United States "initiated a process of disintegration in Vietnam" and accused the CIA of an attempted coup against the Diem government.[86] Indeed, on 1 November 1963 Diem and his brother were kidnapped, assassinated, and replaced by a military junta, later evidenced to be planned and conducted by the CIA at the Kennedy administration's direction.[87] Interestingly, Saigon station chief John H. Richardson was recalled to Washington one month earlier on 5 October, possibly as a way of providing some level of plausible deniability for the coup.[88] To provide some perspective on the significance of the coup to the U.S. military mission in Indochina, Secretary of Defense McNamara and the DCI made monthly trips to Saigon starting the month after the coup to evaluate the new provisional government's war efforts and the MAC-V's progress therein.[89]

Another dangerous aspect of reliably collecting intelligence on the VC in South Vietnam, as well as on persons aligned with the North, in the unfolding situation in Vietnam was the increasing number of terrorist attacks against U.S. military persons in 1964. In May an explosion in Saigon harbor sank a 9,800-ton U.S. Navy aircraft transport ship.[90] Countless other instances targeted U.S. military personnel with bombing and small-arms attacks in broad daylight. Operational policy did not change because of these threats, but intelligence collection was not easily conducted under these circumstances.

A paradox emerged. While the United States desperately needed intelligence to gauge the course of the war—that up until then was a North and South war—it also accepted greater risk through U.S. involvement and the inadvertent exposure to the American public. The United States' role exemplifies the ambiguity of the term "crisis" because by 1963 the U.S. military conducted combat operations in Vietnam even as the official mission remained to only advise and assist the South Vietnamese military in its efforts.

The End of the Beginning

The Gulf of Tonkin incident and the following Gulf of Tonkin Resolution (effectively committing the United States to a broader military engagement) signified the end of the proxy war in Southeast Asia and the end of the subtle indirect approach that the earlier years of the crisis required. While the campaigns that followed in the ensuing years proved to be colossal tragedies, the naval services' HUMINT capabilities and roles were altered forever. The early 1960s in Southeast Asia proved to be the opening of a new U.S. acceptance of newly authorized military use of clandestine capabilities. Despite the previously rare conduct of Navy and Marine Corps clandestine intelligence operations—save for the occasional operations in conjunction with the CIA or the OSS before that—intelligence gathering and its role in the intelligence community changed.

In December 1965, as an inevitable culmination, the increasing role that military intelligence played in the national security mission overall—whether autonomously or under the discretion of the CIA as the national intelligence manager—the secretary of the Navy, Paul Nitze (undoubtedly, at the request of the secretary of defense and the DCI), provided the Navy with a formal guidance memo to collect, control, and coordinate clandestine intelligence.[91] Nitze's unprecedented direction was extraordinary because the term "clandestine" had never been used in official Navy correspondence or directives. While classified Top Secret, the documents were at least an internal communication to the naval intelligence community to expand its clandestine aptitude beyond the agency. Still under the authority of the National Security Act of 1947, the Nitze memo defined "clandestine operations," "cover," "cover stories," "target countries," "third-world operations," "case officers," "operational data," and "command authorities."[92] This was an enormous change for the Fleet because it meant that naval intelligence officers would forever be more closely aligned with the civilian intelligence community. Of the terms, "cover" (both official and nonofficial) exemplified the definitive difference between the methods with which the Fleet conducted HUMINT historically and those employed in the near future under the guise of organizations such as Task Force 157. Task Force 157 was the first exclusively clandestine intelligence organization the Navy ever operated, distinguished primarily from previous operations because it used nonofficial cover and other aspects of tradecraft similar to those used by the CIA.[93]

Conclusion

HUMINT fulfilled a fundamental role in the U.S. prosecution of the early part of the Vietnam War. Indeed, like any counterinsurgency, it was a localized war among the people with strategic outcomes indecipherable on a day-to-day basis. In fact, this made calculating the value of intelligence even more difficult. However, the intelligence collected during the early years of the Vietnam crisis did not resemble any the Fleet experienced in years past (at least since the Philippines campaign in the Spanish-American War or the so-called Banana Wars of the 1920s). The state of naval intelligence therefore constituted a paradox. On one hand, the institution of HUMINT in the Navy significantly matured. On the other hand, it mattered very little in relation to the outcome of the crisis. Ultimately, President Johnson committed an astonishing number of forces to a war that many believed was already lost.

While the Fleet conducted HUMINT for several decades (at least since the ONI's establishment), the U.S. experience in Southeast Asia provided a catalyst for which the Navy clearly codified its use, including clandestine HUMINT, as an authorized capability. HUMINT's official establishment was preceded by real-world events in that acted as clear conditions for deeper institutional support in a broader context. Few, however—including Fleet intelligence officers—believed in the decisive value of HUMINT. The ensuing war reinforced this point. The establishment of Task Force 157 embodied the proponents for expanding its use and its utility in obtaining enemy secrets to achieve a comparative advantage for the Fleet's relative power. This underscores the unique nature of what it means to collect HUMINT for naval purposes: while the methods and tradecraft may be similar to, if not the same as, those used by CIA case officers, the end use would generally serve Navy and Marine Corps interests.

Conclusion

Pivotal Legacy

This book has documented the historical record of U.S. naval human intelligence (HUMINT) during crises with China while considering the Navy and Marine Corps' relationship with intelligence through three questions: What role did naval HUMINT play in East Asia over the course of four distinct crises? How was this institutionally enabled? What advantages did it help produce? Specifically, it addresses collection practices, the resulting intelligence, institutional changes, and significant shifts in policy. The selection of cases covers periods in which Western naval forces were present in East Asia when a crises—defined from the Western perspective—was at hand. In all cases but the Taiwan crises, a war was underway, but the West was not directly involved in fighting. The mission of military units was instead to observe or provide noncombat support (e.g., advise and assist) to another country's military.

The role that naval HUMINT played during the Sino-Japanese war of the 1930s, the Chinese Civil War (1945–49), the Taiwan crises (1954–55 and 1958), and the Kennedy-Johnson containment policy in Indochina (1961–65) was at times significant in its ability to inform decision-making. Its utility to operations was sometimes both clear and debatable, however, due to poor preparation (both institutionally and operationally) and the ultimate use of intelligence by decision-makers. As Michael Warner points out of the Vietnam War, sometimes even with tremendous preparation, intelligence proves to be a colossal failure.[1] In other instances in which the United States was involved, the intelligence aspects have either been largely ignored in the academic body of literature or told through the eyes of the practitioner in the form of "spy-and-tell" memoirs.[2] Still others have often included intelligence as a by-product, failing to highlight its role in naval operations.[3] Although this research does not focus directly on customer use of intelligence, it is impossible to ignore in some cases, as Richard Betts points to in his work linking intelligence and policy decisions in military confrontation.[4]

The nature of major power navies is to be forward deployed in areas of national concern and for the benefit of national security. This presence enables the collection of information otherwise unavailable to other organizations throughout the intelligence community, and without significant challenges. While this is assumed to be true in the signals domain, it is true in the human domain as well. The use of the ship, as well as ashore-deployed positions, offers the possibility of being physically present. To collect strong, reliable naval HUMINT, navies must be forward deployed and, for the most part, ashore where humans tend to be. This, however, underscores the access paradox. While physical access to an area or region is required to develop human sources, often the dangers of being present prohibit the access to the very sources of value, as was certainly the case in the Taiwan crises. Furthermore, due to ever-existent risks, both physically and in terms of secrecy, this is always the case to some degree.

The relationship between crisis management and intelligence is interdependent. While crises cannot necessarily be averted with better intelligence, the latter informs the former so a country can manage its policy in relation to the outcome. This is dependent upon several factors, including intelligence priority requirements, personnel, enemy willingness to escalate, and—most of all—national priorities, as seen throughout the cases in this research. As shown, there is often a disconnect between otherwise valuable intelligence and the outcome of crises. Still, the two are connected by the decisions made or not made by the primary customers of intelligence—namely, the national security decision apparatus. Moreover, the interdependence between the machinations of crisis and intelligence was also clearly present in other crises, such as the War Scare of 1983 (or Able Archer), the Cuban Missile Crisis, and the Suez Crisis of 1956.

The nature of the crisis matters and bears on the kind of intelligence that leaders require. The cases in this research underscore four different types of roles the United States played in crises: strategic observer (the Asiatic Fleet in the pre–World War II era), damage control (Chinese Communist Revolution), active containment (Taiwan crises), and clandestine containment (U.S. policy in Southeast Asia in the early 1960s). The unifying theme in these crises is the threat of escalation and deeper involvement, factors that intelligence informed in each case. To reiterate a directly related axiom to this, valuable intelligence is not synonymous with the impact or customer uses of such intelligence. It is unclear, however, who determines value. Therefore, valuable intelligence can be produced *and* poor decisions can be made simultaneously, in contradiction to or in spite of one another. So while this builds on Betts' and others' assumptions of their interdependence, it seeks to separate them from the reality that leaders—despite intelligence—are often prone to panic, hesitation, and disregard, accidentally or otherwise, as was demonstrated in each of the cases.[5]

I propose two primary conclusions in the study of institutional and operational dynamics of naval HUMINT for the U.S. Navy. Ultimately, the research underscores that peacetime and crisis periods—as opposed to war—enable the development of sources and the collection of HUMINT in ways that wartime cannot, primarily for the fact that hostility is less and targets are more accessible. While each of the cases illustrate this tendency, institutional shortcomings (e.g., parochialism) and strategic mismanagement periodically dilute the impact of intelligence. As the Taiwan crises in chapters 5 and 6 show access to sources close to an enemy regime is also clearly driven by the physical access of intelligence personnel to those sources.

Access to political and military personnel, facilities, and other resources in enemy or third-country territories are primary factors in the ability to collect accurate, reliable information and produce finished intelligence. By far, this was the most fundamentally reinforced assumption surrounding this research, as is evident in each of the cases. When access is acquired and later lost or denied, reacquiring it is not as simple as it might have been previously, which was the case in the Taiwan crises. The number of potential sources diminishes. Moreover, the likelihood that a hostile nation protects itself through improved counterintelligence increases, along with its desire to increase its own foreign intelligence collection abilities. Although imperfect in terms of explaining the history of naval HUMINT overall, these cases explored a wide range of explanations for its role in a discrete region and an institutional community that experienced tremendous change over the course of thirty years.

Second, the practice of naval intelligence—specifically HUMINT—was an effect of a duality of priorities and evolving institutional norms within the Fleet. On one level, HUMINT activity and its effects were an outgrowth of the Navy's purpose in the United States' objectives in the world—namely, to project power and influence while holding true to Western democratic norms. Navies of great powers, such as the Royal Navy and the U.S. Navy of these periods, could do this. On another level, HUMINT in the Fleet was an effect of radically and periodically changing priorities at the national level, while leaders continued to rely heavily on the Navy—through forward-deployed positions—to collect meaningful intelligence that enabled decision-making in relation to adversaries.

As chapter 4 established, and chapters 5 through 7 expanded upon, the creation of the CIA and the establishment of a subordinated community did not simplify the management of HUMINT as much as it was intended to do. Institutions have cultural norms and parochial interests, and the Navy's long-established practices did not change overnight. This was not helped by the fact that the ONI was a comparable centralized predecessor to the OSS and CIA. While ultimately the naval HUMINT community evolved within the post-1947 construct, it did so through multiple trials, some detailed in the preceding cases.

In the case of the Western presence in China during the decade prior to World War II, U.S. naval HUMINT as a discipline was still in its infancy. Indeed, the term "HUMINT" would not be part of the lexicon until the early 1960s. Broadly, outside of the naval intelligence community (including the ONI and all subordinate units), HUMINT was treated as a peripheral action conducted for general situational awareness but hardly as central to how the Navy and Marine Corps fought and prepared for war. This is an institutional phenomenon captured at times in the literature as well as within the archival record.[6] This changes considerably with heightened global tensions and DNI William Puleston's (1934–37) timely reforms, as presented in chapter 1.

Examining units collecting intelligence during the Sino-Japanese War revealed some interesting insights. First, it appears evident from the archival record that, while afloat units such as the Yangtze Patrol collecting a considerable amount of intelligence on Japanese and Chinese Nationalist activity along the coast and inland waters—indeed, they covered a vast territory in a short period—the ONI relied more on the intelligence of the naval attaché in Nanking and the 4th Marine Regiment in Shanghai. This is understandable to some extent. The requirements during this period were more often to monitor activity ashore, such as the disposition of the Chinese Nationalist regime and the activities of the Japanese invading military. This coupled with the fact that the attaché and the Marine units had greater access to sources and could develop them for longer periods than the afloat units.

The contrast between ashore and afloat units underscores a paradox in naval intelligence. Institutionally, naval HUMINT is perhaps flawed to begin with because ship-based units—the heart and soul of the Navy—are never deployed in one place for very long. While afloat units often produced detailed studies of ports, enemy capabilities, and dispositions, political and military activity ashore were of more consistent value to customers in Washington, such as the DNI, evidenced by the subject matter of intelligence seen in the appendix. This also became evident across each of the crises studied in this research. War (and the escalation of tension preceding war) brings with it a completely different set of requirements, ideally those focused more on the operational activities of enemy units. To illustrate this point, consider the degree to which code-breaking and radio signals became important with the onset of World War II and the difficulty of conducting HUMINT once bullets started flying.

One of the unfortunate oversights of the prewar-period literature on China was the unmitigated lack of intelligence reporting on Mao Zedong's growing Communist movement.[7] Whether by the naval attaché in Nanking, the naval patrol units, or the Marines guarding the U.S. post at the International Legation in Shanghai, surprisingly little reporting on the Chinese Communists occurred. It is unclear whether this lack of emphasis was directed from the ONI or from each unit's fundamental misunderstanding of the wave behind Communism in general. Another possibility, however, is the issue of access, as explained previously. The danger in attempting to target, develop, and run sources inside Mao's inner circle was likely prohibitive, especially considering the United States' aversion to open conflict during this period. At any rate, intelligence during this period focused on Japanese capabilities and actions as well as the Chinese Nationalists' will to oppose them. This is understandable from a conventional military perspective (i.e., why would one choose to focus on the forces that are not officially in power?). Moreover, this could have further complicated Western understanding of Chinese Communism later. Therefore, while HUMINT was useful for purposes of developing situational awareness and preparing for future conflict, its use was also constrained.

Given the range of subjects that naval attachés and the Marines addressed during the Sino-Japanese War and the kinds of high-level sources discussed (e.g., Madam Chiang, T. V. Soong, and Tai Li), three explanations about intelligence management during this period are apparent. First, units in theater often drove the agenda by the kinds of intelligence they could most easily and expediently produce. Second, while this should not be overstated, by subordinate units at least partially driving the collection process, the DNI and other decision-makers (e.g., the secretary of the Navy and chief of naval operations) could carefully refine the kinds of intelligence targets they believed were important, as seen in the case of DNI Hayne Ellis (1931–34). Finally, while the absence of evidence of prioritized requirements does not mean they did not exist, there is some evidence to suggest a desire to use forward units to explore alternative requirements. Moreover, as this might appear to contradict the claim that the ONI (and thus the naval intelligence establishment) was a very centralized system prior to the war, requirement exploration on the DNI's part does not negate the fact that policy, training, institutional expertise, and higher-level strategy was highly centralized. As tensions between Japan and the West increased after 1939, requirements became more refined and derived from the ONI, further institutionalizing the naval intelligence establishment's prewar preparations.

As this book underscores, most notably in chapter 3 on the naval presence in China after World War II, HUMINT serves a different function in crisis than it does in war. This is likely more so the case with naval HUMINT because in war the Navy will focus the bulk of its operations at sea. In general, HUMINT is a unique kind of intelligence that requires the security, and access that wartime conditions prohibit, at least when it comes to the most sensitive of sources and targets. As the post–World War II case infers, unlike in war—where officers and enlisted personnel often give their lives to obtain the intelligence required to support decision-makers and operating forces—peace and crisis provide the needed cover that officialdom enables. Other forms of intelligence enjoy the safety of a stand-off position with which collection is enabled. War presents HUMINT with a susceptibility to open targeting by counterintelligence forces and the outright killing of agents. For these reasons, the post–World War II period—both in Washington and with the Navy and Marine Corps' continued presence in China during the Chinese Civil War—deeply contrasts with the period of the war. Naval intelligence in war has been studied exhaustively, but in crisis, less so.

A portion of the effort in this research explored the institutional fallout resulting from the end of the war with Japan and the deterioration of the Navy's relationship with Chiang Kai-shek's Kuomintang regime through the Sino-American Cooperative Organization (SACO). SACO garnered significant intelligence during the war in China, and the relationships with people, such as Tai Li, Chiang's head of the Jun Tong (Bureau of Investigation and Statistics, one of several Nationalist intelligence bodies), proved invaluable, as the body of research on the naval presence in China during the war has widely underscored.[8] As the Chinese Communists gained greater power, the Nationalists under Chiang fought to hold onto power, and Soviet influence in China increased, the ability for U.S. naval intelligence personnel to gather intelligence was greatly constrained. At the same time, the contested presence of Navy and Marine Corps forces in the country afforded valuable intelligence insight into the direction by which the Communist presence proceeded in the region. HUMINT following World War II was generally at an inflection point, in which business as usual was diverging from the changing winds in Washington.

While crises such as Western policy during the Chinese Civil War complicate the development of sources, the lingering military mission in the Far East was not the only challenge for the Navy and its intelligence enterprise in the years following World War II. The Marshall Mission, Marines monitoring the demobilization of Japanese forces in Manchuria, and the gradual dissolution of the U.S. naval presence in China all occurred while the entire U.S. national security apparatus experienced unprecedented changes. While the entire process was not complete until 1948—and arguably later, with the formation of the NSA—the Truman administration embarked upon the job of centralizing intelligence in January 1946 with the establishment of the Central Intelligence Group. Additionally, the military in general was going through a postwar institutional shock with tremendous budget and personnel cuts. The scramble on the part of Navy elites, such as DNI Thomas Inglis and Rear Adm. Sidney Souers—who Truman appointed the first Director of Central Intelligence—to shape the intelligence community was clear. Infighting between the Navy and Army was almost inevitable.

While the post–World War II case shows little in the way of immediate effects that the CIA's establishment had on the ONI or the naval intelligence community, this is understandable in its context. To be sure, naval intelligence was indeed affected institutionally, but operations in China were very disconnected with events in Washington. As the case concludes, this resulted in some chaos in the ability to manage and prioritize intelligence. Organizations such as the ONI attempted to find their way in a new world order in which the DNI was no longer the central authority but a player among a group of intelligence leaders now ultimately serving the

Director of Central Intelligence. While this had its downsides—certainly in contrast to the Navy's unmitigated history of centralized authority—naval intelligence practitioners eventually found a greater role in national intelligence, such as the national intelligence estimates that would soon come to be the standard. The practice of intelligence—certainly naval intelligence—did not keep pace with the policy and institutional changes among the bureaucracy before the last units were pushed out of China in 1949 with the ascent and final victory of the Chinese Communists over the Kuomintang. This meant that the lessons learned from the postwar presence in China would be considered within a new institutional framework.

Naval HUMINT during crises was again put to the test in the early Cold War period. The Taiwan crises of the 1950s brought the threat of the use of nuclear weapons between the West and the Communist Bloc. While the 1954–55 crisis was a display of the challenges and advantages of how the intelligence community established sources in and around Taiwan, the 1958 crisis demonstrated that they were generally of less relevance in the event of escalation and conflict termination. Again, the theme of access is relevant in this case. Ultimately, the most useful sources the Navy and Marine Corps found were those sympathetic to the Communist mainland on the Kinmen and Matsu islands and, more importantly, those with whom they liaised within the Kuomintang regime. None were developed on the Chinese mainland proper.

Still, as the 1958 crisis shows, the identification of new sources and the exploitation of existing ones held little value when decisions needed to be made at a heightened pace. As the case illustrates, Admiral Smoot's high-level sources were important, but they ultimately revealed more about the Taiwan leadership than Chinese Communist decision-making. This is another consistent theme in the Fleet's navigation of intelligence challenges during crises. Obviously, intelligence on the enemy is the primary mission, but occasionally this is far more prohibitive than the risk to access will allow. Moreover, it is possible that the more important targets during these crises were Chiang Kai-shek and his regime, which eventually yielded the realization that the Taiwan navy was not willing to continue fighting. Without Smoot's relationships with the Taiwan navy, it is possible that U.S. decision-makers in Washington would have unnecessarily escalated in 1958. In a sense, HUMINT was a decisive factor in the crisis, but it had little to do with developing sources in relation to the enemy. Instead, the case reflects the dark murkiness of crises and alliance relations in general in the Cold War, and the limitations of determining adversarial intentions.

For both the Taiwan Patrol Force and the Military Assistance and Advisory Group in Taiwan, the use of HUMINT sources were not integral in revealing the degree of Beijing's reliance on deceptive tactics for strategic gain (e.g., alternate-day bombing of the islands). The loss of access to sources on the Chinese mainland—or, more accurately, the fact that they never existed in the first place—following the Communist takeover in 1949 only added to the blindness in which Western intelligence found itself during the Taiwan crises. Ultimately, while HUMINT was important in discerning how Western support for Taiwan should continue, it was less useful in producing insights on Mao's intentions or a resolution to the crises advantageous to the West. To illustrate this, the offshore islands problem continued in the ensuing years, along with the need for better intelligence on the Chinese regime, yet this was nearly impossible without greater access to indigenous assets. While there are naval HUMINT lessons to learn from these crises—most notably the partnership between the CIA and the Navy and the liaison relationship with Taiwan government—the crises once again underscore the importance of being physically present to develop sources.

The case of the naval presence in the crises in Indochina (1959–65) explores a clandestine side of containment in Southeast Asia. This occurred in the years before general-purpose forces deployed to Vietnam, in which the Navy and Marine Corps experienced a new kind of contribution to policy. Ultimately, this changed the naval intelligence institution from the inside out. The stakes were increasingly high at this point in the Cold War as the Chinese (and, indirectly, the Soviets) counteractively supplied the Pathet Lao and Viet Minh efforts to establish long-term Communist footholds in the region. The use of naval units for collecting intelligence among the population and behind enemy lines was dangerous; such efforts were previously the work of the CIA. As the demand for intelligence increased, so grew the sensitivity of missions. Ultimately, this showed the unique value of HUMINT in crises in which contact with the enemy—and, thus, access to sources around the enemy—is experienced through the tool of secrecy.

The significance of the Kennedy-Johnson years on naval intelligence is that it solidified the modern evolution of the Navy and Marine Corps' role in the intelligence community that began prior to World War II. HUMIINT was a fundamental aspect of the U.S. prosecution of the crises in Indochina before the situation evolved into an all-out war. Indeed, like any counterinsurgency, it was a localized war among the people, where strategic inflection points were unclear from day to day. Ultimately, this made calculating the value of intelligence even more difficult. However, the intelligence collected during the early years of the Vietnam experience was different from what the Fleet experienced in years past because it represented more than the Fleet's awareness of an enemy or its capability. Chinese military general Sun Tzu (771–256 BC) refers to the "divine manipulation of the threads," which implies the use of all kinds of spies to affect a desired outcome.[9] This constituted an institutional paradox. On one hand, the institution of HUMINT in the Navy matured significantly. On the other, it mattered relatively little in relation to the outcome of the crisis. Still, it was this context in which the secretary of the Navy, Paul Nitze, granted the Navy official authorities to conduct clandestine intelligence in 1965. Ultimately, this changed the practice of naval HUMINT from a sideline task to a more fundamental part of the national mission, a culmination of a long institutional history decades in making. Still, as the history of this crisis (and the ensuing war) shows us, no amount of intelligence could save America from its policy failures.

Historically, U.S. naval HUMINT was not a central factor in whether the Navy and Marine Corps achieved victory in battle. Indeed, that is not its utility. Instead, HUMINT serves as an aggregate tool used repeatedly, sometimes with well-planned and purposeful regard and other times in an ad hoc manner. It certainly mattered, but the context in which it was employed also mattered. The archival record shows that it garners the best results when access to reliable enemy sources is greater, which is generally enabled during peace and in crises, not during war or when denied access by the enemy. Exceptions to this have been noted, but the issue of access is directly related to the nature of forward-deployed Navy operations. Institutionally, HUMINT will never be a primary focus of the Navy—that is not the role it is supposed to play—but the historical record shows it played a significant part in informing decision-makers at critical moments in crises in which the stakes impacted national security.

Appendix

Naval Attaché Reports (1930-41)

Naval Attaché Reports (1930–41)

Subject	1930	1931	1932	1933	1934	1935	1936	1937	1938	1939	1940	1941
Chinese strategic plans, policies, and concepts		1	1				1		1			
Counterintelligence and foreign intelligence	2		3		4	16	18	4	4	3		
Economy, resources, and commercial infrastructure	8	6	21	18	18	15	8	10	4	3	1	1
Enemy activity in third countries	4			1		4	3	2	13			2
Foreign relations	4	5	6	4	5	7	6	4	6		1	5
Geologic and hydrographic survey	2	1	7	1	2	2	5	2	4	2		
Geopolitics, disposition, and posture	3	2	2	3	2	4	5	1	1	1		5
Internal politics and leadership	16	10	24	7	9	22	21	18	12	5	1	1
Japanese strategic plans, policies, and concept	7		5	2	6	3	3		1			7
Life of the intelligence officer	1	4	2		1	2			1	1		
Military actions	5	7	16	1	2	1	2	13	9	3	2	9

Naval Attaché Reports (1930–41) *continued*

Subject	1930	1931	1932	1933	1934	1935	1936	1937	1938	1939	1940	1941
Oceania	1	2		2	2	10	8					
Order of Battle / Training	3	1	5	2	6	14	11	13	14	10	1	
Ports, bases, and maritime information	7	3	2	3	2	11	5	8	6			1
Shipbuilding, acquisitions, and budgets	7	6	6	4	6	1	3	6	2	1		
Signals and cryptology	4		2		1	3						
U.S. policy, tradecraft, and management	2	4	2	1	1	3	2	6	10	4	4	6
Totals	76	52	104	49	67	118	101	87	88	33	10	37

Notes

Introduction

1. For an account of the Marine Corps as a naval institution leading into World War II, see David J. Ulbrich, *Preparing for Victory: Thomas Holcomb and the Making of the Modern Marine Corps, 1936–1943* (Annapolis, MD: Naval Institute Press, 2011), 285. For more information on the intelligence relationship during World War II, see Roger Dingman, *Deciphering the Rising Sun: Navy and Marine Corps Codebreakers, Translators, and Interpreters in the Pacific War* (Annapolis, MD: Naval Institute Press, 2009), 384.
2. Historical works about several aspects of the CIA are cited throughout this thesis. One of the more notable ones was Arthur Darling's *The Central Intelligence Agency: An Instrument of Government, to 1950* (University Park: Pennsylvania State University Press, 1990).
3. Mahan's work of the late nineteenth century characterized the claim that great nations require great navies to protect commerce and present a formidable threat to other nations' navies through the deployment of battleship squadrons. This was done through decisive fleet battles. See Alfred Thayer Mahan, *The Influence of Sea Power upon History, 1660–1783* (Boston: Little, Brown, 1890).
4. For a work on naval operational intelligence in World War II and the Cold War, see Christopher Ford and David Alan Rosenberg, *The Admirals' Advantage: U.S. Operational Intelligence in World War II and the Cold War* (Annapolis, MD: Naval Institute Press, 2005), 219.
5. For a thorough discussion of the potential for naval intelligence research at the end of the Cold War, see John B. Hattendorf, *Ubi Sumus? The State of Naval and Maritime History* (Newport, RI: Naval

War College, 1994), 419. Also see John Prados, *Combined Fleet Decoded* (New York: Random House, 1995). British accounts of naval intelligence are vastly explored as well. For a classic account of how the Admiralty innovated the cryptanalysis discipline during World War I, see Patrick Beesly, *Room 40: British Naval Intelligence 1914–1918* (Oxford: Oxford University Press, 1984), 352.

6. John Keegan, *Intelligence in War: The Value and Limitations of What the Military Can Learn about the Enemy* (London: Vintage, 2004), 99–143.

7. Since earlier times, when armies in Egypt and others across the Eastern empires first used sea craft, nation-states went to sea to affect their power over people and territories. As armies needed information about each one's rivals, they often sent emissaries to meet with the enemy, both for diplomatic reasons and for collecting secret information from the enemy. See Hans Delbrück, *Warfare in Antiquity: History of the Art of War*, vol. 1, trans. Walter J. Renfroe Jr. (Lincoln: University of Nebraska Press, 1990), 251.

8. This is due to various reasons, including continued classification, lost or stolen materials, and poor recordkeeping.

9. For a U.S. institutional account of how the missions of coordinating HUMINT and SIGINT were given to the CIA and NSA in the early Cold War as well as the implications for agencies such as the Office of Naval Intelligence (ONI), see Roger Hilsman, *Strategic Intelligence and National Decisions* (Glencoe, IL: Free Press, 1956), 28, 37.

10. Concerning covert operations in the Far East and Pacific, see William B. Breuer and Douglas MacArthur, *MacArthur's Undercover War: Spies, Saboteurs, Guerrillas, and Secret Missions* (Edison, NJ: Castle, 2005), 257. For an examination of enemy intelligence in the Pacific, see Ken Kotani and Chiharu Kotani, *Japanese Intelligence in World War II* (Oxford: Osprey, 2009), 232. For a thorough account of the U.S.–Chinese intelligence relationship during the war from a Chinese perspective, see Qi Xisheng, *Allies at Swords' Points: The Sino–U.S. Military Cooperative Relationship during the Pacific War Period (1941–1945)* (Taipei: Linking, 2011), 694. For an authoritative history of the OSS during the war, see Kermit Roosevelt, *War Report of the OSS (Office of Strategic Service)* (New York: Walker, 1976), 261.

11. For a complete discussion of the differences of intelligence application in war and peace, see Peter Jackson and Jennifer Siegel, *Intelligence and Statecraft: The Use and Limits of Intelligence in International Society* (Westport, CT: Praeger, 2005), 302.
12. There are countless examples of the differences in intelligence use during war and peace. For example, John Prados traces the how various twentieth-century U.S. presidents used intelligence to further policies during the Cold War. See John Prados, *Presidents' Secret Wars: CIA and Pentagon Covert Operations since World War II* (New York: Morrow, 1986), 480.
13. Consider one of the quintessential works on how the U.S. national security complex was established in the years following World War II. See Amy B. Zegart, *Flawed by Design: The Evolution of the CIA, JCS, and NSC* (Stanford, CA: Stanford University Press, 1999), 336.
14. John Keegan spoke of the limitations of conducting intelligence collection in time of war in his case on Nazi development of the V2 rocket. See Keegan, *Intelligence in War*, 221–257. Also see Richard K. Betts, "Analysis, War, and Decision: Why Intelligence Failures Are Inevitable," *World Politics* 31 (October 1978): 61–89.
15. This kind of structural approach has generally been effective in past works. See Huw Dylan, *Defense Intelligence and the Cold War: Britain's Joint Intelligence Bureau, 1945–1964* (Oxford: Oxford University Press, 2014), 256. Also see Percy Cradock, *Know Your Enemy: How the Joint Intelligence Committee Saw the World* (London: John Murray, 2002), 362. Specifically relevant to this research, Cradock looks at cases including the Berlin Blockade (1948), Korean War, Sino–Soviet Dispute, and American involvement in Vietnam.
16. Several thousand pages of archival research collected at the National Archives in the course of this research were not used. While historically located on a single local computer at the National Archives in College Park, Maryland, the CIA began transitioning CREST to an Internet-based database in 2016. About half of the research found in CREST was retrieved on-site at College Park and half through the online database.
17. For example, among others, these included the Texas Tech University Vietnam Center and Archive, the Wilson Center Digital Archive, and the Pedro Loureiro Collection at the University of Southern California

Digital Library, the latter of which included several records essential to the examination of pre–World War II intelligence.

18. For instance, it is discussed very minimally in Jeffrey Dorwart's seminal work on the first three decades of the ONI. See Jeffrey M. Dorwart, *The Office of Naval Intelligence* (Annapolis, MD: Naval Institute Press, 1979), 216. Also, in Stedman Chandler's work, published just after World War II, it appears as though naval spying for operational (or "frontline") intelligence was indeed a discipline, but perhaps one that required little more than a handbook to engage in it. See Stedman Chandler and Robert W. Robb, *Front-Line Intelligence* (Washington, DC: U.S. Marine Corps, 1986), 192.

19. It should be noted that officers selected for duty as an embassy attaché undergo HUMINT training not by the Navy but by the DIA, under which they then fall directly in that role.

20. See specifically Packard's chapter on HUMINT as well as the chapter on naval attachés: Wyman H. Packard, *A Century of U.S. Naval Intelligence* (Washington, DC: Office of Naval Intelligence and Naval Historical Center, Department of the Navy, 1996), 58–93, 130–35.

21. Dennis L. Noble, "A U.S. Naval Intelligence Mission to China in the 1930s: Operations in Another Time," *Studies in Intelligence* 50, no. 2 (2006), https://www.cia.gov/resources/csi/static/Naval-Intel-China-Mission.pdf.

22. Crisis studies began as a substantive discipline in the Cold War in which part of the struggle was carried out in the context of nuclear deterrence and part through violent proxy wars in the third world. For a discussion of the causes of war under these circumstances, see Bernard Brodie, *War and Politics* (New York: Macmillan, 1973), 276–340.

23. For a theoretical discussion of crisis in international affairs, see Warren Phillips and Richard Rimkunas, "The Concept of Crisis in International Politics," *Journal of Peace Research* 15, no. 3 (1978): 259–72.

24. This was generally the case in a substantively thorough examination of crisis research. See Richard W. Parker, "An Examination of Basic and Applied International Crisis Research," *International Studies Quarterly* 21, no. 1 (1977): 225–46.

25. How one considers quick-onset crises versus longer-term ones is subjective and worth further analysis. For instance, see the official CIA history of Able Archer (1983) and how Soviet nuclear alert

and U.S. psychological operations combined to create a crisis over a number of days. Benjamin B. Fischer, *A Cold War Conundrum: The 1983 Soviet War Scare* (Langley, VA: Center for the Study of Intelligence, 2007), https://www.cia.gov/resources/csi/static/Cold-War-Conundrum.pdf. Also see David Gioe, Len Scott, and Christopher Andrew, eds., *An International History of the Cuban Missile Crisis: A 50-Year Retrospective* (London: Routledge Studies in Intelligence: 2014).

26. Arthur N. Gilbert and Paul Gordon, "Crisis Management: An Assessment and Critique," *Journal of Conflict Resolution* 24, no. 4 (1980): 641–64. Some have attempted to use a crisis as an opportunity to pursue decisive military options, such as the Air Force chief of staff, Gen. Curtis LeMay, during the Cuban missile crisis. Graham Allison and Philip Zelikow, *Essence of Decision: Explaining the Cuban Missile Crisis*, 2nd ed. (New York: Longman, 1999), 226–27.

27. Rose McDermott, Jonathan Cowden, and Cheryl Koopman, "Framing, Uncertainty, and Hostile Communications in a Crisis Experiment," *Political Psychology* 23, no. 1 (2002): 133–49.

28. For instance, the use of guerillas or covert action to avert or change the course of a crisis might have negative consequences and create an escalatory environment. See J. K. Zawodny, "Guerrilla and Sabotage: Organization, Operations, Motivations, Escalation," *Annals of the American Academy of Political and Social Science* 341 (May 1962): 8–18.

29. Kemp Tolley, *Yangtze Patrol: The U.S. Navy in China* (Annapolis, MD: Naval Institute Press, 1971), 329.

30. While the sinking of the *Panay* was publicized as an accident and the Japanese aviator who bombed it was severely punished, the situation was grave and could have resulted in a much harsher U.S. response. For a history of the sinking of the *Panay*, see Hamilton Darby Perry, *The Panay Incident: Prelude to Pearl Harbor* (Toronto, ON: Macmillan, 1969), 295.

31. Chen Jian, *Mao's China and the Cold War* (Chapel Hill: University of North Carolina Press, 2001), 167–70.

32. For example, while there was military use of force (and people died), the Taiwan events of the 1950s have been treated as crises. See Richard Bush, *At Cross Purposes: U.S.–Taiwan Relations since 1942* (Abingdon, U.K.: Routledge, 2004).

33. For a thoughtful, modern discussion of intelligence, see Gregory F. Treverton, Seth G. Jones, Steven Boraz, and Phillip Lipscy, *Toward a Theory of Intelligence: Workshop Report* (Santa Monica, CA: RAND, 13 February 2006), 35. Related to this, also see Michael Warner, "Wanted: A Definition of 'Intelligence,'" *Studies in Intelligence* 46, no. 3 (2002).
34. David Omand, "Securing the State: A Question of Balance" (transcript, Chatham House, 8 June 2010), https://www.chathamhouse.org/sites/default/files/public/Meetings/Meeting%20Transcripts/080610davidomand.pdf, 2. Also see David Omand, *Securing the State* (Oxford: Oxford University Press, 2014), 288.
35. Packard, *A Century of U.S. Naval Intelligence*, xix.
36. The term "actions" is often eschewed in military intelligence references because it connotes activities that are regularly associated with the CIA and NSA. A choice was made in the research for this book to include it because there are countless instances in which the Navy was involved in the planning, operations, or oversight of such activities. "Activities" has sometimes replaced verbs such as "influence," as in Michael Warner's definition of it: "Intelligence is secret state or group activity to understand or influence foreign entities." See Warner, "Wanted."
37. L. V. Scott and R. Gerald Hughes, eds. *Intelligence, Crises and Security: Prospects and Retrospects* (London: Routledge, 2008), 256. Also see Richard Betts, *Soldiers, Statesmen, and Cold War Crises* (New York: Columbia University Press, 1991), 326. For an earlier, and important, work on this level of escalation, see George Armand Furse, *Information in War: Its Acquisition and Transmission (Parts I–IV)* (London: W. Cloves & Sons, 1895).
38. Some allude to the fact that intelligence is not the sole weapon of victory. It has limitations. Where in some cases operational planning could win a battle even if the intelligence is mediocre, intelligence is simply a tool for decision-making. See Sherman Kent, *Strategic Intelligence: For American World Policy* (Hamden, CT: Archon, 1965), 252. Kent defines strategic intelligence as "the kind of knowledge our state must possess regarding other states in order to assure itself that its cause will not suffer nor its undertaking fail because its statesmen and soldiers plan and act in ignorance."
39. Ford and Rosenberg, *The Admirals' Advantage*, 219.

40. Richard K. Betts, *Enemies of Intelligence: Knowledge and Power in American National Security* (New York: Columbia University Press, 2007), 241.
41. Clive Jones, "Where the State Feared to Tread: Britain, Britons, Covert Action and the Yemen Civil War, 1962–64," in Scott and Hughes, *Intelligence, Crises and Security*, 65–85. Also see Gregory F. Treverton, *Covert Action: The CIA and the Limits of American Intervention in the Postwar World* (London: Tauris, 1988), 28–31, 234–35; and Loch K. Johnson, *Intelligence: Critical Concepts in Military, Strategic & Security Studies* (London: Routledge, 2011), 1,776.
42. Barry Posen explored the roots of inadvertent escalation in both nuclear and conventional crises in the later part of the Cold War. Many of its tenets are applicable to historical cases. See Barry Posen, *Inadvertent Escalation: Conventional War and Nuclear Risks* (Ithaca, NY: Cornell University Press, 1992), 280.
43. In his work on Western naval intelligence, Richard Deacon describes the means by which Benjamin Franklin used the first attaché system to gather, manipulate, and share intelligence with the American Continental Army, his French allies, and the British, particularly as it related to commercial shipping. See Richard Deacon, *The Silent War: A History of Western Naval Intelligence* (London: Grafton Books, 1978), 13–26.
44. See Keegan's chapter on radio intelligence during World War I titled "Wireless Intelligence." Keegan, *Intelligence in War*, 99–143.
45. The U.S. naval attaché system began the same year the ONI was established, with the assignment of Lt. Cdr. French E. Chadwick to the U.S. embassy in London. See Packard, *A Century of U.S. Naval Intelligence*, 59.
46. Keeping in mind that ambassadors outrank chiefs of stations, some embassies worked closer with CIA stations than others. Sometimes this relationship depends on the post and the degree to which leadership in Washington compels them to work together. Karl Lott Rankin's account of his time as U.S. ambassador to China discussed the embassy's relationship with intelligence services; see Karl Lott Rankin, *China Assignment* (Seattle: University of Washington, 1964), 343.
47. There is a substantial body of work on the relationship between the civilian intelligence services, particularly during World War II. For example, for more detail on Linda Kush's work on the Sino-American Cooperative Organization's (SACO, originally known as the

Naval Group China) relationship with the OSS during World War II, see Linda Kush, *The Rice Paddy Navy: US Sailors Undercover in China* (Oxford: Osprey, 2012), 294. For an OSS account of the relationship, see Roosevelt, *War Report of the OSS*, 261. For a discussion of CIA's relationship with the military during the Vietnam War, see Michael Warner, "'U.S. Intelligence and Vietnam': The Official Version," *Intelligence and National Security* 25, no. 5 (2010): 611–37.

48. Chief of Naval Operations, *History of Navy HUMINT (Human Source Intelligence) 1974*, 200071, declassified 6 August 1991, National Security Archives, http://www2.gwu.edu/~nsarchiv/NSAEBB/NSAEBB46/.

49. Arthur Darling, "With Vandenberg as DCI," *Studies in Intelligence* 12, no. 3 (1996).

50. Zegart, *Flawed by Design*, 167–81.

51. On the controversy of domestic spying, see Jeffery M. Dorwart, *Conflict of Duty: U.S. Navy's Intelligence Dilemma, 1919–1945* (Annapolis, MD: Naval Institute Press, 1983), 71–85. For more information on the controversy of domestic intelligence that involved the U.S. Navy during the years just following World War I, see Dorwart, *Conflict of Duty*, 10–18; also see Packard, *A Century of U.S. Naval Intelligence*, 300–305.

52. See Noble, "A U.S. Naval Intelligence Mission to China in the 1930s."

53. Roger Thompson, *Lessons Not Learned: The U.S. Navy's Status Quo Culture* (Annapolis, MD: Naval Institute Press, 2007), 288.

54. Jeffrey T. Richelson, "Task Force 157: The U.S. Navy's Secret Intelligence Service, 1966–77," *Intelligence and National Security* 11, no. 1 (1996): 106–45.

55 This structure is similar to the one in Steve Levine and Michael Hunt's *Arc of Empire: America's War in Asia from the Philippines to Vietnam* (Chapel Hill: University of North Carolina Press, 2012).

56. For a unique work on U.S. naval presence in China in the interwar years and the shape of this informal intelligence, see William Reynolds Braisted, *Diplomats in Blue: U.S. Naval Officers in China, 1922–1933* (Gainesville: University Press of Florida, 2009), 560.

57. Particularly descriptive of this is Packard's chapters on electronic intelligence and imagery intelligence, in that a technological revolution occurred in the interwar years (particularly 1935–38) in the areas of radar communications and sensors and aerial reconnaissance. Packard, *A Century of U.S. Naval Intelligence*, 94–106, 194–97.

58. For an extensive discussion of the impact of radar intelligence on the Joint Intelligence Center for Pacific Ocean Areas and allied victory against Japan, see Jeffrey M. Moore, *Spies for Nimitz: Joint Military Intelligence in the Pacific War* (Annapolis, MD: Naval Institute Press, 2004), 236–38, 280. As Moore highlights, however, despite the abundance of information that signals data provided in the war, failures often occurred. He classified intelligence failures into four categories: those resulting from process errors, those resulting from a commander not paying attention to the intelligence provided, those resulting from a lack of consideration of the guidance provided by a commander, and those resulting from effective deception by the enemy.
59. Of the various accounts of both wartime and peacetime naval HUMINT found in the body of literature, most are either narrative histories, memoirs, or romanticized accounts of individual naval spies, attachés, and flag officers. This contrasts the fact that works related to SIGINT often discuss the discipline itself and its role across the entire fleet. See Ronald Lewin, *Ultra Goes to War: The Secret Story* (London: Hutchinson, 1978).
60. The surface warfare officer and the fighter aviator are generally the two communities that most often rise to prominent leadership positions in the Navy. More recently, submariners have garnered similar influence.
61. For discussions on the intelligence officer in the historical context of greater Navy career tracks, see Packard's chapters titled "Organization and Personnel" and "Officer Training in Naval Intelligence." Packard, *A Century of U.S. Naval Intelligence*, 330–43, 365–77, respectively. Beyond this, one other volume treats the career track issue (particular in the Cold War) with tangential anecdotes, but again mostly focusing on the SIGINT story. See Peter A. Huchthausen and Alexandre Sheldon-Duplaix, *Hide and Seek: The Untold Story of Cold War Naval Espionage*, (Hoboken, NJ: Wiley, 2009).

Chapter 1. Intelligence in the Interwar Years

1. While U.S. foreign policy evolved into a more militarily competitive one later in the 1930s, as the threat of Japanese expansion in

the Pacific intensified, U.S. isolationism marked the better part of the decade in which naval forces in the Far East largely applied a "hands-off" approach to the Japanese military. FDR knew that—despite Tokyo's trend toward confrontation with the West over the long term—he faced a depression-era Congress ultimately unwilling to grant him expanded powers to mitigate the threat. See Department of State, Office of the Historian, *Milestones: 1921–1936: The Great Depression and U.S. Foreign Policy*, accessed 7 December 2015, https://history.state.gov/milestones/1921-1936/great-depression.

2. J. D. Hittle, "The Marine Corps Battalion Intelligence Service," *Marine Corps Gazette* 25, no. 4 (November 1941).

3. Unlike today, prior to World War II, the ONI had operational control of the naval attachés at embassies and could task them according to Navy intelligence priorities.

4. Department of State, *A Guide to the United States History of Recognition, Diplomatic, and Consular Relations, by Country, since 1776, China*, Office of the Historian, available at https://history.state.gov/countries/china.

5. FDR was personally an avid consumer of naval intelligence in a way most other U.S. presidents were not. See Christopher Andrew, *For the President's Eyes Only: Secret Intelligence and the American Presidency from Washington to Bush* (New York: Harper Collins, 1995), 75–122. Andrew pointed out that FDR was fascinated by HUMINT since his days as assistant secretary of the Navy, often getting deeply involved in the ONI's collections and covert operations (76–77). Also see Hal Vaughan's work on the FDR-directed pre–World War II covert operation in northern Africa, which eventually enabled Operation Torch. Hal Vaughan, *FDR's 12 Apostles: The Spies Who Paved the Way for the Invasion of North Africa* (Guilford, CT: Lyons, 2006), 311.

6. See, for example, Kemp Tolley, *Yangtze Patrol: The U.S. Navy in China* (Annapolis, MD: Naval Institute Press, 1971). The pre–World War II period is less often an area of focus simply because there are fewer records, which is directly correlated with the fact that there were fewer American forces and less activity in the region.

7. Edwin P. Hoyt, *The Lonely Ships: The Life and Death of the Asiatic Fleet* (New York: David McKay, 1976). Also see Michael Schaller, *The U.S. Crusade in China, 1938–1945* (New York: Columbia University

Press, 1979). For a memoir history of naval intelligence, which underscores the treatment of the term "naval intelligence" during the 1930s Navy as being what one would today consider HUMINT, see Tolley, *Yangtze Patrol.*
8. Jeffrey M. Dorwart, *Conflict of Duty: The U.S. Navy's Intelligence Dilemma, 1919–1945* (Annapolis, MD: Naval Institute Press, 1983), 3–93.
9. For more information on the atrophied intelligence capabilities of the U.S. Navy in the interwar years, see Wyman H. Packard, *A Century of U.S. Naval Intelligence* (Washington, DC: Office of Naval Intelligence, 1996), 42–43.
10. Packard, *A Century of U.S. Naval Intelligence,* 522; also see Dorwart, *Conflict of Duty,* 320.
11. This is in direct contrast to the databasing systems the U.S. intelligence community later relied on to track the reliability and credibility of each individual source.
12. For instance, in a report for a Lt. J. S. Chitwood in May 1939, the officer reports the source as a "personal observation," implying it was he who personally gathered the information in the report. USS *Mindanao,* "Subject: Japan, Canton, China, Ships—Special Types (Boats)," *Intelligence Report,* Serial number 45–1, 16 May 1939, RG 38, Entry 98, Box 929, NARA, via the Pedro Loureiro Collection at the University of Southern California Digital Library.
13. Office of Naval Intelligence, *Weekly Summary,* 5 April 1941, OP-16-F-2, RG 38, Entry 98, Box 331, NARA.
14. Department of State, Office of the Historian, Foreign Relations of the United States Diplomatic Papers, 1935, *The Far East,* vol. 3: *The Far Eastern Crisis,* accessed 10 August 2018, https://history.state.gov/historicaldocuments/frus1935v03/comp1.
15. The archival record shows this, more often in the form of aggressive Japanese intelligence collection (and, later, sabotage operations) against the West. See Director of Naval Communications to Director of Naval Intelligence, 7 April 1932, OP-20-O, (SC) A7-2, RG 38, NARA. Also see Commandant, Thirteenth Naval District to CNO (Director of Naval Intelligence) (Japanese Situation; 13th Naval District), 18 October 1935, 13ND-16/67 (Ng), RG 38, NARA.
16. It was agreed that the United States and United Kingdom would each have 500,000 tonnes, and Japan would have 300,000 tons.

17. Daniel Marx Jr., "American Shipping and the Sino-Japanese War," *Far Eastern Survey* 8, no. 14 (5 July 1939): 159–65. Also see Andrew Kelly, "The Sino-Japanese War and the Anglo-American Response," *Australian Journal of American Studies* 32, no. 2 (December 2013): 27–43.
18. At earliest, one would consider the so-called Far East Station. See Robert E. Johnson, *Far East Station: The U.S. Navy in Asian Waters, 1800–1898* (Annapolis, MD: Naval Institute Press, 1979).
19. This was clear in FDR's published letters. See Elliott Roosevelt, *The Roosevelt Letters*, vol. 3: *1928–1945* (London: George G. Harrap, 1952), 201, 228–29.
20. Tony Saich, *From Rebel to Ruler: One Hundred Years of the Chinese Communist Party* (Cambridge, MA: Belknap Press of Harvard University Press, 2021), 67–73. Also see James E. Sheridan, *China in Disintegration* (New York: Free Press, 1975), 171–73.
21. The Nanking decade began with Generalissimo Chiang Kai-shek taking Nanking from warlord Sun Chuanfang in 1927 and moving the Republic of China's capital from Beijing (also referred to as Peking or Peiping) to Nanking. It ended with the Japanese invasion in December 1937 in what is referred to as the Nanking massacre. See Sheridan, *China in Disintegration*, 207–44.
22. The Japanese invasion of Manchuria ostensibly resulted in the Hoover–Stimson Doctrine. See Richard N. Current, "The Stimson Doctrine and the Hoover Doctrine," *American Historical Review* 59, no. 3 (April 1954): 513–42.
23. "The Fourth Regiment of Marines was reinforced by a detachment of eight officers and 326 Marines and by the Marine Detachment of the USS *Houston*." C. H. Metcalf, "The Marines in China," *Marine Corps Gazette* 22, no. 3 (September 1938). The 31st Army Regiment was also temporarily transferred from the Philippines, arriving in Shanghai on 5 February 1932.
24. Alan Armstrong's book *Preemptive Strike* examines in masterful detail the plan (Joint Board Plan 355) that FDR endorsed on 23 July 1941 to preemptively attack Japanese supply lines and provide the Chinese with 150 manned bombers and 350 fighters with which to disrupt Japanese actions in the Far East. See Alan Armstrong, *Preemptive Strike: The Secret Plan That Would Have Prevented the Attack on Pearl Harbor* (Guilford, CT: Lyons, 2006), 285.

25. This is significantly different from how nondemocratic societies tended to use intelligence. For instance, consider the way Stalin used intelligence produced by KGB predecessor organizations NKVD, MGB, and MVD, particularly under chiefs Lavrenti Beria and Vsevolod Merkulov. See Christopher M. Andrew and Oleg Gordievsky, *KGB: The Inside Story of Its Foreign Operations from Lenin to Gorbachev* (New York: HarperPerennial, 1991), 107–72.
26. Dorwart, *Conflict of Duty*, 47–57.
27. The CNO directly referenced the policy in an archived memorandum later in 1939. See CNO to unnamed recipient, 20 November 1939, OP-16-B-3, A8-5/QQ/Gorin, M., RG 38, Entry 98, Box 43, NARA.
28. Packard, *A Century of U.S. Naval Intelligence*, 13, 334.
29. Packard, *A Century of U.S Naval Intelligence*, 334.
30. As will be evident in the myriad sources throughout this research, countless incidents depict the DNI directly interacting with units subordinate to CINCAF.
31. No specific guiding directive was found as to how this came about and under which DNI, but it was deduced by the fact that ONI occasionally reported information to subordinate units of the Fleet that local units had not already reported or found in the free press.
32. Packard, *A Century of U.S. Naval Intelligence*, 67–70.
33. A. Viola Smith, Trade Commissioner, "Industrial Explosives," 23 October 1937, No. 48, RG 38, Entry 98, Box 74, NARA.
34. Smith, "Industrial Explosives."
35. Records of sources in the archives were rare during this period, but when they were found, they were hardly formatted and minimally descriptive.
36. This was evident in much of the correspondence between the DNI and units in the Far East as well as in correspondence between the DNI and the chief of naval operations. For instance, see Director of Naval Intelligence to Chief of Naval Operations, "Subject: Intelligence Information—Cooperation of Officers of Merchant Marine Naval Reserve," 28 March 1940, RG 38, Entry 98, Box 134, NARA.
37. DNI Captain Hayne Ellis to Commander Archer M. R. Allen (USS *Stewart*), 6 January 1934, OP-16, RG 38, Entry 98, Box 134, NARA.
38. Ellis to Allen.

39. Such was evidenced in his message to CINCAF in March 1932 in which he requested information on the identity of Chinese commanders, unit strengths, and locations on behalf of the War Department. See Director of Naval Intelligence to Commander in Chief, Asiatic Fleet, 11 March 1932, RG 38, Entry 98, Box 134, NARA.
40. Dorwart devoted a significant amount of effort to discussing Puleston's changes to the ONI structure and policy. See Dorwart, *Conflict of Duty*, 59–90.
41. In the course of the research, records of the naval districts were found, but few if any were concerned with the Sino-Japanese War.
42. Department of the Navy, "Director of Naval Intelligence to Fourth Regiment, USMC Expeditionary Force," 17 February 1932, RG 38, Entry 43, Box 134, NARA.
43. W. D. Puleston, Captain (Director of Naval Intelligence) to Commander-in-Chief, U.S. Fleet, "State of Training Japanese Fleet," Office of Naval Intelligence, 20 March 1935, OP-1a-8-11, A8-3/SF39(S-8), RG 38, Entry 98, Box 136, NARA.
44. Puleston to Commander-in-Chief.
45. Rear Admiral R. L. Ghormley, Chief of War Plans Division, Office of the Chief of Naval Operations to President, Naval War College, 2 August 1939, OP-CS-CTB S.1.37 (SC)A7-3(1), Serial 309, RG 80, NARA. See also Packard, *A Century of U.S. Naval Intelligence*, 379–81; the official list of Naval War College (1918–41) studies is available in the National Archives in Washington, DC. Of the studies included throughout the 1930s (128), 47 directly concerned Japan and Japanese military capabilities. Many others dealt with Japan in global context amongst analyses of other nations' military capabilities.
46. Ghormley to President, Naval War College.
47. Office of Naval Intelligence, "Memorandum for the Secretary, General Board: Present Strength of Italian, German, and Japanese Navies in comparison with United States' authorized tonnage as used by War Plans Division," 30 October 1939, OP-16B-C, (SC)A8-2/QS/5, RG 38, NARA.
48. W. J. Holmes, *Double-Edged Secrets: U.S. Naval Intelligence Operations in the Pacific during World War II* (Annapolis, MD: Naval Institute Press, 2013).
49. Office of Naval Intelligence, *Weekly Summary*, 5 April 1941.

50. Clearly, the United States did not support the status quo but went much further to impose an oil embargo on Japan in July 1941. See Jeffrey Record, *Japan's Decision for War in 1941: Some Enduring Lessons* (Carlisle Barracks, PA: Strategic Studies Institute, U.S. Army War College, February 2009).
51. Office of Naval Intelligence, Far East Section, *Weekly Summary*, 28 December 1940, OP-16-F-2, RG 80, NARA.
52. Office of Naval Intelligence, Far East Section, *Weekly Summary*, 22 February 1941, OP-16-F, RG 80, NARA.
53. Chief of Naval Operations (ONI), "Information Collected by the Division of Naval Intelligence—Dissemination and Application of," 18 March 1940, OP-16-F, A8/EN3-10, Serial No. 110916, RG 38, NARA.
54. CNO (ONI), "Information Collected."
55. Chief of Naval Operations to Naval Attaché, "Subject: Secret Communication between Naval and Military Attachés," 14 January 1930 (Declassified 26 March 2015), RG 38, Entry 98, Box 53, NARA.
56. For example, the *Weekly Summary* referenced in note 54 used intelligence reporting derived from sources from the Asiatic Fleet Headquarters, the attaché in Nanking, and the Yangtze Fleet.
57. Office of Naval Intelligence, Far East Section, *Weekly Summary*, 9 September 1941, OP-16-F-2, RG 80, NARA.
58. ONI, *Weekly Summary*, 9 September 1941.
59. ONI, *Weekly Summary*, 9 September 1941.
60. ONI, *Weekly Summary*, 9 September 1941.
61. Document exploitation later became an explicit function within the HUMINT mission. See, for example, Headquarters Department of Army, *Intelligence* (FM 2-0), May 2004, 6-1.
62. Office of Naval Intelligence, Far East Section, *Weekly Summary*, 25 January 1941, OP-16-F-2, RG 80, NARA.
63. See Carolle J. Carter, *Mission to Yenan: American Liaison with the Chinese Communists, 1944–1947* (Lexington: University of Kentucky, 1997), 211–19. Also see Maochun Yu, *OSS in China: Prelude to Cold War* (Annapolis, MD: Naval Institute Press, 1996).
64. Office of Naval Intelligence, *Weekly Summary*, 16 March 1941, OP-16-F-2, RG 38, Entry 98, Box 68, NARA.
65. Office of Naval Intelligence, *Weekly Summary*, Far East, 10 May 1941, OP-16-F-2, RG 38, Entry 98, Box 68, NARA.

66. The *Panay* incident was probably the beginning of this reality, but provocations by Western shipping and the eventual U.S. oil embargo of Japan exacerbated the underlying problem.
67. CNO to Commander-in-Chief, Asiatic Fleet, "Intelligence Report—Cruise to Australia," 30 August 1934, OP-38-A-XW/8/29, (SC) A8-2, RG 38, Entry 98, Box 13, NARA.
68. Office of Naval Intelligence, "Promulgating Letter for ONI 22 (Notes on Espionage, Counter-Espionage and Passport Control)," 18 February 1935, OP-16-X, A16/CNO, (SC)A7-2(i), RG 38, Entry 98, Box 61, NARA.
69. C. E. Courtney (Director of Naval Communications) to Director of Naval Intelligence (Instruction in Security for Senior Officers), 4 February 1938, OP-20-GS, (SC) A7-2(2)/A6, RG 38, NARA.

Chapter 2. Collection and Observation in the Second Sino-Japanese War

1. Department of the Navy, *Annual Reports of the Navy Department for the Fiscal Year (Including Operations to November 15, 1931)* (Washington, DC: Government Printing Office, 1931), RG 38, NARA.
2. This was more often the case in the years preceding Captain Puleston as the DNI.
3. Wyman H. Packard, *A Century of U.S. Naval Intelligence* (Washington, DC: Office of Naval Intelligence, 1996), 391–93.
4. S. D. McCaughey (USS *Smith Thomson*), *Wei Hai Wei* (Intelligence Report), 12–13 August 1933, Serial No. 1–33, RG 38, Entry 98, Box 1033, NARA. Also see Walter E. Brown (USS *Whipple*), "Wei Hai Wei, China," Serial No. 1–33. 5–6 August 1933, RG 38, Entry 98, Box 1033, NARA.
5. Commander J. M. Creighton, *Ta Wah Petroleum Company, Ltd., Tientsin, China*, U.S. Asiatic Fleet, Serial Number 490-15, 11 December 1935, RG 38, EN 98, Box 995, NARA.
6. For example, the naval attaché felt free to send a memo directly to the commanding officer of the *Panay* during the hostilities of November 1937. See J. M. McHugh, Assistant Naval Attaché (Nanking) to Commanding Officer, USS *Panay*, 20 November 1937, Secret file

#a-1/100, RG 38, EN 81, Box 281, NARA. Also see Department of the Navy, "Director of Naval Intelligence to Fourth Regiment, US Marine Expeditionary Force," 17 February 1932, NARA, RG 38, Entry 43.
7. J. D. Hittle, "The Marine Corps Battalion Intelligence Service," *Marine Corps Gazette* 25, no. 4 (November 1941).
8. The Marine regiment's intelligence personnel most often fulfilled the role of observer sources or supplied the sources for ONI weekly summaries published after 1939. For more on the command structure during this period, see W. G. Winslow, *The Fleet the Gods Forgot: The U.S. Asiatic Fleet in World War II* (Annapolis, MD: Naval Institute Press, 2014), 3–4.
9. Lt. Cdr. R. M. Ihrig, USS *Augusta*, "Central Aircraft Factory," *Intelligence Report* (Serial no. 32-27), USS *Augusta*, 16 November 1936, RG 38, Entry 81, Box 67, NARA.
10. Office of Naval Intelligence, *Weekly Summary*, 15 May 1941, OP-16-F-2, RG 80, NARA.
11. ONI, *Weekly Summary*, 15 May 1941.
12. Office of Naval Intelligence, *Weekly Summary*, 31 May 1941, OP-16-F-2, RG 80, Entry 98, Box 68, NARA.
13. Barbara Tuchman discussed some typical overt activities in her chapter on the attaché office during the Sino-Japanese War, 1937–1939. See Barbara W. Tuchman, *Stilwell and the American Experience in China, 1911–45* (New York: Macmillan, 1971), 164–200. See also James Lilley and Jeffrey Lilley, *China Hands* (New York: Public Affairs, 2004), 3–47.
14. In the hundreds of pages discovered in the National Archives covering this period of the naval attaché, Stilwell's name was rarely mentioned. This could be for the same reason that the naval attaché reported through two chains of command (the Department of State and ONI).
15. McHugh to Commanding Officer, USS *Panay*, 20 November 1937.
16. McHugh to Commanding Officer, USS *Panay*, 20 November 1937.
17. Department of the Navy, "J. M. McHugh, Assistant Naval Attaché (Nanking) to Director of Naval Intelligence," Washington, DC (Japanese aviation material), 26 November 1937, Secret file #a-1/100, RG 38, EN 81, Box 281, NARA.

18. Department of the Navy, "J. M. McHugh, Assistant Naval Attaché."
19. McHugh to Commanding Officer, USS *Panay*, 20 November 1937.
20. Department of the Navy, "J. M. McHugh, Assistant Naval Attaché."
21. Department of the Navy, "J. M. McHugh, Assistant Naval Attaché."
22. Department of the Navy, "J. M. McHugh, Assistant Naval Attaché."
23. Department of the Navy, "J. M. McHugh, Captain, USMC (Assistant Naval Attaché) to Rear Admiral Ralston S. Holmes, USN, Director of Naval Intelligence," 3 March 1938, File a-1/102, Hankow, China, RG 38, Entry 81, Box 281, NARA.
24. Department of the Navy, "J. M. McHugh, Captain."
25. Department of the Navy, "J. M. McHugh, Captain." Dr. Wen was also found in the official Chinese government registry as a member of the Central Executive Committee later in 1942. See Chinese Ministry of Information, *Chinese Government Directory*, Chongqing, 1943, RG 38, Entry 98C, Box 10, NARA.
26. Department of the Navy, "J. M. McHugh, Captain."
27. Department of the Navy, "J. M. McHugh, Captain."
28. Department of the Navy, "J. M. McHugh, Captain."
29. See Ted Morgan, *FDR: A Biography* (New York: Simon and Schuster, 1985), 691–92.
30. John Prados, *Combined Fleet Decoded* (New York: Random House, 1995), 25–56.
31. The U.S. National Archives and Records Administration in Washington, DC, provided the author with a complete database of naval attaché report citations and archival record data on 25 March 2015. According to the National Archives, the database (including 20,814 titles) is the most complete of the period from 1900 to 1939.
32. Despite the Navy's clear interest in expanding the capability, this was still years before the expansion of signals technology as a means of collecting information for intelligence that took place in the early part of World War II. See Prados, *Combined Fleet Decoded*.
33. The importance of the attaché role in prewar reporting cannot be understated. Past research and memoir accounts underscored the unique position the job incurred. For example, for an account from a former British assistant military attaché in Berlin prior to World War II (and later director of general intelligence), see Kenneth Strong, *Intelligence at the Top: The Recollections of an Intelligence Officer* (London: Cassell,

1968). Also see Huw Dylan, *Defense Intelligence and the Cold War: Britain's Joint Intelligence Bureau, 1945–1964* (Oxford: Oxford University Press, 2014).
34. Ihrig, USS *Augusta*, 16 November 1936.
35. Prados, *Combined Fleet Decoded*, 7–10.
36. United States Asiatic Fleet, Destroyer Division Thirteen, USS *Barker*, *Intelligence Report on Military Characteristics of Weihaiwei, China*, Chefoo, China, 15 September 1935, RG 38, Entry 98, Box 1033, NARA.
37. United States Asiatic Fleet, *Intelligence Report on Military Characteristics of Weihaiwei, China*.
38. United States Asiatic Fleet, *Intelligence Report on Military Characteristics of Weihaiwei, China*.
39. For instance, in 1931 the ONI furnished CINCAF with information on a source inside China (W. H. Jansen, of Industrial and Educational Films), who would be willing to obtain and sell films showing intimate details of the Chinese army and navy for three dollars per foot. Director of Naval Intelligence to Commander-in-Chief, US Asiatic Fleet, USS *Houston*, 6 July 1931, OP-16-A, RG 38, Box 191, File A8–2/EF16, NARA.
40. W. S. Anderson, Director of Naval Intelligence to Chief of Naval Operations, "Subject: Intelligence Information—Cooperation of Officers of Merchant Marine Naval Reserve," 28 March 1940, RG 38, NARA.
41. For an enlightening essay on the value and challenges of employing merchant marines in intelligence, see Art Haberstich, *The Mariner as Agent*, Center for the Study of Intelligence, Approved for Release 1994, CIA Historical Review Program, 18 September 1995, available at https://www.cia.gov/resources/csi/static/The-Mariner-as-Agent.pdf.
42. Anderson to Chief of Naval Operations, "Subject: Intelligence Information," 28 March 1940.
43. Anderson to Chief of Naval Operations, "Subject: Intelligence Information," 28 March 1940.
44. U.S. Naval Reserve, "Captain H. Copeland (USNR) to Captain Hartigan," 29 March 1940, OP 30A-HGC, RG 38, NARA.
45. USNR, "Captain H. Copeland (USNR) to Captain Hartigan."
46. For a U.S. Navy perspective of the intelligence threat faced by Japan in the 1930s, see Ellis Zacharias, *Secret Missions: The Story of an Intel-*

ligence Officer (Annapolis, MD: Naval Institute Press, 2003), 448. The Fleet withheld classified documents from distribution to the Asiatic Fleet as far back as 1930 for fear of interception by the Japanese. Director of Intelligence to Commander in Chief, Asiatic Fleet, *Naval Message*, 21 May 1932, RG 38, NARA. During the 1930s the ONI became increasingly aware of both foreign and domestic infiltration of U.S. government personnel and facilities by the Japanese agents and those with an allegiance to Tokyo. Commandant, Thirteenth Naval District to CNO (Director of Naval Intelligence), "Japanese Situation; 13th Naval District," 18 October 1935, 13ND-16/67 (Ng), RG 38, NARA.

47. For a history of U.S. missionaries in China and relationships with the Chinese Nationalists prior to the 1930s, see Michael V. Metallo, "American Missionaries, Sun Yat-sen, and the Chinese Revolution," *Pacific Historical Review* 47, no. 2 (1978): 261–82. Also see Bruce S. Greenawalt, *Missionary Intelligence from China: American Protestant Reports, 1930–1950* (Chapel Hill: University of North Carolina Press, 1974).

48. Office of Naval Intelligence, *Weekly Summary*, 31 August 1940, RG 80, NARA.

49. Both the *Leatherneck* and the *Gazette* are U.S. Marine Corps publications with articles generally written by active duty, reserve, or retired Marines. Because their circulation consists generally of the U.S. naval community, potentially sensitive topics were often discussed with little regard for operational security, the way one might take into consideration today.

50. Samuel B. Griffith, "North China, 1937," *Marine Corps Gazette* 22, no. 4 (1938). Also see C. H. Metcalf, "The Marines in China," *Marine Corps Gazette* 22, no. 3 (September 1938).

51. Griffith, "North China, 1937."

52. Franklin Roosevelt frequently corresponded with Prime Minister Churchill as well as Secretary of State Cordell Hull on the strategic importance of confronting the Japanese threat. See Elliott Roosevelt, *The Roosevelt Letters*, vol. 3: *1928–1945* (London: George G. Harrap, 1952), 228–229 and 398–421.

53. This is most likely the result of FDR's fight with isolationists in Congress, such as Senator Robert Taft. See Morgan, *FDR: A Biography*, 602.

54. L. V. Scott and R. Gerald Hughes, *Intelligence, Crises and Security: Prospects and Retrospects* (London: Routledge, 2008), 256. Also see Richard K. Betts, *Soldiers, Statesmen, and Cold War Crises* (New York: Columbia University Press, 1991), 326.
55. Department of the Navy, "Chief of Naval Operations (DNI) to Commander in Chief, U.S. Fleet," 16 November 1935, OP-16-B, Serial 3351, RG 38, NARA.
56. Department of the Navy, "Chief of Naval Operations (DNI) to Commander in Chief, U.S. Fleet," 16 November 1935.
57. The United States generally supported an isolationist policy in the 1930s, and no amount of Roosevelt's influence to intervene convinced the opposition otherwise. Even Roosevelt's call for a "quarantine" of nations pursuing extraterritorial gains met with little interest. See Department of State, *American Isolationism in the 1930s*, Office of the Historian, accessed 2 January 2016, https://history.state.gov/milestones/1937-1945/american-isolationism.
58. Commandant, U.S. Naval Station Guam to CINC, Asiatic Fleet, "Activities of Japanese on the Island of Guam," 28 March 1929, RG 38, NARA.
59. Commandant, U.S. Naval Station Guam to CINC, Asiatic Fleet, "Activities of Japanese." "Source of information: Native of Guam recently returned from Saipan. Credibility—3.0." The report provided details of the numbers, dispositions, and military reinforcements of the Japanese administered islands. "It is estimated that the population of Saipan is 14,000 Japanese, 4000 Chamorros. . . . The Chamorran population is mistreated and mistrusted" (2). At the time there were only fifty-seven Japanese-born residents on the island.
60. Office of Naval Intelligence, *Weekly Summary*, 8 March 1941, OP-16-F-2, RG 80, NARA.
61. Office of Naval Intelligence, *Weekly Summary*, 14 June 1941, OP-16-F-2, RG 80, NARA.
62. Commander, Asiatic Fleet, "CINC Asiatic to NAVINTEL (ONI)," 28 February 1931, RG 38, NARA. For a definitive history of isolationist policy in the 1930s, see Manfred Jonas, *Isolationism in America 1935–1941* (Ithaca, NY: Cornell University Press, 1966), 312. For an alternative analysis of isolationism, see Bear Braumoeller's work in which Braumoeller discounts isolationism as "myth"

but contends that U.S. intervention in the 1930s largely focused on regions outside of the Asia Pacific. Bear F. Braumoeller, "The Myth of American Isolationism," *Foreign Policy Analysis* 6 (2010): 349–71.
63. Suddenly, in February 1932, the ONI was interested in the ensuing events. The DNI wrote to the 4th Regiment: "War Department desires following information: Chinese reinforcements recently moving by rail or road into Shanghai . . . what Chinese troops remain in Hangchow." Department of the Navy, "Director of Naval Intelligence to 4th Regiment," US Marine Expeditionary Force, Shanghai, China, 8 February 1932, NARA RG 38, Entry 98, Box 277.
64. William M. Miller and John H. Johnstone, *A Chronology of the United States Marine Corps*, Vol. 1, *1775–1934*, (Washington, DC: Historical Division Headquarters, U.S. Marine Corps, 1965), 128.
65. K. M. Lammers to 4th Regiment, SOP Shanghai, COMDESRON 5, Blackhawk, COMDT 16th, COMYANGRAT, 31 January 1932, RG 38, NARA. As of February 1932 the Marines in Shanghai totaled 1,700 and the Army's 31st Infantry detachment totaled 1,100. Meanwhile, the British army in Shanghai totaled 3,850. Military Intelligence Division (G-2), War Department General Staff, *Intelligence Summary*, 12 February 1932, RG 80, A8-1/E W (320212), NARA.
66. "Director of Naval Intelligence to 4th Regiment," US Marine Expeditionary Force, Shanghai, China, 8 February 1932, NARA RG 38, Entry 98, Box 277.
67. Commander, Asiatic Fleet, "CINC Asiatic Fleet—Am Minister China—USS *Tulsa* (Naval message)," 7 March 1932, RG 38, NARA.
68. Commander Mine Division Three to CINAF, "Observations of Activities," 7 February 1932, RG 38, Box 276, NARA.
69. Director of Intelligence to Commander in Chief, Asiatic Fleet, *Naval Message*, 21 May 1932.
70. For instance, in 1932 the ONI had 23 naval officers. By 1939 the ONI grew to 111 personnel (49 officers and 43 civilians at the headquarters, and 19 officers deployed, not including naval attachés). See Packard, *A Century of U.S. Naval Intelligence*, 343.
71. Carolyn A. Tyson, *A Chronology of the United States Marine Corps, 1935–1946*, vol. 2 (Washington, DC: History and Museums Division, Headquarters, U.S. Marine Corps, 1965), 2.

72. Commander, Asiatic Fleet, "CINCAF (Untitled Cable)," 6 December 1937, RG 38, Entry 81, Box 281, NARA.
73. Commander, Asiatic Fleet, "CINCAF (Untitled Cable)." This point was contradicted later the same day when CINCAF reported (exact source unknown) that the Chinese claimed they strengthened positions for the defense of the Kuyung Wuhu Line northwest of Nanking. CINCAF, 6 December 1937, NPG 1223, RG 38, Entry 81, Box 281, NARA.
74. CINCAF, 6 December 1937, NPG 1223, RG 38, Entry 81, Box 281, NARA.
75. CINCAF, 6 December 1937, NPG 1223, RG 38, Entry 81, Box 281, NARA.
76. Office of Naval Intelligence, *Weekly Summary*, 31 May 1941. Subsequently, Ambassador Grew in Tokyo protested Japanese seizure of U.S. equipment in Haiphong.
77. Tuchman, *Stilwell and the American Experience in China*, 150.
78. This is not to say that the United States did not have historically established relations with China, but it is evident the relationship was far more transactional than Washington's relationship with London and Paris.
79. Office of Naval Intelligence, *Weekly Summary*, 20 October 1940, OP-16-F-2, RG 80, NARA.
80. Commander, Asiatic Fleet, "CINCAF to ACTSECNAV," 25 July 1939, RG 127, Entry 38A, NARA.
81. Commander, Asiatic Fleet, "CINCAF to ACTSECNAV."
82. Office of Naval Intelligence, *Weekly Summary*, 16 August 1941, OP-16-F-2, RG 80, NARA.
83. ONI, *Weekly Summary*, 16 August 1941.
84. ONI, *Weekly Summary*, 16 August 1941.
85. Alexander George, "United States–Japan Relations Leading to Pearl Harbor," in *Forceful Persuasion: Coercive Diplomacy as an Alternative to War* (Washington, DC: United States Institute of Peace Press, 1991), 19–23.
86. Office of Naval Intelligence, *Weekly Summary*, 5 July 1941, OP-16-F-2, RG 80, NARA.
87. ONI, *Weekly Summary*, 8 March 1941.
88. Office of Naval Intelligence, *Weekly Summary*, 16 March 1941, OP-16-F-2, RG 80, NARA.

89. Office of Naval Intelligence, *Weekly Summary*, 22 March 1941, OP-16-F-2, RG 80, NARA.
90. Office of Naval Intelligence, *Weekly Summary*, 10 July 1941, OP-16-F-2, RG 80, NARA.
91. Office of Naval Intelligence, *Weekly Summary*, 23 August 1941, OP-16-F-2, RG 80, NARA.
92. ONI, *Weekly Summary*, 14 June 1941.
93. Office of Naval Intelligence, *Weekly Summary*, 30 August 1941, OP-16-F-2, RG 80, NARA.
94. ONI, *Weekly Summary*, 30 August 1941.
95. Jeffrey Dorwart discussed this at length in his chapter "New Deal for Intelligence." See Jeffrey M. Dorwart, *Conflict of Duty: The U.S. Navy's Intelligence Dilemma, 1919–1945* (Annapolis, MD: Naval Institute Press, 1983), 320.
96. Office of Naval Intelligence, *Weekly Summary*, 4 January 1941, RG 38, NARA.
97. Office of Naval Intelligence, *Weekly Summary*, 5 April 1941, RG 38, NARA.
98. ONI, *Weekly Summary*, 23 August 1941.
99. Office of Naval Intelligence, *Weekly Summary*, 22 May 1941, OP-16-F-2, RG 80, NARA.
100. ONI, *Weekly Summary*, 23 August 1941.
101. ONI, *Weekly Summary*, 23 August 1941.
102. Office of Naval Intelligence, *Weekly Summary*, 9 April 1941, OP-16-F-2, RG 80, NARA.
103. Office of Naval Intelligence, *Weekly Summary*, 7 June 1941, OP-16-F-2, RG 80, NARA.
104. ONI, *Weekly Summary*, 15 May 1941.
105. ONI, *Weekly Summary*, 23 August 1941.
106. CNO to unnamed recipient, 20 November 1939, OP-16-B-3, A8-5/QQ/Gorin, M., RG 38, Entry 98, Box 43, NARA.
107. Fred Borch summarized it in his 2003 work. See Fred L. Borch, "Comparing Pearl Harbor and 9/11: Intelligence Failure? American Unpreparedness? Military Responsibility?" *Journal of Military History* 67, no. 3 (2003): 845–60.

Chapter 3. Legacies of World War II and the Resumption of the Chinese Civil War, 1942–49

1. Earnest May studied this dichotomy in his research on post–World War II Western relations with China. See Earnest R. May, *The Truman Administration and China, 1945–1949* (New York: Lippincott, 1975), 221.
2. Harold M. Tanner, *The Battle for Manchuria and the Fate of China: Siping 1946* (Bloomington: Indiana University Press, 2013), 15–47.
3. Henry I. Shaw, *The United States Marines in North China, 1945–1949*, Historical Branch, G-3 Division, Headquarters, U.S. Marine Corps, 1960, 29.
4. There is scant evidence in the archival record showing the reaction of naval forces in the Pacific theater to the changes going on in Washington. A good example to underscore this is Lawrence Salisbury's research on aid to China during the civil war, in which the author makes little to no connection with the changes going on in national security policy in Washington. See Lawrence E. Salisbury, "New Aid to China," *Far East Survey* 17, no. 8 (1948).
5. This period was best contextualized for the Navy as the culmination in 1949 of the so-called Revolt of the Admirals, in which top Navy leadership openly opposed the Truman administration's attempt to do away with naval aviation in favor of the Air Force's strategic bombing approach. See Jeffrey G. Barlow, *Revolt of the Admirals: The Fight for Naval Aviation, 1945–1950* (Washington, DC: U.S. Government Printing Office, 1995), 420.
6. See Roy Stratton, *SACO: Rice Paddy Navy*, 2nd ed. (New York: U.S. Press & Graphics, 2004), 56.
7. Theodore H. White and Annalee Jacoby, *Thunder out of China* (New York: William Sloane Associates, 1946), 145–56.
8. Craig Shirley, *December 1941: 31 Days That Changed America and Saved the World* (Nashville, TN: Thomas Nelson, 2013).
9. See Robert F. Piacine, *Pearl Harbor: Failure of Intelligence?* (Newport, RI: Naval War College, 1997). More recently, see comparisons made between Pearl Harbor and 9/11. Fred L. Borch, "Comparing Pearl Harbor and 9/11: Intelligence Failure? American Unpreparedness?

Military Responsibility?" *Journal of Military History* 67, no. 3 (2003): 845–60.

10. Hamilton Darby Perry, *The Panay Incident: Prelude to Pearl Harbor* (Toronto: Macmillan, 1969).
11. Christopher Ford and David Alan Rosenberg, *The Admirals' Advantage: U.S. Operational Intelligence in World War II and the Cold War* (Annapolis, MD: Naval Institute Press, 2005).
12. John Prados, *Combined Fleet Decoded* (New York: Random House, 1995), 316–22.
13. See Ray C. Hunt and Bernard Norling, *Behind Japanese Lines: An American Guerilla in the Philippines* (Lexington: University of Kentucky Press, 1986). Also see Roger Hilsman, *American Guerilla: My War behind Japanese Lines* (Washington, DC: Potomac Books, 1990).
14. Richard Helms with William Hood, *A Look over My Shoulder: A Life in the Central Intelligence Agency* (New York: Random House, 2003), 82–91.
15. Jeffrey M. Moore, *Spies for Nimitz: Joint Military Intelligence in the Pacific War* (Annapolis, MD: Naval Institute Press, 2004), 137.
16. The U.S. Naval War College recently released the complete eight-volume journal of Admiral Nimitz, his so-called Gray Book, and much of it focuses on his thoughts on intelligence during the war. See Command Summary of Fleet Admiral Chester W. Nimitz, USN Nimitz "Gray Book" 7 December 1941–31 August 1945 (Bolton Landing, NY: American Naval Records Society, 2010), www.ibiblio.org/anrs/docs/D/D7/nimitz_graybook1.pdf.
17. Stratton, *SACO: Rice Paddy Navy*, 67–68.
18. Linda Kush, *The Rice Paddy Navy: U.S. Sailors Undercover in China* (Oxford: Osprey, 2012), 32–41.
19. For example, along with source operations, the U.S. Army doctrine on HUMINT includes debriefing, liaison operations, and interrogation all within the scope of HUMINT. See Headquarters, Department of the Army, *HUMINT Intelligence Collector Operations* FM 2-22.3 (FM 34–52), September 2006.
20. Wyman H. Packard, *A Century of U.S. Naval Intelligence* (Washington, DC: Office of Naval Intelligence, 1996), 124–25.

21. For example, in late 1944, JICPOA sent 130 stolen Japanese documents (presumably from post-battle recovery operations) for processing, translation, and further analysis. See Packard, *A Century of U.S. Naval Intelligence*, 47.
22. Eric A. Feldt, *The Coastwatchers: Operation Ferdinand and the Fight for the South Pacific* (N.p.: Carousel Books, 2019), 269.
23. Odd Arne Westad, *Decisive Encounters: The Chinese Civil War, 1946–1950* (Stanford, CA: Stanford University Press, 2003), 141–43.
24. John L. Gaddis, *Strategies of Containment: A Critical Appraisal of Postwar American National Security Policy* (New York: Oxford University Press, 1982), 54–88. Packard discusses the Navy's postwar mindset on this. Packard, *A Century of U.S. Naval Intelligence*, 26–28, 131–32.
25. Imagery intelligence (IMINT) and measurement and signature intelligence (MASINT) were still years away from being used with regularity.
26. For example, the basic parameters of radar signal processing have remained generally the same throughout the history of SIGINT. See Richard G. Wiley, *Electronic Intelligence: The Interception of Radar Signals* (Dedham, MA: Artech House, 1985).
27. This is apparent in looking at the Central Intelligence Group's National Intelligence Authority requirements on collection on China in February 1947. See Central Intelligence Group, "National Intelligence Authority, NIA Directive No. 8, National Intelligence Requirement—China," 12 February 1947, CIA CREST Database.
28. David Finkelstein, *Washington's Taiwan Dilemma, 1949–1950: From Abandonment to Salvation* (Annapolis, MD: Naval Institute Press, 2014). Also see the CIA's estimate of the situation from November 1948. Central Intelligence Agency, "Possible Developments in China," 19 November 1948, ORE 27-48, CIA CREST Database.
29. For instance, while the validity of intelligence gathered by North Korean defectors is often hailed as valuable to the United States' understanding of the Kim regime, the fact that they no longer reside in North Korea renders their ability to assess the current state of the regime is at least slightly dubious.
30. David W. Becker, *Coming in From the Cold . . . War: Defense HUMINT Services Support to Military Operations Other Than War* (Fort Leavenworth, KS: U.S. Army Command and General Staff College, 2000).

31. Richard K. Betts discusses this in *Soldiers, Statesmen, and Cold War Crises* (New York: Columbia University Press, 1991), 183–208.
32. "A Report to the National Security Council—NSC 68," 12 April 1950, President's Secretary's File, Truman Papers, The Truman Library, https://www.trumanlibrary.gov/library/research-files/report-national-security-council-nsc-68?documentid=NA&pagenumber=1. Also see Bostdorff's history of the Truman Doctrine and its long-term strategic effects. Denise M. Bostdorff, *Proclaiming the Truman Doctrine: The Cold War Call to Arms* (College Station: Texas A&M University Press, 2008), 206. For a full collection of the documents that led to the containment strategy as well as the policy itself and analysis by then-director of policy planning at the State Department, Paul Nitze, see S. Nelson Drew, ed, *NSC-68: Forging the Strategy of Containment*, 2nd ed., (Washington, DC: Institute for National Strategic Studies, 1996), 137.
33. Truman to the Secretaries of State, War, and Navy, 22 January 1946, Truman Papers, Truman Library. Also see Sarah-Jane Corke, *U.S. Covert Operations and Cold War Strategy: Truman, Secret Warfare, and the CIA, 1945–1953* (New York: Routledge, 2008), 256.
34. Central Intelligence Group, "National Intelligence Authority Directive 1, Policies and Procedures Governing the Central Intelligence Group," 8 February 1946, CIA CREST Database. Also see Sidney W. Souers (Executive Secretary of the National Security Council) to National Intelligence Authority, "Progress Report on the Central Intelligence Group," 7 June 1946, CIA CREST Database.
35. National Security Act of 1947, 26 July 1947, Pub. L. 80-253, 61 Stat. 495.
36. For a definitive history of the debate and establishment of the Central Intelligence Group and later the CIA, see Arthur Darling, *The Central Intelligence Agency: An Instrument of Government, to 1950* (University Park: Pennsylvania State University Press, 1990), 509.
37. Beyond the 12 March 1947 speech he gave announcing the Truman Doctrine, President Truman rarely ever used the phrase "cold war."
38. Chen Jian, *Mao's China and the Cold War* (Chapel Hill: University of North Carolina Press, 2001), 17–37.
39. This was discussed in detail in James E. Sheridan, *China in Disintegration* (New York: Free Press, 1975). Also see William W. Stueck, *The Road to Confrontation: American Policy toward China and Korea, 1947–1950* (Chapel Hill: University of North Carolina Press, 1981).

40. Salisbury, "New Aid to China," 89–92.
41. As Nancy Bernkopf Tucker's work on American diplomats in China discusses, the U.S. Navy placed external survey detachments throughout China during the war to collect intelligence and supply the Nationalists with Communist secret codes and radio transmitters. The Communists discovered one of them in Mukden, and eight American operatives were arrested. Nancy B. Tucker, *China Confidential: American Diplomats and Sino-American Relations, 1945–1996* (New York: Columbia University Press, 2001), 41, 506n22.
42. Moore, *Spies for Nimitz*, 59–60.
43. The idea of centralizing intelligence emerged as early as September, discussed elsewhere in this chapter. See Corke, *U.S. Covert Operations and Cold War Strategy*.
44. See Department of State, *A Guide to the United States History of Recognition, Diplomatic, and Consular Relations, by Country, since 1776, China*, Office of the Historian, available at https://history.state.gov/countries/china.
45. While this chapter discusses several other works, it is useful to contrast a few of them here. For instance, Carolle Carter's final chapter discusses how OSS and the Dixie Mission lost the intelligence network access they developed during World War II by April 1946. See Carolle J. Carter, *Mission to Yenan: American Liaison with the Chinese Communists, 1944–1947* (Lexington: University of Kentucky, 1997), 296. Maochun Yu's work provides a similar account. See Maochun Yu, *OSS in China: Prelude to Cold War* (Annapolis, MD: Naval Institute Press, 1996), 340. As a means of discussing intelligence in the opening conflict of the Cold War, Matthew Aid discusses the remnants of U.S. access in China following World War II. See Matthew Aid, "U.S. HUMINT and COMINT in the Korean War: From the Approach of War to the Chinese Intervention," *Intelligence and National Security* 14, no. 4 (1999): 17–63.
46. For example, John Lewis Gaddis clarifies this in his history of the evolution of containment policy over the course of the Cold War. See Gaddis, *Strategies of Containment*, 432.
47. For a political science perspective on the institutional underpinnings of this change, see Amy B. Zegart's seminal work *Flawed by Design: The Evolution of the CIA, JCS, and NSC* (Stanford, CA: Stanford University Press, 1999), 336.

48. This was discussed in May, *The Truman Administration and China, 1945–1949*.
49. Fleet Admiral, US Navy, "Subject: Continuation of SACO Agreement," United States Fleet, Headquarters of the Commander in Chief, 20 August 1945, RG 38, Entry 543, Box 99, NARA.
50. Jeffrey C. Metzel, Naval message, 6 August 1945, RG 38, Entry 98C, Box 10, NARA. SACO was often referred to as the "Friendship Project" in diplomatic settings.
51. The widespread perception of the close relationship between Miles and Chiang led Madame Chiang to call upon Miles to advise him on Chinese Nationalist policy during the Korean War. See M. E. Miles, "Memorandum for File, Subj: Conversation with Madame Chiang Kai-Shek" (Declassified 16 June 1976), Department of the Navy, Office of the Chief of Naval Operations, OP-27/dmh, 12 December 1952, RG 313, Entry 1492, NARA.
52. T.V. Soong to Secretary of Navy, 27 August 1945, RG 38, Entry 98C, Box 9, NARA.
53. A memorandum of Navy Headquarters on 28 August 1945 clearly indicated this. See A. E. Becker Jr., "For F-1, Subject: Concluding of SACO Agreement" (Declassified 27 December 2015), Department of the Navy, Headquarters, 28 August 1945, RG 38, Entry 98C (A1), NARA.
54. For instance, the U.S. forces China theater deputy chief of staff sent the commander of the Seventh Fleet in Shanghai a "non-concur" memorandum in December. See Paul W. Caraway (Brigadier General, GSC) to Commander, Seventh Fleet, Shanghai, China, 15 December 1945, A14–7 (F-0–1/mk) AG 322-Clandestine (Declassified 28 December 2015), RG 38, Entry 98C, Box 12, NARA.
55. Caraway to Commander, 15 December 1945. Also see United States Naval Group, China, *Study of the Termination of the SACO Agreement*, 11 November 1945, RG 38, Entry 98C, Box 9, 54464–54477, NARA.
56. CG U.S. Forces China Theater Chungking China to War Department, 14 September 1945 (Declassified 29 December 2015), RG 38, Entry 98C, Box 11, NARA.
57. G. C. Marshall, "Memorandum for Admiral King," 17 September 1945 (Declassified 28 December 2015), RG 38, Entry 98C, Box 10, NARA.

58. Admiral C. M. Cooke, "Memorandum for F-O, Subject: Rear Admiral Miles," 24 September 1945 (Declassified 28 December 2015), RG 38, Entry 98, Box 10, NARA.
59. J. C. Metzel to Admiral Charles Cooke, "Subject: Wedemeyer and Miles," 22 September 1945 (Declassified 28 December 2015), RG 38, Entry 98C, Box 10, NARA.
60. Department of the Navy, "Commander G. B. Berger to Captain Metzel," 27 September 1945 (Declassified 28 December 2015), RG 38, Entry 98C, Box 10, NARA.
61. The records of these correspondences over naval message traffic were extremely difficult to accurately cite due to a lack of formal subject line, often without addressees other than nicknames (Miles' nickname was Mary), and signatures with only a first name. A generic citation is offered as: Metzel to Miles, 25 August to 27 September 1945 (Declassified 29 December 2015), RG 38, Entry 98C, Box 11, NARA. Metzel remained in Chongqing to close the NGC headquarters, which moved to Nanking along with the Generalissimo and Tai Li following V-J Day.
62. Metzel to Miles, 25 August to 27 September 1945.
63. Joint Chiefs of Staff, "JCS 1290/5," 15 October 1945, RG 38, Entry 98C, Box 23, NARA.
64. For a treatise on the Marshall mission, see Steven I. Levine, "A New Look at American Mediation in the Chinese Civil War: The Marshall Mission and Manchuria." *Diplomatic History* 3, no. 4 (1979): 349–75.
65. Department of State, Dean Acheson (Acting Secretary of State) to James Forrestal (Secretary of the Navy), 22 December 1945, RG 38, Entry 98C, Box 9, NARA.
66. R. A. Spruance (Commander in Chief, US Pacific Fleet) to Commander, Seventh Fleet, "Subject: Sino-American Special Technical Cooperative Agreement—Proposed Termination Agreement" (Declassified 28 December 2015), 3 January 1946, Serial: 0001, RG 38, Entry 98C, Box 10, NARA.
67. Carolle J. Carter wrote a substantial history of the Dixie Mission. See Carter, *Mission to Yenan*, 296. For a comprehensive history of Naval Group, China's intelligence activities, its relationship with Tai Li, and the building of SACO, see Kush, *Rice Paddy Navy*, 294. Also see Stratton, *SACO: Rice Paddy Navy*, 408.

68. Yu, *OSS in China*, 340. Donovan was favored by FDR, but his influence waned with the Truman administration.
69. For an account of the rivalries, see Barbara W. Tuchman, *Stilwell and the American Experience in China, 1911–45* (New York: Macmillan, 1971), 621.
70. Linda Kush discusses this and the fact that Miles held a deep affinity for Tai as well as the Chinese Nationalist cause beyond the war with Japan. See Kush, *Rice Paddy Navy*, 46–56. Also see Stratton, *SACO: Rice Paddy Navy*.
71. This was both for personal reasons and what Miles believed were national interests. See Kush, *Rice Paddy Navy*, 252–56.
72. Sheridan, *China in Disintegration*, 269–70.
73. Harvey Klehr and Ronald Radosh, *The Amerasia Spy Case: Prelude to McCarthyism* (Chapel Hill: University of North Carolina Press, 1996), 280.
74. See S. M. Plokhy, *Yalta: The Price of Peace* (London: Penguin, 2011), 496.
75. Jian, *Mao's China and the Cold War*, 14–20.
76. Kush, *Rice Paddy Navy*, 46–52.
77. Tuchman, *Stilwell and the American Experience*, 513–14.
78. Tuchman, *Stilwell and the American Experience*, 492–97.
79. Harold Tanner, "Chinese Civil War, 1945–1949," *Military History*, February 2012, http://www.oxfordbibliographies.com/view/document/obo-9780199791279/obo-9780199791279-0031.xml. Also see Tang Tsou, *America's Failure in China, 1941–50* (Chicago: University of Chicago Press, 1963), 632.
80. Ralph W. Donnelly, Gabrielle M. Neufeld, and Carolyn A. Tyson, *A Chronology of the United States Marine Corps, Corps*, Vol. 3, *1947-1964*, Historical Division, Headquarters, U.S. Marine Corps, Washington, DC, 1971, 9.
81. Department of State, *Guide to the United States History of Recognition*.
82. See Packard, *A Century of U.S. Naval Intelligence*, 131. Packard describes the ILO's discreet contact in mainland China with Ching Hung Pang, "a secret society and progenitor of the Kuomintang." For a later account of how the U.S. naval intelligence presence in China following the war enabled CIA operations during the Korean War, even after the United States left China with the Communist rise to

power in 1949, see Frank Holober, *Raiders of the China Coast: CIA Operations during the Korean War* (Annapolis, MD: Naval Institute Press, 1999).
83. For an account of early U.S. Cold War covert action against China, see John Prados, *Safe for Democracy* (Chicago: Ivan R. Dee, 2006), 124–44. Also see Richard J. Aldrich, Gary Rawnsley, and Ming-Yeh T. Rawnsley, "Introduction: The Clandestine Cold War in Asia, 1945–65," in *The Clandestine Cold War in Asia, 1945–65: Western Intelligence, Propaganda, and Special Operations*, edited by Richard J. Aldrich, Gary Rawnsley, and Ming-Yeh T. Rawnsley (London: Frank Cass, 2000), 1–14. Although polemical in places, William Blum's work is a thorough and well-researched work, particularly in its depiction of U.S. covert policies in Burma and Tibet. See William Blum, *Killing Hope: U.S. Military and CIA Interventions since World War II* (Monroe, ME: Common Courage, 1995), 457.

Chapter 4. Blackout in China

1. For example, the first naval intelligence manual since World War II was not published until 1949. See Office of the Chief of Naval Operations, Office of Naval Intelligence, *Naval Intelligence Manual*, 1949, ONI 19(B), June 1949 (Declassified 28 December 2015), RG 38, Entry 98C, Box 25, NARA.
2. The Intelligence Advisory Board was originally established with the creation of the Central Intelligence Group but carried over in the first few years of the CIA. It was headed by the DCI, and its members included the intelligence heads of each of the military services, a representative from State, and one from the FBI. Michael Warner, "The Creation of the Central Intelligence Group," *Studies in Intelligence* 39, no. 5 (1996).
3. The Central Intelligence Group (established in January 1946) and the CIA were young organizations with their own problems to address, not least of which was finding an appropriate role at the top of a community in which established interests preceded them.
4. For a history of U.S. Asiatic Fleet's experience in World War II, see W. G. Winslow, *The Fleet the Gods Forgot: The U.S. Asiatic Fleet in World War II* (Annapolis, MD: Naval Institute Press, 2014), 344.

5. Both the Third and Seventh Fleets continue to be OPCON to Pacific Fleet today.
6. Jeffrey M. Moore, *Spies for Nimitz: Joint Military Intelligence in the Pacific War* (Annapolis, MD: Naval Institute Press, 2004), 1–25. For a substantive analysis of the history of Joint Intelligence Centers (JIC), with descriptions of JICPOA and the other JICs during World War II, see James D. Marchio, "The Evolution and Relevance of Joint Intelligence Centers: Support to Military Operations," *Studies in Intelligence*, Center for the Study of Intelligence 49, no. 1 (2005), https://www.cia.gov/resources/csi/static/Evolution-Joint-Intel-Centers.pdf.
7. Moore, *Spies for Nimitz*, 32.
8. Moore, *Spies for Nimitz*, 33–34.
9. This could have also been a result of the institutional scrutiny the ONI experienced following the Pearl Harbor attack. See Robert F. Piacine, *Pearl Harbor: Failure of Intelligence?* (Newport, RI: Naval War College, 1997), 102.
10. Wyman H. Packard, *A Century of U.S. Naval Intelligence* (Washington, DC: Office of Naval Intelligence, 1996), 26–28.
11. Packard, *A Century of U.S. Naval Intelligence*.
12. *Advanced Changes to the U.S. Navy Regulations, 1920*, 20 June 1946, RG 38, Entry 98C, Box 23, NARA. Also see OP-32, "Command Narrative and Quarterly Summary Report, 1 July 1946–30 September" (as cited in Packard, *A Century of U.S. Naval Intelligence*, 26n162).
13. Office of Naval Intelligence, "OP-32X to Commandant, Marine Corps," ONI Day File, Serial Number 05950P32, 3 September 1946, RG 38, Entry 98C, Box 16, NARA.
14. This is particularly interesting considering the relative influence and notoriety the Marine Corps experienced because of the war in the Pacific and its numerous victorious battles against the Japanese. For the first time in its history, the position of the commandant was raised to the rank of general (four star) in January 1944.
15. Thomas B. Inglis (Rear Admiral) to Chief of Naval Operations, 1 November 1948, Ser. 13601P32, RG 38, NARA.
16. Warner, "The Creation of the Central Intelligence Group," 111–20.
17. Arthur B. Darling, "With Vandenberg as DCI," *Studies in Intelligence* 12, no. 3 (1996).

18. E. K. Wright (Colonel, GSC) Memorandum for Admiral Inglis, "Subject: Engineering Drawing and Detailed Calculations on New Russian Rocket Propelled Artillery Shell," Central Intelligence Group, 7 January 1947 (Declassified 30 December 2015), RG 38, Entry 98C, Box 14, NARA.
19. Naval Attaché Manila, "Subject: Central Intelligence Group Personnel in Embassy Manila—Assignment of," 23 May 1947 (Declassified 27 August 1992), RG 38, Entry 98C, Box 14, NARA.
20. Marchio, "The Evolution and Relevance of Joint Intelligence Centers."
21. During the postwar period, intelligence reporting from China showed a ratio of roughly four to one in favor of Soviet-related subjects over all other intelligence subjects.
22. Donovan memo to Truman, 13 September 1945, Office of Strategic Services in Michael Warner, ed., *The CIA under Harry Truman* (Langley, VA: Center for the Study of Intelligence, 1994). The CIA CREST database includes the "Creating Central Intelligence" collection, which houses many of the key documents of this period. See "Freedom of Information Act Electronic Reading Room," n.d., https://www.cia.gov/library/readingroom/collection/creating-global-intelligence.
23. ONI, "OP-32X to Commandant, Marine Corps."
24. This was examined in a special issue of *Intelligence and National Security*. See Richard J. Aldrich, Gary D. Rawnsley, and Ming Yeh T. Rawnsley, "Introduction: The Clandestine Cold War in Asia: 1945–1965," *Intelligence and National Security* 14, no 4 (December 1999): 1–14. A book was later published with a more extensive version of this research. Richard J. Aldrich, Gary Rawnsley, and Ming-Yeh T. Rawnsley, eds., *The Clandestine Cold War in Asia, 1945–65: Western Intelligence, Propaganda, and Special Operations* (London: Frank Cass, 2000), 298.
25. This included the existing power dynamics of the Army and Navy but also the increased influence of the Marine Corps (although it remained under the Department of the Navy).
26. Harold R. Stark, ADM, USN, to Frank Knox, Secretary of the Navy, 12 November 1940, in Stark Papers, 1, also referred to as Plan Dog Memo, Franklin D. Roosevelt Presidential Library and Museum, http://docs.fdrlibrary.marist.edu/psf/box4/a48b01.html.

27. The beginning of the discussion about centralized intelligence is marked with a memorandum Bill Donovan sent to Truman on 18 September 1945 pleading with the president to not disband the OSS. Truman did just that weeks later and began discussions about the establishment of the Central Intelligence Group (established in January 1946). See Donovan memo to Truman, 13 September 1945.
28. U.S. Marine Corps, "1948 Facts on File (FOF)," 98E, as cited in Ralph W. Donnelly, Gabrielle M. Neufeld, and Carolyn A. Tyson, *A Chronology of the United States Marine Corps*, Vol. 3, *1947–1964*, Vol. 3, *Marine Corps Historical Reference Pamphlet*, Historical Division Headquarters, U.S. Marine Corps, Washington, DC.
29. For instance, the Army clause of the Constitution states: "The Congress shall have Power to . . . raise and support Armies, but no Appropriation of Money to that Use shall be for a longer Term than two Years. . . ." United States Constitution, Article I, Section 8, Clause 12.
30. Modern U.S. "jointness" dates to 1986 with the Goldwater–Nichols Act, which established regional combatant commanders with OPCON of all forces of the services in a particular geographic region. For an insider's history of the development and debate that occurred during its drafting, see James R. Locher, *Victory on the Potomac: The Goldwater–Nichols Act Unifies the Pentagon* (College Station: Texas A&M University Press, 2002), 524. For an analysis of how Goldwater-Nichols created unforeseen problems for command and control and organizational structures, also see Christopher Bourne, "Unintended Consequences of the Goldwater-Nichols Act," *Joint Forces Quarterly*, Spring 1998.
31. Richard Frank, *Guadalcanal: The Definitive Account of the Landmark Battle* (New York: Random House, 1990), 840.
32. NARA maintains a complete list of these studies. Also see Central Intelligence Group, "Survey of the Joint Intelligence Study Publishing Board (JISPB)," 20 April 1946, C16 Directive, CIA CREST Database.
33. Mao corresponded with some regularity with Roosevelt, even congratulating him on his election win in November 1944. Franklin D. Roosevelt to Mao Tze-tung, "Thanking Mao for congratulations on winning election," 14 November 1944, Box 88, File 14, Western History Collections, Patrick J. Hurley Collection, University of

Oklahoma Libraries. No direct exchanges between Truman and Mao were found in the Truman Archives. However, Mao and Ambassador Hurley did converse from time to time, as did George Marshall during the Marshall Mission period.

34. Albert C. Wedemeyer to Mao Tse-tung, "American intelligence unit captured by Communists," 7 July 1945, RG 38, Entry 98C, Box 31, NARA.
35. Office of Naval Intelligence, "Strength Distribution of the Chinese Communist Army," December 1945 (53929), RG 38, Entry 98C, Box 12, NARA.
36. E. A. Buchanan (Lieutenant Commander), "Subject: Communist Activity in Kwantung," *Intelligence Report*, 27 September 1946, Monograph no. ONI 104-400, BID 3144.0200 (Declassified 29 December 2015), RG 38, Entry 98C, Box 11, NARA.
37. Naval Attaché to Chief of Naval Intelligence, "Subj: Transportation assistance afforded Chinese Communists by United States Information Service," 29 November 1945, Serial: s-61, RG 38, Entry 98C, Box 9, NARA.
38. Naval Attaché to Chief of Naval Intelligence, "Subj: Transportation assistance."
39. Naval Attaché to Chief of Naval Intelligence, "Subj: Transportation assistance."
40. Office of Strategic Services, *Organizations in China*, April 1946, RG 226, Entry UD-WX 1569, Box 92, NARA.
41. Naval Attaché, Nanking, China, Intelligence Report, "China—Sino-Soviet Philanthropic Association," 5 April 1946 (Declassified 20 March 2016), ONI-104-500; 202-300; BID-3164.0503; 5800.0000, RG 38, NARA.
42. Dieter Heinzig, *The Soviet Union and Communist China 1945–1950: The Arduous Road to the Alliance* (Milton Park, Abingdon, U.K.: Routledge, 2015).
43. Naval Attaché, Nanking, China, "Subject: Manchuria Situation, 1 April 1946 (Declassified 28 December 2015), RG 38, Entry 98c, Box 11, NARA.
44. Naval Attaché, "Subject: Manchuria Situation."
45. Naval Attaché, Nanking, China, "Subject: Military movement from southern China," 5 October 1946 (Declassified 29 December 2015), RG 38, Entry 98C, Box 11, NARA.

46. Although they had guarded coalfields, the U.S. mission was more clearly articulated in September 1946. Chinese Nationalist forces guarded the coalfields from then on. Henry I. Shaw Jr., *The United States Marines in North China*, Historical Branch, G-3 Division, Headquarters, U.S. Marine Corps, 1960, 16.
47. Donnelly, Neufeld, and Tyson, *A Chronology of the United States Marine Corps*, Vol. 3: *1947–1964*, Historical Division, Headquarters, U.S. Marine Corps, Washington, DC, 1971, 3.
48. David Finkelstein, *Washington's Taiwan Dilemma, 1949–1950: From Abandonment to Salvation* (Annapolis, MD: Naval Institute Press, 2014), 392. Also see William W. Stueck, *The Road to Confrontation: American Policy toward China and Korea, 1947–1950* (Chapel Hill: University of North Carolina Press, 1981), 336.
49. Donnelly, Neufeld, and Tyson *Chronology of the United States Marine Corps*, Vol 3, *1947–1964*, 1.
50. While more aid went to the Kuomintang ($2 billion between 1945 and 1949), this remained a major point of contention. See Russell D. Buhite, "'Major Interests': American Policy toward China, Taiwan, and Korea, 1945–1950," *Pacific History Review* 47, no. 3 (August 1978): 425–51. Also see Lawrence E. Salisbury, "New Aid to China," *Far East Survey* 17, no. 8 (1948): 89–92.
51. Shaw, *The United States Marines in North China*, 18.
52. Shaw, *The United States Marines in North China*, 22.
53. Steven I. Levine, "A New Look at American Mediation in the Chinese Civil War: The Marshall Mission and Manchuria," *Diplomatic History* 3, no. 4 (1979): 349–75.
54. The Marines alone had two divisions in Northern China. See Shaw, *The United States Marines in North China*. Also consider the notion that the CIA likely used the military's vast footprint in the Far East to assess Chinese military capabilities. Central Intelligence Agency, *Chinese Communist Capabilities for Control of All China*, 10 December 1948, NIE 58, ORE 77–48, CIA CREST Database.
55. C. M. Cooke Jr. (Chief of Staff, US Fleet, Headquarters of the Commander in Chief), "Subject: U.S. Naval Group China," 8 August 1945, RG 38, 54396, NARA.

56. J. C. Metzel (Friendship Project Officer) to Vice Chief of Naval Operations, Via Deputy Chief of Naval Operations (Operations), n.d., approximately March 1946, RG 38, Entry 98C, Box 10, NARA.
57. T. V. Soong to Secretary of the Navy (James Forrestal), Col. Sinju Pu Hsiao to represent Soong in Washington, 3 September 1945, RG 38, Entry 98C, Box 9, NARA.
58. J. C. Metzel to Admiral Ramsey, "Subject: Future Cooperation with Chinese Navy," 10 August 1946, RG 38, Entry 98-C, Box 10, NARA.
59. Colonel Sinju Pu Hsiao to Admiral D. C. Ramsey, 15 April 1947, RG 38, Entry 64, Box 17, NARA.
60. Ralph W. Donnely, Gabriele N. Neufeld, and Carolyn A. Tyson, *A Chronology of the United States Marine Corps*, Vol. 3, *1947–1960*, (Washington, DC: Historical Division Headquarters, U.S. Marine Corps, 1971), 3. Also see "North China Marine," *Marine Corps Gazette* 33, no. 6 (10 January 1948).
61. "North China Marine."
62. "North China Marine."
63. Henry Aplington II, "North China Patrol," *Marine Corps Gazette* 33, no. 6 (1949).
64. Aplington, "North China Patrol," 55.
65. Henry I. Shaw, "The United States Marines in North China, 1945–1949" (Quantico, VA: Historical Branch, G-3 Division, Headquarters Branch, U.S. Marine Corps, 1968), 28.
66. Donnelly, Neufeld, and Tyson *Chronology of the United States Marine Corps*, Vol. 3, *1947–1964*, 8.
67. For these reasons, the archival records on the naval attaché (Nanking) are extremely limited.
68. CNO, ONI, *Naval Intelligence Manual*, 1949.
69. Odd Arne Westad, *Decisive Encounters: The Chinese Civil War, 1946–1950* (Stanford, CA: Stanford University Press, 2003), 167–68, 181–214.
70. Harold Tanner, *Where Chiang Kai-shek Lost China: The Liao-Shen Campaign, 1948* (Bloomington: Indiana University Press, 2015); and Harold Tanner, *The Battle for Manchuria and the Fate of China, Siping 1946* (Bloomington: Indiana University Press, 2013).
71. Naval Attaché (Chungking) to Chief of Naval Intelligence, "Organization and Recent Activities of the O.G.P.U. in Shanghai," 29

November 1945, EN3–11(K)/A-6, Serial: S-62 (Declassified 21 February 2016), RG 38, Entry 98C, Box 11, NARA.
72. Naval Attaché (Chungking) to CNO, "Organization and Recent Activities."
73. War Department, Office of the Assistant Secretary of War, Headquarters, Strategic Services Unit, China Theater, APC 907, X-2 Branch, "Summary Report on Intelligence Organizations in the Canton–Hong Kong–Macau Area," 15 January 1946 (Declassified 2 November 1996), RG 38, Entry 56, Box 129, NARA.
74. John S. Service, U.S. Army Observer, China, "Contact between the Chinese Communists and Moscow," letter dated 23 March 1945 (Declassified 20 March 2017), RG 38, NARA.
75. Naval Attaché, Nanking, China, Intelligence Report [Source: Official of Chinese Ministry of Foreign Affairs], "China—Russian Activity in China," 5 April 1946 (Declassified 20 March 2016), RG 38, NARA.
76. Naval Attaché, Nanking, China, Intelligence Report [Source: Various], "Manchuria—Manchurian Situation, week ending 7 April 1946," 8 April 1946 (Declassified 20 March 2016), Serial: 10-S-46, Monograph No. ONI-106-100 BID-8000, RG 38, Entry 98C, Box 11, NARA.
77. Naval Attaché, Nanking, China, Intelligence Report, "China—Sino-Soviet Philanthropic Association," 5 April 1946.
78. Soviet Internal Affairs was the People's Commissariat for Internal Affairs' successor as of early 1946.
79. Naval Attaché, Nanking, China, Intelligence Report, "Soviet Secret Activities in T'ien-Ching (Tientsin)," 12 April 1946 (Declassified 20 March 2016), ONI-104-500, 215-400, Bid-3164.0600, 3164.0300, RG 38, NARA.

Chapter 5. New Model Intelligence and Holding Steady with the Nationalists

1. The People's Liberation Army is an umbrella term that includes the PLA navy and air force as well as the ground forces. The term for "army" in Mandarin is 军事 (*junshi*), which translates to "military affairs."

2. M. H. Halperin, *The 1958 Taiwan Straits Crisis: A Documented History*, RM-4900-ISA (Santa Monica, CA: RAND, 1966, declassified, March 18, 1975). Another more recent source focused on the strategic, cultural dynamics of deterrence in each of the Taiwan crises (treating 1954–55 and 1958 as wholly separate crises). See Shu Guang Zhang, *Deterrence and Strategic Culture Chinese-American Confrontations, 1949–1958* (Ithaca, NY: Cornell University Press, 1992), 302.
3. Edward J. Marolda, *Ready Seapower: A History of the U.S. Seventh Fleet* (Washington, DC: Naval History and Heritage Command, 2012), x.
4. As described from primary Chinese sources in Pang Yang Huei's *Strait Rituals: China, Taiwan and the United States in the Taiwan Crises, 1954–1958* (Hong Kong: Hong Kong University Press), 177–85.
5. For a history of how the CIA initially managed intelligence estimates and integrated the intelligence collected by the services early in the Cold War, see Arthur Darling, *The Central Intelligence Agency: An Instrument of Government, to 1950* (University Park: Pennsylvania State University Press, 1990), 420–21.
6. Matthew Aid and Jeffrey T. Richelson, *U.S. Intelligence and China: Collection, Analysis and Covert Action*, National Security Archives, undated paper, accessed 14 September 2014. http://nsarchive.chadwyck.com/collections/content/CI/intell_and_china_essay.pdf.
7. "The Taiwan Straits Crises: 1954–55 and 1958," Office of the Historian, accessed 21 October 2017, https://history.state.gov/milestones/1953-1960/taiwan-strait-crises. Also see Walter Pincus, "Eisenhower Advisors Discussed Using Nuclear Weapons in China," *Washington Post*, 30 April 2008; and Bernard Brodie, *Strategy in the Missile Age* (Santa Monica, CA: RAND, 2007), 444.
8. I learned in my off-the-record discussions with a former intelligence officer at the American Institute in Taiwan that this remained true for several decades after the 1950s crises.
9. Matthew Aid and Jeff Richelson explored U.S. SIGINT and IMINT intelligence in China during the Cold War. See Aid and Richelson, *U.S. Intelligence and China*.
10. The CIA's CREST database maintains a broad collection of U.S. photo reconnaissance over mainland China and the strait during both crises. See Freedom of Information Act Electronic Reading Room, https://www.cia.gov/readingroom/collection/china-collection.

11. The 1954–55 crisis was never resolved following the PRC's end of the shelling of Jinmen Island in May 1955. At the same time, the island was still a disputed territory. See Bernard Cole, *Taiwan's Security: History and Prospects* (Abingdon, U.K.: Routledge, 2006). Also see Richard Bush, *At Cross Purposes: U.S.–Taiwan Relations since 1942* (Abingdon, U.K.: Routledge, 2004), 304.
12. Wyman H. Packard, *A Century of U.S. Naval Intelligence* (Washington, DC: Office of Naval Intelligence, 1996), 415–17.
13. "Recommendation for Assistance to Greece and Turkey," Address of the President of the United States, 12 March 1947, Truman Library, https://www.trumanlibrary.gov/library/research-files/address-president-congress-recommending-assistance-greece-and-turkey.
14. George Kennan, "The Charge in the Soviet Union (Kennan) to the Secretary of State," 22 February 1946, 861.00/2-2246: Telegram, NSA Archive, http://nsarchive.gwu.edu/coldwar/documents/episode-1/kennan.htm.
15. See Roger B. Jeans, *The CIA and Third Force Movements in China during the Early Cold War* (Lanham, MD: Lexington, 2017). Also see Thomas F. Troy, *Donovan and the CIA: A History of the Establishment of the Central Intelligence Agency* (Frederick, MD: University Publications of America, 1981).
16. Directives periodically revised and updated, codifying the relationship between the CIA and the military, were all largely outgrowths of the CIA's original charter, Section 202 of the National Security Act of 1947. For a brief history of the charter, see L. Britt Snider, *The Agency and the Hill: CIA's Relationship with Congress, 1946–2004* (Washington, DC: Center for the Study of Intelligence, 2008), https://www.cia.gov/resources/csi/static/The-Agency-and-Hill.pdf.
17. Central Intelligence Agency, "Critical Situations in the Far East," ORE 58-50, CIA CREST Database, 12 October 1950 (Declassified 23 January 1978).
18. CIA, "Critical Situations in the Far East."
19. Office of Naval Intelligence, "Office of Naval Intelligence Contribution to: SE-10—Soviet Capabilities for Surprise Attack on the Continental United States before July 1952," CIA CREST Database, n.d. (Declassified 31 October 2002).

20. This assumption—which eventually evolved into the domino theory—is fraught with fallacy and has been debated ad infinitum. For instance, see John Lewis Gaddis' classic work, *Strategies of Containment: A Critical Appraisal of Postwar American National Security Policy* (New York: Oxford University Press, 1982).
21. William J. Donovan, "Strategic Services in 'Cold War,'" *Naval War College Review*, September 1953, 32.
22. For instance, consider how former DCI Allen Dulles treated the threat of Communism's spread in his historical memoir. Allen Dulles, *The Craft of Intelligence: America's Legendary Spy Master on the Fundamentals of Intelligence Gathering in the Free World* (New York: Lyons, 2005), 44–48.
23. Jay Taylor, *The Generalissimo: Chiang Kai-shek and the Struggle for Modern China* (Cambridge, MA: Belknap Press of Harvard University Press, 2011), 752.
24. Commander, Taiwan Patrol Force, US Seventh Fleet (COMPATFOR7THFLT), Command History, 1954, RG 313, Entry 1615, Box 289, NARA.
25. See S. Nelson Drew, ed., *NSC-68: Forging the Strategy of Containment*, 2nd ed. (Washington, DC: Institute for National Strategic Studies, 1996), 137.
26. For an extensive analysis of how U.S. Navy commanders formed requirements in the Cold War, see Christopher Ford and David Alan Rosenberg, *The Admirals' Advantage: U.S. Operational Intelligence in World War II and the Cold War* (Annapolis, MD: Naval Institute Press, 2005), 219.
27. For example, the primary intelligence publication that the Taiwan Patrol Force contributed in the aftermath of the 1958 crisis was a net assessment of Taiwan navy capabilities in comparison to PLA Navy capabilities. See Naval Forces, Far East, *GRC Navy Force Levels*, 20 October 1958 (Declassified 9 April 1958), RG 313, UD 1615, Box 9184, NARA.
28. Central Intelligence Agency, Untitled, CIA Cable, October 1950, CIA CREST Database, CIA-RDP78-01617A006100020075-7 (Declassified 20 March 1978).
29. Consider the fact that, in 1950, the Pacific Fleet commander reorganized these activities. Commander in Chief, Pacific Fleet to Chief of

Naval Operations, "Subject: Reorganization of Clandestine Activities, Covert Operations and Unconventional Warfare within the Far East Command," Pacific Fleet, November 1950 (Declassified 9 April 2018), RG 313, Entry 1340, Box 58, NARA. Also see John B. Dwyer, *Scouts and Raiders: The Navy's First Special Warfare Commandos* (New York: Praeger, 1993), 224.

30. For a complete history of the Chinese leadership's decision to enter the Korean conflict, see Chen Jian, *China's Road to the Korean War: The Making of the Sino-American Confrontation* (New York: Columbia University Press, 1996), 339.

31. For more on the risks and dangers to the collection in the Cold War, see Roger Hilsman's chapter on the operators. See Roger Hilsman, *Strategic Intelligence and National Decisions* (Glencoe, IL: Free, 1956), 36–56.

32. Office of the Chief of Naval Operations, Office of Naval Intelligence, *Naval Intelligence Requirements—Periodic Summary (NIRPS)*, ONI Instruction 003820.21, Change 1, 11 June 1952, RG 38, Entry 4, Box 6 (Declassified 18 July 2016), NARA.

33. For example, see Department of State, Office of the Historian, "Memorandum by the Assistant Secretary of State for Far Eastern Affairs (Robertson) to the Secretary of State (1952–1954, Volume XII, Part 1, East Asia and the Pacific)," 25 October 1954, *Foreign Relations of the United States*.

34. See Michael D. Swaine, "Understanding the Historical Record," in *Managing Sino-American Crises: Case Studies and Analysis*, ed. by Michael D. Swaine, Tuosheng Zhang, and Danielle F. S. Cohen (Washington, DC: Carnegie Endowment for International Peace, 2006), 2.

35. Swaine, "Understanding the Historical Record."

36. The decision-makers were directors of naval intelligence Rear Adm. Carl F. Espe (December 1952–May 1956) and Rear Adm. Laurence H. Frost (June 1956–September 1960), both members of the Intelligence Advisory Committee under DCI Allen Dulles). For example, see Central Intelligence Agency, "Intelligence Advisory Committee Minutes of Meeting Held in Director's Conference Room, Administration Building Central Intelligence Agency at 1045," 14 December 1954, IAC-M-148 (Declassified 27 February 2003), CIA CREST Database.

37. Central Intelligence Agency, "Intelligence Advisory Committee-Agenda," 13 March 1952, 20 March 1952, 27 March 1952, CIA CREST Database (Declassified 27 February 2003), https://www.cia.gov/readingroom/docs/CIA-RDP85S00362R000200120025-9.pdf.
38. Chief of Naval Operations to Chief of Naval Personnel, "CIA Representative for CINCLANT Staff," 6 April 1955 (Declassified 24 April 2003), CIA CREST Database.
39. This was common when estimates focused on Soviet naval support to the Chinese. For instance, see Central Intelligence Agency, *Relations between the Chinese Communist Regime and the USSR: Their Present Character and Probable Future Courses*, 10 September 1952, NIE-58, CIA CREST Database (Declassified May 2004).
40. This notion is common in a wide range of histories of the agency, not least of which its own official histories. See Arthur B. Darling, "The Birth of Central Intelligence," Center for the Study of Intelligence, Central Intelligence Agency (Declassified and approved for release 22 September 1993). For a general history of the origins of the CIA, see Troy, *Donovan and the CIA*. Also see Evan Thomas, *The Very Best Men: Four Who Dared; The Early Years of the CIA* (New York: Simon & Schuster, 1995), 432.
41. "Remarks of the President, To the Final Session of the CIA's Eighth Training Orientation Course for Representatives of Various Government Agencies," Harry S. Truman, at the Department of Agriculture Auditorium, Washington DC, 21 November 1952, American Presidency Project, UC Santa Barbara, http://www.presidency.ucsb.edu/ws/index.php?pid=14345.
42. U.S. National Security Act, 1947, U.S. Code: Title 10—ARMED FORCES, https://www.law.cornell.edu/uscode/text/10.
43. In response to an early CIA attempt to reign in incongruities in the Cold War intelligence community, the DNI appealed for changes to retain some of the ONI's previous authorities. Ultimately this attempt failed, and the CIA remained the primary agency. See Office of the Chief of Naval Operations, "Memorandum for Director, Central Intelligence Agency, Subject: Comments of the Office of Naval Intelligence on the Report to the National Security Council entitled 'The Central Intelligence Agency and National Organization for Intelligence,' dated 1 January 1949." 21 February 1949, CIA CREST Database (Declassified 22 October 2003).

44. Frank Holober, *Raiders of the China Coast: CIA Operations during the Korean War* (Annapolis, MD: Naval Institute Press, 1999), 253.
45. Commander Carrier Air Group TWO to Commanding Officer, USS *Boxer* (CV-21), "Subj: Action Report of Carrier Air Group TWO (15 October 1950–22 October 1950)," 1 November 1950, NHHC, Declassified.
46. Commander Carrier Air Group TWO to Commanding Officer, USS *Boxer* (CV-21), Subj: Action Report of Carrier Air Group TWO (15 September 1950–2 October 1950), 10 October 1950, NHHC, Declassified.
47. Commander Carrier Air Group TWO, 15 September 1950–2 October 1950.
48. Lyman B. Kirkpatrick (Acting Assistant Director of Operations) to Chief, Coordination, Operations & Policy Staff, "Subject: Naval Intelligence Collection Instructions," Department of the Navy, 25 January 1950, CIA CREST Database (Declassified 28 August 2001).
49. However, it is clear the CIA collected intelligence of a naval nature at times, and the Navy collected intelligence of a political nature at times.
50. Holober, *Raiders on the Korean Coast*, 253.
51. Far East Command, *Intelligence and Related Covert Activities*, General Headquarters, FEC, 4 November 1950 (Declassified 12 May 2008), RG 313, NARA.
52. Director of Central Intelligence, "Memorandum for Director of Naval Intelligence, Subject: Naval Intelligence Instructions," from 12 January 1950, CIA CREST Database (Declassified 3 July 2003). On the NSCID, see ESPIONAGE AND COUNTERESPIONAGE OPERATIONS, National Security Council Intelligence Directive No. 5, 12 December 1947, Washington, DC: National Security Council.
53. NSC Intelligence Directive No. 9, 1 July 1948, Washington, DC: National Security Council.
54. National Security Agency, Center for Cryptologic History, *The Origins of NSA*, n.d., https://www.nsa.gov/portals/75/documents/about/cryptologic-heritage/historical-figures-publications/publications/NSACSS/origins_of_nsa.pdf?ver=2019-08-09-091926-677.
55. Capt. George R. Phelan, "Introduction to Command Intelligence," *Naval War College Review*, December 1953, 34.

56. Phelan, "Introduction to Command Intelligence," 34.
57. Kent's own views and theory of intelligence were presented in his pioneering work on strategic intelligence. See Sherman Kent, *Strategic Intelligence for American World Policy* (Hamden, CT: Archon, 1965), 226.
58. Anonymous, "Strategic Intelligence for American World Policy / The Future of American Secret Intelligence," *Marine Corps Gazette* 34, no. 5 (May 1950).
59. This was evident in the Navy's perception of its role in covert operations. See Commander in Chief, Pacific Fleet to CNO, "Subject: Reorganization of Clandestine Activities."
60. Jeffrey M. Moore, *Spies for Nimitz: Joint Military Intelligence in the Pacific War* (Annapolis, MD: Naval Institute Press, 2004), 280.
61. By the 1958 crisis, the MAAG-T (formerly MAAG FORMOSA) established the Kinmen Advisory Team to more closely work with the Taiwan navy and marine corps. This also enabled an expanded ability to develop sources. See Senior Marine Advisor to Captain Charles Dininokr, "Subject: Temporary Additional Duty Kinmen Advisory Team," Navy section MAAG-Taiwan, 12 September 1958 (Declassified 9 April 2018), RG 313, UD 1615, Box 9184, NARA.
62. Commander, Taiwan Patrol Force (COMTAIWANPATFOR), *Command History*, 10 August 1959, RG 38, NARA.
63. Far East Command was disbanded in July 1957, and from there on reporting went directly from U.S. Taiwan Defense Command to the Seventh Fleet.
64. This was a result of the easing of U.S.–China relations and the rapprochement that occurred following the 1979 Taiwan Relations Act. United States Congress, The Taiwan Relations Act (TRA), Pub. L. 96-8, 93 Stat. 14, enacted April 10, 1979; H.R. 2479.
65. Commander, First Fleet to Chief of Naval Operations (Director of Naval Intelligence), "Subject: Organization and Operation of Staff Intelligence Activities," Commander, First Fleet, July 1954 (Declassified 9 April 2018), RG 313, Entry 1340, Box 58, NARA.
66. Commander, First Fleet to CNO, "Subject: Organization and Operation."
67. Commander in Chief, Pacific Fleet to CNO, "Subject: Reorganization of Clandestine Activities."

68. The Special Plans Branch of the Joint Staff J2 was the equivalent of today's "J2X," which coordinates intelligence-related special operations and reconnaissance.
69. Commander in Chief, Pacific Fleet to CNO, "Subject: Reorganization of Clandestine Activities."
70. Command, Naval Forces Far East to Chief of Naval Operations, "Subject: Personnel Allowance for Special Support Activities, Naval Forces, Far East, request for," 18 December 1954 (Declassified 9 April 2018), RG 313, Entry 1340, Box 58, NARA.
71. Commander, Pacific Fleet to Commander in Chief Pacific, "Subject: Formosa Liaison Center, Additional Personnel for," 8 January 1954 (Declassified 9 April 2018), RG 313, Entry 1340, Box 58, NARA.
72. Central Intelligence Agency, "Memorandum for Assistant for Operations, Subject: Naval Intelligence Collection Instructions," 20 January 1950, CIA CREST database (Declassified 7 May 2002).
73. Central Intelligence Agency, Chief, Liaison Division Collection and Dissemination, "Memorandum for the Director of Naval of Intelligence, Subject: Release of Department of the Navy Intelligence," 27 September 1954, CIA CREST Database (Declassified 2 September 1999).
74. Central Intelligence Agency, Office of National Estimates, "Subject: Draft Terms of Reference: NIE-27: Chinese Communist Capabilities and Intentions with Respect to Taiwan," 7 February 1951, CIA CREST Database (Declassified 31 August 2001).
75. CIA, Office of National Estimates, "Subject: Draft Terms of Reference."
76. Office of Naval Intelligence, "Memorandum for: Training Liaison Officers, Subject: Nominations for US Naval School, Naval Intelligence," 1 November 1954, CIA CREST Database (Declassified 22 January 2002).
77. ONI, "Memorandum for: Training Liaison Officers."
78. The Farm began operating in 1951. For one of the first public news stories on the Farm, see Miles Copeland, "How the CIA Trains Its Recruits Down on 'the Farm' in Virginia," *Richmond Times Dispatch*, 25 August 1974, CIA CREST Database, https://www.cia.gov/readingroom/docs/CIA-RDP88-01350R000200810007-8.pdf.

79. *All Hands: The Bureau of Naval Personnel Information Bulletin*, July 1949, no. 389, NHHC, https://media.defense.gov/2019/Apr/10/2002112366/-1/-1/1/AH194907.pdf.
80. Central Intelligence Agency, "Basic Training Agreement between Central Intelligence Agency and Department of the Navy," 3 October 1951 (Declassified 27 August 2001), CIA CREST Database.
81. CIA, "Basic Training Agreement."

Chapter 6. Reading the Chinese Communists through Taipei

1. For an account of how President Truman and Gen. Douglas MacArthur disagreed on this matter, and the latter was insubordinate to the former, see David McCullough, *Truman* (New York: Simon & Schuster, 1992), 796–97.
2. COM7THFLT, "Report of Operations, Jul–Dec 1953," 15, RG 38, Box 383, NARA.
3. Central Intelligence Agency, "Naval Intelligence School in Kuangtung Province," 27 August 1951 (Declassified 4 December 2001), CIA CREST Database.
4. COM7THFLT, "Report of Operations, Dec 1953–Jun 1954," RG 38, Box 383, NARA.
5. "Appreciation of the Ability of the Chinese Nationalist Navy to Effect a Blockade of Communist Territorial Waters" (Declassified), Intelligence Division, Naval Staff, Admiralty, FO371/75902, 9 July 1949, TNA/UK, cited in Bruce A. Elleman, *High Seas Buffer: The Taiwan Patrol Force, 1950–1979* (Newport, RI: Naval War College, 2012).
6. "Appreciation of the Ability."
7. Commander in Chief U.S. Pacific Fleet to Chief of Naval Staff, Australia, "Subject: Supplement to the Radford Collins Agreement," U.S. Pacific Fleet, 5 June 1954, RG 313, NARA.
8. Office of Naval Intelligence, "The Southeast China Coast Today," *ONI Review* (February 1953), 51–60, RG 38, Box 415, NARA.
9. Statement issued by President Truman, 27 June 1950, Harry S. Truman Archives.
10. Following Truman's commitment of naval forces to both the Korean theater and for the defense of Taiwan, Commander, Pacific Fleet,

was required to pull additional forces from the west coast for Task Force Yoke in July 1950. See "Korean War: Chronology of US Pacific Fleet Operations, June-December 1950," NHHC, 10 April 2015, https://www.history.navy.mil/content/history/nhhc/research/library/online-reading-room/title-list-alphabetically/k/korean-war-chronology/june-dec-1950.html.
11. Chen Jian, *Mao's China and the Cold War* (Chapel Hill: University of North Carolina Press, 2001), 166.
12. Central Intelligence Agency, "Replacement of CH'EN I by Sung Shih-lun as Commander for Taiwan Invasion; Chinese Communist Plans Regarding Taiwan Invasion," 13 October 1950 (Declassified 7 July 1978), CIA CREST Database.
13. Director of Naval Intelligence to Director of Central Intelligence Agency, "Subject: Non-Communist Shipping in the China Trade, January through October 1951," Department of the Navy, 14 November 1951 (Declassified 7 October 2003), CIA CREST Database.
14. Xiao Jinguang, "The Taiwan Campaign Was Called Off," 30 June 1950, CCFP, p. 155, cited in Jian, *Mao's China and the Cold War*.
15. Zhou Jun, "The Party Central Committee's Decision on the Strategic Transition from the War of Liberation to the War to Resist America and Assist Korea," *Dangshi yanjiu ziliao*, no. 4 (1992): 15, Wilson Center Digital Archive (WCDA).
16. Edward J. Marolda, *Ready Seapower: A History of the U.S. Seventh Fleet* (Washington, DC: Naval History and Heritage Command, 2012), 34.
17. Marolda, *Ready Seapower*, 34.
18. CIA, "Replacement of CH'EN I."
19. Marolda, *Ready Seapower*, 33.
20. Marolda, *Ready Seapower*, x.
21. Wyman H. Packard, *A Century of U.S. Naval Intelligence* (Washington, DC: Office of Naval Intelligence, 1996), 415.
22. Far East Command, *Intelligence and Related Covert Activities*, General Headquarters, 4 November 1950 (Declassified 12 May 2008), RG 313, NARA.
23. Marolda, *Ready Seapower*, 26.
24. Jian, *Mao's China and the Cold War*, 116.
25. David Tsui, *China's Military Intervention in Korea: Its Origins and Objectives* (Bloomington, IN: Trafford, 2015), 117–18.

26. CIA, "Replacement of CH'EN I."
27. Central Intelligence Agency, "Situation at Liuchou Airfield; East China Navy Command," 30 November 1950 (Declassified 11 August 2003), CIA CREST Database.
28. ComCruDiv One, "US Navy Operation Order No. 7–50," 7 October 1950, Post-1946 Operation Plans, Task Force 72, NHHC, cited in Elleman, *High Seas Buffer*.
29. COM7THFLT, "Report of Operations, Mar 1951–Mar 1952," RG 313, NARA.
30. COM7THFLT, "Report of Operations, Mar 1951–Mar 1952."
31. For instance, see Central Intelligence Agency, *The Situation in Korea*, National Intelligence Estimate, 20 May 1954, CIA CREST Database.
32. Central Intelligence Agency, "Memorandum for the Record: Interagency Agreement with the Navy," 5 May 1954, CIA CREST Database.
33. Central Intelligence Agency, *National Intelligence Digest*, 1 November 1952, (Declassified 21 September 2007), 27–30, CIA CREST Database.
34. Central Intelligence Agency, "Chinese Communist Central Military Council Order to Expedite Reorganization of the Navy and Air Force," *Information Report*, 14 August 1953 (Declassified 17 January 2006), CIA CREST Database.
35. "Mao Zedong to Su Yu, Zhang Zhen, Zhou Jingming, and the CCP East China Bureau," 14 June 1949, *CCFP*, 117, as cited in Jian, *Mao's China and the Cold War*, 165.
36. Mao Zedong to Zhou Enlai, 10 July 1949, *CCFP*, cited in Jian, *Mao's China and the Cold War*, 166n9.
37. ONI, "The Southeast China Coast Today," 51–60.
38. Adm. Robert B. Carney, "Security of the Offshore Islands Presently Held by the Nationalist Government of the Republic of China," Memorandum to Joint Chiefs of Staff (Top Secret), 30 July 1953, appendix, Strategic Plans Division, box 289, NHHC, Washington, DC.
39. Carney, "Security of the Offshore Islands."
40. Ralph W. Donnelly, Gabrielle M. Neufeld, and Carolyn A. Tyson, *A Chronology of the United States Marine Corps*, Vol. 3, *1947–1964* (Washington, DC: Historical Division Headquarters, U.S. Marine Corps, 1965), 29.
41. There is evidence to suggest, however, that Marine intelligence personnel had interrogated Chinese prisoners of war during the Korean

War, and integrated information educed from them into finished intelligence reports. Pat Meid and James M. Yingling, *Operations in West Korea*, vol. 5 (Washington, DC: Headquarters, U.S. Marine Corps, Historical Division, 1972), 85.
42. "Statement by the President on the Situation in Korea," 27 June 1950, Harry S. Truman Library and Museum, https://www.trumanlibrary.gov/library/public-papers/173/statement-president-situation-korea#.
43. Central Intelligence Agency, *Activities of Chinese Communist Army and Navy at Shanghai, Foochow, and Wenchow*, 2 June 1954 (Declassified 22 November 2005), CIA CREST Database. Also see Central Intelligence Agency, Office of Current Intelligence, *Current Intelligence Bulletin*, 24 June 1954 (Declassified 1 June 2005), CIA CREST Database.
44. Marolda, *Ready Seapower*, 40.
45. Mao Zedong at enlarged meeting of the CCP Politburo, July 7, 1954, in Zhang Baijia and Jia Qingguo, "Steering Wheel, Shock Absorber, and Probe in Confrontation: Sino-American Ambassadorial Talks as Seen from the Chinese Perspective," WCDA.
46. The works of Ralph Sawyer significantly contributed to the body of research into modern Chinese military theory drawing on a long tradition of deception and indirect approaches to warfare. See Ralph D. Sawyer, *The Tao of Deception* (New York: Basic Books, 2007), 489.
47. Baijia and Jia, "Steering Wheel, Shock Absorber," 355.
48. Central Intelligence Agency, *Chinese Communist Plans Proceed with Taiwan Invasion*, 11 July 1950 (Declassified 9 September 1999), CIA CREST Database.
49. Certainly the degree to which the Communist Bloc used deception and political warfare was not fully understood by Western intelligence at that point in the Cold War. See "Telegram, CCP Central Committee to Zhou Enlai, Concerning Policies and Measures in the Struggle against the United States and Jiang Jieshi after the Geneva Conference," 27 July 1954, WCDA, https://digitalarchive.wilsoncenter.org/document/telegram-ccp-central-committee-zhou-enlai-concerning-policies-and-measures-struggle.
50. Most of the material found in this research existed in archives that acquired material from the Chinese mainland several decades after the crisis. This included the Wilson Center Digital Archive (WCDA) and the Hoover Institution's archives.

51. For an exceptional history of Chinese deception in military doctrine, see Sawyer, *The Tao of Deception*.
52. It was later realized that the ship had been seized by the Chinese Nationalist navy. CIA, Office of Current Intelligence, *Current Intelligence Bulletin*, 24 June 1954. Also see National Security Council, *Disruption of Soviet Shipping in Far East Following Seizure of Tuapse*, NSC Briefing, 13 July 1954 (Approved for release 26 August 2003), RG 80, NARA.
53. "Memorandum of Conversation, between Soviet Premier Georgy M. Malenkov and Zhou Enlai," 29 July 1954, WCDA.
54. National Security Council, *Disruption of Soviet Shipping*.
55. PLA archives at the PLA Academy of Military Science, in Li Xiaoping, "PLA Attacks and Amphibious Operations during the Taiwan Straits Crises of 1954–1955 and 1958," Conference on PLA Warfighting, 1949–199, as referenced in Allen S. Whiting, "China's Use of Force, 1950–96, and Taiwan," *International Security* 26, no. 2 (Fall 2001): 108. The Kinmen Island group is also referred to as "Jinmen" in some of the archival records. In the interest of standardization, it is referred to as Kinmen. Kinmen Island is also referred to as Quemoy.
56. June Teufel Dreyer, "A History of Cross-Strait Interchange," in *Crisis in the Taiwan Strait*, ed. by James R. Lilley and Chuck Downs (Washington, DC: National Defense University Press, 1997), 13–45.
57. Deng Lifeng, *Jianguo hou junshi xingdong quanlu* [Complete record of military operations after the founding of the state] (Taiyuan: Shanxi People's Press, 1994), 207, as cited in Mark A. Ryan, David Finkelstein, Michael A. McDevitt, eds., *Chinese Warfighting: The PLA Experience since 1949* (Abingdon, U.K.: Routledge, 2003), n51.
58. Marolda, *Ready Seapower*, xi.
59. As referred to in O. Edmund Clubb, "Sino-American Relations and the Future of Formosa," *Political Science Quarterly* 80, no. 1 (March 1965), 8.
60. Mutual Defense Treaty between the United States and the Republic of China, 2 December 1954, Yale Law School, Lillian Goldman Law Library, http://avalon.law.yale.edu/20th_century/chin001.asp.
61. Richard F. Grimmett, "Instances of Use of United States Armed Forces Abroad, 1798–2004" (Washington, DC: Congressional Research

Service, Library of Congress, October 5, 2004), NHHC, https://www.history.navy.mil/research/library/online-reading-room/title-list-alphabetically/i/use-of-armed-forces-abroad-1798-2004.html.

62. Packard, *A Century of U.S. Naval Intelligence*, 415–16. Packard states this in his history of U.S. naval intelligence, but he provided no direct source. The author's credibility, however, is due to his service as the chief of the Collection and Dissemination branch at the ONI during this period.

63. Central Intelligence Agency, "Memorandum for the Director of Central Intelligence, Subject: NIE 100-4-55: Communist Capabilities and Intentions with Respect to the Offshore Islands, the Pescadores, and Taiwan through 1955, and Communist and Non-Communist Reactions with Respect to the Defense of Taiwan," 16 March 1955 (Declassified 3 September 2013), CIA CREST Database.

64. "Summary of the Views of Afro-Asian Countries on the Taiwan Issue at the Afro-Asian Conference," 27 May 1955, PRC FMA 207-00018-01, 1–4, obtained by Amitav Acharya and translated by Yang Shanhou, WCDA, http://digitalarchive.wilsoncenter.org/document/114694.

65. CHMAAG FORMOSA [China: Military Assistance Advisory Group, Formosa] to CINCPAC [Commander-in-Chief of the Pacific Fleet], Navy Telegram, 3895, 17 April 1955, Office of Chinese Affairs files, RG 313, NARA.

66. The standard process that would become universal—namely, plan, collect, process/exploit, analyze, and disseminate—was not yet clearly evident.

67. M. H. Halperin, *The 1958 Taiwan Straits Crisis: A Documented History*, RM-4900-ISA (Santa Monica, CA: RAND, 1966; declassified March 18, 1975).

68. For a dual historical/international relations examination of the 1950s crises, see Shu Guang Zhang, *Deterrence and Strategic Culture: Chinese-American Confrontations, 1949–1958* (Ithaca, NY: Cornell University Press, 1992). Richard Bush's work on U.S.-Taiwan relations since 1942 also covers the crises at length. See Richard Bush, *At Cross Purposes: U.S.-Taiwan Relations since 1942* (Abingdon, U.K.: Routledge, 2004). Thomas Christensen's work puts U.S.-Taiwan relations in a Cold War perspective, underscoring the Kuomintang importance to containment policy. See Thomas J. Christensen, *Useful Adversaries:*

Grand Strategy, Domestic Mobilization, and Sino-American Conflict, 1947–1958 (Princeton, NJ: Princeton University Press, 1996).
69. Packard, *A Century of U.S. Naval Intelligence*, 416.
70. This was done under the guise of the Friendship, Commerce, and Navigation Treaty of 1948.
71. Command, Taiwan Patrol Force to Chief of Naval Operations, "Subject: Operating Force Staff Intelligence Activity Report," 11 April 1958 (Declassified 10 April 2018), RG 313, UD 1615, Box 9184, NARA.
72. Command, Taiwan Patrol Force to Chief of Naval Operations.
73. Commander, Taiwan Patrol Force to Commander, Seventh Fleet, "Subject: Operations in Taiwan Straits Situation," 30 October 1958 (Declassified 10 April 2018), RG 313, EN 1615, Box 9184, NARA.
74. Far East Command (Headquarters), Policy Directive No. 9–5, *FEC ECM Policy*, 31 December 1956 (Declassified 10 April 2018), RG 313, UD 1615, Box 9184, NARA.
75. Commander ECMRON One to Commander Task Force 72, "Subject: Plans for the Employment of the AN/ALQ-23 Countermeasure Set," 15 March 1957 (Declassified 10 April 2018), RG 313, UD 1615, Box 9184, NARA. The surface combatant version of the AN/ALQ-23 was the SLQ-23, which was also introduced around the same time.
76. Headquarters, Far East Command, Policy Directive No. 9-6, Functions and Composition of the JEF, 31 December 1958 (Declassified 10 April 1958), RG 313, NARA.
77. Commander, Taiwan Patrol Force to Commander, Destroyer Flotilla, Western Pacific, "Subject: Magnetic Tape Recorders in West Pacific Destroyers, Installation of," 22 March 1958 (Declassified 10 April 2018), RG 313, UD 1615, Box 9184, NARA.
78. Central Intelligence Agency, *Probable Chinese Communist and Soviet Intentions in the Taiwan Strait Area*, National Intelligence Estimate, no. 100-11-58, 16 September 1958 (Declassified June 2004), CIA CREST Database.
79. Letter, Mao Zedong to Peng Dehuai and Huang Kecheng, 27 July 1958, WCDA, http://digitalarchive.wilsoncenter.org/document/117011.pdf?v=f33d871dedc21e2ccdc637d4dcb7cfab.
80. Halperin, *The 1958 Taiwan Straits Crisis*.

81. "History of the Strategic Air Command, January 1958–30 June 1958," Historical Study No. 73 (Declassified through FOIA), Air Force Historical Research Center, Maxwell Air Force Base, AL.
82. Central Intelligence Agency, "Minutes of Meeting Held in IAC Conference Room, Administration Building Central Intelligence Agency, at 1045, 26 AUGUST 1958," CIA CREST Database, https://www.cia.gov/readingroom/document/cia-rdp61-00549r000300090006-8.
83. CIA, "Minutes of Meeting Held in IAC Conference Room."
84. Department of State, Office of the Historian, "Memorandum from the Commander, U.S. Taiwan Defense Command (Smoot) to the Chief of General Staff, Republic of China (Wang)," Taipei, September 4, 1958, Washington National Records Center, RG 84, Taipei Embassy Files: FRC 68 A 5159, Lot 62 F 83 (declassified), https://history.state.gov/historicaldocuments/frus1958-60v19/d65.
85. Even with significant support from Soviet air power (including foreign military sales), this was a prohibitive endeavor for the PLA Air Force at the time.
86. Mao Zedong to Peng Dehuai (Instructions), 18 August 1958, WCDA.
87. While there is speculation of this in NIEs and other intelligence reports in years preceding the 1958 crisis, none of the estimates published in the months preceding the crisis gave serious credence to this possibility.
88. Halperin, *The 1958 Taiwan Straits Crisis*.
89. Central Intelligence Agency, "Probable Developments in the Taiwan Strait Area," Special National Intelligence Estimate, SNIE 100-9-58, 26 August 1958, Department of State, Office of the Historian, https://history.state.gov/historicaldocuments/frus1958-60v19/d47.
90. CIA, "Minutes of Meeting Held in IAC Conference Room."
91. William P. Bundy, "Validity Study of NIE 100-4-55: Communist Capabilities and Intentions with Respect to the Offshore Islands and Taiwan through 1955, and Communist and Non-Communist Reactions with Respect to the Defense of Taiwan, Published 16 March 1958," Intelligence Advisory Committee, 24 May 1956 (Declassified 15 August 2012), CIA CREST Database.
92. Central Intelligence Agency, *Probable Developments in the Taiwan Strait*, National Intelligence Estimate, Number 100-9-58, 15 September 1958 (Declassified 16 May 2005), CIA CREST Database.

93. Xu Yan, *Jinmen Zhizhan shilao chubian* [A preliminary collection of historical materials about the Jinmen and Dengbu battles] (Taipei: Guoshiguan, 1979), 561–63, as cited in Jian, *Mao's China and the Cold War*.
94. Halperin, *The 1958 Taiwan Straits Crisis*.
95. Richard Bissell Jr., Project Director, Central Intelligence Agency, "Memorandum for Director of Central Intelligence, Subject: Deployment of Detachment C to Japan," 10 December 1956 (Declassified June 2004), CIA CREST Database.
96. Secretary of the Navy to Director of Central Intelligence, Allen Dulles, 5 December 1958, CIA CREST Database.
97. Chief of Naval Operations to Director of Central Intelligence, "Overflights of the China Coast, Requests For," 9 September 1958 (Declassified 27 August 2001), CIA CREST Database, https://www.cia.gov/readingroom/docs/CIA-RDP61S00750A000500040074-0.pdf
98. Gregory Pedlow and Donald Welzenbach, *The Central Intelligence Agency and Overhead Reconnaissance: The U2 and Oxcart Programs, 1954–1974* (New York: Skyhorse, 2016), 211–20.
99. CIA, "Minutes of Meeting Held in IAC Conference Room."
100. Joint Chiefs of Staff to the Commander in Chief, Pacific (Felt) (Telegram from the), 25 August 1958, Department of State, *Foreign Relations of the United States, 1958–1960, China*, vol. 19, https://history.state.gov/historicaldocuments/frus1958-60v19/d44.
101. Halperin, *The 1958 Taiwan Straits Crisis*.
102. CIA, "Probable Developments in the Taiwan Strait Area," Special National Intelligence Estimate, SNIE 100-9-58.
103. Halperin, *The 1958 Taiwan Straits Crisis*.
104. Jian, *Mao's China and the Cold War*, 116.
105. Donnelly, Neufeld, and Tyson, *A Chronology of the United States Marine Corps*, Vol. 3, *1947–1964*, 38.
106. Jian, *Mao's China and the Cold War*, 116.
107. Mao Zedong at the Fifteenth Meeting of the Supreme State Council (Speech), 8 September 1958, WCDA.
108. "Letter, Central Committee of the Communist Party of the Soviet Union to the Chinese Communist Party, on the Soviet Union's Readiness to Provide Assistance to China in the Event of an Attack," 27 September 1958, WCDA, http://digitalarchive.wilsoncenter.org/document/117028.

109. "Memorandum of Conversation of Mao Zedong with Six Delegates of the Socialist Countries, China, 2 October 1958," History and Public Policy Program Digital Archive, GARF f. 9576, op. 18, 1958, d. 26, l, 312–22, obtained and translated by Austin Jersild, WCDA, http://digitalarchive.wilsoncenter.org/document/116826.

110. Letter, Mao Zedong to Huang Kecheng and Peng Dehuai, 6 October 1958, History and Public Policy Program Digital Archive, Zhonggong zhongyang wenxian yanjiushi, ed., *Jianguo yilai Mao Zedong wengao* [Mao Zedong's manuscripts since the founding of the People's Republic of China], vol. 7 (Beijing: Zhongyang wenxian chubanshe, 1992), 437, http://digitalarchive.wilsoncenter.org/document/117023; Zhou Enlai's Conversation with S. F. Antonov on the Taiwan Issue (Meeting Minutes excerpt), 5 October 1958, History and Public Policy Program Digital Archive, *Zhou Enlai waijiao wenxuan* [Selected works of Zhou Enlai on diplomacy] (Beijing: Zhongyang wenxian chubanshe, 1990), 262–67, WCDA, http://digitalarchive.wilsoncenter.org/document/117018; and "Message to the Compatriots in Taiwan," *Renmin ribao* (*People's Daily*), 6 October 1958, WCDA.

111. Commander, Task Force 72 to U.S. Taiwan Defense Command, "Subject: Orientation of CHINAT Resupply Operations in Event of Resumption Artillery Fire Kinmen," 15 October 1958 (Declassified 9 April 2018), RG 313, UD 1615, Box 9184, NARA.

112. Naval Forces, Far East, *GRC Navy Force Levels*, 20 October 1958 (Declassified 9 April 1958), RG 313, UD 1615, Box 9184, NARA.

113. Few, if any, Taiwan perspectives on Communist mainland sources survived or were published.

114. Central Intelligence Agency, "Need for Intelligence on ChiCom Activities Opposite Taiwan" (Declassified 18 August 2003), 22 August 1961, CIA CREST Database.

Chapter 7. Kennedy and the Dominoes

1. For the years 1959–61, the CIA CREST Database as of 11 May 2018 shows 459 reports with "Soviet Union" in the title, 3,463 with "China" in the title, 291 with "Russia" in the title, 281 with "nuclear" in the title, and 744 with "missile" in the title. The large disparity between the

number of reports referring to the Soviet Union or Russia and those referring to China can be explained by the level of specificity in those reports on the Soviet Union or Russia (e.g., stating the "SS-5 missile") versus those focused on China or Chinese military capabilities.

2. Mao Lin, "China and the Escalation of the Vietnam War, *Journal of Cold War Studies* 11, no. 2 (Spring 2009): 35–69. Also see Mark Moyar, *Triumph Forsaken: The Vietnam War, 1954–1965* (New York: Cambridge University Press, 2006).

3. Xiaoming Zhang, "The Vietnam War, 1964–1969: A Chinese Perspective," *Journal of Military History* 60, no. 4 (October 1996): 731–62.

4. Mao Zedong, "The Role of the Chinese Communist Party in the National War, October 1938," speech delivered at the Sixth Plenary Session of the Sixth Central Committee of the Chinese Communist Party, in *Selected Works of Mao Tse-tung*, https://www.marxists.org/reference/archive/mao/selected-works/volume-2/mswv2_10.htm.

5. This was discussed at length in Gaddis' treatment on containment. John L. Gaddis, *Strategies of Containment: A Critical Appraisal of Postwar American National Security Policy* (New York: Oxford University Press, 1982), 198–236. Eisenhower first mentioned the domino theory in a press conference on 7 April 1954, specifically referring to Southeast Asia.

6. For example, see Paul Maddrell's *Spying on Science: Western Intelligence in Divided Germany, 1945–1961* (Oxford: Oxford University Press, 2006). Also see Oleg Penkovsky, *The Penkovsky Papers*, trans. by Edward Crankshaw (London: Collins, 1965).

7. For various reasons, the CIA's recruitment pipeline during this time was at a low point. More importantly for those who were successfully recruited and eventually Farm-trained case officers, career tracks were unpredictable, at least compared with the military. See Emmet D. Echols (Director of Personnel) to Deputy Director (Support), "Subject: JOT [Junior Officer Recruitment] Recruitment," 19 September 1961, https://www.cia.gov/readingroom/docs/CIA-RDP80-01826R000300050025-1.pdf.

8. Secretary of the Navy to Distribution List [e.g., CINCLANTFLT, CINCPACFLT, COMNAVFORJAPAN], "Subj: Instructions for the Coordination and Control of the Navy's Clandestine Intelligence

Collection Program," 7 December 1965 (Declassified 13 July 1990), National Security Archive, https://nsarchive2.gwu.edu/NSAEBB/NSAEBB520-the-Pentagons-Spies/EBB-PS01.pdf. Task Force 157 has been studied before, but its historical context has not. Also see Jeffrey T. Richelson, "Task Force 157: The U.S. Navy's Secret Intelligence Service, 1966–77," *Intelligence and National Security* 11, no. 1 (1996): 106–45.

9. See Michael Warner, "'US Intelligence and Vietnam': The Official Version," *Intelligence and National Security* 25, no. 5 (2010): 611–37.

10. Joshua Kurlantzick's work on the U.S. role in Laos provides significant evidence that the U.S. military played a central part in the "CIA war." Conversely, while the CIA was certainly involved, the Seventh Fleet, special operations forces, and the III Marine Expeditionary Force also contributed important parts, as did Amb. William Sullivan in Vientiane. See Joshua Kurlantzick, *A Great Place to Have a War: America in Laos and the Birth of a Military CIA* (New York: Simon & Schuster, 2016), 323.

11. For instance, see Thomas A. Ahern, *Vietnam Declassified: The CIA and Counterinsurgency* (Lexington: University Press of Kentucky, 2012). Also see Max Boot's work on Edward Lansdale. Max Boot, *The Road Not Taken: Edward Lansdale and the American Tragedy in Vietnam* (New York: Liveright, 2018). For a naval intelligence–specific memoir work, see Douglass H. Hubbard, *Special Agent, Vietnam: A Naval Intelligence Memoir* (Washington, DC: Potomac, 2006).

12. Secretary of the Navy to Distribution List, "Instructions for the Coordination and Control."

13. See, for instance, William Blum, *Killing Hope: U.S. Military and CIA Interventions since World War II* (Monroe, ME: Common Courage, 1995), 144–45.

14. Chengzhi Yin, "China's Military Assistance to North Vietnam Revisited," *Journal of American–East Asian Relations* 26 (2019): 226–56.

15. Richard A. Mobley and Edward J. Marolda, *Knowing the Enemy: Naval Intelligence in Southeast Asia* (Washington, DC: Department of the Navy, Naval History and Heritage Command, 2015), 100.

16. A large body of evidence suggests that intelligence served both as a catalyst for escalation and as a burden for domestic perspectives. The use and manipulation of intelligence (sometimes referred to as

"cherry-picking") by leaders from Gen. William Westmoreland to Secretary of Defense Robert McNamara is widely acknowledged. See, for example, H. R. McMaster, *Dereliction of Duty: Johnson, McNamara, the Joint Chiefs of Staff, and the Lies That Led to Vietnam* (New York: Harper Perennial, 1998), 480.
17. The term "Indochina" is used here to broadly refer to Vietnam, Laos, and Cambodia collectively, in the context of the crises associated with them.
18. Lawrence Freedman, *Kennedy's Wars: Berlin, Cuba, Laos, and Vietnam* (Oxford: Oxford University Press, 2000), 560.
19. U.S. Marine Corps, Historical Branch, G-3 Division Headquarters, *General Chronology of Events in Vietnam, 1945–1964*, 9 October 1964 (Declassified 9 April 2018), RG 127, EN 984145, Box 98, NARA.
20. This is characterized in the Marine Corps' Anti-Guerilla Operations doctrine, produced in 1961. See U.S. Marine Corps, *Anti-Guerilla Operations in South East Asia, Commander in Chief Far East Land Forces*, January 1963, RG 127, EN 984145, Box 198, NARA. It was also clear that the CIA included Navy and Marine Corps units in several aspects of its covert campaign against North Vietnam, many records of which remain classified. For a well-researched history of this with some of the available archival records, see Richard H. Shultz, *The Secret War against Hanoi: Kennedy's and Johnson's Use of Spies, Saboteurs, and Covert Warriors in North Vietnam* (New York: HarperCollins, 1999), 390.
21. Peter Wyden, *Bay of Pigs: The Untold Story* (New York: Simon & Schuster, 1979), 86, 125–31. Also see Wyman H. Packard, *A Century of U.S. Naval Intelligence* (Washington, DC: Office of Naval Intelligence, 1996), 32.
22. Defense Intelligence Agency, *A Brief History: Committed to Excellence in Defense of the Nation* (Washington, DC: DIA History Office, 1996), 7, https://www.govinfo.gov/content/pkg/GOVPUB-D5_200-PURL-LPS49168/pdf/GOVPUB-D5_200-PURL-LPS49168.pdf.
23. John Prados, *Safe for Democracy* (Chicago: Ivan R. Dee, 2006), 736.
24. Christopher Andrew, *The World Was Going Our Way: The KGB and the Battle for the Third World* (New York: Basic Books, 2006), 736.
25. For an overview of the early rationale for covert policy under Truman, see Sarah-Jane Corke, *U.S. Covert Operations and Cold War Strategy: Truman, Secret Warfare, and the CIA, 1945–1953* (New York:

Routledge, 2008), 256. Although partly about postcolonial perturbations in the third world, the British approach to covert policy also partially rooted in a similar containment policy. See Clive Jones, "Where the State Feared to Tread: Britain, Britons, Covert Action and the Yemen Civil War, 1962–64," in *Intelligence, Crises and Security: Prospects and Retrospects*, ed. by L. V. Scott and R. Gerald Hughes, 65–85 (London: Routledge, 2008). Also see Richard J. Aldrich, "British Intelligence and the Anglo-American 'Special Relationship' during the Cold War," *Review of International Studies* 24, no. 3 (July 1998): 331–51.

26. The Taylor Committee Investigation of The Bay of Pigs, 1961 (rev. ed., 1984), National Security Archives, https://nsarchive2.gwu.edu/NSAEBB/NSAEBB355/bop-vol4.pdf.

27. The so-called Church Committee (after the chairman, Sen. Frank Church) was the shorthand for Senate Select Committee to Study Governmental Operations with Respect to Intelligence Activities. The final report is available at https://www.intelligence.senate.gov/resources/intelligence-related-commissions.

28. Clayton Laurie and Andres Vaart, eds., *CIA and the Wars in Southeast Asia 1947–75*, Studies in Intelligence (Washington, DC: Center for the Study of Intelligence), August 2016, https://www.cia.gov/resources/csi/static/8893cd9ddceaad19edf3c14516bcd6a7/CIA-Wars-Southeast-Asia.pdf.

29. William Colby, *Honorable Men: My Life in the CIA* (New York: Simon & Schuster, 1978).

30. For a complete first-person account of the political covert operations the CIA conducted around this time, see Larry Devlin's account of the assassination of Lumumba in the Belgian Congo and the installation of Mobutu Sese Seko. Larry Devlin, *Chief of Station, Congo: Fighting the Cold War in a Hot Zone* (New York: Public Affairs, 2008).

31. Many of the works cited in this research have debated whether it *was* a U.S. war at this point. For example, see John Prados, *The Hidden History of the Vietnam War* (Chicago: Ivan R. Dee, 1998).

32. Other countries involved in the region included Britain, France, South Korea, and Taiwan.

33. U.S. Marine Corps, *General Chronology of Events in Vietnam*, 9 October 1964.
34. This was broadly discussed in John Prados' seminal work on the secret side of the U.S. experience in Vietnam. See Prados, *Hidden History*.
35. Countless records on this topic exist in the State Department's historical archives. For instance, see Department of State, Office of the Historian, "Director of the Bureau of Intelligence and Research (Hughes) to the Secretary of State" (Research Memorandum), Washington, September 11, 1963, https://history.state.gov/historicaldocuments/frus1961-63v04/d92.
36. Peter T. Leeson and Andrea Dean, "The Democratic Domino Theory," *American Journal of Political Science* 53, no. 3 (2009): 533–51.
37. Boot, *Road Not Taken*, 768. Also see Warner Smith, *Covert Warrior: Fighting the CIA's Secret War in Southeast Asia and China, 1965–1967: The Vietnam War Memoir of Warner Smith* (Novato, CA: Presidio, 1996), 296.
38. The volume talks at length about clandestine warfare, intelligence networks in Vietnam, and the role of the Navy and Marine Corps in the broader crisis and war context. New York Times Company, *The Pentagon Papers: The Secret History of the Vietnam War* (New York: Racehorse, 2017), 810.
39. Central Intelligence Agency, "Considerations in the Establishment of a Defense Intelligence Agency," 21 April 1961 (Approved for release 29 May 2003), CIA CREST Database.
40. Attempts were made in this research, of course, to bridge this divide through efforts of Kennedy's call for the Taylor Commission and Edward Lansdale's official, yet vague, postmilitary retirement role in Saigon in 1963. See Taylor Committee Investigation of The Bay of Pigs. Also see Boot, *Road Not Taken*.
41. Jeffrey Richelson's research at the National Security Archives in Washington uncovered the earliest known uses of the term "HUMINT" outside of the CIA starting in the early 1960s. Jeffrey T. Richelson, "The Pentagon's Spies, Newly Available Documents Trace Evolution of Spy Units through Obama Administration," National Security Archive Electronic Briefing Book No. 520 (Updated July 6, 2015), https://nsarchive2.gwu.edu/NSAEBB/NSAEBB520-the-Pentagons-Spies/.

42. For the definitive history of the Bay of Pigs and its effects on intelligence policy, see Wyden, *Bay of Pigs*, 352.
43. Colby, *Honorable Men*.
44. NSC 10/2, 18 June 1948, authorized the Office of Policy Coordination to conduct covert operations. See Michael Warner, ed., *The CIA under Harry Truman* (Langley, VA: Center for the Study of Intelligence, 1994).
45. Thomas L. Ahern Jr., *The Way We Do Things: Black Entry Operations into North Vietnamese*, Center for the Study of Intelligence, Central Intelligence Agency (Declassified), 2005, 7, CIA CREST Database.
46. Thomas L. Ahern, *CIA and the House of Ngo, 1954–63*, Center for the Study of Intelligence, Central Intelligence Agency, 2000, CIA CREST Database.
47. Graham A. Cosmas, *MAC-V: The Joint Command in the Years of Escalation, 1962–1967*, The United States Army in Vietnam (Washington, DC: United States Army Center of Military History, 2006), https://www.history.army.mil/catalog/pubs/91/91-6.html.
48. For an excellent history of special operations (including Navy SEAL and Marine special reconnaissance units) in North Vietnam and Laos, see Ahern, *The Way We Do Things*.
49. U.S. Military Assistance Command, Vietnam, Studies and Observations Group, *Annex A, Command History, 1964* (Saigon: MAC-V-SOG, 1965; declassified), U.S. Army Center of Military History.
50. Naval Forces, Vietnam, was established in 1965.
51. George F. Howe, "The Early History of NSA," undated internal NSA history, National Security Agency (declassified), https://www.nsa.gov/portals/75/documents/news-features/declassified-documents/cryptologic-spectrum/early_history_nsa.pdf.
52. For a history of the Seabee experience in Vietnam, see Thomas A. Johnston and Kenneth E. Bingham, *Seabee Teams in Vietnam 1963–1968: 13 Man Teams That Helped Rural Vietnamese and Who Fought Alongside the Special Forces* (N.p.: CreateSpace, 2012). Also see Mark Divine and Allyson Edelhertz Mechate, *The Way of the SEAL: Think Like an Elite Warrior to Lead and Succeed* (New York: Reader's Digest, 2016).
53. Commander Amphibious Force, Pacific Fleet, CTF 16, *PACFLET 1-61, Exercise Greenlight, Phase III (Final Report)*, 30 October 1961 (Declassified), The Vietnam Center and Archive, Texas Tech University.

54. Commander Amphibious Force, Pacific Fleet, CTF 16, *PACFLET 1-61*.
55. New York Times Company, *The Pentagon Papers*, 54–67.
56. *Headquarters, U.S. Military Assistance Command, Vietnam, Command History 1964* (Declassified, sanitized version) (Washington, DC: Defense Technical Information Center database, 1968).
57. It was deemed that photo interpreters were needed—not immediately, but over the next few years. See Headquarters, Fleet Marine Force, Atlantic, "Subject: Fleet Marine Force Organization Test Program, Phase II, Unit Studies, Intelligence Specialist Teams, Photo Interpreters (Mid-range, 1962–1968)" (Declassified), RG 127, Entry 984145, Box 107, NARA.
58. Leon Cohan Jr., "Intelligence and Viet-Nam," *Marine Corps Gazette* 50, no. 2 (February 1966).
59. Fleet Marine Force, Atlantic, G2 Section, "Subject: Organization and Employment of Interrogation-Translation and Interpreter Teams," 30 March 1961 (Declassified 9 April 2018), RG 127, Entry 984145, Box 107, NARA.
60. Dirk Anthony Ballendorf and Merrill Bartlett, *Pete Ellis: An Amphibious Warfare Prophet, 1880–1923* (Annapolis, MD: Naval Institute Press, 1997).
61. Fleet Marine Force, Atlantic, G-2 Section, "Subject: Organization of the Counterintelligence Team, Fleet Marine Force," 30 March 1961, RG 127, Entry 984145, Box 108, NARA.
62. Fleet Marine Force, Atlantic, G-2 Section, "Organization of the Counterintelligence Team."
63. Charles Thomas, Secretary of the Navy to Allen Dulles, Director of Central Intelligence, 3 December 1956, CIA CREST Database.
64. G. McNulty, Lieutenant Commander, Training Branch, Office of Naval Intelligence to Orientation Office, CIA, 1 February 1961 (Approved for release 8 May 2002), CIA CREST Database.
65. B. E. Wiggin, Captain (USN), to Matthew Baird, Director of Training, Central Intelligence Agency, 15 March 1961 (Approved for release 8 May 2002), CIA CREST Database.

Chapter 8. Preparing Intelligence for Deeper Involvement

1. U.S. Marine Corps, Historical Branch, G-3 Division Headquarters, *General Chronology of Events in Vietnam, 1945–1964*, 9 October 1964 (Declassified 9 April 2018), RG 127, Entry 984145, Box 98, NARA.
2. U.S. Marine Corps, *General Chronology of Events in Vietnam*.
3. Although separated (FMF-P on Camp Smith and the Pacific Fleet at Makalapa on Oahu), FMF-P was the subordinate Marine Corps component to the commander of the Pacific Fleet.
4. The service chiefs and secretaries were also not considered in the operational chain of command.
5. For instance, Commanding General, Fleet Marine Force, Pacific to Commandant of the Marine Corps, "Subj: Quarterly Combat Readiness Report of Ground Units," Headquarters, Fleet Marine Force, Pacific, 11 May 1960, U.S. Marine Corps History Division Vietnam War Documents Collection, The Vietnam Center and Archive, Texas Tech University. In FMF-P's case, the commander oversaw I Marine Division and III Marine Division, among several other adjacent units, such as Marine air wings.
6. Edwin Moise, *Tonkin Gulf and the Escalation of the Vietnam War* (Chapel Hill: University of North Carolina Press, 1996), 304.
7. U.S. Marine Corps, *General Chronology of Events in Vietnam*.
8. On the debate over the war, see Robert S. McNamara, *Argument without End: In Search of Answers to the Vietnam Tragedy* (New York: Public Affairs, 2000); on the idea that the United States wanted to help South Vietnam, consider the chapter titled "Conflict, Dissent, and Moderation" in Robert L. Gallucci, *Neither Peace nor Honor: The Politics of American Military Policy in Viet-Nam* (Baltimore: Johns Hopkins University Press, 1975), 12–34.
9. Richard H. Shultz, *The Secret War against Hanoi: Kennedy's and Johnson's Use of Spies, Saboteurs, and Covert Warriors in North Vietnam* (New York: HarperCollins, 1999), 390.
10. Commander, United States Military Assistance Command, Vietnam, "Subj: Possible VC Anti-Aircraft Weapon Capability (SRI-62-57)," MACJ21, 3800 Ser: 0628 dtd 26 December 1962, included as enclosure in Commanding General, Aircraft, Fleet Marine Force,

Pacific to Commandant of the Marine Corps, "Subj: Command Diary; submission of" [CTE 79.3.3.6], 4 April 1963 (Declassified), The Vietnam Center and Archive, Texas Tech University.
11. Commander, MAC-V, "Subj: Possible VC Anti-Aircraft Weapon Capability."
12. Commander, Task Element 79.3.3.6 to Commander, MAC-V, "Subj: Evaluation of Helicopter Tactics and Techniques Report," 10 January 1963, included as enclosure in Commanding General, Aircraft, Fleet Marine Force, Pacific to Commandant of the Marine Corps, "Subj: Command Diary; submission of" [CTE 79.3.3.6], 4 April 1963 (Declassified), The Vietnam Center and Archive, Texas Tech University.
13. Commander, MAC-V, "Subj: Possible VC Anti-Aircraft Weapon Capability."
14. John L. Plaster, *SOG: The Secret Wars of America's Commandos in Vietnam* (New York: Nal Caliber, 2010), 7.
15. Plaster, *SOG*, 7, 315.
16. U.S. Military Assistance Command Vietnam, Studies and Observations Group, *Annex A, Command History, 1964*, Saigon: MAC-V-SOG, 1965 (Declassified), The Vietnam Center and Archive, Texas Tech University.
17. Colby discussed this in his autobiography. See William Colby, *Honorable Men: My Life in the CIA* (New York: Simon & Schuster, 1978), 137–40.
18. MAC-V, Studies and Observations Group, *Annex A, Command History, 1964*.
19. MAC-V, Studies and Observations Group, *Annex A, Command History, 1964*.
20. Michael Lee Lanning and Ray W. Stubbe, *Inside Force Recon: Recon Marines in Vietnam* (Guilford, CT: Stackpole, 1989), 37–39.
21. Plaster, *SOG*, 10.
22. Moise, *Tonkin Gulf*.
23. Commander, United States Military Assistance Command, Vietnam, "Subject: Chien Thang (National Pacification Program)," 20 April 1964 (Declassified 14 April 2018), RG 38, EN 98C, Box 13, NARA. The National Pacification Program later became the Civil Operations and Revolutionary Development Support in 1967.

24. Commander, United States Military Assistance Command, Vietnam, MACJ2 3800 Ser: 00202 dtd 11 October 1962, "Subject: Intelligence Estimate, Period October 1962–February 1963," included as enclosure in Commanding General, Aircraft, Fleet Marine Force, Pacific to Commandant of the Marine Corps, "Subj: Command Diary; submission of" [CTE 79.3.3.6], 4 April 1963 (Declassified), The Vietnam Center and Archive, Texas Tech University.
25. For instance, it is sometimes unclear when estimations include the actual VC versus only population-based guerillas. Additionally, it is often unclear whether guerillas were transports from the North or persons from the South with an affinity for the North Vietnamese cause.
26. U.S. Military Assistance Command Vietnam, Studies and Observations Group, *Annex N, Command History, 1965* (Saigon: MAC-V-SOG, 1966), The Vietnam Center and Archive, Texas Tech University.
27. For more on the ban of reconnaissance flights during this period, see Thomas Tobin, *Last Flight from Saigon*, USAF Southeast Asia Monograph, ser. 1, vol. 4, mono. 6 (Washington, DC: U.S. Government Printing Office, 1978).
28. MAC-V, Studies and Observations Group, *Annex A, Command History*.
29. These target lists were completely focused on people rather than infrastructure or any other kind of fixed target.
30. MAC-V, Studies and Observations Group, *Annex A, Command History*.
31. Headquarters, U.S. Military Assistance Command, Vietnam, *Command History 1964* (Declassified, Sanitized version), DTIC database, referencing: CINCPAC to COMUSMAC-V, DTG 260341Z Sep 64, File MACJ3 (S), Ltr, Hq MAC-V, Ser 0076A, 25 February 64, "Subj: Report on Recommendations Pertaining to Infiltration into SVN of VC Personnel, Supporting Materials, Weapons and Ammunition."
32. Headquarters, MAC-V, *Command History 1964*.
33. MAC-V, Studies and Observations Group, *Annex A*.
34. Capt. Robert H. Whitlow, USMCR, *U.S. Marines in Vietnam: The Advisory & Combat Assistance Era, 1954–1964* (Washington, DC: History and Museums Division Headquarters, U.S. Marine Corps, 1977), https://www.usmcu.edu/Portals/218/U_S_%20Marines%20in%20Vietnam_The%20Advisory%20and%20Combat%20Assistance%20Era%201954-1964%20%20PCN%2019000306400.pdf. Also see Chet Decker, "Operation Shufly," *Leatherneck*, April 2002, 36–39.

35. U.S. Marine Corps, *General Chronology*.
36. U.S. Marine Corps, *General Chronology*.
37. Lanning and Stubbe, *Inside Force Recon*, 33–39.
38. Task Element 79.3.3.6 (Intelligence Officer), "Subj: Progress Report," Memorandum 2: DFA: brb 3800 dtd 23 January 1963, included as enclosure in Commanding General, Aircraft, Fleet Marine Force, Pacific to Commandant of the Marine Corps, "Subj: Command Diary; submission of" [CTE 79.3.3.6], 4 April 1963, The Vietnam Center and Archive, Texas Tech University.
39. Task Element 79.3.3.6 (Intelligence Officer), "Subj: Progress Report."
40. Task Element 79.3.3.6 (Intelligence Officer), "Subj: Progress Report."
41. Task Element 79.3.3.6, "Subj: Comments on Countering Heliborne Landings and Raids," Captured translated Viet Cong Document [TE 79.3.3.6], undated enclosure in Commanding General, Aircraft, Fleet Marine Force, Pacific to Commandant of the Marine Corps, "Subj: Command Diary; submission of" [CTE 79.3.3.6], 4 April 1963 (Declassified), The Vietnam Center and Archive, Texas Tech University.
42. Task Element 79.3.3.6, "Subj: Comments on Countering Heliborne Landings and Raids."
43. Task Element 79.3.3.6, "Subj: Comments on Countering Heliborne Landings and Raids."
44. Task Element 79.3.3.6, *Task Element 79.3.3.6 Command Diary, 1 Nov 1963–1 Oct 1964*, p. 34 (Declassified), The Vietnam Center and Archive, Texas Tech University.
45. Task Element 79.3.3.6 (Intelligence Officer), "Subj: Progress Report."
46. 1st Lt. D. G. Marr, "Subj: Problems Faced by Task Element 79.3.3.6 in the event of an attempted Coup d'état in Vietnam," 2 January 1963, included as enclosure in Commanding General, Aircraft, Fleet Marine Force, Pacific to Commandant of the Marine Corps, "Subj: Command Diary; submission of" [CTE 79.3.3.6], 4 April 1963 (Declassified), The Vietnam Center and Archive, Texas Tech University.
47. United States Marine Corps, *The Marines in Vietnam: 1954–1973: An Anthology and Annotated Bibliography*, 2nd. ed. (Washington, DC: History and Museums Division Headquarters, U.S. Marine Corps, 1985), 17.
48. Fleet Marine Force Pacific, Senior Advisor, I Corps, "MAGTN-IC dtd 23 Nov 1962, Subj: VC Anti-American Activity," included as

enclosure in Commanding General, Aircraft, Fleet Marine Force, Pacific to Commandant of the Marine Corps, "Subj: Command Diary; submission of" [CTE 79.3.3.6], 4 April 1963 (Declassified), The Vietnam Center and Archive, Texas Tech University. The source of this intelligence was the chief of Da Nang Security Office. See Fleet Marine Force Pacific, Security Officer, Northern Area, Intelligence Bulletin No. 1852/CSDB.IM, "Subj: Viet Cong Anti-American Activity," included as enclosure in Commanding General, Aircraft, Fleet Marine Force, Pacific to Commandant of the Marine Corps, "Subj: Command Diary; submission of" [CTE 79.3.3.6], 4 April 1963 (Declassified), The Vietnam Center and Archive, Texas Tech University.

49. Fleet Marine Force Pacific, Security Officer, Northern Area, Intelligence Bulletin No. 1852/CSDB.IM, "Subj: Viet Cong Anti-American Activity."
50. Fleet Marine Force Pacific, Security Officer, Northern Area, Intelligence Bulletin No. 1852/CSDB.IM, "Subj: Viet Cong Anti-American Activity."
51. Fleet Marine Force Pacific, Security Officer, Northern Area, Intelligence Bulletin No. 1852/CSDB.IM, "Subj: Viet Cong Anti-American Activity."
52. Task Element 79.3.3.6. "Weekly OPSUM TE 79.3.3.6 Period 11–17 June 1964, Task Element 79.3.3.6" (Declassified), The Vietnam Center and Archive, Texas Tech University.
53. Task Element 79.3.3.6 (Intelligence Officer), "Subj: Progress Report."
54. CTF 79.3.3.6, Operation Shufly Summaries, 11–17 June 1964 (Declassified), The Vietnam Center and Archive, Texas Tech University.
55. Task Element 79.3.3.6 (Intelligence Officer), "Subj: Progress Report."
56. Task Element 79.3.3.6 (Intelligence Officer), "Subj: Security Survey of Task Element 79.3.3.6," Memorandum 2, 31 Dec. 1962, included as enclosure in Commanding General, Aircraft, Fleet Marine Force, Pacific to Commandant of the Marine Corps, "Subj: Command Diary; submission of" [CTE 79.3.3.6], 4 April 1963 (Declassified), The Vietnam Center and Archive, Texas Tech University.

57. Task Element 79.3.3.6, After Action Reports 1 November 1963, U.S. Marine Corps History Division Vietnam War Documents Collection, The Vietnam Center and Archive, Texas Tech University.
58. Task Element 79.3.3.6, After Action Reports.
59. Marine Corps Operation Analysis Group, *Characteristics of U.S. Marine Corps Helicopter Operations in the Mekong Delta*, MCOAG Study 1 (Alexandria, VA: Center for Naval Analyses, 1962, declassified).
60. Marine Corps Operation Analysis Group, *Characteristics of U.S. Marine Corps Helicopter Operations*.
61. Intelligence Officer to Commander, Marine Aircraft Group 16, Task Element 79.3.3.6, "Subject: Progress Report," 23 January 1963 (Declassified), U.S. Marine Corps History Division Vietnam War Documents Collection, The Vietnam Center and Archive, Texas Tech University.
62. This was the case during the covert war period, February through August 1964. See New York Times Company, *The Pentagon Papers: The Secret History of the Vietnam War* (New York: Racehorse, 2017), 241–314.
63. The ONI later established its Kennedy Irregular Warfare Center specifically for irregular, warfare-centric intelligence.
64. Chief, Naval Advisory Group, Military Assistance Command, Vietnam to Commander, United States Military Assistance Command, Vietnam, "Subject: Historical Review, Naval Advisory Group Activities, May 1965," 21 June 1965 (Declassified 9 April 2018), RG 313, NARA.
65. Chief, Naval Advisory Group, "Historical Review, Naval Advisory Group Activities, May 1965."
66. As the NAVGP Historical Review of Activities from April 1965 stated: "In the Vietnamese mind, whether that of a Viet Cong or a government supporter, every 'Westerner' casts the shadow of French Colonialism." Naval Advisory Group, "Historical Review, Naval Advisory Group Activities," April 1965 (Declassified 9 April 2018), RG 38, Entry 98C, Box 12, NARA.
67. Headquarters, MAC-V, *Command History 1964*.
68. SEAL Advisor to Chief, Naval Advisory Group, Military Assistance Command, Vietnam, "Subject: Report of LDNN Participation at

Vung Row Bay," 24 February 1965 (Declassified 9 April 2018), RG 38, Entry 98C, Box 13, NARA.
69. Chief, Naval Advisory Group, Military Assistance Command, Vietnam to Commander, United States Military Assistance Command, Vietnam, "Subject: Historical Review, Naval Advisory Group Activities, March 1965," 30 April 1965 (Declassified 9 April 2018), RG 38, Entry 98C, Box 13, NARA.
70. Chief, Naval Advisory Group, "Subject: Historical Review, Naval Advisory Group Activities, March 1965."
71. SEAL Advisor to Chief, Naval Advisory Group, "Subject: Report of LDNN Participation."
72. SEAL Advisor to Chief, Naval Advisory Group, "Subject: Report of LDNN Participation."
73. This was a concern in 1975 with the Church Commission, again in 1988 with the Iran–Contra affair, and again in the post-9/11 years with the wars in Iraq and Afghanistan. See Stuart D. Lyle, "The Militarization of Intelligence: Can the Military Perform Covert Action More Effectively Than the Intelligence Community," *American Intelligence Journal* 20, no. 2 (2012): 79–83.
74. Plaster, *SOG*, 3.
75. Department of State, Office of the Historian, National Security Memorandum 52, Washington, May 11, 1961, https://history.state.gov/historicaldocuments/frus1961-63v01/d52.
76. Vinh Truong, *Vietnam War: The New Legion*, vol. 1 (Bloomington, IN: Trafford, 2010), 154.
77. For a history of SEALs in Vietnam, see Daryl Young, *The Element of Surprise: Navy SEALs in Vietnam* (New York: Ballantine, 1990). Also see Mark Divine and Allyson Edelhertz Mechate, *The Way of the SEAL: Think Like an Elite Warrior to Lead and Succeed* (New York: Reader's Digest, 2016).
78. Plaster, *SOG*, 7.
79. For a complete history of the Phoenix Program, see Mark Moyar, *Phoenix and the Birds of Prey: Counterinsurgency and Counterterrorism in Vietnam* (New York: Bison Books, 2007).
80. The most recent naval intelligence doctrine addressing roles found prior to the crisis in Indochina was the one the Navy had released

in the aftermath of the CIA's establishment. See Office of the Chief of Naval Operations, Office of Naval Intelligence, *Naval Intelligence Manual*, 1949, ONI 19(B), June 1949 (Declassified 28 December 2015), RG 38, Entry 98C, Box 25, NARA.
81. George F. Howe, "The Early History of NSA," undated internal NSA history, National Security Agency (declassified), https://www.nsa.gov/portals/75/documents/news-features/declassified-documents/cryptologic-spectrum/early_history_nsa.pdf.
82. U.S. Marine Corps, *General Chronology of Events in Vietnam*.
83. United States Air Force, "History of the Assistant Chief of Staff, Intelligence, July–December 1967," National Security Archives, George Washington University, Washington, DC, https://nsarchive2.gwu.edu/NSAEBB/NSAEBB520-the-Pentagons-Spies/EBB-PS03b.pdf.
84. United States Air Force, "Air Force Intelligence Responsibilities and Functions," AFR 200-1, 14 February 1964, National Security Archives, George Washington University, Washington, DC.
85. U.S. Marine Corps, *General Chronology of Events in Vietnam*.
86. U.S. Marine Corps, *General Chronology of Events in Vietnam*.
87. John Prados, *JFK and the Diem Coup*, National Security Archive Electronic Briefing Book No. 101, Posted November 5, 2003, https://nsarchive2.gwu.edu/NSAEBB/NSAEBB101/index.htm.
88. U.S. Marine Corps, *General Chronology of Events in Vietnam*.
89. U.S. Marine Corps, *General Chronology of Events in Vietnam*.
90. U.S. Marine Corps, *General Chronology of Events in Vietnam*.
91. Secretary of the Navy to Distribution List (e.g., CINCLANTFLT, CINCPACFLT, COMNAVFORJAPAN), "Subj: Instructions for the Coordination and Control of Navy's Clandestine Intelligence Collection Program," 7 December 1965 (Declassified 13 July 1990), National Security Archive, https://nsarchive2.gwu.edu/NSAEBB/NSAEBB520-the-Pentagons-Spies/EBB-PS01.pdf.
92. Secretary of the Navy to Distribution List, "Instructions for the Coordination and Control."
93. Jeffrey T. Richelson, "Task Force 157: The U.S. Navy's Secret Intelligence Service, 1966–77," *Intelligence and National Security* 11, no. 1 (1996): 106–45.

Conclusion

1. Michael Warner, "'U.S. Intelligence and Vietnam': The Official Version," *Intelligence and National Security* 25, no. 5 (2010): 611–37.
2. Consider Kemp Tolley's somewhat romanticized account of his experiences as a Navy intelligence officer in the Asiatic Fleet during the 1930s. Kemp Tolley, *Yangtze Patrol: The U.S. Navy in China* (Annapolis, MD: Naval Institute Press, 1971).
3. This seemed to be the case with the works on the Taiwan crises. See, for example, Michael D. Swaine, Tuosheng Zhang, and Danielle F. S. Cohen, eds., *Managing Sino-American Crises: Case Studies and Analysis* (Washington, DC: Carnegie Endowment for International Peace, 2006).
4. Richard K. Betts, "Analysis, War, and Decision: Why Intelligence Failures Are Inevitable," *World Politics* 31 (October 1978): 61–89.
5. Betts, "Analysis, War, and Decision."
6. Dennis L. Noble, "A U.S. Naval Intelligence Mission to China in the 1930s," *Studies in Intelligence* 50, no. 2 (2006), https://www.cia.gov/resources/csi/static/Naval-Intel-China-Mission.pdf. Noble captured this well with his depiction of Marine major William A. Worton, who was ill equipped and lacking training when he was sent to China in the 1930s to collect intelligence on Japanese activities there and to liaise with Chiang's director of investigation and statistics, Tai Li.
7. Even the few works focusing on intelligence during this period seem to have brushed over the subject. For example, see W. G. Winslow, *The Fleet the Gods Forgot: The U.S. Asiatic Fleet in World War II* (Annapolis, MD: Naval Institute Press, 2014).
8. See Linda Kush, *The Rice Paddy Navy: U.S. Sailors Undercover in China* (Oxford: Osprey, 2012).
9. Sun Tzu, *The Art of War*, trans. by Lionel Giles (The Project Gutenberg E-book, 1910 edition), chap. 13, no. 8, https://www.gutenberg.org/files/132/132-h/132-h.htm.

Bibliography

Primary Sources

The National Archives and Records Administration (NARA), College Park, Maryland, and Washington, DC

Records of the U.S. Navy, RG 38
Records of the U.S. Navy (Office of Naval Intelligence), RG 80
Records of the U.S. Marine Corps, RG 127
Records of the Office of Strategic Services, RG 226
Records of the Naval Operating Forces, RG 313

Pedro Loureiro Collection at the University of Southern California Digital Library (retrieved via NARA)

Records of the U.S. Navy, RG 38
Records of the U.S. Marine Corps, RG 127

Online Primary Sources

CIA CREST Database of Center for the Study of Intelligence, https://www.cia.gov/readingroom/collection/crest-25-year-program-archive

Harry S. Truman Library and Museum, https://www.trumanlibrary.gov/

Hurley, Patrick J., Collection, Western History Collections, University of Oklahoma, https://legacy-westhist.libraries.ou.edu/locations/docs/westhist/hurley/index.html

Joint Chiefs of Staff, https://www.jcs.mil/Library/

Lillian Goldman Law Library, Yale Law School, Yale University, https://library.law.yale.edu/

Marine Corps History Division, https://www.usmcu.edu/Research/History-Division/

National Security Archives, George Washington University, https://nsarchive.gwu.edu/

Naval History and Heritage Command (NHHC), https://www.history.navy.mil/

U.S. Army Center of Military History, https://history.army.mil/

U.S. Department of State, Office of the Historian, https://history.state.gov/

U.S. Naval War College, https://usnwcarchives.org/

The Vietnam Center and Archive, Texas Tech University, https://www.vietnam.ttu.edu/

Wilson Center Digital Archive (WCDA), https://www.wilsoncenter.org/digital-archive

Selected Secondary Sources

Ahern, Thomas A. *Vietnam Declassified: The CIA and Counterinsurgency.* Lexington: University Press of Kentucky, 2012.

Aid, Matthew. "U.S. HUMINT and COMINT in the Korean War: From the Approach of War to the Chinese Intervention." *Intelligence and National Security* 14, no. 4 (1999): 17–63.

Albion, Robert G. *Makers of Naval Policy, 1798–1947.* Annapolis, MD: Naval Institute Press, 1980.

Aldrich, Richard J. "British Intelligence and the Anglo-American 'Special Relationship' during the Cold War." *Review of International Studies* 24, no. 3 (1998): 331–51.

———. *Intelligence and the War against Japan: Britain, America and the Politics of Secret Service.* Cambridge: Cambridge University Press, 2000.

Aldrich, Richard J., Gary D. Rawnsley, and Ming-Yeh T. Rawnsley. "Introduction: The Clandestine Cold War in Asia, 1945–65." *Intelligence and National Security* 14, no. 4 (1999): 1–14.

———, eds. *The Clandestine Cold War in Asia, 1945–65: Western Intelligence, Propaganda, and Special Operations.* London: Frank Cass, 2000.

Andrew, Christopher. *For the President's Eyes Only: Secret Intelligence and the American Presidency from Washington to Bush.* New York: HarperCollins, 1995.

———. *The Secret World: A History of Intelligence.* New Haven, CT: Yale University Press, 2018.

———. *The Sword and the Shield.* New York: Basic Books, 1999.

Anonymous. "Strategic Intelligence for American World Policy / The Future of American Secret Intelligence." *Marine Corps Gazette* 34, no. 5 (May 1950).

Aplington, Henry, II. "North China Patrol." *Marine Corps Gazette* 33, no. 6 (1949).

Armstrong, Alan. *Preemptive Strike: The Secret Plan That Would Have Prevented the Attack on Pearl Harbor.* Guilford, CT: Lyons, 2006.

Barlow, Jeffrey G. *Revolt of the Admirals: The Fight for Naval Aviation, 1945–1950.* Washington, DC: U.S. Government Printing Office, 1995.

Barnett, A. Doak. *China on the Eve of Communist Takeover.* New York: Praeger, 1963.

Bayly, Christopher A., and Tim Harper. *Forgotten Wars: Freedom and Revolution in Southeast Asia.* Cambridge, MA: Belknap Press of Harvard University Press, 2007.

Becker, David W. *Coming in From the Cold . . . War: Defense HUMINT Services Support to Military Operations Other Than War.* Fort Leavenworth, KS: U.S. Army Command and General Staff College, 2000.

Betts, Richard K. *Enemies of Intelligence: Knowledge and Power in American National Security.* New York: Columbia University Press, 2007.

Biggs, Chester M. *The United States Marines in North China, 1894–1942.* Jefferson, NC: McFarland, 2003.

Blum, William. *Killing Hope: U.S. Military and CIA Interventions since World War II.* Monroe, ME: Common Courage, 1995.

Borisov, O. B., and B. T. Koloskov. *Soviet-Chinese Relations, 1945–1970.* Bloomington: Indiana University Press, 1975.

Bostdorff, Denise M. *Proclaiming the Truman Doctrine: The Cold War Call to Arms.* College Station: Texas A&M University Press, 2008.

Braisted, William R. *Diplomats in Blue: U.S. Naval Officers in China, 1922–1933.* Gainesville: University Press of Florida, 2009.

Breuer, William B., and Douglas MacArthur. *MacArthur's Undercover War: Spies, Saboteurs, Guerrillas, and Secret Missions.* Edison, NJ: Castle, 2005.

Brodie, Bernard. *Strategy in the Missile Age.* Santa Monica, CA: RAND, 2007.

Buhite, Russell D. " 'Major Interests': American Policy toward China, Taiwan, and Korea, 1945–1950." *Pacific History Review* 47, no. 3 (1978): 425–51.

Bush, Richard. *At Cross Purposes: U.S.-Taiwan Relations since 1942.* Abingdon, U.K.: Routledge, 2004.

Carter, Carolle J. *Mission to Yenan: American Liaison with the Chinese Communists, 1944–1947.* Lexington: University of Kentucky, 1997.

Chandler, Stedman and Robert W. Robb. *Front-Line Intelligence.* Washington, DC: U.S. Marine Corps, 1986.

Christensen, Thomas J. *Useful Adversaries: Grand Strategy, Domestic Mobilization, and Sino-American Conflict, 1947–1958.* Princeton, NJ: Princeton University Press, 1996.

Clubb, O. Edmund. "Sino-American Relations and the Future of Formosa." *Political Science Quarterly* 80, no. 1 (March 1965).

Cohan, Leon, Jr. "Intelligence and Viet-Nam." *Marine Corps Gazette* 50, no. 2 (1966).

Colby, William. *Honorable Men: My Life in the CIA.* New York: Simon & Schuster, 1978.

Cole, Bernard. *Taiwan's Security: History and Prospects.* Abingdon, U.K.: Routledge, 2006.

Conboy, Kenneth. *Shadow War: The CIA's Secret War in Laos.* Boulder, CO: Paladin, 1995.

Conboy, Kenneth, and Dale Andrade, *Spies & Commandos: How America Lost the Secret War in North Vietnam.* Lawrence: University Press of Kansas, 2000.

Corke, Sarah-Jane. *U.S. Covert Operations and Cold War Strategy: Truman, Secret Warfare, and the CIA, 1945–1953.* New York: Routledge, 2008.

Cradock, Percy. *Know Your Enemy: How the Joint Intelligence Committee Saw the World.* London: John Murray, 2002.

Craig, Alexander. "The Joint Intelligence Committee and British Strategic Assessment, 1945–1956." PhD diss., University of Cambridge, 1999.

Crozier, Brian. "Beijing and the Laotian Crisis: A Further Appraisal." *China Quarterly*, no. 11 (1962): 116–23.

Darling, Arthur. *The Central Intelligence Agency: An Instrument of Government, to 1950*. University Park: Pennsylvania State University Press, 1990.

———. "With Vandenberg as DCI." *Studies in Intelligence* 12, no. 3 (1996).

Deacon, Richard. *The Silent War: A History of Western Naval Intelligence*. London: Grafton, 1978.

DeForest, Orrin. *Slow Burn: The Rise and Bitter Fall of American Intelligence in Vietnam*. New York: Simon & Schuster, 1990.

Dingman, Roger. *Deciphering the Rising Sun: Navy and Marine Corps Codebreakers, Translators, and Interpreters in the Pacific War*. Annapolis, MD: Naval Institute Press, 2009.

Donovan, William J. "Strategic Services in 'Cold War.'" *Naval War College Review*, September 1953.

Dorwart, Jeffery M. *Conflict of Duty: The U.S. Navy's Intelligence Dilemma, 1919–1945*. Annapolis, MD: Naval Institute Press, 1983.

———. *The Office of Naval Intelligence*. Annapolis, MD: Naval Institute Press, 1979.

Drew, S. Nelson, ed. *NSC-68: Forging the Strategy of Containment*. 2nd ed. Washington, DC: Institute for National Strategic Studies, 1996.

Dreyer, June Teufel. "A History of Cross-Strait Interchange," in *Crisis in the Taiwan Strait*, ed. by James R. Lilley and Chuck Downs. Washington, DC: National Defense University Press, 1997.

Dulles, Allen. *The Craft of Intelligence: America's Legendary Spy Master on the Fundamentals of Intelligence Gathering in the Free World*. New York: Lyons, 2005.

During, Marvin B. *World Turned Upside Down: U.S. Naval Intelligence and the Cold War Struggle for Germany*. Washington, DC: Potomac Books, 2007.

Dwyer, John B. *Scouts and Raiders: The Navy's First Special Warfare Commandos*. New York: Praeger, 1993.

Dylan, Huw. *Defense Intelligence and the Cold War: Britain's Joint Intelligence Bureau, 1945–1964*. Oxford: Oxford University Press, 2014.

Dylan, Huw, David V. Gioe, and Michael S. Goodman. *The CIA and the Pursuit of Security: History, Documents and Contexts*. Edinburgh: Edinburgh University Press, 2022.
Edwards, Fred L. *The Bridges of Vietnam: From the Journals of a U.S. Marine Intelligence Officer*. Denton: University of North Texas, 2000.
Elleman, Bruce A. *High Seas Buffer: The Taiwan Patrol Force, 1950–1979*. Newport, RI: Naval War College, 2012.
Fehrenback, T. R. *This Kind of War*. 2nd ed. Washington, DC: Brassey's, 1998.
Finkelstein, David. *Washington's Taiwan Dilemma, 1949–1950: From Abandonment to Salvation*. Annapolis, MD: Naval Institute Press, 2014.
Fischer, Benjamin B. *A Cold War Conundrum: The 1983 Soviet War Scare*. Langley, VA: Center for the Study of Intelligence, 2007. https://www.cia.gov/resources/csi/static/Cold-War-Conundrum.pdf.
Ford, Christopher, and David Alan Rosenberg. *The Admiral's Advantage: U.S. Operational Intelligence in World War II and the Cold War*. Annapolis, MD: Naval Institute Press, 2005.
Frank, Richard. *Guadalcanal: The Definitive Account of the Landmark Battle*. New York: Random House, 1990.
Freedman, Lawrence. *Kennedy's Wars: Berlin, Cuba, Laos, and Vietnam*. Oxford: Oxford University Press, 2000.
Fuchida, Mitsuo, and Masatake Okumiya. *Midway: The Battle That Doomed Japan*. Annapolis, MD: Naval Institute Press, 1955.
Gaddis, John L. *Strategies of Containment: A Critical Appraisal of Postwar American National Security Policy*. New York: Oxford University Press, 1982.
Gallicchio, Marc S. *The Cold War Begins in Asia: American East Asian Policy and the Fall of the Japanese Empire*. New York: Columbia University Press, 1988.
Gallucci, Robert L. *Neither Peace nor Honor: The Politics of American Military Policy in Viet-Nam*. Baltimore: Johns Hopkins University Press, 1975.
Gill, Peter, Stephen Marrin, and Mark Phythian. *Intelligence Theory: Key Questions and Debates*. London: Routledge, 2009.
Goodman, Michael S. *Spying on the Nuclear Bear*. Palo Alto, CA: Stanford University Press, 2007.

Grant, Zalin. *Facing the Phoenix: The CIA and the Political Defeat of the United States in Vietnam.* New York: Norton, 1991.

Greenawalt, Bruce S. *Missionary Intelligence from China: American Protestant Reports, 1930–1950.* Chapel Hill: University of North Carolina Press, 1974.

Griffith, Samuel B. "North China, 1937." *Marine Corps Gazette* 22, no. 4 (1938).

Halperin, M. H. *The 1958 Taiwan Straits Crisis: A Documented History.* RM-4900-ISA. Santa Monica, CA: RAND, 1966 (Declassified March 18, 1975).

Heinzig, Dieter. *The Soviet Union and Communist China 1945–1950: The Arduous Road to the Alliance.* Milton Park, Abingdon, U.K.: Routledge, 2015.

Henriot, Christian, and Wen-hsin Yeh, eds. *In the Shadow of the Rising Sun: Shanghai under Japanese Occupation.* Cambridge: Cambridge University Press, 2004.

Hilsman, Roger. *Strategic Intelligence and National Decisions.* Glencoe, IL: Free Press, 1956.

Hittle, J. D. "The Marine Corps Battalion Intelligence Service." *Marine Corps Gazette* 25, no. 4 (November 1941).

Holmes, W. J. *Double-Edged Secrets: U.S. Naval Intelligence Operations in the Pacific during World War II.* Annapolis, MD: Naval Institute Press, 2013.

Holober, Frank. *Raiders of the China Coast: CIA Operations during the Korean War.* Annapolis, MD: Naval Institute Press, 1999.

Hoyt, Edwin P. *The Lonely Ships: The Life and Death of the Asiatic Fleet.* New York: David McKay, 1976.

Hubbard, Douglass H. *Special Agent, Vietnam: A Naval Intelligence Memoir.* Washington, DC: Potomac Books, 2006.

Huchthausen Peter A., and Alexandre Sheldon-Duplaix. *Hide and Seek: The Untold Story of Cold War Naval Espionage.* Hoboken, NJ: Wiley, 2009.

Hunt, Ray C., and Bernard Norling. *Behind Japanese Lines: An American Guerilla in the Philippines.* Lexington: University of Kentucky Press, 1986.

Irie, Akira, and Yonosuke Nagai. *The Origins of the Cold War in Asia.* New York: Columbia University Press, 1977.

Jackson, Peter, and Jennifer Siegel. *Intelligence and Statecraft: The Use and Limits of Intelligence in International Society.* Westport, CT: Praeger, 2005.

Jeans, Roger B., *The CIA and Third Force Movements in China during the Early Cold War.* Lanham, MD: Lexington, 2017.

Jian, Chen. "China and the First Indo-China War, 1950–54." *China Quarterly*, no. 133 (March 1993): 85–110.

———. "China's Involvement in the Vietnam War, 1964–69." *China Quarterly*, no. 142 (June 1995): 356–87.

———. *China's Road to the Korean War: The Making of the Sino-American Confrontation.* New York: Columbia University Press, 1996.

———. *Mao's China and the Cold War.* Chapel Hill: University of North Carolina Press, 2001.

Joint Army–Navy Intelligence Study of Formosa (Taiwan). Washington, DC: Joint Intelligence Study Publication Board, 1944.

Johnson, Loch K., and James J. Wirtz. *Intelligence and National Security: The Secret World of Spies: An Anthology.* New York: Oxford University Press, 2008.

Johnson, Robert E. *Far East Station: The U.S. Navy in Asian Waters, 1800–1898.* Annapolis, MD: Naval Institute Press, 1979.

Johnston, Thomas A., and Kenneth E. Bingham. *Seabee Teams in Vietnam 1963–1968: 13 Man Teams That Helped Rural Vietnamese and Who Fought Alongside the Special For*ces. N.p.: CreateSpace, 2012.

Jonas, Manfred. *Isolationism in America 1935–1941.* Ithaca, NY: Cornell University Press, 1966.

Keegan, John. *Intelligence in War: The Value and Limitations of What the Military Can Learn about the Enemy.* London: Vintage, 2004.

Kelly, Andrew. "The Sino-Japanese War and the Anglo-American Response." *Australian Journal of American Studies* 32, no. 2 (December 2013): 27–43.

Kent, Sherman. *Strategic Intelligence: For American World Policy.* Hamden, CT: Archon, 1965.

King, Chen C. *Vietnam and China 1938–1954.* Princeton, NJ: Princeton University Press, 1969.

Klehr, Harvey, and Ronald Radosh. *The Amerasia Spy Case: Prelude to McCarthyism.* Chapel Hill: University of North Carolina Press, 1996.

Kotani, Ken, and Chiharu Kotani. *Japanese Intelligence in World War II*. Oxford: Osprey, 2009.
Kurlantzick, Joshua. *A Great Place to Have a War: America in Laos and the Birth of a Military CIA*. New York: Simon & Schuster, 2016.
Kush, Linda. *The Rice Paddy Navy: U.S. Sailors Undercover in China*. Oxford: Osprey, 2012.
Lanning, Michael Lee, and Ray W. Stubbe. *Inside Force Recon: Recon Marines in Vietnam*. Guilford, CT: Stackpole, 1989.
Leeson, Peter T., and Andrea Dean. "The Democratic Domino Theory." *American Journal of Political Science* 53, no. 3 (2009): 533–51.
Levine, Steven I. "A New Look at American Mediation in the Chinese Civil War: The Marshall Mission and Manchuria." *Diplomatic History* 3, no. 4 (1979): 349–75.
Lewin, Ronald. *The American Magic: Codes, Ciphers and the Defeat of Japan*. New York: Farrar, Strauss & Giroux, 1982.
———. *Ultra Goes to War: The Secret Story*. London: Hutchinson, 1978.
Lilley, James, and Jeffrey Lilley. *China Hands*. New York: Public Affairs, 2004.
Lilley, James R., and Chuck Downs, eds. *Crisis in the Taiwan Strait*. Washington, DC: National Defense University Press, 1997.
Lowenthal, Mark M. *U.S. Intelligence: Evolution and Anatomy*. 2nd ed. Westport, CT: Praeger, 1992.
Lu, Suping. *They Were in Nanjing: The Nanjing Massacre Witnessed by American and British Nationals*. Hong Kong: Hong Kong University Press, 2004.
Lyle, Stuart D. "The Militarization of Intelligence: Can the Military Perform Covert Action More Effectively Than the Intelligence Community." *American Intelligence Journal* 20, no. 2 (2012): 79–83.
Maddrell, Paul. *Spying on Science: Western Intelligence in Divided Germany, 1945–1961*. Oxford: Oxford University Press, 2006.
Mahan, Alfred T. *The Influence of Sea Power upon History, 1660–1783*. Boston: Little, Brown, 1890.
Marchio, James D. "The Evolution and Relevance of Joint Intelligence Centers: Support to Military Operations." *Studies in Intelligence* 49, no. 1 (2005). https://www.cia.gov/resources/csi/static/Evolution-Joint-Intel-Centers.pdf.

Marine Corps Operation Analysis Group, *Characteristics of U.S. Marine Corps Helicopter Operations in the Mekong Delta.* MCOAG Study 1 (declassified). Alexandria, VA: Center for Naval Analyses, 1962.

Marolda, Edward J. *Ready Seapower: A History of the U.S. Seventh Fleet.* Washington, DC: Naval History and Heritage Command, 2012.

Marx, Daniel, Jr. "American Shipping and the Sino-Japanese War," *Far Eastern Survey* 8, no. 14 (5 July 1939): 159–65.

Matsumoto, Haruka I. *The Taiwan Strait Crisis 1954–55 and U.S.–R.O.C. Relations.* IDE Discussion Paper No. 223. Chiba, Japan: Institute of Developing Economies, 2010.

Matthews, Tony. *Shadows Dancing: Japanese Espionage against the West, 1939–1945.* New York: St. Martin's Press, 1993.

May, Earnest R. *The Truman Administration and China, 1945–1949.* New York: Lippincott, 1975.

McDermott, Rose, Jonathan Cowden, and Cheryl Koopman. "Framing, Uncertainty, and Hostile Communications in a Crisis Experiment." *Political Psychology* 23, no. 1 (2002): 133–49.

Metcalf, C. H. "The Marines in China." *Marine Corps Gazette* 22, no. 3 (September 1938).

Millett, Allan R. *Semper Fidelis: The History of the United States Marine Corps.* New York: Free Press, 1991.

Mobley, Richard A., and Edward J. Marolda. *Knowing the Enemy: Naval Intelligence in Southeast Asia.* Washington, DC: Department of the Navy, Naval History and Heritage Command, 2015.

Moise, Edwin. *Tonkin Gulf and the Escalation of the Vietnam War.* Chapel Hill: University of North Carolina Press, 1996.

Montague, Ludwell L. *General Walter Bedell Smith as Director of Central Intelligence, October 1950–February 1953.* University Park: Pennsylvania State University Press, 1991.

Moore, Jeffrey M. *Spies for Nimitz: Joint Military Intelligence in the Pacific War.* Annapolis, MD: Naval Institute Press, 2004.

Morgan, Ted. *FDR: A Biography.* New York: Simon & Schuster, 1985.

Myšička, Stanislav. "Chinese Support for Communist Insurgencies in Southeast Asia during the Cold War." *International Journal of China Studies* 6, no. 3 (2015): 203–30. https://www.researchgate.net/publication/298837423_Chinese_support_for_communist_insurgencies_in_Southeast_Asia_during_the_cold_war.

New York Times Company. *The Pentagon Papers: The Secret History of the Vietnam War*. New York: Racehorse, 2017.

Noble, Dennis L. "A U.S. Naval Intelligence Mission to China in the 1930s." *Studies in Intelligence* 50, no. 2 (2006). https://www.cia.gov/resources/csi/static/Naval-Intel-China-Mission.pdf.

"North China Marine." *Marine Corps Gazette*, January 10, 1948.

O'Toole, G. J. A. *Honorable Treachery: A History of U.S. Intelligence, Espionage, and Covert Action from the American Revolution to the CIA*. Reprint ed. New York: Grove, 2014.

Omand, David. *Securing the State*. Oxford: Oxford University Press, 2014.

———. "Securing the State: A Question of Balance." Transcript. Chatham House, June 8, 2010. https://www.chathamhouse.org/sites/default/files/public/Meetings/Meeting%20Transcripts/080610davidomand.pdf.

Packard, Wyman H. *A Century of U.S. Naval Intelligence*. Washington, DC: Office of Naval Intelligence, 1996.

Parker, Richard W. "An Examination of Basic and Applied International Crisis Research." *International Studies Quarterly* 21, no. 1 (1977): 225–46.

Pedlow, Gregory, and Donald Welzenbach, *The Central Intelligence Agency and Overhead Reconnaissance: The U2 and Oxcart Programs, 1954–1974*. New York: Skyhorse, 2016.

Perry, Hamilton Darby. *The Panay Incident: Prelude to Pearl Harbor*. Toronto: Macmillan, 1969.

Phelan, George R. "Introduction to Command Intelligence." *Naval War College Review*, December 1953, 34.

Phillips, Warren, and Richard Rimkunas. "The Concept of Crisis in International Politics." *Journal of Peace Research* 15, no. 3 (1978): 259–72.

Plaster, John L. *SOG: The Secret Wars of America's Commandos in Vietnam*. New York: Nal Caliber, 2010.

Posen, Barry. *Inadvertent Escalation: Conventional War and Nuclear Risks*. Ithaca, NY: Cornell University Press, 1992.

Prados, John. *The Hidden History of the Vietnam War*. Chicago: Ivan R. Dee, 1998.

———. *Safe for Democracy*. Chicago: Ivan R. Dee, 2006.

Qi Xisheng. *Allies at Swords' Points: The Sino-U.S. Military Cooperative Relationship during the Pacific War Period (1941–1945)*. Taipei: Linking, 2011.

Rankin, Karl L. *China Assignment*. Seattle: University of Washington Press, 1964.

Record, Jeffrey. *Japan's Decision for War in 1941: Some Enduring Lessons*. Carlysle Barracks, PA: Strategic Studies Institute, 2009.

Rice, Edward E. *Wars of the Third Kind: Conflict in Underdeveloped Countries*. Berkeley: University of California, 1988.

Richelson, Jeffrey T. "Task Force 157: The U.S. Navy's Secret Intelligence Service, 1966–77." *Intelligence and National Security* 11, no. 1 (1996): 106–45.

Roosevelt, Elliott. *The Roosevelt Letters*. Vol. 3: *1928–1945*. London: George G. Harrap, 1952.

Rostow, Walt W. "U.S. Policy in the Far East—Communist China." *Naval War College Review*, October 1955.

Ryan, Mark A., David Finkelstein, and Michael A. McDevitt, eds. *Chinese Warfighting: The PLA Experience since 1949*. Abingdon, U.K.: Routledge, 2003.

Salisbury, Lawrence E. "New Aid to China." *Far East Survey* 17, no. 8 (1948).

Schaller, Michael. *The U.S. Crusade in China, 1938–1945*. New York: Columbia University Press, 1979.

Scott, L. V., and R. Gerald Hughes, eds. *Intelligence, Crises and Security: Prospects and Retrospects*. London: Routledge, 2008.

Sheridan, James E. *China in Disintegration*. New York: Free Press, 1975.

Shultz, Richard H. Jr. *The Secret War against Hanoi: Kennedy's and Johnson's Use of Spies, Saboteurs, and Covert Warriors in North Vietnam*. New York: HarperCollins, 1999.

Smith, Warner. *Covert Warrior: Fighting the CIA's Secret War in Southeast Asia and China, 1965–1967: The Vietnam War Memoir of Warner Smith*. Novato, CA: Presidio, 1996.

Sprout, Harold, and Margaret Sprout. *The Rise of American Naval Power, 1776–1918*. Annapolis, MD: Naval Institute Press, 1990.

Steele, Robert D. *On Intelligence: Spies and Secrecy in an Open World*. Fairfax, VA: AFCEA International, 2000.

Stefanick, Tom. *Strategic Antisubmarine Warfare and Naval Strategy.* Lanham, MD: Lexington, 1987.
Stephens, Harold. *Take China: The Last of the China Marines.* Miranda, CA: Wolfenden, 2002.
Stratton, Roy. *SACO: Rice Paddy Navy.* 2nd ed. New York: U.S. Press & Graphics, 2004.
Strong, Kenneth. *Intelligence at the Top: The Recollections of an Intelligence Officer.* London: Cassell, 1968.
Stuart, Douglas. *Creating the National Security State: A History of the Law that Transformed America.* Princeton, N.J.: Princeton University Press, 2012.
Stueck, William W. *The Road to Confrontation: American Policy toward China and Korea, 1947–1950.* Chapel Hill: University of North Carolina Press, 1981.
Sun Tzu. *The Art of War.* Translated by Lionel Giles. Project Gutenberg E-book, 1910 edition. https://www.gutenberg.org/files/132/132-h/132-h.htm.
Swaine, Michael D. "Understanding the Historical Record." In *Managing Sino-American Crises: Case Studies and Analysis*, ed. by Michael D. Swaine, Tuosheng Zhang, and Danielle F. S. Cohen. Washington, DC: Carnegie Endowment for International Peace, 2006.
Swaine, Michael D., Tuosheng Zhang, and Danielle F. S. Cohen, eds. *Managing Sino-American Crises: Case Studies and Analysis.* Washington, DC: Carnegie Endowment for International Peace, 2006.
Tanner, Harold. "Chinese Civil War, 1945–1949." *Military History*, February 2012. http://www.oxfordbibliographies.com/view/document/obo-9780199791279/obo-9780199791279-0031.xml.
Taylor, Jay. *The Generalissimo: Chiang Kai-shek and the Struggle for Modern China.* Cambridge, MA: Belknap Press of Harvard University Press, 2011.
Thomas, Evan. *The Very Best Men: Four Who Dared; The Early Years of the CIA.* New York: Simon & Schuster, 1995.
Thompson, Roger. *Lessons Not Learned: The U.S. Navy's Status Quo Culture.* Annapolis, MD: Naval Institute Press, 2007.
Thorpe, Elliott R. *East Wind, Rain: the Intimate Account of an Intelligence Officer in the Pacific, 1939–49.* Boston: Gambit, 1969.

Till, Geoffrey. *Maritime Strategy in the Nuclear Age.* 2nd ed. Basingstoke, U.K.: Palgrave Macmillan, 1984.

Tolley, Kemp. *Yangtze Patrol: The U.S. Navy in China.* Annapolis, MD: Naval Institute Press, 1971.

Treverton, Gregory F. *Covert Action: The CIA and the Limits of American Intervention in the Postwar World.* London: Tauris, 1988.

Treverton, Gregory F., Seth G. Jones, Steven Boraz, and Phillip Lipscy. *Toward a Theory of Intelligence: A Workshop Report.* Arlington, VA: RAND, 2006.

Troy, Thomas F. *Donovan and the CIA: A History of the Establishment of the Central Intelligence Agency.* Frederick, MD: University Publications of America, 1981.

Truong, Vinh. *Vietnam War: The New Legion.* Vol. 1. Bloomington, IN: Trafford, 2010.

Tsou, Tang. *America's Failure in China, 1941–50.* Chicago: University of Chicago Press, 1963.

Tsui, David. *China's Military Intervention in Korea: Its Origins and Objectives.* Bloomington, IN: Trafford, 2015.

Tuchman, Barbara W. *Stilwell and the American Experience in China, 1911–45.* New York: Macmillan, 1971.

Tucker, Nancy B. *China Confidential: American Diplomats and Sino-American Relations, 1945–1996.* New York: Columbia University Press, 2001.

———, ed. *Dangerous Strait: The U.S.-Taiwan-China Crisis.* New York: Columbia University Press, 2008.

Ulbrich, David J. *Preparing for Victory: Thomas Holcomb and the Making of the Modern Marine Corps, 1936–1943.* Annapolis, MD: Naval Institute Press, 2011.

Valentine, Douglas. *The Phoenix Program.* New York: Open Road Distribution, 2016.

van der Bijl, Nicholas. *Mau Mau Rebellion: The Emergency in Kenya, 1952–1956.* Barnsley, U.K.: Pen and Sword, 2017.

Vaughan, Hal. *FDR's 12 Apostles: The Spies Who Paved the Way for the Invasion of North Africa.* Guilford, CT: Lyons, 2006.

Wakeman, Frederic E. *Spymaster: Dai Li and the Chinese Secret Service.* Berkeley: University of California, 2003.

Walt, Stephen M. *The Origins of Alliances*. Ithaca, N.Y.: Cornell University Press, 1987.
Warner, Michael, ed. *The CIA under Harry Truman*. Langley, VA: Center for the Study of Intelligence, 1994.
———. "The CIA's Office of Policy Coordination: From NSC 10/2 to NSC 68." *International Journal of Intelligence and Counterintelligence* 11, no. 2 (1998): 211–20.
———. "The Creation of the Central Intelligence Group." *Studies in Intelligence* 39, no. 5 (1996).
———. "The Divine Skein: Sun Tzu on Intelligence." *Intelligence and National Security* 21, no. 4 (2006): 483–92.
———. "'U.S. Intelligence and Vietnam': The Official Version." *Intelligence and National Security* 25, no. 5 (2010): 611–37.
———. "Wanted: A Definition of 'Intelligence.'" *Studies in Intelligence* 46, no. 3 (2002).
West, Nigel. *Games of Intelligence*. New York: Crown, 1990.
White, Theodore H., and Annalee Jacoby. *Thunder out of China*. New York: William Sloane Associates, 1946.
Whiting, Allen S. "China's Use of Force, 1950–96, and Taiwan." *International Security* 26, no. 2 (2001).
Wiley, Richard G. *Electronic Intelligence: The Interception of Radar Signals*. Dedham, MA: Artech House, 1985.
Winslow, W. G. *The Fleet the Gods Forgot: The U.S. Asiatic Fleet in World War II*. Annapolis, MD: Naval Institute Press, 2014.
Winters, Francis X. *The Year of the Hare: America in Vietnam, January 25, 1963–February 15, 1964*. Athens: University of Georgia Press, 1997.
Wyden, Peter. *Bay of Pigs: The Untold Story*. New York: Simon & Schuster, 1979.
Young, Daryl. *The Element of Surprise: Navy SEALs in Vietnam*. New York: Ballantine, 1990.
Yu, Maochun. *OSS in China: Prelude to Cold War*. Annapolis, MD: Naval Institute Press, 1996.
Yu, Peter Kien-hong. *The Taiwan Strait: Changing Political and Military Issues*. Singapore: East Asian Institute, National University of Singapore, 1999.
Yuan, Hongbing. *The Taiwan Crisis: China's Plan to Annex Taiwan without a Battle by 2012*. Taipei: Tzung Mei, 2010.

Zacharias, Ellis. *Secret Missions: The Story of an Intelligence Officer.* Annapolis, MD: Naval Institute Press, 2003.

Zawodny, J. K. "Guerrilla and Sabotage: Organization, Operations, Motivations, Escalation." *Annals of the American Academy of Political and Social Science* 341 (May 1962): 8–18.

Zegart, Amy B. *Flawed by Design: The Evolution of the CIA, JCS, and NSC.* Stanford, CA: Stanford University Press, 1999.

Zhang, Shu Guang. *Deterrence and Strategic Culture: Chinese-American Confrontations, 1949–1958.* Ithaca, NY: Cornell University Press, 1992.

Zhang, Xiaoming. "China's Involvement in Laos during the Vietnam War, 1963–1975." *Journal of Military History* 66, no. 4 (2002): 1141–66.

———. "The Vietnam War, 1964–1969: A Chinese Perspective." *Journal of Military History* 60, no. 4 (1996): 731–62.

Index

Able Archer crisis, 8, 193, 210–11n25
Acheson, Dean, 84–85
actions and activities, 9, 212n36
Aid, Matthew, 235n45, 247n9
Air America, 187
Air Force, U.S., 96
American Revolution, 10, 213n43
amphibious operations: intelligence to support, 22; invasion of Taiwan/Formosa by Communist Chinese, 114, 138
Anderson, Franklin, 184
Anderson, Walter, 40, 53
Army, U.S.: disagreement with Navy on military status in China, 83–85, 236n54, 237n61; joint command and control and operations, 96, 242n30; mission and institutional changes for Cold War, 95–96, 241n25, 242n29; relationship with civilian intelligence services, 11, 213–14n47; Shanghai stationing of Army regiment, 27, 58, 218n23, 228n65
Asia: concern about Communism threat and alignment in, 71, 80, 86–87, 97–99, 103–7, 133; Soviet influence and presence in, 80
Asiatic Fleet, U.S.: command structure of Far East intelligence and role of, 31–33, 43–44, 219nn30–31; dissolution of, 90; history of, 239n4; intelligence collection by, 22, 39–42, 43–45, 56, 221n56; response to evolving crisis in the Pacific, 56–58
attachés/naval attachés: Cold War intelligence activities of, 81; command structure of Far East intelligence and role of, 31–33, 43–44, 93, 223n14; coordination and sharing of intelligence between, 34; diplomatic context of work of, 46–47, 56; embassy and attaché move to Nanking, 87; establishment of system for, 213n45; history of use of for intelligence activities, 213n43; HUMINT training for, 6, 210nn19–20; importance of intelligence collection by, 103; intelligence work and activities of, 11, 22, 29, 43, 44, 45, 46–51, 56, 67, 195, 196, 204–5, 221n56, 222–23n6, 223nn13–14, 224–25nn31–33; intelligence work in northern China, 103–6, 245n67; ONI control over, 22, 30, 216n3, 223n14; relationship with host countries and other intelligence services, 11, 213–14nn46–47; reports on activities of, 204–5; value of intelligence collected by, 11
aviation/naval aviation and Revolt of the Admirals, 231n5

Badger, Oscar C., 102
Bay of Pigs and the Cuban missile crisis, 8, 144, 155, 158–59, 160, 163–64, 186, 193, 211n26, 269n40, 270n42
Beijing: intelligence from attaché in, 29, 46–51; Marines stationed in and defense of, 58, 101; mission of naval presence in, 22; move of capital from to Nanking, 218n21
Betts, Richard, 192, 193
Big Comeback, Operation, 135
blockades, 16, 38, 40, 61–62, 129–30, 133
Blum, William, 239n83
Boot, Max, 162, 266n11
Brayton, Charles J., Jr., 101

297

Britain: attaché system and sharing intelligence with, 213n43; avoidance of military involvement in Sino-Japanese War, 21; context of interests related to Sino-Japanese War, 25–29, 60–61, 217n16, 229n78; context of Southeast Asia interests of, 161, 268n32; covert activities and strategy and superpower competition related to Communism threat, 159, 267–68n25; embassy in China, 47, 81; Japan's relationship with, 64; Shanghai stationing of army forces, 27, 228n65

Burke, Arleigh, 145

Cambodia, 154–55, 160–61, 160–63, 172–73, 175, 184, 267n17

Camp Peary, Farm at, 127, 154, 169–70, 254n78, 265n7

Carter, Carolle J., 235n45, 237n67

Carter administration, 125

Center for Naval Analysis, xii, 181

Central Intelligence Agency (CIA): attachés and embassy's relationships with, 11, 213n46; centralization of intelligence under, 3, 12, 80–81, 89–90, 94–95, 118–25, 198–99, 235n43, 241n22, 242n27, 251n43; Cold War clandestine/covert operations of, 158–61, 267–68n25, 268n30; covert actions of in and around China, 88, 239n83; CREST database of, 5, 94, 209n16, 241n22, 247n10, 264–65n1; establishment of, 17, 72, 79, 90, 93–94, 194, 198, 234n36, 239n2, 242n27; Farm at Camp Peary for training officers, 127, 154, 169–70, 254n78, 265n7; history of intelligence operations of, 1, 12, 207n2; HUMINT oversight mission of, 3, 208n9; Indochina clandestine operations of, 154–57, 158, 266n10, 267n20; influence and role in intelligence community, 3, 93–94, 111–12, 186–87, 278–79n80; intelligence operations of, 13–14; leadership role of in U.S. intelligence, 12; national intelligence estimate development by, 36, 111–12, 114, 119, 123–25, 126–27, 247n5, 251n39; Navy training and integration with, 113, 126–27, 169–70, 254n78, 280n6; ONI relationship with, 79, 198–99; opposition to centralized intelligence, 79, 234n36; Phoenix Program, 186, 278n79; relationship with the military, 3, 11, 12, 111–12, 113, 114, 118–22, 118–23, 169–70, 194–95, 198–99, 213–14n47, 248n16, 253n59; Taiwan crises intelligence activities, 129–31, 132, 133–35, 136–37, 138–39, 143–44, 145, 147, 149

Central Intelligence Group (CIG), 12, 93–94, 198, 239nn2–3

Chandler, Stedman, 210n18

Channell, Ralph, 184

cherry-picking, 157, 181–82, 266–67n16, 277n62

Chiang Kai-shek: civil war against Communists, 26–27; defeat of and retreat to Formosa/Taiwan, 78, 81, 87, 88, 107, 129; foreign policy toward, 46–50, 56, 64–66, 68, 98–100, 115–16, 199–200, 244n50. *See also* Taiwan crises

Chiang Kai-shek, Madam, 47–48, 49, 66, 196, 236n51

chief of naval intelligence (CNI), 92, 94

China: airfields built opposite of Taiwan from, 139; economy and currency of, 79, 80, 234n39; establishment of People's Republic of China, 78, 88, 98, 107; foreign policy toward, 60, 85–88, 97–101, 229n78; informal intelligence and naval presence in during interwar years, 16, 214n56; Marines in northern China, 97, 98–102, 244n46, 244n54; military capabilities and advancements of, 264–65n1; mission of naval services in, 71–72; Navy and Marine Corps presence in, 4, 8, 22, 26, 77, 83–88, 218n18, 238–39n82; post–World War II changes in, 79–80; post–World War II foreign relations of, 71; post–World War II relations and policy of U.S. with, 80–88, 238–39n82; relationship with and pivot to Asia, xiii; Soviet influence and presence in northern China, 103–6; VC support from, 155, 157, 161–62; Vietnam and Vietnam War involvement of, 158, 187–88

Chinese Civil War: avoidance of military involvement in, 21, 71; concern about

Communist victory and Communist alignment in Asia, 71, 80; contributions and significance of HUMINT during, 191, 198–99; damage control role of naval forces during, 14–15, 17–18, 193; defeat of Nationalists by Communists, 78, 81, 88, 107; East Asia naval intelligence operations during, 97–107; intelligence about, 64–65; intelligence networks and activities during, 80–81, 88, 235n41, 235n45; limitations on collection and analysis of intelligence during, 198–99; Marshall Mission to negotiate peace to end, 82, 84, 99–100, 198, 237n64; Navy and Marine Corps presence in China during, 8, 77; pause in, 26–27, 64–65; resumption of, 71, 75, 80, 81, 103–4; victory declaration by Mao, 98
Church Committee and Frank Church, 160, 268n27, 278n73
clandestine intelligence organization in Indochina(Task Force 157), 14, 154–56, 189, 190, 265–66n8
Clark, Eugene F., 131–32
coast watching, 76
Coastal Riverine Forces, 166
codes and breaking codes. *See* cryptology
Colby, William, 173–74, 185, 273n17
Cold War: attaché intelligence activities during, 81; CIA covert action of in and around China during, 88, 239n83; CIA covert/clandestine actions during, 158–61, 267–68n25, 268n30; clandestine containment role of naval forces in, 158–61; "cold war" terminology in Truman speech, 80, 234n37; command and control changes in Far East intelligence during, 89–95; containment policy evolution during, 186–87, 235n46; context of interest and intervention in Indochina during, 158–64, 267n20; contributions and significance of HUMINT during, 191, 199–201; East Asia naval intelligence operations during the early Cold War years, 97–107; intelligence and national security structure during, 3, 118–25, 208n9, 251n43; intelligence collection inside China during, 81, 82–88, 106–7, 235n45; intelligence command structure and reporting during, 123–25; intelligence networks, collection, and use during, 115–18, 149nn26–27, 209n12, 235n45, 250n31; literature about intelligence during, 81; Navy thinking on intelligence during, 122–23, 253n57
communications intelligence (COMINT), 121–22, 141
Communism: concern about alignment and spread in Southeast Asia, 153, 154, 155, 156, 159, 161–63, 186, 200–201; concern about threat and alignment in Asia, 71, 80, 86–87, 97–99, 103–7, 114–15, 133, 249n20; containment strategy and superpower competition related to, 113–16, 159, 200, 267–68n25; domino theory and spread of, 114–15, 249n20, 265n5; intelligence about threat from, 94, 114, 241n21; Soviet influence and presence to spread, 71, 80, 85, 114–15, 133, 153, 154, 155, 156, 159, 161–63, 249n20
Communists and Chinese Communist Party: amphibious invasion of Taiwan/Formosa by, 114, 138; Army and OSS support for, 65; civil war against Nationalists, 26–27; concern about Communist alignment in Asia, 71, 80, 86–87, 97–99, 103–7, 133; consolidation and power of, 77, 80, 88, 97–98, 103–7, 238–39n82; intelligence networks with, 80–81, 88, 117, 128, 149, 235n41, 235n45, 247n5; Korean War and Taiwan crises operations of, 128–34; Marshall Mission to negotiate peace between Nationalists and, 82, 84, 99–100, 198, 237n64; Southeast Asia activities to spread Communism, 153, 154, 155, 156, 159, 161–63, 186, 200–201; Soviet assistance to and influence with, 103–7; U.S. response to potential spread of Communism, 71; violence against Americans by, 81–82. *See also* Chinese Civil War; Taiwan crises
Constitution, U.S., 96, 242n29
containment: active containment role of naval forces, 14–15, 17–18, 193; clandestine containment role of naval forces, 14–15, 17–18, 154–57, 193; context

of strategy and intervention in Indochina, 158–64, 267n20; development of policy, 79, 234n32; documents related to strategy and policy, 234n32; domino theory, 114–15, 249n20, 265n5; evolution of policy during Cold War, 186–87, 235n46; intelligence officers for strategy of, 154, 265n7; Southeast Asia activities to counter spread of Communism, 153, 154, 155, 156, 159, 161–63, 186, 200, 200–201; strategy and superpower competition related to Communism threat, 113–16, 159, 200, 267–68n25

Cooke, Charles M., Jr., 83–84

counterinsurgency operations, 76, 158, 172–74, 178, 179–80, 190, 201

counterintelligence activities, 11, 18, 54, 127, 178–79, 180–81, 194, 197, 225–26n46

covert actions: CIA and Navy activities in Taiwan, 133–34; CIA and other agency actions in and around China, 88, 239n83; Cold War covert/clandestine actions, 158–61, 267–68n25, 268n30; manipulation of information and events through, 10; preparations for crisis or conflict between China and the West using, 116, 249–50n29; use of to change course of a crisis, 211n28

crises and conflicts: context of naval HUMINT during, 2–3; definition and characteristics of a crisis, 7–9, 57, 210–11nn22–26, 211n28, 211n32; differences in intelligence collection and use during peace, crisis, or war, 3–5, 23, 44–45, 78–79, 106–7, 193–94, 195, 197, 209nn11–14; dynamics of U.S.–China relations during, 117–18; escalation and deeper involvement threats during, 17–18, 30; historical perspective for preparation for future, xiii–xiv; inadvertent escalation in, 10, 213n42; influence and role of intelligence during, 9–10, 16–18, 192–93, 212nn37–38, 213n42; influence of naval HUMINT during, 2–3, 4–5, 6, 16–18, 106–7; roles of foreign policy during, 14–15, 17–18, 193

cryptology: Armed Forces Security Agency establishment for, 121; codes and breaking Japanese codes, 49–50, 77, 235n41; Communists codes for intelligence collection, 235n41; development of practices and capabilities, 16, 214nn56–57; history of use of by the naval services, 2

Cuba, Bay of Pigs, and the Cuban missile crisis, 8, 144, 155, 158–59, 160, 163–64, 186, 193, 211n26, 269n40, 270n42

Darling, Arthur, 12, 207n2

Deacon, Richard, 213n43

decisions: modernization of intelligence practices to support, 35–42, 55–56; naval HUMINT role in making, 12–13, 22, 191–92, 201–2; pace of making and intelligence to support, 144–48, 149; Taiwan crisis intelligence to support, 118, 149, 250n36, 260–61n68; value of acquiring right information for making, 9–10, 193

Defense Intelligence Agency (DIA), 6, 210n19

Diem regime and Ngo Dinh Diem, 160, 161–62, 164, 172, 177, 179, 180–81, 187–88, 278–79n80

diplomacy: naval attaché relationships and, 46–47, 56; use of to change course of a crisis, 8, 25

director of naval intelligence (DNI): Cold War intelligence activities under, 121; command and structure of Far East intelligence under, 31–33, 43–44, 91–95, 219nn30–31, 223n14; establishment of, 163; Intelligence Advisory Board under, 90, 239n2; Puleston as director, 7, 24, 31, 32, 34, 35–39, 57, 59, 195, 220n40, 222n2; title change to CNI and back to DNI, 92; units for information collection by ONI under during Sino-Japanese War, 22, 23, 24–25, 40–42, 43–56, 217n12

Dixie Mission, 41, 86, 87, 235n45, 237n67, 238n69

document exploitation, 40, 76, 77, 221n61, 233n21

domino theory, 114–15, 249n20, 265n5

Donovan, William "Wild Bill," 13, 86, 87, 115, 238n68, 242n27

Dorwart, Jeffrey, 210n18, 214n51, 220n40

Dulles, Allen, 74, 115, 138, 159, 164, 250n36

Index 301

East Asia: concern about Communism threat and alignment in, 71, 86–87, 97–99, 103–7, 133; intelligence networks and activities in, 81, 235n45; intelligence related to Japanese activities in, 30; mission of naval services in, 72; naval intelligence operations during civil war and early Cold War, 97–107; post–World War II foreign relations in, 71, 231n1; Soviet influence and presence in, 71, 80, 85, 133
Edison, Charles, 33
Eisenhower administration and Dwight D. Eisenhower, 138, 146–47, 148, 154, 161, 265n5
electronic intelligence (ELINT), 4, 74, 122, 141, 166, 214n57
electronic warfare, 141, 261n75
Ellis, Hayne, 34, 35–36, 44, 196, 220n39
Ellis, Pete, 169
embassy attachés. *See* attachés/naval attachés
espionage, 2, 21. *See also* human intelligence (HUMINT)
Exercise Intelligence Center (EIC), 167–68

Far East: clandestine forward-deployed officers and development of local agent networks in, 12; Cold War command and control changes in intelligence in, 89–95; command of intelligence in, 23–24, 29–39, 90–96, 123, 219n27, 219nn30–31, 219nn35–36, 220n39, 220n45; FDR efforts to disrupt Japanese actions in, 218n24; focus and purpose of intelligence about, 30, 33–34, 220n45, 221n56; intelligence for U.S. involvement in, 28–29; mission of naval presence in, 22; naval presence in, 22, 29; post–World War II intelligence conditions in, 71–72, 77–88; stakes in outcome of crises and conflicts in, 16–18
Far East Command, U.S., 124, 131, 253n63
Farm at Camp Peary, 127, 154, 169–70, 254n78, 265n7
Fleet Marine Force, Atlantic (FMFLANT), 168–69, 271n57
Fleet Marine Force, Pacific (FMF-P), 165, 172, 272n3, 272n5

Fleet Marine Force, Western Pacific, 92–93, 100
foreign policy: access to intelligence sources and, 18, 192; Chiang Kai-shek and Nationalists policy of U.S., 46–50, 56, 64–66, 68, 98–100, 115–16, 199–200, 244n50; China policy of U.S., 60, 85–88, 97–101, 229n78; effects of intelligence on policy related to Japan, 23, 24, 56–68; intelligence development, use, misuse, and value in policymaking, 3; Japan policy of U.S., 21, 60–61, 215–16n1, 229n78; pivot to Asia, xiii; post–World War II China relations and policy of U.S., 80–88, 238–39n82; roles of during crises and conflicts, 14–15, 17–18, 193; Taiwan policy of U.S., 111, 112, 136, 138, 146–47, 148, 260–61n68
foreign press and press correspondents, 25, 40, 49, 53, 55, 219n31, 226n49
Formosa. *See* Taiwan (Formosa)
Formosa Liaison Center (Task Force 74), 125
Formosa Patrol Force (Task Force 72), 131, 133, 140–41, 148
Forrestal, James, 84–85, 95–96
France: attaché system and sharing intelligence with, 213n43; context of Southeast Asia interests of, 161, 268n32; embassy in China, 47, 81; weapons from used by VC, 173
Franklin, Benjamin, 213n43
Friendship Project, 100, 236n50. *See also* Sino-American Cooperation Organization (SACO)
Frost, Laurence H., 250n36
future, prediction of, xiv

Gaddis, John Lewis, 235n46, 249n20, 265n5
Gates, Thomas, 158
Gehlen Organization and Reinhard Gehlen, 74
Goldwater-Nichols Act, 242n30
Gray Book (Nimitz), 232n16
Green Berets, 185
Grew, Joseph, 60, 229n76
Gromyko, Andrei, 147
Guam, 57, 227n59

302 Index

guerrilla operations: complexity of anti-guerrilla operations, 166–67; use of to change course of a crisis, 211n28; VC operations intelligence, 173, 174–77, 179–80, 274n25
Gulf of Tonkin incident and resolution, 4, 153, 163m172, 174, 188–89

Halperin, M. H., 140, 142, 145, 247n2
Hardcastle, William H., 183
Helms, Richard, 74
Holmes, Ralson, 34, 39, 40
Hoover-Stimson Doctrine, 218n22
Hopwood, Herbert, 146–47
human intelligence (HUMINT): CIA oversight mission related to, 3, 208n9; contributions and significance of, 12–13, 66–68, 191–202; definition, focus, and purpose of, xi–xiii, 10, 76–77, 163, 232n19; differences in intelligence collection and use during peace, crisis, or war, 3–5, 23, 78–79, 106–7; evolution and maturation of in Indochina and Vietnam, 154–57, 160–61, 163–64, 190; evolution of naval intelligence, xiii–xiv, 3, 7, 10–13, 15–16, 140, 194, 201–2, 213–14nn45–47, 260n66; forward presence for collection of, 10–12, 17, 192; history of collection and use of by the naval services, 1–3, 6–13, 13–14, 208n7, 210nn18–20, 213n43; influence of during crises and conflicts, 2–3, 4–5, 6, 16–18, 106–7; institutional bias toward signals over, 16; institutionalization of, 13–14, 16, 23–24; Navy's relationship with and attitude toward, xii–xiii, 2–3, 7, 14, 21–22; Pacific naval intelligence during World War II, 72–77; processes/activities for, 140, 160–61, 260n66; records and data on, 3, 5–6, 24–25, 192, 208n8, 209–10nn16–17, 217nn11–12, 280n2; relevance of to naval operations, 2; success and failure related to risks associated with, 156–57, 191–92, 266–67n16; term use in Navy, 163, 194–95, 269n41; value of during interwar years, 77–78; value placed on by the Navy and historians, 4–5, 16, 22, 215n59; wartime collection of, 76–77. *See also* sources/human sources
human intelligence (HUMINT) capabilities: clandestine forward-deployed officers and development of local agent networks, 11–12; evolution of naval services, 2; maintenance of by naval services, xii–xiii, 10–13. *See also* training
Hurley, Patrick J., 84, 87, 97

imagery intelligence (IMINT), 112, 141, 145, 168–69, 233n25, 247nn9–10, 271n57
indications and warnings (I&Ws) intelligence, 134, 138, 145
Indochina: CIA clandestine operations in, 154–57, 158, 266n10, 267n20; clandestine containment role of naval forces in, 14–15, 17–18, 154–57, 193; context of interest and intervention in, 158–64, 267n20; contributions and significance of HUMINT in, 191, 200–201; countries included in discussions of, 267n17; end of war in, 188–89; HUMINT evolution and maturation in, 154–57, 160–61, 190; HUMINT importance in, 154; imminent failure in and change in intelligence activities in, 14; Japanese agreement with, 41; limitations on collection and analysis of intelligence in, 200–201; military assistance role in without declaration of war, 161, 268n31; success and failure related to risks associated with operations in, 156–57, 266–67n16; Task Force 157 activities in, 14, 154–56, 189, 190, 265–66n8; training and capabilities for intelligence and HUMINT in, 157, 166–70, 271n57; units and command of intelligence in, 154–56, 158, 165–66, 167, 171–86, 272nn4–5
Inglis, Thomas B., 91–92, 198
intelligence: bias in analysis of, 115–16, 249nn26–27; context-sensitive value of, xii, 9–10, 193; definition, focus, and purpose of, xi–xiii, 9, 212n33, 212n36; definition of in context of crises, 9–10; differences in collection and use during peace, crisis, or war, 3–5, 23,

Index 303

44–45, 78–79, 106–7, 193–94, 195, 197, 209nn11–14; evolution of naval intelligence, xiii–xiv, 3, 10–13, 15–16, 186–87, 194, 201–2, 213–14nn45–47, 278–79n80; function and use of, 29, 219n25; influence and role of during crises and conflicts, 9–10, 16–18, 192–93, 212nn37–38, 213n42; institutionalization of, 13–14; militarization of, 185, 278n73; naval intelligence changes with centralized intelligence system, 89–90, 239n1; Navy's relationship with, 1–3, 21–22, 207n1, 207–8nn4–5; policy failures and, 201; push and pull aspects of intelligence customer versus producer, 34, 35–36; strategic context of, 7, 13–14; timeliness of and importance of timeliness, 9–10, 37–39. *See also* human intelligence (HUMINT); sources/human sources
Intelligence Advisory Board, 90, 239n2
Intelligence Advisory Committee (IAC), 118, 142, 144, 250n36
intelligence capabilities: access to and loss of intelligence sources and, 18, 192; anticipation of need for leading up to World War II, 23–24; assessment of adversary capabilities, xii, 10; atrophy of capabilities during interwar period, xiv, 23, 29–30, 33–34, 59, 217n9, 228n70; Navy and Marine Corps capabilities, xiii–xiv
intelligence community: aversion to surprise and reorganization of, 119, 251n40; centralized intelligence system, 3, 12, 80–81, 89–90, 94–95, 107, 118–25, 198–99, 235n43, 241n22, 242n27, 251n43; changes to command and control of intelligence during interwar/postwar years, 4, 17, 90–96, 113, 118–25, 209n13, 251n40, 251n43; evolution of agencies and organizations in, 186–87, 278–79n80; opposition to call for central intelligence organization, 13, 79, 234n36; relationship between the military and civilian intelligence services, 3, 11, 12, 111–12, 113, 114, 118–22, 118–23, 169–70, 194–95, 213–14n47, 248n16, 253n59
Intelligence Liaison Office, 88, 238–39n82
intelligence officers: leadership positions and Navy career trajectories of, 16,

127, 215nn60–61; types of intelligence officers, 11–12. *See also* training
interwar and postwar periods: atrophy of intelligence capabilities during, xiv, 23, 29–30, 33–34, 59, 217n9, 228n70; changes to intelligence establishment during, 4, 17, 90–96, 209n13; naval strategy, doctrine, and technology changes during, 16, 17, 214nn56–57; post–World War II foreign relations in East Asia, 71, 231n1; post–World War II intelligence conditions in the Far East, 71–72, 77–88; value of HUMINT during, 77–78
Iran-Contra affair, 278n73

Japan: Britain's relationship with, 64; buildup in the Pacific by, 56–58, 227n59; context of Western interests related to imperial expansion interests of, 25–29, 60–61, 217nn15–16, 229n78; control of naval forces in, 90; effects of intelligence on foreign policy of U.S., 23, 24, 56–68; focus and purpose of intelligence about, 30, 33–34, 35–42, 46, 65–68, 220n45, 221n56; foreign policy toward, 21, 60–61, 215–16n1, 229n78; foreign relations and alliances of, intelligence about, 63–66; imperial expansion activities of, 22, 215–16n1; increasing threat of war with and intelligence about threat, 8, 21, 29, 30, 37–42, 56, 59–68, 221n56, 222n66, 226nn52–53; initial invasion of Manchuria by, 4, 26–27, 218n22; limitations on collection and analysis of intelligence about, 62–63; limitations on collection and analysis of intelligence during, 40–42, 55–56, 62–63, 66–68, 73–74, 230n107; mission of naval presence in, 22; post–World War II foreign relations of, 71; prewar buildup and intelligence about activities of, 59–68; surrender of and repatriation of military and civilians, 71–72, 80, 91; U.S. relations with before Pearl Harbor attack, 8, 21. *See also* Sino-Japanese War, Second
Jinmen islands, 248n11, 259n55. *See also* Kinmen (Quemoy) islands
John C. Stennis, xii
Johnson, Felix L., 121

Johnson, Lyndon, 156, 172, 190
Joint Chiefs of Staff, 72, 79, 95–96
Joint Intelligence Center Pacific Ocean Area (JICPOA), 68, 75, 80, 91, 94, 95, 123, 240n6
Joint Intelligence Centers (JCIs), 240n6
Joint Intelligence Study Publishing Board, 96, 242n32
journalists, 25, 40, 49, 53, 55, 219n31, 226n49
Joy, C. Turner, 131

Kennan, George, 114
Kennedy administration and John F. Kennedy: Bay of Pigs and the Cuban operations under, 8, 144, 155, 158–59, 160, 163–64, 186, 193, 211n26, 269n40, 270n42; CIA clandestine operations review under, 160; containment strategy of, 153, 154; context of Indochina crisis under, 161–63; intelligence changes under, 163–64; special operations and clandestine activities preference of, 158
Kennedy Irregular Warfare Center, 277n63
Kenny, William T., 105
Kent, Sherman, 122, 253n57
King, Ernest J., 83
Kinmen (Quemoy) islands, 9, 137, 138, 139, 142, 143, 144–45, 147, 148, 199, 259n55
Kinmen Advisory Team, 253n61
Korea and Korean Peninsula: control of naval forces in, 90; Japanese presence in, 27
Korean War: China's involvement in, 116–17, 132–33, 134, 250n30; CIA operations during, 238–39n82; collection and use of intelligence during, 3–4, 119–21, 148–49, 252n49; Inchon landing operation, 131–32; intelligence networks and activities during, 80; interrogation of Chinese prisoners of war during, 257–58n41; reorientation of Navy and Marine Corps after, 111; Soviet support for China and North Korea and, 106; start of, 130; Taiwan crises relationship to, 128–34, 255n1, 255–56n10; talks to reach an agreement to end, 133

Kuomintang. See Nationalists and Kuomintang
Kush, Linda, 87, 238n70

Lansdale, Edward, 162, 266n11, 269n40
Laos: denial of Chinese support in, 8; Indochina inclusion of, 267n17; intelligence collection and clandestine containment role of naval forces in, 154–55, 156, 157, 160–61, 162, 163, 266n10; intelligence sources in, 160–61; MAC-V operations in, 176, 274n29; Pathet Lao forces in, 157, 161, 162, 163, 173, 200
Lejeune, John, 169
liberation, wars of, 154

MacArthur, Douglas, 132, 255n1
Maddox, 174
Magruder, John, 65
Manchuria: drawback of Soviet forces in, 98–99; Japanese occupation of, 42; Japan's initial invasion of, 4, 26–27, 58–59, 218n22; Soviet invasion of, 71, 92, 104
Mao Zedong: Army and OSS support for, 65; civil war against Nationalists, 26–27; civil war victory declaration by, 98; correspondence with Roosevelt, 242–43n33; deception strategy of, 136–37, 145, 149, 200, 258n46, 258–59nn49–51; Great Leap Forward policies of, 129, 148; Korean War and Taiwan policy under, 128–34; Korean War involvement under, 116–17, 132–33, 134–35, 250n30; proposal for meeting with Roosevelt, 87; Soviet assistance and ties to, 103–6; Taiwan crises strategy of, 134–39, 142–44, 147–48. See also Taiwan crises
Marine Brigade, 9th, 87
Marine Brigade, Second, 45–46, 67
Marine Corps, U.S.: deployment to and mission in northern China, 97, 98–102, 135, 244n46, 244n54; expeditionary ethos of and intelligence training in, 168–69; integration of Marine Corps intelligence under CNI, 92, 240n14; Korean War role of, 131–32, 135; Taiwan crises role of, 135. See also Navy and Marine Corps, U.S.

Marine Division, 1st, 100, 101–2
Marine Regiment, 4th: Beijing stationing of and defense mission of, 58; Chinese prisoners of war interrogations by, 135, 257–58n41; command structure of Far East intelligence and role of, 31–33, 43–44; intelligence from, 24, 29, 43, 44, 45–46, 55–56, 67, 195, 196, 223n8; Shanghai stationing of and defense mission of, 7, 27, 45, 58–59, 195, 196, 218n23, 228n65
Market Time, Operation, 171, 182–85
Marshall Mission and George C. Marshall, 82, 84, 99–100, 198, 237n64
Matsu island, 137, 138, 139, 143, 199
McHugh, J. M., 47–49
McNamara, Robert, 158–59, 164, 173, 176, 188, 266–67n16, 272n8
merchant marines, 53–54, 55, 225n41
Metzel, J. C., 84, 100–101, 237n61
Midway, Battle of, 16, 74
Miles, Milton, 48, 75, 76, 83–84, 85–87, 236n51, 237n61, 238nn70–71
militarization of intelligence, 185, 278n73
Military Assistance Advisory Group, Taiwan (MAAG-T, MAAG Formosa), 124, 125, 146, 149, 200, 253n61
Military Assistance Advisory Group, Vietnam (MAAG-V), 158, 161, 165, 167, 171–72
Military Assistance Command-Vietnam (MAC-V): command and reporting chain in Indochina, 165–66, 167, 175–76; intelligence and clandestine operations of, 155, 156, 157, 158, 164, 165–66, 172–77; Laos operations of, 176, 274n29; MAAG-V replacement with, 171, 172; reorganization of, 175–76; Special Operations Group under, 185–86; Studies and Observations Group (SOG), 158, 165–66, 172–74, 179, 185–86
military intelligence, 9, 212n36
missionaries, 54–55, 64–65, 226n47

Nanking: intelligence from attaché in, 24, 29, 43, 45, 46–51, 67, 103–6, 195, 196, 245n67; Japanese invasion of and massacre in, 26, 27, 60, 218n21; Marines stationed in, 46, 102; mission of naval presence in, 22; move of capital from Beijing to, 218n21; U.S. embassy and attaché move to, 87
national intelligence estimates (NIEs), 36, 111–12, 114, 119, 123–25, 126–27, 247n5, 251n39
National Pacification Program, 174–75, 273n23
National Security Act (1947), 17, 72, 79, 89, 91–92, 95–96, 122, 123
National Security Agency (NSA), 3, 121–22, 166, 186–87, 208n9
National Security Council, 72, 79
National Security Council Memorandum 68 (NSC 68), 79, 88, 234n32
National Security Intelligence Directive 9, 121–22
national security organization and policy: centralized management of, 90; changes under Truman administration, 79, 80–81, 82, 95–96, 119, 122–23, 234n36, 241n25; evolution of during Cold War, 186–87; influence and role of naval intelligence in, 3, 79, 90–96, 113, 118–25, 251n43; intelligence mission of naval services role in, 72, 231nn4–5; naval HUMINT role in, 12–13; post–World War II changes in, 72; structure and evolution of, 3, 14, 17
Nationalists and Kuomintang: civil war against Communists, 26–27; defeat of and retreat to Formosa/Taiwan, 78, 81, 87, 88, 107, 129; disintegration of, 98–99; foreign policy toward, 46–50, 56, 64–66, 68, 98–100, 115–16, 199–200, 244n50; importance of intelligence relationship with, 85–88; intelligence networks and activities with, 80–81, 82–88, 88, 112, 115–16, 235n41, 235n45; Korean War and Taiwan crises operations of, 128–34; Marshall Mission to negotiate peace between Communists and, 82, 84, 99–100, 198, 237n64; naval attaché office relationship with, 46–50; strength of and presence on mainland, 78, 233nn27–28; support for and military assistance to, 30, 60, 100, 115–16, 229n76, 244n50. *See also* Chinese Civil War; Taiwan crises

national-level intelligence, 72, 90, 119, 123–25, 126–27, 231nn4–5
Naval Advisory Group (NAVGP), 158, 166, 167, 171, 182–85
naval analysis, xi
naval attachés. *See* attachés/naval attachés
Naval Group, China (NGC), 41, 48, 68, 72, 75–76, 82–87, 166, 213–14n47, 237n67, 238n69
Naval Intelligence School, Anacostia, 170
Naval War College, Newport, 170
Navy and Marine Corps, U.S.: authority for clandestine operations by, 155; aversion to change by and traditions and culture of, 14; disagreement with Army on military status in China, 83–85, 236n54, 237n61; forward deployment of and access to information by, 10–12, 17, 192, 201–2; influence and role in intelligence community, 3, 79, 90–96, 107, 113, 118–25, 251n43, 253n59; institutional biases for Fleet assets, 7, 195; integration of Marine Corps intelligence under CNI, 92, 240n14; intelligence training for officers and sailors, 6–7, 113, 126–27, 166–70, 195, 210nn18–20, 280n6; joint command and control and operations, 96, 242n30; leadership positions and career trajectories in, 16, 215nn60–61; mission and institutional changes for Cold War, 95–96, 241n25; personnel shortfalls for intelligence, 167–68; power projection and missions of, 1–2, 14, 207n3; presence in China, 4, 8, 22, 26, 77, 83–88, 218n18, 238–39n82; relationship with civilian intelligence services, 3, 11, 12, 111–12, 113, 114, 118–22, 118–23, 169–70, 194–95, 198–99, 213–14n47, 248n16, 253n59; training and integration with CIA, 113, 126–27, 169–70, 254n78, 280n6
Nimitz, Chester, 1, 45, 75, 77, 82, 91, 123, 232n16
Nitze, Paul, 154, 189, 201
nuclear weapons, Taiwan crises and threat of use of, 17, 112, 117, 133, 138, 142, 146–47, 148, 149, 154, 199

Office of Naval Intelligence (ONI): changes in and modernization of under Puleston, 23–24, 32, 34, 35–39, 55–56, 59, 195, 220n40, 228n70; CIA relationship with, 79, 198–99; Cold War intelligence activities of, 119–22; collection, analysis, and management of intelligence in the Far East by, 23–24, 29–39, 219n27, 219nn30–31, 219nn35–36, 220n39, 220n45; command and organizational structure of Far East intelligence, 31–33, 43–44, 91–95, 123, 219nn30–31, 223n14; command structure and reporting during Cold War, 123–25; disarray in, 29–30; domestic spying by, 13, 214n51; influence and role in intelligence community, 79, 91–92, 93–95, 198–99, 208n9, 240n9; mission of, 13; national-level intelligence role of, 90; Pacific naval intelligence during World War II under, 73–77, 240n9; postwar changes to mission and organizational structure of, 91–95; units for information collection by during Sino-Japanese War, 22, 23, 24–25, 40–42, 43–56, 217n12
Office of Strategic Services (OSS): dissolution of, 79, 93, 95, 242n27; Dixie Mission under, 41, 86, 87, 235n45, 237n67, 238n69; history of during World War II, 208n10; influence and role in intelligence community, 3; intelligence during World War II under, 74; intelligence operations of, 13–14; relationship with the military, 3, 11, 194–95, 213–14n47
oil embargo, 30, 56, 61, 221n50, 222n66
operational intelligence, 1–2, 4, 6, 9, 74, 77, 92, 120, 122, 146, 207n4
Operational Intelligence Course for Foreign Officers, 170

Pacific Fleet, U.S. (PACFLT), 90–91, 123, 124, 125, 141, 166
Packard, Wyman, 6–7, 214n57, 260n62
Panay, 8, 26, 42, 46, 47–48, 60, 74, 211n30, 222–23n6, 222n66
peace: continuum between war and, 7–8; differences in intelligence collection and use during peace, crisis, or war, 3–5, 23,

44–45, 78–79, 106–7, 193–94, 195, 197, 209nn11–14
Peng Dehuai, 143, 147
Pentagon Papers, 163, 269n38
People's Liberation Army (PLA): capabilities and advancements of, 264–65n1; deception strategy of Mao and, 136–37, 145, 149, 200, 258n46, 258–59nn49–51; forces included in, 246n1; Korean War operations of, 132–33; Taiwan crises role of, 111, 136–39, 142–48, 262n85
Perez, Joseph, 184
Phelan, George R., 122
Phoenix Program, 186, 278n79
photo reconnaissance, 141, 175, 247n10. *See also* imagery intelligence (IMINT)
Posen, Barry, 213n42
postwar periods. *See* interwar and postwar periods
Prados, John, 51–52, 209n12, 269n34
press, media, and press correspondents, 25, 40, 49, 53, 55, 219n31, 226n49
Pride, Alfred M., 138
Puleston, William, 7, 24, 31, 32, 34, 35–39, 57, 59, 195, 220n40, 222n2

Quemoy (Kinmen) islands, 9, 137, 138, 139, 142, 143, 144–45, 147, 148, 199, 259n55

radar communications and intelligence, 10, 214–15nn57–58, 233n26
radio technology and communications, 2, 10, 21
Ramsey, D. C., 100–101
Richardson, John H., 188
Richelson, Jeffrey "Jeff," 163–64, 247n9, 269n41
Roosevelt administration and Franklin D. Roosevelt (FDR): concern about threat from Japan, 56, 226nn52–53, 227n57; correspondence with Mao, 242–43n33; efforts of to disrupt Japanese actions in Far East, 218n24; Japan policy under, 215–16n1; naval intelligence use by, 22, 216n5; proposal for meeting with Mao, 87
Ryukyu Islands, 143

Salisbury, Lawrence, 231n4
Sawyer, Ralph, 258n46, 259n51
Sea, Air, and Land Teams (SEALs), 166, 174, 182, 183, 184–86, 185–86, 270n48, 278n77
Seabees, 166, 270n52
Service, John, 86–87, 104–5
Seventh Fleet, U.S.: Combined Task Forces 76 and 77, 166, 167, 182; command and reporting chain in Indochina, 166, 167; headquarters of, 87, 90; Indochina intelligence and clandestine operations of, 155, 157, 266n10; intelligence activities of in China, 85; intelligence activities of in Taiwan, 124, 253n63; Marine Corps forces under, 92–93; operational control of, 90, 240n5; PLA attacks on in Taiwan strait, 136; Taiwan crises role of, 111, 117, 129, 130–31, 133, 134–35, 137–38, 140–41, 142–47; Taiwan defense role of, 136, 146–47; Tonkin Gulf Yacht Club name for, 182
Shanghai: development of network of agents in, 7; intelligence from attaché in, 46–51; intelligence from Marines in, 24, 29, 43, 44, 45–46, 55–56, 223n8; Japanese invasion of and massacre in, 8, 26, 27–28, 52, 58; Marines stationed in and defense of, 7, 27, 45, 58–59, 67, 102, 195, 196, 218n23, 228n65; mission of naval presence in, 22
Shufly, Operation (Task Element 79.3.3.6, MAG 16), 154–55, 158, 163, 165, 167, 171, 177–82
signals intelligence (SIGINT): contributions and significance of during World War II, 16, 17, 77, 215n58; development of practices and capabilities, 16, 214–15nn56–58; failures of, 215n58; history of use of by the naval services, 2, 14; institutional bias toward, 16, 17, 215nn58–59; NSA oversight mission related to, 3, 121–22, 208n9; use of by naval services, 10, 40; use of during Cold War, 112, 247n9; value of during interwar years, 78, 106, 233n25–26
Sino-American Cooperation Organization (SACO), 41, 65, 72, 75, 82–87, 93, 100, 197–98, 213–14n47, 236n50, 237n67

Sino-Japanese War, Second: collection of HUMINT during, 21–22, 23; context of U.S. and British interests related to, 22–23, 25–29, 60–61, 217nn15–16, 229n78; contributions and significance of HUMINT during, 191, 194–98; influence and role of intelligence during, 21, 22, 56–68; limitations on and failures of collection and analysis of intelligence during, 40–42, 55–56, 62–63, 66–68, 73–74, 196–98, 230n107; Navy and Marine Corps presence in China during, 8; offensive marking official beginning of, 59–63; processes for and value of intelligence during, 23–24, 216–17nn6–7; sources and methods of intelligence during, 22, 24–25, 40–41, 46, 217nn11–12; strategic observer status of naval forces during, 14–15, 17–18, 193; units for information collection during, 22, 23, 24–25, 40–42, 43–56, 217n12

Smith, Holland, 77

Smoot, Roland, 142–43, 149, 199–200

SOG (Studies and Observations Group), 158, 165–66, 172–74, 179, 185–86

Souers, Sidney, 198

sources/human sources: access to and loss of access to, 18, 73, 75, 78–79, 85–88, 149, 192, 193–94, 233n29; accuracy of intelligence from, 18, 68, 78, 233n29; credibility and reliability of, 18, 24–25, 41, 68, 217n11; Indochina operations sources, 160–61, 164, 183–84, 277n66; Japanese prisoners of war as, 75–76; nonmilitary personnel as, 53–56, 64–65, 225n39, 225n41, 226n47; Pacific campaign sources, 75–77, 77, 233n21; physical presence for development of, 149, 200; post–World War II sources in the Far East, 78–79, 112; Sino-Japanese War intelligence sources, 22, 24–25, 40–41, 46, 196, 217nn11–12; Taiwan crises sources, 144, 148, 149, 200, 264n113; VC intelligence sources, 161, 183–85

South China Patrol: command structure of Far East intelligence and role of, 31–33, 43–44; intelligence collection by, 40–42, 43, 51–53, 55–56; intelligence from, 25

Southeast Asia: clandestine containment role of naval forces in, 17–18, 154–57; concern about Communism alignment and spread in, 153, 154, 155, 156, 159, 161–63, 186, 200–201; context of U.S. and Allied interests in, 161–64, 268n32; Tonkin Gulf incident and resolution in, 4, 153, 163m172, 174, 188–89. *See also* Indochina

Soviet Union: clandestine and influence campaigns in China by, 89; drawback of forces in Manchuria, 98–99; function and use of intelligence in, 219n25; influence and presence in northern China, 103–6; influence and presence to spread Communism in Asia and East Asia, 71, 80, 85, 114–15, 133, 153, 154, 155, 156, 159, 161–63, 249n20; invasion of Manchuria by, 71, 92, 104; military capabilities and advancements of, 153, 264–65n1; post–World War II foreign relations of, 71; Southeast Asia activities to spread Communism, 153, 154, 155, 156, 159, 161–63, 186, 200–201; Taiwan crises involvement of, 137, 140, 147, 148, 259n52; VC support from, 161–62

special operations forces, 165, 174, 184–86, 185–86, 266n10, 270n48

Special Plans Branch, Joint Staff J2, 125, 254n68

Special Support Activities, Naval Forces (Far East), 125

Spruance, Raymond A., 85

spying, 13, 21, 210n18, 214n51. *See also* human intelligence (HUMINT)

stealing foreign information, xi

Stillwell, Joseph "Vinegar Joe," 47, 223n14

strategic intelligence, 9, 122, 212n38, 253n57

Struble, Arthur Dewey, 131

Studies and Observations Group (SOG), 158, 165–66, 172–74, 179, 185–86

Suez Crisis, 193

Sun Tzu, 201

Swaine, Michael, 117–18

Switchback, Operation, 160, 173–74

Tai Li, 48, 65, 75, 76, 197, 236n51, 237n67, 238n70

Index

Taiwan (Formosa): airfields built opposite of, 139; amphibious invasion of by Communist Chinese, 114, 138; defeat of Nationalists and retreat to, 78, 81, 88; defense of by U.S., 9, 111, 136, 138, 146–47; foreign policy toward, 111, 112, 136, 138, 146–47, 148, 260–61n68; independence of, 114–15, 139; threat of Communist control of, 114–15

Taiwan crises: active containment role of naval forces during, 14–15, 17–18, 193; contributions and significance of HUMINT during, 191, 192, 280n3; deception strategy of Mao and PLA during, 136–37, 145, 149, 200, 258n46, 258–59nn49–51; escalation of and intelligence to support decisions during, 144–48, 149; failure of intelligence during, 144–48; intelligence command structure and reporting during, 123–25, 166; intelligence in the 1954-55 crisis, 134–39, 148–49, 199, 257–58n41, 258–59nn49–52, 260n62, 262n87; intelligence in the 1958 crisis, 140–49, 199–200, 261n70; intelligence networks and activities during, 80, 111–13, 115–18, 128, 149, 247n2, 247nn9–10, 249n27; intelligence to support decision-makers during, 118, 149, 250n36, 260–61n68; kinetic operations in 1958 crisis, 144–48; Korean War relationship to, 128–34, 255n1, 255–56n10; liaison relationship between U.S. and Taiwan military commands during, 140–41, 261n70; limitations on collection and analysis of intelligence during, 199–200; Mao and Communist's intelligence strategy during, 134–35; negotiations to end, 139; nuclear weapons use threat during, 17, 112, 117, 133, 138, 142, 146–47, 148, 149, 154, 199; provocations and invasion threat as basis for, 111, 113, 248n11; Soviet involvement in, 137, 140, 147, 148, 259n52; U.S. response to, 8–9, 134–38; U.S.-Taiwan relations and decisions to affect outcome of, 112, 247n8

Taiwan Defense Command, U.S. (USTDC), 124, 138, 140–41, 141, 142–43, 144, 166, 253n63

Taiwan Patrol Force, 124, 125, 130, 133, 138, 140, 149, 200, 249n27, 253n64

Taiwan Relations Act, 253n64

Task Element 79.3.3.6 (MAG 16, Operation Shufly), 154–55, 158, 163, 165, 167, 171, 177–82

Task Force 72 (Formosa Patrol Force), 131, 133, 140, 140–41, 148

Task Force 74 (Formosa Liaison Center), 125

Task Force 157 (clandestine intelligence organization in Indochina), 14, 154–56, 189, 190, 265–66n8

Taylor, Maxwell, 160, 269n40

Third Fleet, U.S., 90, 240n5

Thomas, Gould, 105

Thompson, Roger, 14

Tien Mang, Operation, 176

Tokyo, 29, 73

Tolley, Kemp, 280n2

Tonkin Gulf incident and resolution, 4, 153, 163m172, 174, 188–89

training: Farm at Camp Peary for training officers, 127, 154, 169–70, 254n78, 265n7; HUMINT training for attachés, 6, 210nn19–20; intelligence training for officers and sailors, 6–7, 113, 126–27, 166–70, 195, 210nn18–20, 280n6; Navy training and integration with CIA, 113, 126–27, 169–70, 254n78, 280n6

Truman administration and Harry Truman: centralization of intelligence under, 94–95, 241n22, 242n27; "cold war" terminology in speech by, 80, 234n37; containment strategy related to Communism threat, 113–14, 154, 159, 200, 267–68n25; intelligence community changes under, 119; Korean War and Taiwan policy under, 128–34, 255n1, 255–56n10; national security organization changes under, 79, 80–81, 82, 95–96, 119, 122–23, 234n36, 241n25; naval aviation and Revolt of the Admirals under, 231n5; post–World War II foreign relations under, 71

Truman Doctrine, 79, 113–14, 122–23, 154, 234n32, 234n37

Tuchman, Barbara, 223n14, 238n69

Tucker, Nancy Bernkopf, 235n41

Tuyen, Tran Kim, 164

United States (U.S.): avoidance of military involvement in Sino-Japanese War, 21, 60–61, 67–68, 215–16n1, 227n57; domestic spying by ONI, 13, 214n51; isolationist policy of, 215–16n1, 226n53, 227–28n62, 227n57; Japan relations with before Pearl Harbor attack, 8, 21

Viet Cong (VC): Chinese and Soviet support for, 155, 157, 161–62; counterinsurgency operations and, 158, 172–74, 178, 179–80, 190, 201; counterintelligence activities of, 180–81; fight for unification of Vietnam by, 157; French weapons used by, 173; intelligence on capabilities of, 173, 174–82, 274n25; intelligence sources of, 161, 183–85; Pathet Lao forces support by, 162, 173; removal from Laos, 162

Viet Minh, 163, 164, 185, 200

Vietnam and Vietnam War: accuracy and reports on operations and cherry-picking,, 157, 181–82, 266–67n16, 277n62; China's involvement in, 158, 187–88; context of interest and intervention in, 158–64, 172, 267n20, 268n32, 272n8; contributions and significance of HUMINT during, 191, 200–201; counterinsurgency operations in, 158, 172, 172–74, 173, 178, 179–80, 190, 201; early U.S. involvement in Vietnam and escalation to war, 8; end of war, 188–89; fight for unification of Vietnam by VC, 157; history of, 162–63, 269n38, 269n40; HUMINT evolution and maturation in, 154–57, 160–61, 190; Indochina inclusion of Vietnam, 267n17; intelligence collection and clandestine containment role of naval forces in, 4, 154–55, 156, 158, 160–61, 267n20; intelligence sources in Vietnam, 160–61, 164, 183–84, 277n66; limitations on collection and analysis of intelligence during, 200–201; success and failure related to risks associated with operations in, 156–57, 266–67n16; units and command of intelligence in Vietnam, 154–56, 158, 165–66, 167, 171–86, 272nn4–5

Vung Ro Bay operation, 184–85

war: continuum between peace and, 7–8; differences in intelligence collection and use during peace, crisis, or war, 3–5, 23, 44–45, 78–79, 106–7, 193–94, 195, 197, 209nn11–14; HUMINT collection during, 76–77

Warner, Michael, 191–92, 212n36

Washington Naval Conference agreement, 26, 217n16

Wedemeyer, A. C., 83, 84

Weekly Summary reports, 25, 37–38, 46, 221n56, 223n8

Wen, Y. C., 49, 224n25

Westmoreland, William, 266–67n16

Wisner, Frank, 164

World War I, 2

World War II: collection and use of intelligence during, 3–4, 208n10, 209n14; failure of intelligence before Pearl Harbor attack, 67–68, 73–74, 119, 231–32n9, 240n9; importance of SIGINT operations during, 16, 17, 77, 215n58; increasing threat of and intelligence about war with Japan before U.S. entrance in, 8, 21, 29, 30, 37–42, 56, 59–68, 221n56, 222n66, 226nn52–53; intelligence command structure and reporting during, 123; intelligence requirements during, 2; limitations on collection and analysis of intelligence during, 77; operational intelligence requirements during, 74, 77, 207n4; Pacific naval intelligence during, 72–77; Pearl Harbor attack by Japan, 26, 56, 67–68, 73–74; wartime footing and intelligence preceding Pearl Harbor attack, 39–42, 59–68, 221n56, 222n66

Worton, William, 7

Worton, William A., 280n6

Yangtze Patrol: command structure of Far East intelligence and role of, 31–33, 43–44; intelligence collection by, 40–42, 43, 51–53, 55–56, 195, 221n56; intelligence from, 25

Yeager, H. E., 166–67

Zegart, Amy, 13, 235n47

Zhou Enlai, 87, 97, 118, 130, 134–35, 136, 147

About the Author

Brian J. Ellison, PhD, has nearly two decades of experience leading research in national security, in which he has specialized in Chinese strategic affairs, naval warfare, and intelligence. His work has led to significant policy, operational, and institutional changes within the Office of the Secretary of Defense, the Navy, the Marine Corps, and the intelligence community. Before joining the Johns Hopkins University Applied Physics Laboratory, he was a senior research scientist at the Center for Naval Analysis, where he provided on-site research and analytic support to the commanders of Fleet Forces Command; Carrier Strike Group Three; Marine Corps Forces Pacific (MARFORPAC); Marine Forces, Korea; and Regional Command East (Afghanistan). In 2014 he was awarded the Commendation for Meritorious Civilian Service by Commander, MARFORPAC for his research and analysis of the Marine Corps' organizational challenges in the Indo-Pacific. His study for Fleet Forces and OPNAV N2/N6 on the Navy's HUMINT enterprise led to near-term changes in the United States' shift to great power competition. He earned a PhD in war studies from Kings College, London, and an MA in international security from American University.

The **Naval Institute Press** is the book-publishing arm of the U.S. Naval Institute, a private, nonprofit, membership society for sea service professionals and others who share an interest in naval and maritime affairs. Established in 1873 at the U.S. Naval Academy in Annapolis, Maryland, where its offices remain today, the Naval Institute has members worldwide.

Members of the Naval Institute support the education programs of the society and receive the influential monthly magazine *Proceedings* or the colorful bimonthly magazine *Naval History* and discounts on fine nautical prints and on ship and aircraft photos. They also have access to the transcripts of the Institute's Oral History Program and get discounted admission to any of the Institute-sponsored seminars offered around the country.

The Naval Institute's book-publishing program, begun in 1898 with basic guides to naval practices, has broadened its scope to include books of more general interest. Now the Naval Institute Press publishes about seventy titles each year, ranging from how-to books on boating and navigation to battle histories, biographies, ship and aircraft guides, and novels. Institute members receive significant discounts on the Press' more than eight hundred books in print.

Full-time students are eligible for special half-price membership rates. Life memberships are also available.

For more information about Naval Institute Press books that are currently available, visit www.usni.org/press/books. To learn about joining the U.S. Naval Institute, please write to:

Member Services
U.S. Naval Institute
291 Wood Road
Annapolis, MD 21402-5034
Telephone: (800) 233-8764
Fax: (410) 571-1703
Web address: www.usni.org

www.ingramcontent.com/pod-product-compliance
Lightning Source LLC
Jackson TN
JSHW022345231025
92958JS00001B/1